Medicolegal Issues in Pediatrics

7th Edition

Author

Committee on Medical Liability and Risk Management

Editors

Steven M. Donn, MD, FAAP
Gary N. McAbee, DO, JD, FAAP

American Academy of Pediatrics
141 Northwest Point Blvd
Elk Grove Village, IL 60007-1019

American Academy of Pediatrics Department of Marketing and Publications Staff

Maureen DeRosa, MPA
Director, Department of Marketing and Publications

Mark Grimes
Director, Division of Product Development

Sandi King, MS
Director, Division of Publishing and Production Services

Jason Crase
Editorial Specialist

Leesa Levin-Doroba
Manager, Publishing and Production Services

Linda Diamond
Manager, Art Direction and Production

Kevin Tuley
Director, Division of Marketing and Sales

Marirose Russo
Manager, Practice Services Marketing

Seventh Edition—2012
Sixth Edition—© 2004 as *Medical Liability for Pediatricians*
Fifth Edition—© 1995 as *Medical Liability for Pediatricians*
Fourth Edition—© 1989 as *An Introduction to Medical Liability for Pediatricians*
Third Edition—© 1986 as *An Introduction to Medical Liability for Pediatricians*
Second Edition—© 1985 as *An Introduction to Medical Liability for Pediatricians*
First Edition—© 1975 as *An Introduction to Medical Liability for Pediatricians*

Library of Congress Control Number: 2011900506
ISBN: 978-1-58110-584-1
MA0591

The recommendations in this publication do not indicate an exclusive course of treatment or serve as a standard of medical care. Variations, taking into account individual circumstances, may be appropriate.

This publication is for informational purposes only. It is not intended to constitute legal advice. An attorney should be consulted if legal advice is desired.

Listing of resources does not imply an endorsement by the American Academy of Pediatrics. The American Academy of Pediatrics is not responsible for the content of the resources mentioned in this publication. Web site addresses are as current as possible but may change at any time.

Brand names are furnished for identification purposes only. No endorsement of the products mentioned is implied.

Copyright © 2012 American Academy of Pediatrics. All rights reserved. No part of this publication may be reproduced, stored in a retrieval system, or transmitted, in any form or by any means, electronic, mechanical, photocopying, recording, or otherwise, without prior written permission from the publisher. Printed in the United States of America.

11-40/0411

1 2 3 4 5 6 7 8 9 10

Committee on Medical Liability and Risk Management, 2010–2011

Steven M. Donn, MD, FAAP, Chairperson

Jeffrey L. Brown, MD, FAAP

Jonathan M. Fanaroff, MD, JD, FAAP

Jay P. Goldsmith, MD, FAAP

Jose Luis Gonzalez, MD, JD, MSEd, FAAP

David Marcus, MD, FAAP

William M. McDonnell, MD, JD, FAAP

Robert A. Mendelson, MD, FAAP

Stephan R. Paul, MD, JD, FAAP

Insurance Consultant

Holly Myers, JD

Staff

Julie Kersten Ake

In addition, the editors and the Committee on Medical Liability and Risk Management wish to acknowledge the following individuals who contributed or authored chapters in the manual: Andrew R. Hertz, MD, FAAP; Daniel R. Neuspiel, MD, MPH, FAAP; Parul Divya Parikh, MPH; James L. Lukefahr, MD, FAAP; Sandeep K. Narang, MD, JD; and Nancy D. Kellogg, MD, FAAP.

The editors and the Committee on Medical Liability and Risk Management thank the following for the critical review and input they provided: Committee on Adolescence, Committee on Child Abuse and Neglect, Committee on Fetus and Newborn, Committee on Genetics, Committee on Hospital Care, Committee on Infectious Diseases, Committee on Injury and Violence Prevention, Committee on Pediatric Emergency Medicine, Council on Clinical Information Technology, Council on Communications, Council on Community Pediatrics, Council on Environmental Health, Council on School Health, Section on Administration and Practice Management, Section on Adolescent Health, Section on Breastfeeding, Section on Child Abuse and Neglect, Section on Emergency Medicine, Section on Genetics and Birth Defects, Section on Infectious Diseases, Section on Hematology and Oncology, Section on Perinatal Pediatrics, Section on Rheumatology, Section on Telehealth Care, Section on Urology, Section on Young Physicians, and Senior Section.

Table of Contents

Preface

Medical liability continues to be a fact of life for pediatricians. Despite a multitude of advances in diagnosis and treatment over the past 25 years, pediatricians are the 10th most frequently sued specialty physician and have the fifth highest average indemnity payment in closed claims paid over this time. One in 3 pediatricians will be sued, including 1 in 10 for care delivered during training.

Despite these sobering facts, medicolegal education remains at a disappointingly low level, as longer curricular subjects continue to be compressed into shorter training periods. Pediatricians are seldom prepared when served with a lawsuit. Fundamental knowledge of medicolegal principles is part of the business end of medicine and is becoming nearly as important as scientific knowledge to the successful practice of pediatrics.

We have been privileged to edit *Medicolegal Issues in Pediatrics,* the seventh iteration of this manual. For those who were familiar with the sixth edition, *Medical Liability for Pediatricians,* many changes and enhancements will be obvious since that edition published 8 years ago. We have expanded the scope of the manual as well as the number of chapters. We have covered the gamut of medical liability and risk management as it applies to pediatric practice, giving the reader a foundation in medicolegal pediatrics. Many of the changes occurring since the sixth edition, including the increased use of electronic health records and newer fraud and abuse laws, as well as a new chapter on child abuse, have been incorporated into this seventh edition.

The expanded scope is reflected in the new title, *Medicolegal Issues in Pediatrics.* All of the chapters have been updated, many have been expanded, and current references have been included to suggest additional information and resources. Chapters have undergone extensive peer review from various American Academy of Pediatrics (AAP) members, and we thank them for their efforts.

While we and our contributors have attempted to be comprehensive, we are by no means exhaustive, and practitioners will need to remain vigilant in keeping pace with a rapidly evolving field. Nevertheless, we offer an overview on a wide range of medicolegal topics that affect the practice of pediatrics at all levels.

We are grateful to past and present members of the AAP Committee on Medical Liability and Risk Management (COMLRM) and to our other contributors, who freely gave their time and expertise in the preparation of this volume. We are also grateful to John Curran, MD, FAAP, who thoroughly reviewed the entire manuscript on behalf of the AAP Board of Directors and made helpful suggestions. We are especially appreciative of the long-standing efforts of Julie Kersten Ake, senior health policy analyst and our staff person at the AAP, who has been the glue that holds the COMLRM together.

Steven M. Donn, MD, FAAP
Gary N. McAbee, DO, JD, FAAP

CHAPTER 1

Overview of Medical Liability

Stephan R. Paul, MD, JD, FAAP

. . . .

KEY CONCEPTS

- Cost of Liability
- Civil Law
- Costs of Medical Malpractice Litigation
- Efficiency of the Tort System
- Pediatric Claims
- Litigation Time
- Insurance Premiums
- Medical Liability Reform
- Health Courts
- American Academy of Pediatrics Position on Tort Reform
- Informed Consent
- Consent by Proxy
- Assent
- Duty to Warn
- Managed Care Liability

United States health care may be the envy of the world, but it is not flawless. Despite the drive for innovation and excellence that gives rise to advances and miracle cures, medical errors persist. United States health care is also the most costly of all industrialized nations. In 2009, expenditures in the United States on health care surpassed $2.3 trillion, which translates to $7,681 per person or 16.2% of the nation's gross domestic product

(GDP), up from 15.9% in 2007.[1] Meanwhile, the number of Americans without health insurance continues to grow, although some significant improvement is anticipated with recent health care reform legislation.[2] Such reforms, however, have become highly politicized and may be difficult to legislate in the current political environment. Curbing excessive litigation should be a critical element of the reform package if it is to provide real relief and help all Americans gain access to better and more affordable health care.

Cost of Liability

Americans spend proportionately far more per person on the costs of litigation than do citizens of any other country in the world. United States tort costs are higher than the average of all developed countries and represented 2.1% (Table 1-1) of the US GDP in 2007.[3] From the early 1950s to the early 1990s, US tort costs rose by a factor of almost 100. By contrast, US economic output (GDP) grew only 20-fold over the same period. Thus, in nearly 60 years, tort costs have grown faster than the US economy.[3] The US tort system cost $252 billion in 2007, which translates to $835 per person or $9 more per person than in 2006.[3] Since 1996, tort costs for medical malpractice have been climbing annually. From 1951 to 2005, the average annual increase in tort costs exceeded the increase in the GDP in most years. From 2003 through 2007, the rate of growth significantly decreased[4] (Table 1-1). Although not all experts agree, some acknowledge that this deceleration may be directly related to the

Table 1-1. Growth of US Tort Costs and Gross Domestic Product[3]

Year	Average Annual Tort Costs	Increase in Gross Domestic Product
1951–1960	11.6%	6.0%
1961–1970	9.8%	7.0%
1971–1980	11.9%	10.4%
1981–1990	11.8%	7.6%
1991–2000	3.2%	5.4%
2001	14.7%	3.2%
2002	13.4%	3.4%
2003	5.5%	4.7%
2004	5.7%	6.9%
2005	0.5%	6.3%
2006	-5.6%	6.1%
2007	2.1%	4.8%
2008	1.1%	3.3%
58 years (1950–2008)	8.9%	6.9%

identification of a malpractice crisis and concomitant tort reform.[5] Critics of the concept that tort reform does little to control health care costs often negate the potential effect reform has on issues such as defensive medicine.[6]

Civil Law

If someone is injured or suffers a loss as a result of another person's negligence, the injured person is entitled to speedy, adequate compensation. If the injured person does not receive that compensation, he or she has the right to present his or her case through a court of law by filing a *tort* lawsuit. This is a basic principle of the US system of justice. When it functions properly, this system benefits every citizen in 3 ways: first, it mandates that injured people are compensated in an attempt to "make them whole"; second, it assigns responsibility for damage—and the cost associated with it; and third, it deters careless behavior by putting people at financial risk for their wrongdoing. Making sure that compensation can be secured through the civil justice system is central to making the United States a fair, compassionate, and safe society.

Like any other right, the civil justice system can be abused and distorted, lessening its value or even imposing hidden, unwarranted costs. When the civil justice system is used improperly, valuable health care products and services can become much more costly or even unavailable, simply because unwarranted lawsuits make it too expensive for people to provide them. Abusive litigation can clog the courts with needless cases, adding years to the time needed to get a fair hearing on a valid claim. Clearly health care reform must be tied to reforming the tort system.

Costs of Medical Malpractice Litigation

Despite the magnitude of spending, the tort system functions very poorly in meeting its compensation objective. Based on data from 2008, a recent study showed that greater than 40% of the national malpractice liability cost is for administrative expenses and does not compensate victims of malpractice.[7] Similarly, a 2006 study found there were even higher costs of litigating a claim, ie, 54% of the compensation to the injured party.[8] Studies consistently show that most claims filed have no merit and that many claims with merit are never filed at all.[9,10]

The 2008 American Medical Association Physician Practice Information Survey found that 65% of malpractice claims filed were dropped, dismissed, or withdrawn.[11] Furthermore, a recent well-publicized study has shown that 37% of payments were made in cases in which there were no medical errors.[8] Claims in this study sample cost more than $449 million, with total indemnity costs of $376 million and defense costs of almost $73 million. In addition, the psychologic costs to accused malpractice defendants is difficult to quantify. Physicians suffer severe psychologic stress in this situation, ultimately affecting their clinical practice and job satisfaction.[12]

The hidden costs of malpractice also include *defensive medicine,* the tendency to over-order diagnostic tests to avoid future litigation. In several surveys of more than 2,000 physicians, nearly all (more than 90%) reported practicing defensive medicine.[13-15] *Assurance behavior,* such as ordering tests, performing diagnostic procedures, and referring patients for consultation, was very common (92%).[13] Among practitioners of defensive medicine who detailed their most recent defensive act, 43% reported using imaging technology in clinically unnecessary circumstances. Avoidance of procedures in patients with a high probability of pursuing litigation was also widespread. Forty-two percent of respondents reported that they had taken steps to restrict their practice in the previous 3 years, including eliminating procedures prone to complications, such as trauma surgery, and avoiding patients who had complex medical problems or were perceived as litigious.[13] Defensive practice correlated strongly with respondents' lack of confidence in their liability insurance and perceived burden of insurance premiums.[14,15] It is difficult to quantify the exact cost of defensive medicine. A 2003 report from the US Congressional Budget Office (CBO) estimates potential savings from defensive medicine of $54 billion.[16]

Efficiency of the Tort System

Most victims of medical error do not file a claim—US Senate testimony found that only 1 in 7 of those who were injured by medical negligence ever filed a claim, and most claims litigated at trial (69.5%–73.7%) result in no payment to the patient.[17] Trial rates for medical malpractice cases usually range between 7% and 10% of lawsuits. These include cases in which defendants prevail—approximately 7 or 8 trials in 10.[17] Data have shown that 65% of claims are dropped, dismissed, or withdrawn; 25.7% of claims are settled; 4.5% of claims are handled through alternative dispute resolution; and only 5% are tried (90% of which are decided for the defendant).[18] The statistics for pediatric claims are similar. Sixty-eight percent of claims are dropped, withdrawn, or dismissed; 27% are settled in favor of the plaintiff; and 5% of claims went to trial.[19]

In cases that go to trial, most result in a decision for the defendant.[17,20] Even though few cases go to trial or are settled, it still costs a significant amount to defend each claim. Claims that did not lead to payments incurred average defense costs of $22,163 for cases dropped, withdrawn, or dismissed, compared with $100,000 for claims that went to trial.[18,21] Pediatrics is the fourth highest among 28 specialties in terms of mean defense expenses.[18,22] Furthermore, although even fewer cases result in awards, it is the unpredictability of those awards that makes liability insurance premiums soar. The number of large verdicts is increasing rapidly. The mean award rose more than 200% from 1996 to 2002.[23]

Pediatric Claims

In 2007–2008, a survey by the American Medical Association revealed that there were 36 medical malpractice claims per 100 pediatricians. Only 27.3% of pediatricians reported that they had ever been sued, and only 5.4% had been sued 2 or more times. During a 24-year period (1985–2009), there were 247,073 closed claims reported to the Physician Insurers Association of America data-sharing project.[20] Pediatricians account for 2.90% of these claims, making it 10th among the 28 specialties in terms of the number of closed claims.[11,22] From February 1, 2004, through December 31, 2005, a total of 30,195 malpractice payments were made on behalf of practitioners in the United States; 14% of those payments were child related, according to the National Practitioner Data Bank.[24] During this 23-month period, $1.73 billion was paid for malpractice cases involving children. The average child-related malpractice payment was significantly greater than an adult-related malpractice payment ($422,000 vs $247,000); however, child-related indemnity payments were only half as likely to occur, compared with adult-related indemnity payments. Failure to diagnose was the leading reason for child-related payments (18%), followed by improper performance (9%), delay in diagnosis (9%), and improper management (6%). Approximately 40% of all malpractice awards were the result of surgical or obstetric issues.

The most common conditions for which pediatricians are sued and the average indemnity payments are listed in Table 1-2.[25]

Table 1-2. Average Pediatric Malpractice Claims by Patient Condition

Condition	Average Indemnity (for All Claims), $
1. Brain-damaged infant	440,379
2. Meningitis	437,423
3. Routine infant or child health check	155,039
4. Respiratory problems in newborns	270,607
5. Appendicitis	116,285
6. Pneumonia	239,531
7. Specified non-teratogenic anomalies	186,708
8. Premature birth	250,031
9. Birth	286,407
10. Asthma	193,414

Litigation Time

The litigation system is expensive, but at the same time, it is slow and provides little benefit to patients injured by medical errors. For most injured patients, therefore, the litigation process, while offering the remote chance of an excessive judgment, provides little real benefit, even for those who file claims and pursue them. The average length of time between occurrence of the injury and closure of the claim was 5 years.[8]

Insurance Premiums

The cost of excesses of the litigation system affects the cost of malpractice insurance coverage. Significant increases in premium costs are evident in most specialties. However, these increases have varied widely across states; some have seen increases of 30% to 75% since the late 1990s, albeit rates have decreased consistently between 2006 and 2009.[26]

The insurance crisis may be less acute in states that have reformed their litigation system. For example, states with limits of $250,000 or $350,000 on noneconomic damages have average combined highest premium increases of 12% to 15%, compared with 44% in states without caps on noneconomic damages.[26] In testimony before the US Government Accountability Office, it was found that insurers in states that enacted caps on noneconomic damages had losses 17% lower than those of insurers in other states, and that premiums were 6% lower.[27] In addition, losses and premiums of insurers in states where punitive damages were not allowed were 16% and 8% lower than losses and premiums of insurers in states that allowed punitive damages.[27]

Medical Liability Reform

According to a previous US CBO report in 1998, tort reform would result in a savings of $1.5 billion over 10 years.[28] In 2009, this report was updated to 10-year savings of $54 billion.[16] Medical liability experts lauded the CBO report as a confirmation of the need for tort reform. National tort reform could mean significant cost savings across the entire health care system. For instance, the CBO put forth the assessment, "Lower medical malpractice costs would contribute to slower growth in Medicare spending," as a result of changes in malpractice premiums used to calculate payment rates for hospitals, physicians, and other health care professionals.[28] The CBO also projected that Medicaid spending would decline as state payment rates adjust to lower costs for liability insurance. Everyone bears the burden of high medical liability costs because they also increase the cost of health care, requiring more out-of-pocket payments, insurance premiums, and federal taxes for government health care programs such as Medicaid and Medicare.

Escalating insurance premiums are debilitating the US health care delivery system by forcing physicians to practice defensive medicine or limit the services they offer.[29] In addition, physician dissatisfaction with medicine during a liability crisis has a direct effect on the delivery of care. Each malpractice crisis raises issues relating to physician access and affordability.[30] Comprehensive medical liability reform is needed today if physicians are to continue providing quality health care tomorrow.

In the early 1970s, California faced a malpractice-induced access crisis like that facing many states now and threatening others. California enacted comprehensive changes to make its medical liability system more predictable and fair. The American Academy of Pediatrics (AAP) has proposed reforms (see "American Academy of Pediatrics Position on Tort Reform" on page 8) based on the California Medical Injury Compensation Reform Act of 1975

(MICRA).[31] This is one of the most extensive tort reform acts at the state level in this country. These include caps on noneconomic damages; elimination of joint and several liability; offsets of awards from collateral sources; reasonable limits on statutes of limitations; and limits on attorney contingency fees. The most important component of these reforms is the $250,000 cap on noneconomic damages.

These reforms have helped reduce the direct costs of medical malpractice; malpractice premiums in California decreased in direct response to MICRA.[32] These reforms have survived all questions of constitutionality.[33-35] Even the cap on noneconomic damages, which was not adjusted for inflation, has been held to be constitutional.[36] These reforms have saved California residents billions of dollars in health care costs. Since the enactment of MICRA, the liability insurance market in California has stabilized and remained stable. Insurance rates for California physicians are among the lowest in the nation.[37]

Since MICRA, almost every state has enacted some type of statutory reform in an effort to discourage filing and adjudication of frivolous lawsuits. For example, Pennsylvania enacted effective tort reform that prohibited *venue shopping,* ie, filing a lawsuit in an area known to have plaintiff-friendly juries rather than filing in the area where the alleged malpractice actually occurred.[38]

Damage Caps

Many states have enacted some type of cap on damages recoverable in medical liability cases.[39] These include a cap on noneconomic damages such as recovery for pain and suffering, loss of marital companionship, and loss of consortium. Noneconomic damages are nebulous and impossible to quantify, so legislators believe that some reasonable limits must be placed on recovery. Punitive damages are rare, intended to punish the defendant for negligent behavior, but also are not quantifiable and are therefore capped. Some states have a cap on total damages, including economic damages, and a few states index damage caps at the rate of inflation or some other economic indicator.[40]

Damage caps can be an effective way of stabilizing the liability insurance market by prohibiting excessive awards, which can result in increased liability insurance premiums for all physicians and ultimately may result in access problems for patients, if physicians leave for other locations. Caps strike a balance between compensating injured patients for damages impossible to quantify and encouraging the availability of health care in general. States were quick to follow California's lead, enacting some form of cap on recoverable damages. Currently, approximately half of states have enforceable damage caps, although future legal challenges to their constitutionality are possible. Other jurisdictions have ruled that damage caps are a violation of individuals' constitutional rights to jury trials or access to courts. Supreme courts in Illinois,[41] Georgia,[42] and Wisconsin[43] have issued rulings to this effect. In other states (among them, Pennsylvania), statutes have not been enacted because the state constitution theoretically prohibits capping damages.

Periodic Payments of Damages

Periodic payments of damages are required in some states, allowing a defendant to pay the claimant a fixed amount periodically until the death of the claimant. Other states do not mandate periodic payment and permit a lump-sum payment, yet allow any party to a lawsuit to request periodic payments. The court in some states must order such payment if requested; in other states, the court may exercise discretion in determining whether periodic payment is appropriate.

A periodic payment arrangement generally benefits physicians and insurers, who are sometimes required to pay huge verdicts that primarily benefit a claimant's beneficiaries. This prevents the need to pay out a large amount of money after a claimant's death.

Abolition of Collateral Source Rule

In states that have the *collateral source* rule, juries are prohibited from hearing evidence that the claimant has been compensated from other collateral sources (eg, insurance) for injuries incurred from medical malpractice. Often, this means that the claimant collects twice for injuries. For public policy reasons, the rule exists so as to encourage people to become adequately insured.

In jurisdictions that have abolished the collateral source rule, juries are permitted to consider evidence that a plaintiff has been compensated from another collateral source in determining the damages payable to a claimant. In other states, evidence about collateral sources may be introduced but only after a verdict is rendered. The judge then uses this information in determining the award. Courts in these states are more informed when determining how much a claimant should be compensated to make himself or herself "whole." This information is helpful in determining the amount of damages that are fair to a plaintiff. Complicating this issue is whether health insurers can *subrogate* (ask to be reimbursed from the legal judgment) to reclaim the part of the judgment that was paid by the health insurance company for the injury.

Limitations on Attorneys' Fees

Plaintiffs' attorneys' fees, which are typically a percentage of the amount received at settlement or trial, are capped in some states. A few states apply a sliding scale based on the total amount of damages awarded in a case.

Reasonable limits on attorneys' fees benefit injured persons by helping to ensure that the injured parties receive their fair share of damages. Without limits, the most seriously injured persons or their beneficiaries may not see the amount of compensation that others receive in states with limits. Limits may also discourage frivolous lawsuits because they make it less lucrative to pursue cases without merit.

Statute of Limitations

State laws specify when an action for medical malpractice must be commenced. This is known as the *statute of limitations,* and time varies among states. Generally, the statute of limitations begins to accrue at the time of the alleged negligent act that caused the injury, when an injury is discovered or should have been discovered, or some combination of the two. States with shorter statutes of limitations limit health care professionals' risk of potential liability. It is optimal to have a short yet reasonable statute of limitations, permitting injured parties or their representatives adequate time to pursue litigation without unreasonably subjecting health care professionals to litigation many years after the alleged malpractice incident.

Many states also have a definite time frame within which claims must be commenced, especially relating to pediatrics. Important to pediatricians is that most state laws distinguish time frames for minors. Usually, these laws require actions to be commenced within a set number of years after the alleged malpractice incident involving the minor. However, a minor still retains the statute of limitations of an adult when that minor reaches the age of majority or legal adulthood, usually 18 years. If a lawsuit has not been filed on the minor's behalf while a minor, he or she may still be able to file as an adult when the age of majority is reached as long as the minor files within the statute of limitations for an adult. This is why pediatric medical records need to be retained for such a long period. Also, there may be a different statute of limitations if the lawsuit includes a wrongful death action. Finally, many states distinguish claims brought by persons deemed "incompetent" by reason of mental illness, imprisonment, or disability by extending or *tolling*

the statute of limitation until the cause for the "incompetence" has ended.

Alternative Dispute Resolution

See Chapter 15 for a discussion of alternative dispute resolution.

Affidavits or Certificates of Merit

An affidavit or certificate of merit is a procedural pretrial tool that some states employ to limit adjudication of frivolous lawsuits that burden the court system. It is required in approximately half of the states. These documents generally may be filed by a plaintiff or defendant in a medical liability action and must be filed within a definite time frame. The plaintiff must file an affidavit or certificate of merit along with the complaint to establish that the claim is justified. In other states, plaintiffs must file such a certificate following a defendant's answer to the complaint. It is usually signed by a health care professional who qualifies under state law as an expert witness.

One potential area of tort reform involves the consequences of expert testimony, including the provision of affidavits or certificates of merit. The majority of medical malpractice lawsuits are dropped without any payment, yet wasteful defense costs are still incurred. If a case is supported by an expert and is subsequently dismissed or dropped, should there be some consequence to the individual stating that malpractice occurred? Courts have held that individual associations can discipline members who provide irresponsible expert testimony.[44] If there are consequences to the individuals providing affidavits or certificates of merit in cases in which there is no negligence, this testimony will be more reliable and provided with more care.

Some recent state court decisions have held that mandatory filing of affidavits or certificates of merit are unconstitutional.[45–47] These courts have held that the affidavit or certificate of merit requirement essentially requires plaintiffs to submit evidence supporting their claims before they even have an opportunity to conduct discovery and obtain such evidence; the statute requiring an affidavit or certificate of merit unduly burdens the right of medical malpractice plaintiffs to conduct discovery and, therefore, violates their right to access the courts; and the statute changes the procedures for filing pleadings in a lawsuit, thereby jeopardizing the court's power to set court procedures.

Health Courts[48,49]

Specialized courts, similar to bankruptcy and patent law, have been suggested as part of tort reform programs. Theoretically, these specialized health courts would help to correct the failings of our existing medical justice system by providing more consistent rulings on the standard of care that would promote greater communication about errors. The hallmark of this approach is the use of trained judges who have health care expertise, akin to the use of specialized judges in federal tax court. Continuing training and education would ensure that judges remained current in their understanding of health care issues.

American Academy of Pediatrics Position on Tort Reform[50]

The AAP encourages the federal government to provide grant funding for demonstration projects to test alternative dispute resolution mechanisms. The AAP also supports comprehensive medical liability reform at state and federal levels. Specifically, the AAP recommends

- State statutes of limitation of 2 years with the toll beginning from the occurrence (rather than discovery) of an injury, and establishment of a child's majority at age 6 years for the purpose of medical liability.
- Periodic payments of future damages exceeding $100,000.

- Noneconomic damages capped at a reasonable amount.
- There should be mandatory offsets for collateral sources (with credit for out-of-pocket costs of collateral sources).
- Use of a sliding scale for plaintiff lawyer fees.
- A fair share rule that allocates damage awards fairly and in proportion to fault.
- Punitive damages should be awarded only if there is "clear and convincing" evidence that the injury meets the standard set by each jurisdiction and for acts for which the defendant is directly responsible. In those cases, punitive damages should be limited to a reasonable amount.

The AAP supports the allocation of federal grants to enable the exploration of state- or local-based demonstration of pilot programs that have the potential to improve the current litigation climate through measures that could expedite equitable resolutions of disputes and contribute to the reduction of litigation costs and the practice of defensive medicine. These alternatives include expert witness qualifications, health courts, early disclosure and compensation programs, administration of a determination of compensation model, and liability protections for use of evidence-based medicine guidelines.[50]

Informed Consent

Medical decisions used to be made exclusively by physicians. This paternalistic approach has been abandoned; now, physicians accept the concept that patients are entitled to make their own decisions about their health. For many patients and family members, personal values affect health care decisions, and physicians have a duty to respect the autonomy, rights, and preferences of their patients and their surrogates. This is obviously tempered in pediatrics, in that children do not have the legal capacity to make decisions about health care. Generally, it is the child's parents or legal guardians who have the legal authority or right to give informed consent for health care of their child. Because children are not making informed decisions about their own health care, the doctrine of informed consent as it relates to pediatrics has been interpreted to be one of *informed permission.*[51]

The doctrine of informed consent reminds us to respect persons by fully and accurately providing information relevant to exercising their decision-making rights. Violations of the informed consent doctrine have led to litigation using theories of negligence or battery (an unwanted/unsolicited touching). Physicians must include at least the following elements in their discussions involving informed consent[52,53]:

1. *Provision of information.* Patients should have explanations, in understandable language, of the nature of their ailment or condition; the nature of proposed diagnostic test(s) or treatment(s) and the probability of their success; the existence and nature of the risks involved; as well as the existence, potential benefits, and risks of alternate test(s) or treatment(s) and the benefits and risks of no test(s) or treatment(s).
2. *Assessment of the patient's understanding of this information.*
3. *Assessment, if only tacit, of the capacity of the patient (parent) to make the necessary decision(s).*

It behooves the pediatrician to be aware that a practitioner can be held liable for scenarios involving inadequate informed consent.[54] In fact, recent cases have underscored the notion that a cause of action based on inadequate informed consent differs from one based on medical malpractice (negligence), and that a cause of action alleging inadequate informed consent is valid even if the medical care was not determined to be substandard.[55,56]

There are situations in which an adolescent minor can give informed consent without the involvement of a parent. These exceptions to the general rule of informed consent are addressed in detail in Chapter 9.

Consent by Proxy

There will be circumstances in which a parent or legal guardian cannot accompany a child to a physician visit. This triggers the doctrine of *consent by proxy,* which allows parents or legal guardians to delegate another to give consent for them for evaluation or treatment of the child. Thus, consent by proxy has potential liability problems for those who care for children. The AAP issued a clinical report on consent by proxy for nonurgent pediatric care.[57] Although uncommon, physicians have been held liable in scenarios involving consent by proxy.[58]

Assent

Decision-making involving the health care of older children and adolescents should include, to the greatest extent feasible, the assent of the patient. Even in situations in which one should not and does not solicit the agreement or opinion of minors, involving them in discussions about their health care may foster trust and a better physician-patient relationship, and perhaps improve long-term health outcomes.

Assent should include at least the following elements[51]:

1. Helping the patient achieve a developmentally appropriate awareness of the nature of his or her condition.
2. Telling the patient what he or she can expect with tests and treatment(s).
3. Making a clinical assessment of the patient's understanding of the situation and the factors influencing how he or she is responding (including whether there is inappropriate pressure to accept testing or treatment).

4. Soliciting an expression of the patient's willingness to accept the proposed care. For this final point, it is noted that no one should solicit a patient's views without intending to weigh them seriously. In situations in which the patient will have to receive medical care despite his or her objection, the patient should be told that fact and should not be deceived.

In a research setting, assent is required for adolescents of a certain age.[59]

Duty to Warn

Traditionally, the law states that a physician has a legal duty only to the patient. However, courts have expanded that duty to third parties other than the patient in situations involving the protection of a third party who may be placed at risk of injury by the patient. Current examples of this expanded rule include a physician's duty to warn a specific third party about potential harm threatened by a patient,[60] a physician's duty to warn a third party who may be at foreseeable risk for contracting a sexually transmitted or communicable disease,[61] and a physician's duty to warn about the risks of driving while taking medication or with epilepsy.[62] Several courts and commentators have supported a duty to warn patients at foreseeable risk of inheriting a genetic disease.[63-65]

A difficulty faced by pediatricians is the conflict between the duty to warn and tenets of patient confidentiality. According to Institute of Medicine guidelines,[66] several criteria must be met before confidentiality can be broken. First, all attempts to elicit voluntary disclosure must have failed. Secondly, there must be a high probability of irreversible harm. The pediatrician can be entangled in an ethical and legal dilemma, for which there is no easy algorithm. Legal consultation may be necessary to sort out these difficult cases.

Managed Care Liability

Because of the rapid rise in health care costs, many employers, state Medicaid programs, and other purchasers of health care have turned to managed care organizations (MCOs) to control costs and provide care. In fact, managed care has become the predominant form of health care in many parts of the United States. More than 170 million Americans receive health care coverage or benefits through some type of managed care setting.[67] By 2007 about 20% of these services were directly provided by health maintenance organizations (HMOs), while the majority were served through other managed arrangements, 60% in preferred provider organizations (PPOs) and 13% in point-of-service plans. National HMO enrollment has significantly increased, plateauing in 2000 and stabilizing over the first decade of this century (Figure 1-1).

Managed care organizations have introduced prepayment and negotiated fees for services as alternatives to traditional fee for service. The HMO is generally a prepaid plan whereby primary care physicians are paid on a monthly capitated basis for each enrollee, who in turn pays a relatively nominal coinsurance payment for medical service. The PPO is a provider group, traditionally assembled by an insurance company but increasingly organized by physicians or entrepreneurs, that provides services on a discounted basis to consumers.

Managed care has changed significantly in the last decade. As managed care continues to change, so will the legal pitfalls that pediatricians may encounter. Pediatricians are responsible for keeping up with this ever-evolving area of medical care and continuing to offer the best medical care possible at the least possible risk to patients and providers.

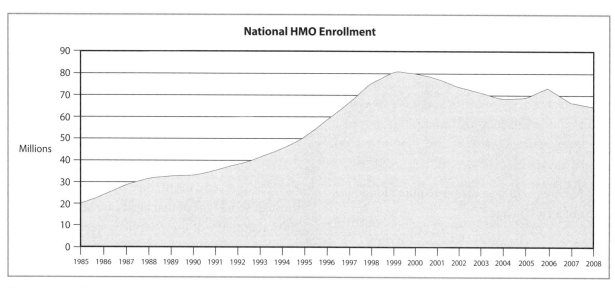

Figure 1-1. National Health Maintenance Organization Enrollment[68]

Resource Control Issues

Before the advent of managed care, pediatricians made decisions about a patient's treatment based primarily on what the pediatrician perceived were the patient's medical needs, wishes, and financial resources. Because of the public's increased awareness of the high cost of medical care, its demand to curb those costs, and fiscal methods used by managed care to meet these demands, the pediatrician can often be placed in a very uncomfortable and legally risky position. Managed care organizations use a variety of methods to limit health care resources, such as referrals, testing, and medication. Earlier forms of managed care often placed the physician in the unenviable position of having to preapprove all referrals, tests, and emergency department visits to control costs. While some of these pre-approvals have been relaxed, they remain an area of legal exposure for the plan and physician.

Pediatrician Issues

- Pediatricians should document all conversations about utilization review issues.
- Pediatricians should use the entire appeal process to render the most appropriate care for their patients.

- In the rare case that a pediatrician cannot reach a reasonable agreement with utilization reviewers, the pediatrician should discuss with the patient the option of paying independently for medical care received outside of his or her insurance coverage. If the patient chooses to refrain from receiving the non-covered care, it is important to document this *informed refusal.*

Another way in which an MCO may involve itself in the referral process is by limiting specialists to whom a primary care physician can refer. It is important that a pediatrician be able to refer a patient for diagnostic or therapeutic services to another physician, or any other provider of health care services permitted by law to furnish such services, whenever the primary care pediatrician believes that this may benefit the patient.[69,70] The primary care pediatrician should base these referrals on individual competence and ability to perform services needed by the patient. A physician should not refer a patient unless the physician is confident that the services provided by the referral will be performed competently and in accordance with accepted scientific standards and legal requirements. For this reason, it is important that pediatricians be allowed to refer to pediatric medical subspecialists and pediatric surgical specialists.

Incentive Programs

Although a direct relationship between the effectiveness of incentive programs in affecting physician behavior and decreasing medical costs has never been proven, some MCOs continue to use them. Courts and state legislatures have looked at the issues associated with financial incentives. At this time, incentives have been found to be legal but still pose a risk. It is difficult for physicians to defend their position in cases in which direct financial gain appears to be attached to medical decision-making. A program that is not tied to utilization alone but also to quality of care is far superior to a program that does not consider quality.

Managed Care Liability Suits

In the 1990s, there was a plethora of litigation in which MCOs were sued for improper denial of care. These were defeated largely through the contention that MCOs were exempt from state-related malpractice litigation and that this preemption was related to the federal regulation as delineated in the Employee Retirement Income Security Act (ERISA).[71] Preemption, in effect, requires the lawsuit to be filed in federal court under the provisions of ERISA rather than in state courts where different state rules of law may apply. Congress enacted this 1974 law to replace a patchwork scheme of state regulations with a uniform set of federal regulations for employer-based benefit plans. For decades it has effectively shielded MCOs from similar efforts on the part of states to regulate employer-based health care coverage.

This ERISA preemption only applies to MCOs if the health care plan is provided through an employer, and usually only to plans that are self-insured. Health plans insured through outside insurance, government or church-sponsored plans, and individually held health plans are generally subject to state insurance law and not preempted, and lawsuits can be filed in state courts. Likewise, plans not offered through employment are also

outside the scope of ERISA. But for those health care plans covered by ERISA, the preemption has the effect of reducing liability risk to MCOs (eg, eliminates state claims such as a personal injury/malpractice claim based on the insurance company's fraud, negligence, or bad-faith breach of contract). A claim based on the federal ERISA law limits recovery of damages to the value of the benefit claimed and does not permit recovery for economic and noneconomic losses. Thus, claims under ERISA have limited recovery.

In 1987, the US Supreme Court held that ERISA preemption provisions are "deliberately expansive" and that the phrase "relates to" that is in the law should be interpreted broadly.[72] As a result, from 1974 to 1994, courts held that if a claim "relates to" an employee benefit plan, it is preempted by ERISA. However, in rendering its 1987 decision, the Supreme Court did not establish any rules clarifying the meaning of that phrase. Thus, federal and state courts have been left to grapple with ERISA application to managed care, often reaching varying and at times conflicting opinions. Yet some general criteria for determining whether a particular claim is subject to ERISA exist.

Since 1997, courts have applied the same principles in making their decisions and thereby have reached consistent, although not identical, conclusions. The trend is to draw a distinction between those types of claims disputing the quantity of benefits provided versus those disputing the quality of benefits. Most courts have ruled that claims related to malpractice pertain to the quality of heath care received by a plan enrollee and are not preempted by ERISA, and state medical liability laws are applicable. On the other hand, claims challenging an MCO decision to deny benefits pertaining to the quantity of health care benefits that an enrollee receives are covered by ERISA.

The effect of the ERISA preemption in a claim against an HMO reached the US Supreme Court in 2000 in what is considered a significant holding in this area of the law. In *Pegram v Herdrich*,[73] the court decided that an HMO's financial incentive schedule, which rewards its affiliated physicians for minimizing medical care, does not per se violate the law. The court determined that decisions governing the quantity of health care provided do implicate ERISA and that decisions governing the quality of health care (ie, medical malpractice) do not.

In 1997, Texas became the first state to pass a managed care right-to-sue law. The Texas law[74] did the following: established a statutory cause of action against MCOs that impose negligent treatment decisions on patients; barred MCOs from retaliating against physicians who advocated a particular course of treatment for their patients in opposition to the plan's policies; and provided patients a right of independent review of medical treatment to determine medical necessity. Subsequently, other states, including Georgia, California, Washington, Oklahoma, West Virginia, Oregon, Arizona, and Maine, have enacted similar statutes. New Mexico allows direct lawsuits against MCOs but does so through its consumer protection laws rather than as part of its general health care statutes. These statutes were ultimately held to be preempted by ERISA. In *Aetna v Davila*[75] and *Cigna v Calad*,[76] the US Supreme Court held unanimously that ERISA was intended to preclude state legislation that might provide additional legal remedies to injured patients. The court held that utilization decisions that contradict decisions of the patient's physician and allegedly adversely affect patient care were covered by ERISA. Thus, recovery of damages would be limited to an ERISA recovery. That court, as well as others, prevailed on the US Congress to revisit an "unjust and increasingly tangled ERISA regimen." This decision has led to the belief that, at least until Congress revisits the issue, managed care is immunized against liability suits.[77]

Summary

As state reforms can and have been repealed, overturned, or declared unconstitutional by state supreme courts, the AAP believes that comprehensive federal and state legislation must be enacted to ensure lasting medical liability reform. Without medical liability tort reform, the insurance market will remain unstable. If physicians cannot get affordable liability insurance, this may significantly affect health care access and affordability. Whatever the outcome of the most recent medical liability crisis, it is important that pediatricians remember this lesson: understanding medical liability insurance, risk management, and complex health care regulations is too important to be delegated to office staff or professional advisors. Pediatricians need to be schooled in these issues if they are to make informed decisions on medical liability insurance companies and their coverage. Other potential liability issues relate to informed consent, consent by proxy, and duty to warn third parties. Pediatricians have also been "managing" managed care relationships for a long time now. There is great complexity of medicolegal issues within various managed care environments. Pediatricians must be aware of the legal risks that need to be managed in these situations. To negate understanding of all of these issues places pediatricians' livelihood at risk.

References

1. National Health Expenditure Data: Historical. Centers for Medicare and Medicaid Services Web site. http://www.cms.gov/NationalHealthExpendData/02_NationalHealthAccountsHistorical.asp. Accessed June 14, 2011

2. Cortese D, Korsmo JO. Health care reform: why we cannot afford to fail. *Health Aff (Millwood)*. 2009;28(2):w173–w176

3. Towers-Perrin-Tillinghast. 2008 Update on U.S. Tort Cost Trends. http://www.towersperrin.com/tp/getwebcachedoc?webc=USA/2008/200811/2008_tort_costs_trends.pdf. Accessed June 14, 2011

4. Towers-Perrin-Tillinghast. 2006 Update on U.S. Tort Cost Trends. http://www.towersperrin.com/tp/getwebcachedoc?webc=TILL/USA/2006/200611/Tort_2006_FINAL.pdf. Accessed June 14, 2011

5. Gonzalez JL. Texas' medical liability landscape improves after tort reform enacted. *AAP News*. 2010;31(5):20

6. Baker T. *The Medical Malpractice Myth*. Chicago, IL: University of Chicago Press; 2005

7. Mello MM, Chandra A, Gawande AA, Studdert DM. National costs of the medical liability system. *Health Aff (Millwood)*. 2010;29(9):1569–1577

8. Studdert DM, Mello MM, Gawande AA, et al. Claims, errors and compensation payments in medical malpractice litigation. *N Engl J Med*. 2006;354(19):2024–2033

9. United States Congress Joint Economic Committee; Vice Chairman Jim Saxton. *Liability for Medical Malpractice: Issues and Evidence: A Joint Economic Committee Study*. May 2003. http://www.house.gov/jec/tort/05-06-03.pdf. Accessed June 14, 2011

10. Localio AR, Lawthers AG, Brennan TA, et al. Relation between malpractice claims and adverse events due to negligence. Results of the Harvard Medical Practice Study III. *N Engl J Med*. 1991;325(4):245–251. http://www.nejm.org/doi/pdf/10.1056/NEJM199107253250405. Accessed June 14, 2011

11. American Medical Association. Physician Practice Information Survey, 2007/2008. http://www.ama-assn.org/ama/pub/physician-resources/solutions-managing-your-practice/coding-billing-insurance/the-resource-based-relative-value-scale/physician-practice-information-survey. Accessed June 14, 2011

12. James JM, Davis WE. *Physicians' Survival Guide to Litigation Stress: Understanding, Managing, and Transcending a Malpractice Crisis*. Lafayette, CA: Physician Health Publications; 2006

13. Studdert DM, Mello MM, Sage WM, et al. Defensive medicine among high-risk specialist physicians in a volatile malpractice environment. *JAMA*. 2005;293(21):2609–2617. http://jama.ama-assn.org/content/293/21/2609.full.pdf+html. Accessed June 14, 2011

14. Bishop TF, Federman AD, Keyhani S. Physicians' views on defensive medicine: a national survey. *Arch Intern Med*. 2010;170(12):1081–1083

15. Tancredi LR, Barondess JA. The problem of defensive medicine. *Science*. 1978;200(4344):879–882

16. Elmendorf DW. Letter to the Honorable Orrin G. Hatch. http://cbo.gov/ftpdocs/106xx/doc10641/10-09-Tort_Reform.pdf. Accessed June 14, 2011

17. Testimony of Neil Vidmar, Russell M. Robinson, II, Professor of Law, Duke Law School, before The Senate Committee on Health, Education, Labor and Pensions. Hearing on Medical Liability: New Ideas for Making the System Work Better for Patients, June 22, 2006. http://www.law.duke.edu/features/pdf/vidmartestimony.pdf. Accessed June 14, 2011

18. Physician Insurers Association of America. *Claims Trend Analysis*. Rockville, MD: Physician Insurers Association of America; 2009

19. Carroll AE, Buddenbaum JL. Malpractice claims involving pediatricians: epidemiology and etiology. *Pediatrics*. 2007;120(1):10–17

20. Congressional Budget Office. Limiting tort liability for medical malpractice. *CBO Economic and Budget Issue Brief*. January 8, 2004. http://www.cbo.gov/doc.cfm?index=4968&type=1. Accessed June 14, 2011

21. Kain ZN, Caldwell-Andrews AA. What pediatricians should know about child-related malpractice payments in the United States. *Pediatrics*. 2006;118(2):464–468. http://pediatrics.aappublications.org/content/118/2/464.full.pdf+html. Accessed June 14, 2011

22. Physicians Insurers Association of America. *Claim Trend Analysis*. Rockville, MD: Physicians Insurers Association of America; 2005

23. Doran BJ, ed. *Medical Malpractice Verdicts, Settlements and Statistical Analysis*. Updated ed. Horsham, PA: Jury Verdict Research; 2005

24. National Practitioner Data Bank, A.M. Best & Co (as cited by Americans for Insurance Reform), Centers for Medicare & Medicaid Services

25. McAbee GN, Donn SM, Mendelson RA, McDonnell WM, Gonzalez J, Ake JK. Medical diagnoses commonly associated with pediatric malpractice lawsuits in the United States. *Pediatrics*. 2008;122(6):e1282–e1286. http://pediatrics.aappublications.org/content/122/6/e1282.full.pdf+html. Accessed June 14, 2011

26. Annual Rate Survey. *Medical Liability Monitor*. October 2009

27. Hillman RJ, Allen KG. *Medical Malpractice Insurance: Multiple Factors Have Contributed to Premium Rate Increases. Testimony before the Subcommittee on Wellness and Human Rights, Committee on Government Reform, House of Representatives.* Washington, DC: United States General Accounting Office; 2003. GAO-04-128T. http://www.gao.gov/new.items/d04128t.pdf. Accessed June 14, 2011

28. Congressional Budget Office. Preliminary cost estimate, HR 4250 Patient Protection Act of 1998. July 24, 1998. http://www.cbo.gov/ftpdocs/7xx/doc701/hr4250.pdf. Accessed June 14, 2011

29. Viscusi WK, Born PH. Damage caps, insurability, and the performance of medical malpractice insurance. *J Risk Insur.* 2005;72(1):23–43

30. Mello MM, Studdert DM, DesRoches CM, et al. Caring for patients in a malpractice crisis: physician satisfaction and quality of care. *Health Aff (Millwood).* 2004;23(4):42–53

31. Medical Injury Compensation Reform Act (MICRA) (1975). Cal Civ Code §3333.1

32. American College of Physicians. Beyond MICRA: new ideas for liability reform. *Ann Intern Med.* 1995;122(6): 466–473

33. *American Bank & Trust Company v Community Hospital,* 36 Cal 3d 359 (1984)

34. *Barme v Wood,* 37 Cal 3d 174 (1984)

35. *Roa v Lodi Medical Group, Inc.,* 37 Cal 3d 920 (1985)

36. *Fein v Permanente Medical Group,* 38 Cal 3d 137; 695 P2d 665; 211 Cal Rptr 368 (1985)

37. Studdert DM, Yang YT, Mello MM. Are damages caps regressive? A study of malpractice jury verdicts in California. *Health Aff (Millwood).* 2004;23(4):54–67

38. Medical Care Availability and Reduction of Error (MCARE) Act, 40 PS §1303.101 et seq

39. Cetra MJ. Damage control: statutory caps on medical malpractice claims, state constitutional challenges and Texas' Proposition 12. *Duq L Rev.* 2004;42:537–558

40. Wisconsin Statutes. Health care liability and injured patients and families compensation. §655.017

41. *Lebron v Gottleib Memorial Hospital,* 930 NE2d 895 (Ill 2010)

42. *Atlanta Oculoplastic Surgery, P.C. v Nestlehutt,* 286 Ga 731; 691 SE2d 218 (Ga 2010)

43. *Ferdon v Wisconsin Patients Compensation Fund,* 284 Wis 2d 573; 701 NW2d 440 (WI 2005)

44. *Austin v American Association of Neurological Surgeons,* 253 F3d 967 (7th Cir 2001)

45. *Putman v Wenatchee Valley Medical Center,* 216 P3d 374 (Wash 2009)

46. *Wimley v Reid,* 991 So2d 135 (Miss 2008)

47. *Summerville v Thrower,* 369 Ark 231, 253 SW3d 415 (Ark 2007)

48. Tobias CW. Health courts: panacea or palliative? *U Rich L Rev.* 2005;40:49–52

49. Chow E. Health courts: an extreme makeover of medical malpractice with potentially fatal complications. *Yale J Health Policy Law Ethics.* 2007;7(2):387–427

50. Advocating for medical liability reform. American Academy of Pediatrics Web site. http://www.aap.org/visit/advocate1.htm. Accessed June 15, 2011

51. American Academy of Pediatrics Committee on Bioethics. Informed consent, parental permission, and assent in pediatric practice. *Pediatrics.* 1995;95(2):314–317

52. Appelbaum PS, Lidz CW, Meisel A. *Informed Consent: Legal Theory and Clinical Practice.* New York, NY: Oxford University Press; 1987

53. Stevens-Simon C. Assent in pediatric research. *Pediatrics.* 2006;118(4):1800–1801. http://pediatrics.aappublications. org/content/118/4/1800.full.pdf+html. Accessed June 15, 2011

54. Vukadinovich DM. Minors' rights to consent to treatment: navigating the complexity of state laws. *J Health Law.* 2004;37(4):667–691

55. *Bubb v Brusky,* 768 NW2d 903 (WI 2009)

56. *McQuitty v Spangler,* 976 A2d 1020 (Md. 2009)

57. McAbee GN, American Academy of Pediatrics Committee on Medical Liability and Risk Management. Consent by proxy for nonurgent pediatric care. *Pediatrics.* 2010;126(5):1022–1031

58. *Tabor v Scobee,* 254 SW2d 474 (Ky 1951)

59. Public Health and Welfare, Institutional Review Boards; Ethics Guidance Program. 42 USC §289

60. *Tarasoff v Regents of the University of California,* 551 P2d 334 (Cal 1976)

61. *Shephard v Redford Community Hospital,* 151 Mich App 242, app den'd, 431 Mich 872 (1988)

62. *Harden v Dalrymple,* 883 F Supp 963 (D Del 1995)

63. *Pate v Threlkel,* 661 So2d 278 (Fla 1995)

64. *Safer v Pack,* 677 A2d 1188, cert den'd, 683 A2d 1163 (NJ 1996)

65. Andrews LB, Fullarton JE, Holtzman NA, Motulsky AG, eds. *Assessing Genetic Risks: Implications for Health and Social Policy.* Washington, DC: National Academy Press; 1994

66. McAbee GN, Sherman J, Davidoff-Feldman B. Physician's duty to warn third parties about the risk of genetic diseases. *Pediatrics.* 1998;102(1):140–142

67. Managed care state laws and regulations, including consumer and provider protections. National Conference of State Legislatures Web site. http://www.ncsl.org/IssuesResearch/Health/ManagedCareStateLaws/tabid/14320/Default.aspx. Updated March 2008. Reposted May 2010. Accessed June 15, 2011

68. Positioning you for change in health care. Managed Care On Line Web site. http://www.mcol.com. Accessed June 15, 2011

69. Nelson RP, Minon ME, eds. *A Pediatrician's Guide to Managed Care.* Rev ed. Elk Grove Village, IL: American Academy of Pediatrics, 2001

70. Council on Ethical and Judicial Affairs. Referral of patients, 3.04. In: *Code of Medical Ethics of the American Medical Association: Current Opinions with Annotations: 2010-2011 ed.* Chicago, IL: American Medical Association; 2010

71. Protection of Employee Benefit Rights, Congressional Findings and Declaration of Policy. 29 USC §1001 et. Seq

72. *Pilot Life Insurance Company v Dedeaux,* 481 US 41(1987)

73. *Pegram v Herdrich,* 530 US 211 (2000)

74. *Texas Civil Practice & Remedies Code,* §88.001 et. Seq

75. *Aetna Health Incorporated v Davila,* 542 US 200 (2004)

76 *Cigna HealthCare of Texas, Incorporated v Calad,* 540 US 1175 (2004)

77. Bloche MG. Back to the '90's—the Supreme Court immunizes managed care. *N Engl J Med.* 2004;351(13):1277–1279

CHAPTER 2

Anatomy of a Medical Malpractice Lawsuit and the Defendant Pediatrician

Jeffrey L. Brown, MD, FAAP

KEY CONCEPTS

- Warning Signs
- Responding to an Incident
- Managing a Formal Claim
- Working With the Defense Attorney
- Making Settlement Decisions
- Discovery Procedures
- Deposition
- Going to Trial
- Tips on Being an Effective Witness

An *adverse event* or incident is any event that creates the possibility of a medical malpractice lawsuit. The actions that physicians take in this early stage can be extremely important. A delay in reporting a suspected problem can make it difficult to prepare a strong defense. This chapter outlines early signs of potential lawsuits, common mistakes physicians make when they are concerned that the patient may initiate a lawsuit, how physicians can work effectively with liability insurers, and other important considerations.

Pediatricians should review what is stated in their professional liability policies about reporting claims. The insured physician is usually required to notify the carrier as soon as a claim is made or suspected. Pediatricians are sometimes afraid that their premiums will increase or that their policies will be canceled as the result of early notification of an incident or claim. There may be a legitimate concern in some instances, but the benefits of early notification clearly outweigh the disadvantages because the insurance company can begin examining the case for merit and prepare the defense if necessary. In addition, pediatricians can obtain guidance on the proper way to conduct themselves during the litigation process.

Sometimes pediatricians just want the problem to go away, or think that once they notify the insurer, the company will just take care of the problem. A good response to any incident requires the pediatrician and the carrier's claims manager to work together. There are times when a quick and quiet settlement may not be the most prudent course of action. For example, it is important to consider the implications of the National Practitioner Data Bank (NPDB)—any insurance company payments, including settlements, made on a physician's behalf from a malpractice claim must be reported to the NPDB. These are entered under the physician's name and retained permanently. Hospitals and other health care facilities are required to check NPDB records for affiliated physicians when reviewing their privileges, and even small payments made to settle frivolous lawsuits might affect hospital and managed care credentialing.

Warning Signs

An unexpected poor outcome and complications of medical treatment have the greatest potential for resulting in a lawsuit. The pediatrician should be aware of the possibility of a lawsuit when a patient or family makes a *direct complaint* to the doctor or expresses extreme dissatisfaction about the care or outcome. When the physician receives a letter from an attorney that requests information and records about a patient's treatment, written authorization (which often accompanies the letter) from the patient is required before any information should be released. Only copies of the requested records (eg, radiographs, test results) should be sent, and the original documents should be retained for safekeeping. It is also wise to keep a list of requests for medical records that document when they were provided, to whom they were sent or given, and for what purpose.

Be aware of problems that can lead to dissatisfaction with care that may result in a lawsuit. When a patient refuses a recommended medical test or procedure, be sure to document discussions about the importance of the test or procedure, the risks and benefits of available treatments and no treatment, and why the test or procedure was refused. In some instances, it may be prudent to have the patient sign a refusal form. Patients who do not keep scheduled follow-up visits should be noted, and efforts to contact the patient to reschedule should also be documented. Those who fail to pay bills or seem to be unusually slow in paying for services may already be dissatisfied. When a representative from the practice politely contacts the patient to express concern or offer a payment schedule, it may ease the tension and restore confidence in the physician. Be cautious before offering to forgive a debt entirely, especially when there has been a poor outcome, because it may be interpreted as a sign of guilt should the patient decide to sue anyway. In addition, debt forgiveness (eg, unpaid co-payments or deductibles) must be done in conformity with state and federal law and managed care contracts.

Responding to an Incident

Sometimes a simple act of humility in response to an incident can help avoid a lawsuit. If a patient has experienced an unexpected bad outcome, some experts recommend that you explain what happened to the patient and family with honesty and empathy. Above all, do not avoid contact with the patient or family after a poor outcome. It creates the impression that you are uncaring, incompetent, or both.

Advise your liability insurance carrier whenever there is an unexpected poor outcome. This will give the company a head start should a malpractice claim be filed later. Physicians who have a claims-made policy will only be covered for those claims that are *reported* during the policy period, so early reporting has an additional benefit for them. If the event occurred at a hospital, its risk or incident manager should also be told about the problem.

The patient's medical record should be reviewed as early as possible to avoid recollections becoming blurred over time. Remember that any written or recorded information given to the insurance company is not privileged and is subject to discovery. However, communication between the physician and his defense attorney is protected by attorney-client privilege.

If a formal claim has been filed, the physician should never attempt to negotiate directly with the patient or the patient's attorney. Any discussion with the plaintiff's attorney should be avoided unless your attorney consents, which is unlikely. These discussions may seriously undermine a good defense. If some contact with the patient or family concerning the incident does occur, the physician should make contemporaneously written notes of precisely what was said. Also, any correspondence about the incident should be saved in a file separate from the patient's medical records.

Managing a Formal Claim

A *lawsuit* begins when the plaintiff (patient or family) files a *notice of intent, formal complaint,* or *declaration.* This is a legal document that consists of *allegations,* the legal basis to support a claim for medical malpractice against the defendant(s), and a *request for damages* or other relief. Once a notice, complaint, or declaration has been filed, the defendant will be served with a *summons* that is attached to the notice, complaint, or declaration. It requires the defendant to file a response, usually known as an *answer,* within a specified period.

When the physician receives a summons, she should notify the professional liability insurance company immediately. The insurer will assign an attorney to defend the case and respond appropriately to the complaint or declaration. The physician should deliver the summons (including the attached complaint or declaration) to the defense attorney or insurance carrier and keep a photocopy. Using the defendant physician as a resource, the attorney will prepare a *written answer* that responds to each of the allegations and issues, and will file it within the time prescribed by the summons (usually within 30 days of the date the summons was received). Failure to file an answer on time may result in a *default judgment* against the defendant, and this failure to respond to allegations or issues may be considered an admission of culpability.

Some defense attorneys will ask the defendant to prepare a thorough analysis of the case. This could include a detailed evaluation of all medical files, correspondence, radiographs, and laboratory test results. The defendant may also be asked to prepare a chronologic review of the medical data, including everything known about the patient and course of treatment. These materials that are developed at the request of the attorney in preparation for litigation are not subject to discovery by the plaintiff's counsel because they are considered attorney-client

work product. All of this information should be kept in a file completely separate from the patient's medical and business records.

Medical records should not be altered in any way. There are times when it might seem tempting to add a clarifying statement to the record that says a test was ordered or a historical question was asked and answered—because it was. This should never be done. Evidence of alteration can lead to a loss of credibility in court as well as a substantial increase in the size of an award. In many cases, altered records (even when the facts are accurate) will render a case indefensible. Sophisticated scientific techniques are now available that show when an alteration has occurred. Altering medical records may result in sanctions against the medical license and may also be a crime (misdemeanor).

Defendant physicians may also be asked to serve as a medical educational resource for their own defense team. In this role, the physician reviews textbooks and medical articles relating to the medical issues in the case and conducts computer database searches. It may be beneficial to educate the defense team about the scientific strengths and weaknesses of the medical aspects of the case. To be properly prepared for trial, defense attorneys need to be aware of differing medical viewpoints, alternative treatments, and opinions that may be given by opposing expert witnesses. Not every defendant physician or defense attorney is comfortable with this role. Sometimes the defendant needs to keep a healthy distance from his own case to preserve emotional well-being.

The relationships among the defendant physician, malpractice insurance representative, and defense attorney should be honest, open, and truthful. To mount a successful defense, good teamwork is required, and good relationships will help decrease the likelihood that unanticipated facts or opinions will come as a surprise during the trial.

Above all, the defendant pediatrician needs to stay calm, remain as objective and professional as possible, and try to be open to new strategies that will help her case. A first reaction to a summons may be surprise, anger, panic, guilt, or self-doubt. Being hostile and overreacting to the situation is not productive and has the potential to interfere with a good result.

Working With the Defense Attorney

In most cases, the insurance company will choose the defense attorney. An appointment should be arranged to meet with that attorney as soon as possible after the lawsuit has been initiated. The first meeting can be considered an *evaluation phase.* Any problems discovered at this early stage in the relationship that cannot be resolved directly between the defendant and attorney should be communicated to the insurance company. Most insurance carriers will be very earnest in their attempt to resolve them.

Evaluating the Attorney

The primary objective of the evaluation phase of the attorney-client relationship is to determine whether this attorney is the best person to handle the defense of this case. It would be most unusual for a malpractice insurance carrier to hire a law firm or attorney who is not competent to handle your case—after all, if there is a poor outcome, the insurer will usually have to pay the bill. Nevertheless, there are some considerations that should be kept in mind.

- Does your attorney understand the medicine involved in your case?
- If not, is your attorney willing and motivated to learn the medicine?
- Does your attorney have experience handling similar types of medical malpractice claims?
- What is the reputation of your attorney and his or her law firm?

- Is your attorney well regarded by other legal colleagues and the community as a whole?

A personal attorney for your family or the legal advisor for your medical practice can help you to make this evaluation.

The most prestigious and highly regarded attorneys will not be of much help in your defense if they are consumed with other legal matters. Be very concerned if your attorney always seems too busy or does not seem to have time for you. Cancelled appointments, unreturned phone calls, or frequent interruptions during pretrial preparation meetings should all be a cause for concern.

The defense of medical malpractice claims is a team effort by many law firms and often involves many lawyers within the same firm. Even in such circumstances, the pediatrician should still try to learn how involved the lead defense counsel will be.

- Will the lead counsel personally handle your deposition and those of the opposing expert witnesses and plaintiffs?
- Will the lead counsel be the primary attorney at the actual trial?
- What is the projected role of the law firm's associates and paralegals in handling your defense?

Sometimes the insurance company has an agreement that specifies the exact involvement of the lead counsel in the defense of claims and minimizes uncontrolled involvement of associates and paralegals. If you are having difficulty getting answers to these questions, contact the insurance company directly.

Personality can play a role in building a successful attorney-client relationship. You do not have to be a close, personal friend of your attorney, but you should be able to communicate well and feel that your personalities are compatible.

Cases involving multiple defendants are common in pediatrics. Insurance companies may suggest that the same attorney provide the defense for several defendants in the case. This may save money for the insurer and be more efficient but is generally not in your best interest; be aware that potential conflicts of interest may occur. For example, when there is a factual dispute between you and the other codefendants, ask the attorney how this will be handled so that potential benefits for you will not be sacrificed to the common defense. There also may be a conflict of interest for an attorney who is representing the hospital and physician.

It is hoped that after this evaluation phase the defendant and defense attorney will begin to function as a defense team with a clear understanding of each person's role and responsibilities.

Your Responsibilities

The main responsibilities of the defendant pediatrician are to be cooperative and participate in the defense of the case. Try to learn as much as possible about how the legal process works in medical liability cases. Your attorney is an expert on this litigation process, so listen carefully to what he or she has to say at its various stages.

Medical liability litigation is very time consuming. You should plan in advance to set aside time from your schedule to work on your own defense. Even though you are the defendant pediatrician, you are also one of the medical experts for the defense team. You should offer to provide medical input and evaluate your role in preparing the medical defense. For example, you can research and provide medical literature relevant to the case. You can help your attorney to carefully review and understand the medical records and your treatment rationale. You can summarize and review alternative treatments that you considered and rejected, and help your attorney to evaluate the medical strengths and weaknesses of your case.

Visual aids and exhibits can sometimes be helpful in educating the jury about the science and medicine involved; their possible use should be discussed with your attorney. Also, you should offer to help

your attorney identify noted experts on the condition involved in your case, especially those who are known to agree with your management and point of view. Finally, you can offer to help your attorney with the selection of a jury; in small communities you may have background information about prospective jurors that might not be otherwise available.

Maintain an open and honest dialogue with your attorney throughout the lawsuit process. Provide any information that may be pertinent—good and bad. Sometimes physicians are afraid to give bad information to their attorney because they are embarrassed by it or truly believe they made an error. It can be catastrophic to your case if surprise facts surface at the last minute and the defense was not adequately prepared. You should regard yourself as your attorney's legal patient and recognize that he or she needs a complete and honest history to come to a proper diagnosis of the condition of your case. Just as you would with your own physician, do not be shy or unduly deferential; it is always better to ask questions and clear up any misunderstandings.

Your Attorney's Responsibilities

Your attorney has many responsibilities to you during the course of the litigation. Many physicians feel extremely uncomfortable in the role of defendant, and your attorney can help alleviate your anxiety by keeping you abreast of litigation process, explaining the significance of each stage of the proceedings, and thoroughly preparing you for your role in the process.

At the most basic level, the attorney must carefully investigate the evidence and prepare your case by deciding on the best strategies and tactics to defend it. He or she must consider all of the factors that could win or lose your case, such as the status of medical records, severity of the injury, and magnitude of potential damages the plaintiff may be awarded. Your attorney also will consider the appearance and credibility of the plaintiff and the plaintiff's witnesses, your appearance and credibility, the quality of your witnesses, and the credibility of expert witnesses for both sides. Any arrogant demeanor by you will be noted because it will not bode well in front of a jury. Other variables include the ability and experience of the plaintiff's attorney and the trial judge assigned to the case, as well as potential biases that the judge may have. The venue in which the case is to be tried is also important—some areas tend be "plaintiff friendly" and grant larger awards than others. Caliber of the jurors and track record of similar cases previously settled or tried to a verdict in your jurisdiction will also be pertinent.

Making Settlement Decisions

Whether your case should be settled will be discussed almost from the time an incident occurs until there is a final verdict—and sometimes beyond. Although a *settlement* usually is not a formal part of pretrial or trial procedures, substantially more cases are settled rather than contested at trial, so you should be aware of what a settlement is, when it can be used, and what your rights are.

A settlement is an agreement made between parties to an incident, claim, or lawsuit that resolves their legal dispute. A settlement often is a financial disposition of a case without a decision being made on its merits. In most instances, a monetary payment is made to the plaintiff in exchange for a *release,* a legal document that absolves the defendant from all past, present, and future liability in connection with the incident.

Most releases specifically state that the settlement by the defendant is not an admission of fault or guilt. Regardless of this, any settlement that results in a payment of any amount on your behalf by an insurance company or anyone other than yourself must be reported to the NPDB. (See Chapter 18 for a discussion of the implications of having these data reported.)

There are substantial costs and risks to both sides involved in litigating a case to a conclusion. The longer a case lasts, the more time, effort, and money are expended, so a settlement may be advantageous to both parties in the suit.

Settlement Perspectives

Each of the participants in the litigation process has reasons for preferring a settlement. The judge hearing the case wants to clear the court's calendar and dispose of cases quickly. To accomplish this, the judge may require the parties to participate in a pretrial settlement conference. Some states require that all cases go through alternative procedures before trial in an effort to settle. In some cases, the judge may actively serve as settlement mediator. The insurance carrier has a financial interest in the settlement of the case. A settlement would limit defense costs and establish a fixed sum for payment. When a settlement occurs, an uncertain jury verdict is eliminated and both sides know exactly what the result will be.

The possibility of a settlement may be discussed at any time, but when a case is settled at the incident stage, this process often is referred to as *aggressive incident management.* The mechanics of this type of settlement differ from those of settling a formal claim.

Settlement of an Incident

You will play a primary role in achieving a settlement at this early stage. The decision to make a settlement offer to your patient is made by the insurance carrier or hospital. In exchange for a release, some financial compensation to the patient is usually given, and there may also be an offer to provide future medical treatment for the patient's condition at no additional cost.

Settlement of a Formal Claim

Attorneys play a primary role in settling a case once a *formal claim* is filed. The plaintiff's attorney typically makes a monetary demand for settlement to the defense attorney. The defense attorney, after consultation with the insurance company, responds with denial, acceptance, or a *counteroffer*. If a counteroffer is made, negotiations may continue until the parties arrive at an acceptable settlement figure. Demands or counteroffers can be made at any time, even if settlement negotiations have previously broken down.

The insurance company also plays a critical role. *The insurance company retains the authority to negotiate all settlements.* The defense attorney can only accept a settlement demand or make a counteroffer with the consent of the insurance carrier.

Your rights concerning the settlement decision are contained in the policy. You may not have the right to accept or reject a settlement depending on the terms of your malpractice insurance policy. Sometimes a discounted rate is offered if you waive your right to consent to a malpractice settlement. The insurance carrier and defense attorney can agree to settle without your consent, but you should be consulted about your opinions on the matter. Defendants who do have that right will be consulted before any offers or counteroffers of settlement are made. You may be asked to sign a written consent to a proposed settlement.

You should review the terms of your insurance policy to determine whether you have the right to accept or reject a settlement. Regardless, your attorney should inform you of all settlement demands and counteroffers. The attorney should present the choices, risks associated with each approach, and alternatives that may be available. Failure to keep you fully advised of settlement negotiations may constitute bad faith on the part of your insurance carrier, especially if the amount of a trial verdict exceeds your coverage. A good-faith letter from your own personal attorney (not your malpractice attorney) may need to be sent to the insurance company if settlement is not reached and the case appears to be proceeding to trial. This letter can protect you in the event that there is a verdict in excess of your policy's limit.

If the amount of the claim does exceed your policy limits, your personal attorney can play a significant role in protecting your interests. He or she will serve as your intermediary on settlement discussions and negotiations to ensure that your rights are protected, and pursue remedies if those rights are breached. Losing a case does not necessarily mean that your insurance company will automatically appeal.

Your attorneys are experienced in this area of settling a lawsuit. They should be able to give you an estimate of your chances of winning at trial. It is rarely wise to try an indefensible case that could have been settled early. On the other hand, to settle a defensible case may set a bad precedent and have adverse implications for your future practice and insurability. Accepting a settlement, especially if you feel you did nothing wrong, is difficult for most physicians, but you should be as realistic and objective as possible. In the end, accepting a settlement is often viewed as a business decision that may not always be seen as fair, but it is still important to make your feelings known to your defense attorney before the decision is finalized. Also, the decision to settle is highly dependent on the strength of your case, which includes opinions of your expert witnesses.

Discovery Procedures

Discovery refers to pretrial procedures used by parties to the lawsuit to gather and learn of evidence so as to develop their respective cases and minimize the element of surprise at the time of the trial. These typically include requests for documents, interrogatories, and depositions, but can also include requests for admission of facts and authenticity of documents. Discovery can eliminate unnecessary issues and enable the parties to settle the case or present it for trial in an efficient manner. Through these discovery procedures, attorneys can assess the strengths and weaknesses of both sides. Because depositions are the most important of discovery procedures for a defendant pediatrician, they will be discussed in a separate section.

Interrogatories

Interrogatories are a set of written questions submitted by one party to the lawsuit to an opposing party, who must answer in writing under oath within a certain period. The answers are admissible at trial under certain circumstances. Interrogatories are more important than most people realize; therefore, your responses must be precise, thorough, and truthful.

Your defense attorney will usually draft the answers to interrogatories based on information you provided in pretrial consultations. You should carefully review with your attorney all of the answers before they are signed and sworn to by you. You and your attorney will have to live with your responses throughout the litigation, and they can be used to cross-examine you at trial.

Request for Admission of Facts

A *request for admission of facts* is a series of factual statements, usually limited in number, served by one party to a lawsuit to another. The party served with the request is required to admit or deny the factual statements, in writing and under oath, within a prescribed period. Once a fact is admitted by an opposing party, that fact is no longer in controversy and can be introduced at trial without having to offer evidence to prove it.

A request for admission of facts is an important discovery procedure that may be overlooked by many defense attorneys. For example, if you are a codefendant who was only marginally involved in the treatment of the plaintiff, a request for admission of facts could provide the basis for a quick

motion for *summary judgment* (ie, a judgment made in your favor, dismissing you from the lawsuit without the necessity of a trial). If you are the primary defendant, a request for admission of facts can still simplify the disputed facts and shorten the ultimate trial. You should consult with your attorney about the advisability of using this discovery procedure and assist him or her in formulating the factual statements for the request.

Request for Admission of Authenticity of Documents

A *request for admission of authenticity of documents* is a request from one party to a lawsuit to another. This request asks the opposing party to admit the authenticity of certain documents. In a medical malpractice lawsuit, the documents usually admitted by this procedure would be the medical records. If the plaintiff has had relevant prior or subsequent treatment from another physician or medical facility, this procedure also can be used to admit those records without the need for testimony from the other physician or medical records librarian. This procedure is beneficial in simplifying the trial itself and procedures related to the introduction of documents at trial.

Deposition

Deposition is oral testimony taken from a witness under oath, not in court but conducted in a manner approved by the court. The testimony is taken before a court reporter, reduced to writing, and often used in court at trial. It may also be videotaped. The deposition is a pretrial discovery procedure and is probably the most important way to investigate the facts and assess the physician's demeanor and credibility. The person whose deposition is being taken is called the *deponent*.

Preparation for your deposition is vital. Your testimony can be used to impeach your credibility if you offer contradictory testimony at trial.

Remember that whatever you say during your deposition is said under oath. If you are not prepared, you may say something that will be repeated at trial that you will regret.

Before your deposition, you and your defense attorney should thoroughly discuss your knowledge of the facts of the case and the subjects on which you may be examined. It cannot be emphasized enough how important it is that you and your attorney devote sufficient time to this preparation. As part of this preparation, you will be instructed by your defense attorney to review the entire history of the case. You need to familiarize yourself with all pertinent medical records, radiographs, test results, and data so that you can refer to this material easily. If you were asked to prepare a chronologic summary of the incident by your defense attorney, you should carefully review it before the deposition. It is also helpful to review the literature in any area of your specialty that may be the subject of questioning. You should have a complete understanding of the alternative treatment options that were available at the time you treated the patient (which may differ from those that are presently available) and be prepared to explain the choice you recommended to your patient.

Effective preparation for your deposition should not be done at the last minute. If your deposition is approaching and you have not heard from your defense attorney, you should call and schedule a pre-deposition conference. Your defense attorney should set aside enough time to thoroughly prepare you for this event. Your attorney should question you and critique your answers. During this rehearsal, your attorney should be able to identify danger areas and weak points in your testimony and suggest alternative language and approaches that you can use.

Your attorney should alert you to possible tactics that may be used by the plaintiff's attorney. In particular, you will be warned of repetitious or leading questions. *Repetitious questions* are calculated to put you on the defensive, wear you down, or irritate you. The same question might be asked over and over again, with only slight changes in wording, with the intent of making you angry, causing you to lose your temper, changing your answer, or having you make a damaging statement. The attorney using leading questions is trying to get a "yes" or "no" response from you when a qualified answer might be more appropriate. The attorney begins his question with "Wouldn't you agree, Doctor..." or "Is it not true, Doctor...." Think for yourself and do not let the opposing attorney put words in your mouth. You do not have to answer these questions with a simple "yes" or "no" response. It is important to stay as calm and composed as possible.

Your defense attorney should warn you of the dangers of *hypothetical questions.* The opposing attorney may ask you to assume certain facts and express an opinion based on those facts. If you do, you may become trapped into becoming an expert witness for the plaintiff. Before answering, make certain that those assumed facts are consistent with this case and your opinion is consistent with your defense.

A common mistake is to boast when you are asked the breadth of your medical reading and knowledge. If you do, you may be held accountable for its content. In addition, opposing counsel may try to get you to define an *absolute standard of care* in your case. You should remind the attorney (and the jury at trial) that each patient and each situation is unique. Do not allow yourself to appear confused by the proceedings. It might suggest to others that you were equally confused while treating your patient.

In preparation for the deposition, you should tell your attorney everything that you remember about the incident. Do not extend this same courtesy to the plaintiff's attorney. *Limit your answers to the question that the plaintiff's attorney asks.* If the question is, "Did you examine Patient A on January 21, 2010?" the correct answer, if you remember, is "yes" or "no." Do not describe why you saw the patient, where the examination took place, or whatever else you remember about that meeting unless you are asked specifically. You do not want to introduce information that the plaintiff's attorney may not have known previously.

Finally, you should be careful about saying that journals, texts, or medical resources are authoritative. Physicians may misinterpret this question to mean, "Is this text written by an authority on the subject?" What the attorney is actually asking is whether what is written in the text or article is correct. If you agree, you will be asked why you did not follow its advice. This is a common trap and you should be prepared to handle it. One way is to work with your attorney to develop a response that appropriately acknowledges a particular document (eg, journal article, policy statement, clinical guideline), person, or entity (eg, American Academy of Pediatrics) as only *one source* of information on that topic or procedure. You can further explain that often these publications include a disclaimer that the recommendations are general and do not reflect an exclusive course of treatment, and that individual circumstances must be taken into account. If the plaintiff's attorney persists with that line of questioning, you can remind the attorney that you do not always agree with everything written by any one author or what is found in any one particular text. When you are questioned about an article or text, ask the plaintiff's attorney to specify the particular section of the text or article, review its language, and carefully consider your position before answering.

Just as you have the right to be present when the plaintiff is being deposed, the plaintiff has the same right at your deposition. Do not be surprised if the plaintiff is present at your deposition. This is occasionally used as an intimidation tactic. This should not change any of the answers that you give in response to questioning, and it is, in fact, good practice if you have to testify at trial.

General purposes of a deposition are as follows:

- *Discovery of facts:* To ascertain the facts and apply the law to those facts.
- *Impeachment:* Documenting a witness's story. If the story changes later, inconsistencies will become obvious.
- *Admissions that would constitute affirmative evidence.*
- *Preservation of the testimony of witnesses.*
- *Learning the identity, demeanor, and credibility of a witness.*
- *Facts and issues are narrowed and clarified.*
- *Evaluating the case for settlement.*
- *Settlement opportunity.*
- *Stipulations:* An agreement between opposing attorneys about issues that are pertinent to the case.

Appropriate Deposition Conduct

You must take your deposition seriously even when it is conducted in an informal atmosphere. If you have a strong case and perform well at the deposition, you may convince the plaintiff's side that its case is too weak to go forward. It may also affect the way your insurer and your own experts view the potential outcome of the case. Most medicolegal commentators believe that the strength of the defendant's testimony is one of the most critical factors in deciding a case. Do not be overly concerned in the event that you do not perform well. We all learn from our mistakes, and it is better to make them here than on the witness stand at trial.

Before You Answer

To be an effective witness, you should listen carefully to the question, weigh your response, and give yourself time to think before answering. Take a short pause before answering a question; it also gives your defense attorney a chance to object to the question, if necessary. If your attorney does object to a question, do not answer it until you are instructed to do so.

If you do not understand a question, ask for it to be repeated or clarified before you respond. If you do not know an answer to a question, it is perfectly all right, indeed preferable, to say, "I don't know." You should not be equivocal in your answers unless uncertainty is inherent in the medicine of the case. Do not ramble or volunteer information that goes beyond the scope of the question. You should not go off on a tangent trying to defend yourself. Your defense attorney will give you that opportunity later in the deposition or at trial.

Although the deposition process may be upsetting, it is important to remain emotionally calm. Do not argue with opposing counsel; that is your defense attorney's job. A deposition can be time consuming, but you should not show exasperation, boredom, or fatigue. Ask for a break if you need one. Because your deposition is being recorded, it is important to speak clearly and distinctly so that you can be understood. Do not act in a patronizing manner to the plaintiff's attorney, even when the questions are simplistic or inappropriate. Sometimes questions are intentionally asked in an overly simplistic way to create the illusion that the plaintiff's attorney knows less than he or she does. Physicians have a tendency to slip into teaching mode and offer more information than was asked in the question. Although the deposition process is often informal, you should dress neatly, be courteous, and remain professional at all times. As the deponent, you will not be able to consult with or ask questions of your attorney during the deposition, but you can ask for a break and during that time meet with your attorney.

Finally, keep in mind that the opposing attorneys in the case may be acquaintances or even friends. You should not become upset if there is friendly banter or conversation between them. Remember, although the practice of law is an adversarial profession by nature, attorneys who are adversaries in court can be friendly when not in court.

Deposing Other Witnesses

Because you are a party to the lawsuit, you do have an absolute right to attend all of the depositions that take place for this lawsuit. This right is frequently disregarded, especially in view of the time constraints of a busy medical practice. When practical, make every effort to be present at the depositions of the plaintiff and the key opposing expert witnesses. Watching others being deposed may help to prepare you for your own deposition, and your presence may make it more likely that the testimony will remain truthful and avoid exaggeration. Plaintiff's experts, in particular, may be reluctant to be critical of your care in your presence. You may also be able to provide on-the-spot assistance to your attorney in his or her examination of the witness.

There may be a significant amount of time and expense involved in attending these depositions (eg, out-of-state travel), but it can be very beneficial. In some cases, your insurance carrier may pay for your expenses to attend the deposition of the plaintiff's expert.

Never forget that you are testifying under oath. From a legal standpoint, your testimony at a deposition is subject to all the responsibilities and penalties of testifying in court.

Finally, it should be noted that not all states require deposing expert witnesses. Some, like Pennsylvania, use expert reports in lieu of depositions, while others, such as New York and Oregon, do not actually disclose the identity of expert witnesses until they appear at trial.

Going to Trial

Plaintiff's Case

The facts of the case are presented to *the trier of fact*—a jury, or a judge in a bench trial—through various witnesses and exhibits. The plaintiff's goal during this phase of the trial is to produce facts that will convince the trier of fact that you were negligent and that your negligence directly caused injury to the plaintiff. The plaintiff must prove all 4 elements of a medical malpractice case: the existence of a legal duty (ie, patient-physician relationship); the breach of that duty (ie, deviation from the standard of care); injury with damages; and that the breach of duty was the legal cause of the injury. The plaintiff has the burden of proving all elements by a *preponderance of the evidence,* ie, it must be more likely true than not (greater than 50%). If the plaintiff has alleged that you committed *gross negligence,* a higher burden of proof—that there is clear and convincing evidence—is imposed on that portion of the claim; this may be required to award punitive damages (rare in a medical malpractice case).

The plaintiff attempts to meet that burden by introducing evidence through witnesses, medical documents, and exhibits. The most critical evidence for the plaintiff usually comes from one or more expert witnesses, who must testify that your care of the plaintiff did not meet the standard of care and that this failure resulted in injury to the plaintiff. A medical standard of care is generally meant to indicate that the care given is the same as that which would have been rendered by a reasonable physician in your medical community with similar training and under the same circumstances.

Directed Verdict

At the completion of the plaintiff's case, the defense will usually make a motion for a *directed verdict.* This is a ruling by the trial judge that as a matter of law, the verdict must be in favor of the defense. If the judge feels that the plaintiff has not introduced enough evidence to demonstrate that the basic elements of medical negligence might have occurred, the judge will grant a directed verdict in favor of the defense. This is an uncommon occurrence, but once granted, the case ends.

Defense Case

If the defense motion for a directed verdict is denied or not requested, it is your responsibility, and that of your codefendants, if any, to present evidence in support of your defense. The defense goal is to demonstrate that there was no negligence or that the plaintiff's injuries were not the direct result of your negligence. Like the plaintiff, the defense attempts to meet this goal by introducing evidence through medical documents, witnesses, and exhibits. Expert witnesses for the defense also are crucial in establishing that the standard of care was met or that the plaintiff's injuries were not the result of a deviation from that standard of care.

Rebuttal Evidence

On completion of the defense case, the plaintiff is entitled to offer *rebuttal evidence.* This is usually limited to new evidence that was introduced during the presentation of the defense case. The plaintiff is given the right of rebuttal under the US system of law because the burden of proof is on the plaintiff.

Direct Examination and Cross-examination of Witnesses

Although plaintiffs and defendants may introduce many types of evidence, the direct testimony of witnesses is among the most important, especially in jury trials. This testimony is elicited by direct examination and cross-examination.

Direct examination is the questioning of a witness by the attorney who has called that witness to the stand. During direct examination, the attorney may not ask leading questions unless the witness is considered to be a *hostile witness,* ie, one who favors the opposing side of the litigation. A leading question is one which is worded in a way that the person answers the way that the questioner wants the question to be answered. Thus, the leading question already suggests the answer or gives information in the question (eg, "Doctor, did you examine the child's abdomen on July 15?"). If the trial judge determines that a witness is hostile, the attorney who called that witness is permitted to treat the questioning as a cross-examination and is allowed to ask leading questions. If you, as a defendant, are called as a witness by the plaintiff's attorney, you will likely be declared and treated as a hostile witness.

Cross-examination is the subsequent questioning by an opposing attorney of a witness who is already on the witness stand. The attorney is allowed to ask leading questions during the cross-examination. However, cross-examination is limited to only the issues raised during the direct examination.

Closing Arguments

The attorneys' final summary is presented to the jury in the *closing arguments*. In a bench trial, closing arguments are still presented to the trial judge, but they are usually shorter and more legalistic. They allow attorneys to summarize their cases and argue why their clients should prevail. The plaintiff's attorney goes first, followed by the defense attorney (or attorneys if there are codefendants). The plaintiff's attorney is given a final opportunity to make a rebuttal argument after defense attorneys have finished.

After the completion of the presentation of the evidence, the defense usually renews its motion for a directed verdict. In a large majority of cases, this motion is denied and the jury is allowed to deliberate before reaching a verdict.

Instructions to the Jury

In a jury trial, the judge instructs jurors on applicable laws, explains legal principles involved, and provides guidelines that govern the jury's deliberations as it attempts to reach a final decision on the case, known as the *verdict*. Instructions typically are uniform and nondiscretionary and are actually read verbatim to the jury from the jury instruction book. The judge will discuss the issue of granting

damages but will also instruct jurors not to consider damages unless they find in favor of the plaintiff.

After completing deliberations, the jury's verdict must be in favor of the plaintiff or defendant. Depending on the state where the trial is being held, the jury verdict may be decided by a simple majority or a two-thirds majority, or it may require a unanimous decision. In the case of multiple defendants, there can be a split verdict that finds in favor of some, but not all defendants. *Damages* must be awarded to the plaintiff when the verdict is in favor of the plaintiff, even if they are in a small amount (known as *nominal damages*). The jury may also hold the plaintiff partially responsible for a bad medical outcome. *Comparative negligence* is a partial legal defense that reduces the amount of damages that a plaintiff can recover based on the degree to which the plaintiff's own negligence contributed to the injury. This is a modification of the *doctrine of contributory negligence,* which disallows any recovery by a plaintiff whose negligence contributed, even minimally, to causing injury. No damages are awarded in the case of a complete defense verdict. At trial, most cases are won by the defendant(s).

Post-verdict

A medical malpractice case does not necessarily end when a verdict is rendered. All of the parties to the lawsuit have a number of options if the verdict is unfavorable. If a verdict has been entered against you as a defendant, your attorneys can ask the trial court to set aside the verdict and grant a new trial; ask the trial court to change the verdict by entering a judgment in your favor; ask the trial court to reduce the amount of the damage award (known as *remittitur);* reopen settlement negotiations with the plaintiff, using the threat of appeal as leverage; or file an appeal.

If the verdict was in your favor (ie, a defense verdict), the plaintiff has a similar range of options.

In some jurisdictions, a plaintiff who won the case can ask the trial judge to increase the amount of damages awarded (known as *additur)*. This is not allowed in the federal court system.

Tips on Being an Effective Witness

As with many endeavors, preparation is the key element to giving effective trial testimony. Begin by reviewing the previous section. All of the suggestions are applicable to your trial testimony. This section will focus on those items that pertain specifically to the trial.

Being present in the courtroom during the entire trial is important because it conveys your concern to the judge and jury. In addition to the facts of the case, a judge or jury is likely to take into consideration your appearance, professionalism, and manner. Remember, it is your testimony at the trial that may be the single most important factor in determining whether you win or lose your case.

Pretrial Preparation

Carefully review the transcripts of your deposition testimony and those of the experts from both sides, especially if they took place a long time ago. You need to have a clear understanding of the strengths and weaknesses of your case before the trial begins.

You also need to spend a substantial amount of time with your attorney preparing for trial. Discuss the most likely questions you will be asked, how best to phrase your answers, and where the most likely pitfalls lie. You might also want to ask about the plaintiff attorney's personality and style of asking questions, and it is often helpful if you have been advised about the court testimony of any other witnesses that have taken the stand before you. If you do not feel comfortable after only one preparatory meeting, it is not unusual to arrange follow-up meetings until you do.

Depending on *your* personality, you might wish to have your family, friends, and even selected members of your staff present during the trial. They may be able to give you moral support in this stressful time, and it might make a favorable impression on the jury.

Trial Testimony

If you and your attorney decide that it is in your best interest to testify on your own behalf, you should take time to consider how to conduct yourself on the stand. Most importantly, you should tell the truth. If the plaintiff's attorney points out that some of your responses were inconsistent, do not become overly anxious; your attorney can give you an opportunity to explain later. There is no reason to panic if you are caught in a mistake.

Be certain you understand a question before you attempt to answer it. You cannot give an accurate answer unless you understand the question. When necessary, you can ask the attorney to repeat the question or to phrase it differently. You are not taking a test; "I don't know" can be a valid answer. Be cautious when responding to leading or repetitive questions, and when you do give an answer, do not volunteer more information than the question calls for. You do not have to accept the opposing counsel's summary of your testimony unless it is accurate.

It is best to speak directly to the jury, and do not talk down to them. Do not be afraid to look at jurors and to speak to them as frankly and openly as you would to a friend or neighbor. Do not use complex medical terminology; rather, speak to the jury as you would speak to the parents of your patients, in language they can understand. On the other hand, you do not want to look to your lawyer for help when you are on the stand. The jury will notice this and get a bad impression.

When the judge asks you a question, you should answer it politely unless your attorney objects, and refer to the judge using the title "Judge" or "Your Honor." You should be articulate—speak clearly and audibly, and avoid annoying mannerisms of speech like mumbling or speaking rapidly using "um" and "you know."

It makes a favorable impression on the court and jury when you are polite and well mannered. You would like jury members to feel that you are the kind of doctor they would like to have caring for them. They will be severely prejudiced against you if you are viewed as arrogant, smug, inconsiderate, or uncaring. No matter how difficult it seems, try not to lose your temper while you are on the witness stand. Do not argue with the attorney on the other side. He or she has the *right* to question you. Studies have demonstrated that physicians are usually viewed favorably by jurors and that the individuals in the courtroom that are the least liked and trusted by the jury are the attorneys and expert witnesses.

It may sound simplistic, but your overall appearance and demeanor at the trial are extremely important. Flashy dress or an expensive suit may suggest that you are successful, but it might also convey to some jurors that you are more interested in making money than in taking care of patients. An untidy appearance might make you look homey to some, but others may feel that you look disorganized, unclean, and unreliable.

Following are some suggestions for making a good impression to the jury:

- When approaching the witness stand, walk with confidence and at a normal pace.
- Sit straight in the witness chair. Slouching may indicate disinterest or sloppy habits.
- Placing your hand over your mouth when you speak makes it look as though you have something to hide.

- Arms folded across the chest may be perceived as looking defensive.
- Tugging at your ears, wringing your hands, biting your fingernails, or fidgeting on the witness stand should be avoided at all costs. It makes you appear nervous and unsure of yourself—not characteristics most people look for in a trusted physician.
- Listen to the question carefully before answering it.
- Answer the specific question honestly and directly without embellishment.
- Look at the jury when answering questions.
- Finally, no matter what has transpired during your testimony or cross-examination, do not show relief, triumph, or defeat when you are excused from the witness stand.

CHAPTER 3

Professional Liability Insurance

Holly Myers, JD

KEY CONCEPTS

- Rates
- Insurance Companies
- Assessing Carriers
- Handling Claims
- Types of Insurance Carriers
- Types of Coverage
- Group Practices
- Evaluating Policies
- Extent of Coverage
- Coverage Requirements
- Fifty Questions to Ask When Buying Insurance

Professional liability insurance is one of the most important and expensive features of practice today. Pediatricians need to make sure they are adequately and continuously insured throughout their careers. Making informed decisions on professional liability insurance is not effortless. It requires time, attention, and a willingness to learn about some rather dry information. Most pediatricians agree that protecting their careers and personal assets from ruin is a worthwhile activity.

Insurance is a system that protects against the risk of individual loss by distributing the burden of losses over a large number of individuals. The distribution of that burden, made in the form of premiums, is based on the law of large numbers. The more individuals insured, the more accurately losses can be predicted. Premium payments contribute to the coverage fund and in turn provide compensation for any members of the group who may suffer from a defined loss. The need for professional liability insurance in medical practice is a fact of life. Medical professional liability insurance is designed specifically to protect physicians, clinics, hospitals, health care facilities, and other health personnel against the financial and legal risks inherent in providing medical care.

A *professional liability insurance* (or medical malpractice insurance) policy is a contract between a physician and an insurer. In exchange for the physician's annual premium, the insurer agrees to defend claims and to pay settlements and awards levied against the physician. There are limits, which vary according to the specific policy, on the amount of money the insurer will pay per claim and for all the claims in the specified period the policy is in effect (usually 1 year).

A *malpractice insurance policy* usually provides 2 kinds of coverage, cost of defense and indemnity. Most policies provide coverage to a physician for costs incurred in defending a lawsuit, even if no payment is ever made to the plaintiff (the patient who initiated the suit). More than two thirds of all claims brought against physicians result in no payment, but defense costs can run into the tens of thousands of dollars. Most importantly, the policy agrees to *indemnify* the patient (ie, reimburse the patient or sometimes a family member) for losses from injury or death sustained as a result of a physician's negligence, if that negligence can be proved in court or the parties agree to settle the case before trial.

Periodically, premiums escalate and medical liability insurance may be less available. This can threaten the financial viability of many health care facilities, including some pediatric practices. Pediatricians need professional liability insurance to protect their assets and peace of mind. Unfortunately, finding affordable insurance has become a major concern for many pediatricians.

Rates

The anticipated losses from claims payouts and defense costs can be estimated, as can the amount of premium needed to build reserves to pay these losses from payouts, defense costs, claims-handling costs, and operating expenses. Companies also need to generate sufficient additional funds to guarantee future solvency.

The process of evaluating the risk and apportioning the degree of risk among individuals in the risk pool is called *underwriting*. Just as health insurers take into account an individual's health status, malpractice insurers consider the liability risks that an individual physician may pose. The underwriter looks at every potential insured physician very closely. Factors important to determining rates are

- Specialty
- Certification
- Years of practice
- Location
- Past claims history
- Other factors

From this information, the insurer calculates a premium for physicians with similar backgrounds, whose day-to-day practice matches closely with other physicians of that specialty. Physicians with claims may be surcharged to obtain coverage.

As premiums are collected, the insurer places amounts that it estimates will be needed over time to pay claims into reserve funds. States also require insurers to maintain surplus funds in the event that reserves become inadequate to pay all claims. These surplus funds and all monies remaining after payment of defense costs and operating expenses are invested to earn additional income.

Insurance carriers group physicians with similar specialties or exposures into rate categories. Fortunately, pediatricians are usually rated within lower-risk categories. Factors such as assisting in surgery or practicing a higher-risk subspecialty such as neonatology may result in a higher classification. It is important to be correctly classified by the insurance carrier.

Another factor affecting insurance premiums is practice location. Rates vary by state and even by city or county of practice. Florida, Pennsylvania, Nevada, Illinois, New York, and the District of Columbia generally have higher than average premiums. Medical liability insurance premiums also vary by area within a state (ie, urban areas tend to have higher rates than rural areas) and by practice setting. For example, physicians in a group practice may receive a discount of 10% or 15%.

Because most pediatricians just leaving residency bring no practice-associated risk with them, they may be entitled to a substantial premium discount. Most companies also set lower rates for part-time work.

Insurance Companies

There are several ways to find a professional liability insurance company.

1. Ask colleagues in your area or American Academy of Pediatrics chapter.
2. Call the state or county medical society and speak to the person who handles professional liability issues.
3. Call the state insurance department and ask for information about medical malpractice insurance.
4. Contact the Physician Insurers Association of America (PIAA) at 301/947-9000 or www.thepiaa.org. This is a trade association of physician-owned or physician-operated medical liability insurers.
5. Contact an insurance broker or independent insurance agent and ask to speak to someone familiar with medical malpractice insurance.

Warning: Do not just look for the company that offers the lowest premiums; look for one that is financially sound and able to pay claims. Before purchasing any professional liability policy, check with the hospital(s) where you have privileges to make sure that a policy from that particular carrier is acceptable as proof of insurance.

Assessing Carriers

Cost is just one of the factors that should influence insurance purchasing decisions. The most important factors include the insurer's financial stability, protections against insolvency, performance record, and claims-handling procedures.

Financial Stability

The recent insolvency of several insurance companies underscores the need for pediatricians to scrutinize the financial stability of their current or prospective insurer. A particularly useful source of information is A.M. Best (www.ambest.com). Throughout the year, insurers are continually

reevaluated and ratings are upgraded, downgraded, affirmed, or placed under review. It is advisable to check the A.M. Best rating against those of other companies that rate professional liability carriers, such as Standard & Poor's, Fitch Ratings, Moody's Investors Service, and Weiss Ratings.

A.M. Best rates companies according to the following scale:

- Secure ratings
  A++ or A+ = Superior
  A or A- = Excellent
  B++ or B+ = Very good

- Vulnerable ratings
  B or B- = Adequate
  C++ or C+ = Fair
  C or C- = Marginal
  D = Very vulnerable
  E = Under regulatory supervision
  F = In liquidation
  S = Rating Suspended

Insurer's Insolvency

Consider what will happen if your insurer becomes insolvent. State guaranty funds offer some protection in these circumstances. Typically all insurance carriers are assessed to finance the state guaranty fund. Only insurers licensed to do business in the state are covered by guaranty funds. Although this protection may be limited, it can be a buffer for physicians whose liability carrier becomes unable to pay claims. When a fund does cover medical liability claims, however, the limits of liability it provides may be lower than the limits the defunct policy had provided. For instance, a pediatrician whose policy provided a liability limit of $1 million per occurrence may live in a state in which the guaranty fund is limited to payments of $100,000 per occurrence.

Performance Record

The state insurance department often provides useful information about specific insurers licensed within the state. A license indicates that the insurer has met that particular state's minimum standards for underwriting insurance. Insurers must file annual statements with the insurance commissioner in each state in which they are licensed or do business. The state also may be able to provide information about how long the company has been licensed in that state, its compliance with state rules and regulations, and the number of complaints lodged against the company. Contact information for state insurance departments can be accessed via the National Association of Insurance Commissioners (www.naic.org).

Handling Claims

Before purchasing liability insurance, find out how the insurer handles claims. Often the procedure is spelled out in a company's promotional material. Look for language that may provide important clues about the insurer's claims-management philosophy. Another way to do this is to consult with colleagues insured by the same carrier. It is especially useful to hear from those who have already experienced a claim and can tell firsthand how the carrier handled it.

Table 3-1 lists more important questions to ask a potential insurer.

Settlement Decisions

The issue of the physician's involvement over settlement decisions has gained significance with the establishment of the National Practitioner Data Bank (NPDB) (see Chapter 18). By federal law, all malpractice indemnity payments made on behalf of physicians for medical malpractice settlements or judgments must be reported to the NPDB regardless of the amount. This includes licensed residents and interns but not unlicensed medical and dental students. Hospitals are required to solicit this information from the NPDB on specific physicians at regular intervals. State licensing boards and certain

Table 3-1. Important Claims-Handling Questions

What to Ask	Why Is It Important?
What happens when a physician reports a claim?	Physicians are entitled to a prompt response to a reported claim from experienced claims personnel. Claims personnel should be able to answer questions and give advice when needed.
What is the claims review process?	Physicians should be told who will review the claim and when, whether other physicians will be involved in the review process, and whether lawyers are involved at the outset. This can be an important factor in determining whether these discussions are privileged communications.
What position does the insurer take on nuisance or frivolous claims?	If the insurer prefers to settle claims without merit simply to avoid further costs, this can have a deleterious effect on the physician's record. Ask the next question.
Will the physician be involved in resolving the claim?	The answer should be yes.
Who makes the decision whether to settle a claim?	Usually, the answer is contained in the policy's consent-to-settle clause. Insurers' approaches vary. Some give a discounted rate if the insured waives the right to consent and have the lawsuit settled on his or her behalf. Some promise that a physician's consent will be obtained before a claim is settled. Others retain total control over the decision. A third approach uses a hammer clause when an insurer wants to settle and a pediatrician does not. The company proceeds with the case but limits claim coverage to the amount of the settlement offer it recommended. If an award eventually is made for more than the initial settlement offer, the insured pediatrician may be personally liable for the difference.

professional societies may request information, and physicians may query their own records. Because each malpractice payment made on behalf of health care practitioners is federally mandated to be reported to the NPDB, pediatricians should evaluate all settlement decisions very carefully. Even the settlement of a nuisance case with no real merit will be reported to the NPDB, no matter how small. This can affect licensure, medical staff privileges, contractual arrangements with managed care organizations, and future insurability by traditional carriers.

High-Low Agreements

A high-low agreement is a contract between the plaintiff and the defendant physician's insurance company before trial or arbitration. The parties agree that if the plaintiff wins the case, the defendant's insurer will pay the high amount, and if the defendant wins, the insurer will pay the low amount. The insurer benefits by limiting its liability to a stated amount; the plaintiff benefits by receiving some compensation regardless of the outcome. If the trial or arbitration results in a finding of *no liability* on the part of the defendant physician, the low amount paid is not reportable to the NPDB because the payment is made pursuant to a contract, not on behalf of the defendant.

Hammer Clauses

If the insurer makes a settlement recommendation but the insured physician rejects it, a hammer clause allows the insurer to limit its exposure to the recommended settlement amount. If the final settlement or verdict exceeds that amount, the physician is liable for the difference. When a hammer clause comes into play, a physician should consult with a personal attorney before accepting or rejecting the insurer's recommendation.

Prejudgment Interest

Many states allow plaintiffs to collect prejudgment interest in tort cases under certain circumstances. This can happen when a physician involved in a civil lawsuit does not attempt to negotiate a settlement in good faith and subsequently loses the case at trial. States compute and award prejudgment interest in different ways. Sometimes the interest begins to be computed on the date the cause of action occurred; sometimes it begins when the physician started or broke off settlement talks. Some insurance policies have provisions exempting them from paying prejudgment interest, leaving the defendant physician responsible.

Types of Insurance Carriers

Insurance carriers include physician-directed companies, commercial carriers, joint underwriting associations (JUAs), risk-retention groups (RRGs), and trusts. Older companies are more easily evaluated, while newer ones have less of a track record.

Physician-Directed Companies

Roughly 60% of physicians in private practice are insured through physician-owned or physician-operated companies. Many of these companies were formed during the malpractice crisis of the mid-1970s, when commercial carriers were forced to increase premiums or withdraw from the market. With few options left for obtaining insurance coverage, physician groups (state medical associations or specialty societies) formed their own insurance companies to bring stability to the market. Unlike other carriers, the mission of the typical physician-owned or physician-operated company is to provide a stable, affordable market for its members. Because of their special knowledge, physician-owners have been able to establish many excellent loss-control programs. The cost to join a physician-owned company may include a non–tax-deductible capital contribution in addition to the premium. It is important to ascertain whether assessments might be made against individual policyholders if the company faced economic peril. The PIAA is an organization of physician-governed professional liability carriers with about 60 member companies More than 60% of physicians, dentists, and hospitals are insured by PIAA companies.

Commercial Carriers

A small number of commercial carriers have long records of providing medical malpractice insurance for individual physicians. The commercial market for clinics and practice groups has shrunk in the last decade with the 2001 exodus of The St. Paul Companies, Inc. The same care should be used in scrutinizing a commercial carrier as any other company.

Joint Underwriting Associations

The malpractice crisis of the 1970s prompted many states to pass laws authorizing state insurance commissioners to establish JUAs, nonprofit risk-pooling associations operated as a branch of the state government to provide medical malpractice insurance. It is common for all the insurers writing liability coverage in a given state to be members of the JUA. Funding and deficit provisions vary from state to state. In some cases insured individuals, as well as member companies, may be assessed to cover any operating deficits.

Some states that created JUAs in the 1970s never appropriated funding for these programs; others deactivated JUAs when the crisis eased. Some states kept JUAs in case a need should arise.

Joint underwriting associations meet a vital insurance need for physicians who cannot obtain liability insurance through the traditional market. Joint underwriting associations cover their operating expenses and pay claims by collecting premiums just as private insurers do. In addition, laws governing JUAs generally require all licensed insurers writing certain types of insurance in that state to

become members of the state JUA, regardless of whether they sell medical liability policies.

Typically JUAs are not covered by state guaranty funds. This can pose an additional risk to physicians. Joint underwriting associations have various contingency plans should deficits arise. One way is through a premium surcharge. Another is to assess policyholders retroactively, up to a specified limited, for deficits accumulated in a given fiscal year. Companies that are members of JUAs also can be assessed when policyholders have been assessed to the maximum allowed by law.

Joint underwriting association rates are sometimes lower than those of other insurers in the same state. This is because they tend to be less closely regulated than other forms of professional liability insurance. Most JUAs cannot reject the application of any physician licensed in a state, so they tend to attract physicians who have been sued more often. This can raise the rates for everyone covered by the JUA.

Risk-Retention Groups

An RRG is a self-insurance mechanism authorized by the Liability Risk Retention Act of 1986, a federal law enacted during another liability insurance crisis. Although many RRGs are financially sound, they are generally far less regulated than traditional insurers. Moreover, RRGs are not protected by state guaranty funds.

An RRG must be owned by its members or by an organization in turn owned by members of the group. Its members must contribute capital to the group, and membership is limited to individuals engaged in similar related businesses or activities.

An RRG must be *domiciled* (ie, incorporated or chartered) and licensed as a liability insurance company in at least one state. Once the RRG has obtained a license in the state in which it is domiciled, it is permitted to solicit business and write insurance in all other states and the District of Columbia. Some states have encouraged the establishment of RRGs. Consequently, many are domiciled and licensed in Vermont, Louisiana, and a few other states that appear to have less-stringent insurance regulations.

Many RRGs are stable, well-run operations. Nevertheless, because only the domiciliary state oversees the RRG closely, problems can arise in other states. There have been cases of fraud and abuse by a few RRGs. Several have been shut down by regulators, leaving physicians without insurance coverage, sometimes with pending unpaid claims. The greatest abuses have been by fly-by-night sellers of purported RRGs or captive insurance companies by direct mail. One way to guard against signing with suspect groups is to make sure that financial data submitted by an RRG are certified by an independent public accountant and include a statement of operation on loss and loss-adjustment expense reserves.

Even though RRGs are generally exempt from insurance regulations outside the state in which they are licensed, states may impose requirements on RRGs doing business in their jurisdiction. Typically these requirements include

- Requiring the RRG to pay premium taxes
- Complying with any state laws on deceptive or fraudulent acts
- Ceasing to do business if an RRG's financial condition is impaired

Initially RRG premiums tend to be lower than those of traditional insurers, largely because RRGs are exempt from the costs of complying with many regulatory requirements. As their liability grows, RRGs are forced to raise premiums accordingly.

Some question whether premiums collected by RRGs will be sufficient to cover future loss. Critics point out that although RRGs can spread their risk across state lines, those programs that insure only one type of physician specialist lose the benefits of spreading risks among large numbers of policy-

holders in different classes of risk. They also suggest that if a physician has a problem with an RRG not licensed in his state, that state's insurance department may have more difficulty responding to a complaint. An RRG does not have to demonstrate an intent to remain active in a state in which it does business but is not licensed.

Pediatricians should consider how the RRG handles claims. It is possible that an RRG that does business nationwide will not maintain claims staff in every state. Therefore, claims handlers may be less adept at working within the framework of local rules. This could delay or compromise the defense of a claim. Some RRGs only offer policies with liability limits that are reduced by the amount of legal expenses incurred in defending a claim. Because those costs can be quite high, such a provision can lower a physician's liability coverage significantly. The average cost to defend a pediatric claim in 2009 was $49,686 (PIAA).

Risk-retention groups cannot participate in state guaranty funds. If the RRG becomes insolvent, there will be no coverage for any liability claims. Federal law requires any RRG insurance policy to note this fact. Most RRG policies are assessable. If premiums collected are insufficient to pay claims, the RRG can demand additional money from policyholders to cover its obligations and stay in business.

Trusts

A trust is another insurance option. Typically, trusts are nonprofit organizations formed with less capital than is required of traditional insurers. Trusts usually are not regulated by state insurance departments and not covered by state guaranty funds. A disadvantage of trusts is that policyholders may be assessed substantially if the trust is hit with huge losses. Because trusts usually start with limited capital, there is a greater risk that the fund balance will be exhausted if claims are higher than anticipated. In this case, physician policyholders must pay additional assessments to replenish operating funds and cover losses.

Important Questions to Ask About Insurers

1. How long has the company been writing medical malpractice insurance?
2. How many physicians does the company insure?
3. Assuming that the coverage is on a claims-made basis, what are the rate projections for the next few years?
4. Will the insured be protected by the state guaranty fund?
5. Is there a possibility of assessments against policyholders?
6. Is an up-front capital contribution required?
7. What loss control assistance is available?
8. Is the insurance program endorsed or sponsored by any medical association?

Types of Coverage

The most common types of traditional professional liability insurance are occurrence and claims made. Two dates are important in determining how these coverages are applied: the date the alleged error or incident occurred and the date the claim was first made.

Occurrence Policy

An occurrence policy provides coverage for an incident that occurs during the term of the policy, regardless of when a claim arising from the incident is made. Occurrence policies are available through select insurance carriers. Although occurrence policies appear to provide the broadest liability coverage, depending on the statute of limitations for minors in that state, they may not provide sufficient financial coverage for a claim that is made many years after the incident. The amount of coverage chosen today may be inadequate for a claim that is made many years in future.

Claims-Made Policy

A claims-made policy provides coverage for claims that are made and reported to the insurance company while the policy is in force. The policy has a retroactive date; there is no coverage for acts or errors that take place before that date.

Typically the retroactive date for a new policy is the same as the inception date of the policy. If the policy is continually renewed, the retroactive date remains the same—the inception date of the first policy. Each renewed policy picks up the exposure of another past year of practice that may or may not include unknown incidents that will result in claims. This is called *prior-acts coverage.*

This gradual increase in exposure to claims is reflected in yearly increases in premiums. After several years the rate is said to be mature and the premiums should become level, except as affected by other factors.

When a physician with claims-made insurance changes insurance companies, it is essential to avoid gaps in coverage by obtaining prior-acts coverage from the new insurer or purchasing *tail* coverage, also called an extended reporting endorsement, from the old insurer.

Tail Coverage

While physicians insured by claims-made policies have the advantage of choosing a limit each year to cover unknown potential claims arising from past acts, they have the disadvantage of needing tail coverage when they stop practicing or when they move. *If a claims-made policy is terminated without tail coverage, there will be no insurance for claims made after the termination date, even if the claims are based on actions that took place during the policy period.*

This is essential coverage if a physician retires, dies, or becomes disabled, and some insurers will provide it at no charge if the insured physician meets certain requirements, such as age and number of years with the insurance company. Tail coverage can also protect a physician who wants to change from a claims-made to an occurrence policy or who is switching to a different company's claims-made policy with no retroactive coverage. Tail coverage can be expensive to purchase—sometimes 3 times the original policy's annual premium.

Claims-Paid Policy

This is a variant of claims-made insurance. A claims-paid policy provides coverage for claims arising from incidents that occur while the policy is in force. *The coverage must be in force at the time the claim is paid.* The advantage is that the premiums can be determined with accuracy because reserving for unknown claims is not necessary. The disadvantage is that for a reported claim to be covered, the insured physician must stay with that insurer until the claim is paid, even if it takes several years.

Tail

The tail of a claim is the time between the incident giving rise to the claim and its ultimate disposition. Although the average interval between the incident from which a malpractice claim arises and its resolution has recently been shortened from 8 to 6 years, it is still considerable. Moreover, because pediatricians treat children (minors under the law) and minors can still sue as adults when they reach the age of majority if no lawsuit has yet been filed, the tail can be measured in decades in some states.

Tail coverage is necessary whenever a physician insured under a claims-made policy changes carriers, becomes disabled, retires, or dies (to protect her estate). Insurance carriers often have strict policies on when tail coverage can be purchased. For instance, some insurance companies only offer the option to purchase tail coverage for 30 days after the termination of the claims-made policy.

Other Coverage Issues

Study the terms of the professional liability policy carefully. The coverage clauses are at the beginning of the policy. They outline the scope of the coverage and identify exclusions. These are too important to overlook.

Important Questions to Ask About Coverage Limitations and Exclusions

1. Are you covered for extracurricular activities (whether paid or unpaid)? Examples include providing sports examinations for the high school basketball team or volunteering (unpaid) at a community health clinic.
4. Does coverage extend to your employees and, if so, what is covered?
5. Is your policy portable if you practice in another state?
6. Is locum tenens coverage available for someone who covers for you temporarily?
7. What are the effects on coverage should you join another group?
8. Does your policy cover you for working in disaster relief in another state?

These questions about coverage should be answered, preferably in writing, before the contract is signed.

Group Practices

If you practice as part of a corporation or partnership, you may want to insure this entity also. Typically, an insurance company requires that all individual physicians in a group be insured with that same company. The physicians and the corporation or partnership will probably be covered on one policy, with separate limits or one limit for all. The additional premium for providing a separate limit for the business entity should be modest, perhaps 10% of the total premium for physicians.

Some policies cover your office staff. These policies will include nonphysician employees, such as nurses, physician assistants, and pediatric nurse practitioners, for little or no additional premium. Some may be required to carry individual policies. To be certain that such professional liability insurance does carry individual coverage, ask for a certificate of insurance.

Residents, as well as other physicians, who join existing groups as employees may have little choice of carrier or coverage. Nevertheless, they should take care to review the details of the insurance policy to make sure it covers all professional activities. If the insurance is on a claims-made basis, be sure that your tail is covered; find out if the insurance you had during residency will cover your tail. If that is not part of the coverage, find out if your new employer will pick up tail coverage for the care you provided during residency. If neither the program nor your future employer will cover the tail, consider buying your own.

Important Questions to Ask Future Employers

- Can the present liability coverage be continued or will it change?
- If yes, can the retroactive date be carried through to the new program?
- What type of coverage is provided?
- What are the policy limits?
- Are there deductibles on policy limits? Who pays the deductible?
- Does the policy provide prior-acts coverage?
- What are the tail coverage provisions?
- Who pays for tail coverage?
- Will tail coverage have lower limits?
- Is there a deductible on tail coverage? Who pays the deductible?
- Approximately what will tail coverage cost if it is necessary to purchase it personally?

- Is it individual coverage or slot coverage? In slot coverage an employer's policy covers positions (eg, 2 pediatricians) rather than named individuals (eg, Dr Smith and Dr Jones). Two or more part-time physicians might fill one slot. If slot coverage, ask the hospital or other entity for a letter confirming your tail coverage if the slot position is eliminated.
- If the policy calls for joint claims investigation and defense, who determines how liability is apportioned among the parties (eg, hospital, managed care organization, defendant physicians, other personnel)?
- Is a physician entitled to a separate attorney if there are irreconcilable differences in a claim being jointly defended?
- Who manages and controls the liability program?
- If it is a self-insured or captive program, is it financially sound?

No Gaps

Before accepting any employment offer, think ahead to the next job. If the current job offer includes claims-made policy, who will cover the tail if you decide to leave in the future? Some employers will negotiate this. For instance, an employer may agree to pay a higher percentage of the cost of the tail coverage for each additional year the pediatrician remains with the practice. *Remember, gap-free coverage is essential.*

Evaluating Policies

Perhaps no written contract is signed more frequently and read less often than the insurance contract. Even when purchasers read the contract, it is more likely to be after a claim has been filed than before the contract was signed.

The primary purpose of any insurance contract is to indemnify the policyholder against certain losses. The essential concept of the insurance contract is the attempt to define those losses that are covered by the insuring agreement and those that are not.

Liability insurance companies generally offer a wide variety of insurance products. Do your homework before purchasing a policy. It may take contacting several carriers or reviewing several policies before finding appropriate coverage. You can ask to see a sample policy including applicable endorsements.

Extent of Coverage

Deciding how much insurance to purchase is a personal decision based on a number of factors, including

- Specialty and the risk it entails
- Practice location
- How much of personal assets you are willing to risk
- Requirements imposed by other contracts
- State legal requirements

A wide range of policy limits is available, from $100,000/$300,000 up to $2 million/$6 million and even higher. The lower number of the policy limits is always the amount an insurer will pay per claim, and the higher number is always the total the insurer will pay in aggregate for all claims during a policy period (eg, 1 year). If a large settlement or judgment is entered against a physician, an insufficient level of coverage could jeopardize personal assets. Some states will provide additional coverage if you maintain hospital privileges.

Coverage Requirements

A number of states have medical liability insurance requirements. These requirements specify the minimum amount of coverage a physician needs to comply with the law. However, physicians are encouraged to consider the 5 factors listed above and consult with an insurance expert to determine appropriate coverage.

In the following states, physicians must carry a minimum amount of insurance (or in some cases, demonstrate financial responsibility):

- Colorado
- Connecticut
- Florida
- Georgia
- Kansas
- Massachusetts
- Pennsylvania
- Rhode Island
- Wisconsin

In the following states, physicians must carry a minimum amount of insurance or level of financial responsibility to be eligible for the protection of a state fund:

- Indiana
- Nebraska
- New Mexico
- North Carolina
- Oregon

In the following states, physicians must be insured to have hospital privileges:

- Arizona
- California
- Indiana
- Missouri

Fifty Questions to Ask When Buying Insurance

Type of Coverage: What Kind of Coverage Is Best for You?

1. Do I understand the difference between occurrence and claims-made coverage?
2. Is occurrence insurance offered?
3. If I go with a claims-made policy, is the policy I am considering a standard claims made, claims paid, or some variation?
4. Do I fully understand the differences among these types of claims-made policies?
5. If I choose a claims-made policy, do I understand the advantages as well as the disadvantages?

Limits: How Do I Determine How Much Coverage to Buy?

6. What amounts of coverage do other pediatricians in similar practices in my area buy?

7. What portion of my personal assets do I want to risk in the event of a large claim?

8. Am I required by hospital bylaws, managed care contracts, or state law to carry a minimum amount of coverage?

Premium: How Much Does It Cost?

9. Is it payable quarterly, semiannually, or annually?

10. Do any discounts apply for taking risk-management courses or for having no claims?

11. Are other discounts available?

12. Will the insurer surcharge me if I have more claims or larger claims payouts than other pediatricians?

13. Does the premium include a charge for prior-acts coverage?

Deductibles

14. What deductibles are available?

15. Should I accept a higher deductible on awards or defense costs in return for premium discounts?

16. Can I handle the economic consequences if I have to absorb the deductible?

17. Does the deductible apply to each claim? Is there an annual aggregate deductible?

What Constitutes a Claim?

18. If I choose a claims-made policy, how does the policy define a claim-triggering coverage?

19. Does coverage begin when I report an adverse incident or only when an actual demand for money or services is received?

20. Does a letter or telephone call from a disgruntled patient or the patient's lawyer constitute a claim?

21. Does a lawyer's request for a patient's records constitute a claim?

22. Does a notice of intent to sue or notice of an actual legal action trigger coverage?

Claims Reporting

23. If the policy stipulates that I must report all incidents and claims in a timely fashion, what is the time limit for reporting?

24. Which incidents and claims must be reported?

25. Can I lose my coverage if I fail to report in the specified time frame?

26. Do I have to notify the insurer in writing of an adverse incident, or is a telephone call sufficient?

27. To whom must I write or speak to report a claim?

28. What documentation must be included with notification of a claim or incident?

29. If I report incidents that may not become claims, will I be surcharged?

Tail Coverage

30. What are the tail-coverage provisions in a claims-made policy?

31. Is there a provision for free tail coverage if I retire, become disabled, or die?

32. Does this free tail coverage require me to stay with a given company for a certain number of years? If so, how long?

33. How does the policy define *disability,* and who makes the disability determination?

34. How old do I have to be to retire and receive free tail coverage?

35. If I do not qualify for free tail coverage, does the company guarantee that I can buy this coverage if I want to change carriers or the company decides to drop me?

36. What is the time limit for buying the tail?

37. How much would tail coverage cost me?

38. Will I be able to pay for it in installments?

39. If I pay in installments, is the original price guaranteed or could the price rise over time?

Cancellation/Nonrenewal

40. Can I terminate my policy at any time?

41. How much notice must I give to cancel?

42. Can the company cancel my coverage or refuse to renew my policy? If so, for what reasons?

43. How much notice does a company need to give me if it cancels or will not renew me?

44. Am I entitled to a refund of premium if I am canceled or not renewed?

Extent of Coverage

45. Does the policy cover only patient injury claims or does it extend to other professional activities such as peer review, credentialing, and utilization review?

46. Does it cover actions brought against me by a state licensure board or hospital?

47. Does the policy cover acts and omissions by my office staff members?

48. Does coverage extend to injuries arising from events such as slips and falls occurring on office premises?

49. Does the policy provide coverage for a locum tenens physician?

50. Is the cost of defense covered in addition to the limit of liability or within the limit?

Summary

Buying professional liability insurance takes time, effort, and care. Pediatricians put their careers at risk when they assume that someone else has taken care of these decisions. Make sure that the carrier is reputable and stable, the policy is adequate, and there are no gaps in coverage.

Bibliography

1. Adapted from: Division of Health Law. *Medical Professional Liability Insurance: The Informed Physician's Guide to Coverage Decisions.* Chicago, IL: American Medical Association; 1998

2. American College of Obstetricians and Gynecologists. Professional liability insurance. In: *Professional Liability and Risk Management: An Essential Guide for Obstetrician-Gynecologists.* 2nd ed. Washington, DC: American College of Obstetricians and Gynecologists; 2008:81–97

3. Division of Quality Assurance. *National Practitioner Data Bank Guidebook.* Rockville, MD: US Department of Health and Human Services, Health Resources and Services Administration; 1996. Publication No. HRSA-95-255

Resources

Physician Insurers Association of America
2775 Research Blvd, Suite 250
Rockville, MD 20850
301/947-9000
www.thepiaa.org

National Association of Insurance Commissioners
Central Office
2301 McGee St, Suite 800
Kansas City, MO 64108-2662
816/842-3600
www.naic.org

CHAPTER 4

Risk Management

Robert A. Mendelson, MD, FAAP

KEY CONCEPTS

- Definition
- Scope
- Why Patients Sue
- Risk Identification Methods
- Risk Management Tour of the Pediatric Office
- Making and Managing Referrals
- Sample Forms and Letters

The escalating severity of medical malpractice awards and the sometimes prohibitive costs of liability insurance have made health care entities increase risk management efforts. Typically 1 in 3 pediatricians is sued for malpractice sometime during her career. This rate has remained relatively unchanged for pediatricians from 1987 to 2007.[1] According to the same survey, 1 in 10 residents and fellows is sued for an event that occurred during training.

In health care settings, risk management is first and foremost a means of improving and maintaining quality patient care and safety. Risk management is proactive in preventing future occurrences and reactive in responding to past adverse events. In a perfect world, pediatricians could practice quality medicine and never have to worry about being sued. However, it is often said that malpractice allegations are more likely to arise from bad outcomes

than bad care. Thus, practicing quality care is no guarantee against malpractice claims. Effective risk management can reduce the likelihood of medical errors in practice settings and minimize losses from malpractice claims.

Definition

Risk management is a systematic process to help identify, evaluate, and address problems that may injure patients, lead to malpractice claims, and cause financial loss to health care entities.[2]

Effective risk prevention depends on the reliable recognition of risk exposure, determination of its causes, implementation of corrective actions, and continual monitoring of risk indicators to determine if risk exposure resolves (Figure 4-1).

Because pediatric practice is so dynamic, the risk management cycle must be continuous and lead to appropriate readjustment and fine-tuning of the process. The full scope of risk management encompasses all organizational activity, operational

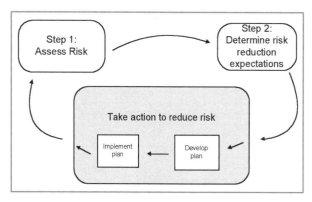

Figure 4-1. Continuous-Cycle Risk Reduction[2]

and clinical, because liability may originate in either area. In developing a risk management program, the practice must make certain that the program has sufficient scope to cover the risk, risk-reduction strategies are appropriate, and the program is documented in written policies and procedures.

Scope

The initial step of risk management is to determine the scope of the risk (Figure 4-1, column 1, and Table 4-1). There are many areas of risk in pediatric care. This chapter focuses on risk management as it relates to the medical care provided in a pediatric practice.

Why Patients Sue

The first step in preventing lawsuits is to understand why patients sue. In general, medical malpractice claims are attributed to

- *An erosion of the physician-patient relationship.* In today's health care environment, it is more difficult to maintain solid relationships with patients and families. Breakdowns in therapeutic alliance may be caused by communication barriers, system changes in health care delivery, reduced time for patient contacts, or other significant changes such as patients changing insurers, patients changing physicians, health care professionals leaving insurance plans, and changes in the family.

Table 4-1. Determining the Scope of Risk[3]

Scope	Definition	Examples
Patient care–related risks	Focuses on direct clinical patient care activities and the consequences of inappropriately or incorrectly performed medical care	• Medication errors • Failure/delay in diagnosis • Patient abandonment • Failure to properly store vaccines
Medical staff–related risks	Focuses on quality improvement activities • Confidentiality • Credentialing and privileging • Disciplinary actions • Business arrangement and incentives • Gatekeeper obligation under managed care plans	• Peer-review activities • HIPAA privacy/security rules
Employee-related risks	Focuses on employer obligations for safe work environment, occupational illness/injury, relevant state workers' compensation laws, federal regulations, discrimination claims, and wrongful termination claims	• OSHA violations (eg, no exposure control plan, failure to provide personal protective equipment for employees at risk for occupational exposure to blood-borne pathogens) • Sexual harassment claims
Property-related risks	Focuses on protection of company assets (eg, building, office equipment, paper and electronic records) from losses caused by disasters	Fires, floods, tornadoes, earthquakes
Financial risks	• Director's and officers' liability • Managed care arrangements • OIG compliance plans to prevent fraud and abuse	Stop-loss coverage in payer contracts, business associates under HIPAA
Other	• General liability issues • Hazardous materials • Biological waste	• Visitor slips and falls in parking lot. • Improper labeling or disposal of hazardous materials in office laboratory.

Abbreviations: HIPAA, Health Insurance Portability and Accountability Act; OIG, Office of Inspector General; OSHA, Occupational Safety & Health Administration.

- *Unrealistic expectations.* Many people still expect a cure for every ailment. Parents expect to have healthy children and they take normal development for granted.
- *Managed care.* The benefits of managed care have come with some costs. Physicians contend that their clinical autonomy has diminished under rigid payer-based policies and procedures.
- *Miracles have risks.* Scientific advances enable cures for conditions that previously were untreatable but simultaneously carry inherent risks of undesirable results or side effects.
- *Need to blame.* An increasingly litigious society seeks to hold someone at fault for injuries or accidents that were previously considered non-preventable tragic events.
- *Financial remedy.* Parents may seek redress through courts even when they know their physicians did nothing wrong because they have no other recourse for obtaining the financial assistance they need to care for their disabled children.[4]
- *Need to determine the truth.* Parents may believe that facts have not been disclosed to them about the care delivered and complications of that care.

The following characteristics unique to pediatrics make risk management more challenging in pediatric settings:

- Relative rarity of many pediatric illnesses
- Limited capacity for communication and cooperation in young children
- High levels of dependency on others (eg, parental observation and assessment of problem)
- Changes in patient (eg, weight, height, physiologic and developmental maturation)
- High-volume specialty (many patients, many visits, many telephone calls, and nonverbal communications, eg, e-mail)

Risk Identification Methods

Effective risk management begins with a system for identifying the specific events likely to result in loss and general clinical areas of risk exposure. The following are some common methods:

Legal Actions

The easiest and most obvious way to identify risk is to assess what ordinary activities of pediatric practices result in lawsuits.

Patient Complaints/Patient Satisfaction Surveys

Reviewing patient complaints is a good way to detect cases involving risk or poor-quality health care. Many organizations have formalized mechanisms for handling patient complaints. Often, descriptive statistics of patient complaints are generated routinely, such as monthly compilation of all complaints by type, clinical or administrative area, and involved staff. A focused review of complaints that suggest risk or poor quality can be a productive undertaking when attempting to discover problematic cases. Occasional random patient satisfaction surveys can also reveal areas of risk (as well as practice strengths).

Billing Disputes

A review of billing disputes is another method of identifying risk and quality deficiencies. Patients often refuse to pay bills because they believe that the care received was substandard and therefore not deserving of payment. Some patients also make accusations of poor quality care simply to justify their refusal to pay for care. This compromises the cost-effectiveness of billing disputes as a risk identification tool. Consequently, detailed clinical review of all cases resulting in a billing dispute should probably be reserved for cases involving large sums of money or significant accusations of substandard quality.

Occurrence (Incident) Reporting

Rather than wait for a legal action, record request, complaint, or billing dispute to initiate the process of risk identification, most practices ask staff to notify the managing partner of the practice should an untoward or unusual incident occur. It is also prudent to notify your medical liability insurer, which may open a file addressing the incident. Often a special form, commonly referred to as an incident report, patient safety report, or variance report, is provided for this purpose. The form indicates the minimum specific information that must be provided about the incident. Although the information contained in the report may be protected from legal discovery by state law, some institutions request that reports of patient harm resulting from medical misdiagnoses, therapies, and procedures be reported verbally rather than in writing. If an incident report is filed, it should not be referenced in the medical record, or it might be deemed discoverable.

Random Medical Record Review

A common practice in the early years of risk management, random medical record reviews involved an unfocused peer review of randomly selected medical records as a quality assurance activity. Random medical record review is less commonly used today because the low yield of positive findings made it cost inefficient. However, a program of random medical record reviews by physicians can be beneficial in educating them about the wide variety of practice styles and approaches present among the providers. Over time, this may lead to group consensus on the identification of less-than-optimal behavior or poor documentation. Some medical liability insurers offer onsite evaluations of practice for risk-reduction purposes. These may include random chart reviews if requested by the practice. Frequently these evaluations result in concrete suggestions for improving risk management.

Occurrence Screening

Because occurrence reporting can be unreliable, some practices identify groups of cases for screening review without depending on reporting from staff. This risk identification method is called occurrence screening. These can be generic screening events that have been identified as areas of concern (eg, unanticipated return visits for the same problem within a specified period, emergency department encounters shortly after an office visit). The mere occurrence of a generic event does not imply the presence of risk or a quality deficiency. Rather, the occurrence event indicator is meant to trigger a careful review to ascertain whether a quality problem or risk exists.

Closed Malpractice Claims

One of the best ways to identify potential risks is to review closed malpractice claims. From time to time the American Academy of Pediatrics (AAP) Committee on Medical Liability and Risk Management will report on trends in closed pediatric malpractice claims. Table 4-2 examines closed malpractice claims in the Physician Insurers Association of America (PIAA) data-sharing system from 1985 to 2009.

According to Table 4-2, the most common medical misadventure among closed pediatric malpractice claims was diagnostic error. This accounted for 32% of all closed pediatric claims, with an average indemnity payment of $279,455 (payment resulting from a settlement or award). The medical misadventure with the highest percentage of paid to closed number of claims (44%) was failure/delay in referral or consultation, with an average indemnity payment of $259,992. It is interesting, though perhaps discouraging, to note that the second most common medical misadventure, occurring in 22% of all closed pediatric malpractice claims, was no medical misadventure. This designation is used to categorize a situation in which there is an absence of an allegation of any inappropriate medical con-

Table 4-2. Closed Pediatric Claims by Medical Misadventure (1985–2009)[5]

Medical Misadventure	Closed Claims	Paid Claims	% Paid to Closed	Average Indemnity	Total Indemnity	% of All Closed Claims
Diagnostic error	2,328	812	35%	$279,455	$226,917,718	32%
No medical misadventure	1,545	101	6%	$339,853	$34,325,159	22%
Improper performance	926	265	29%	$216,846	$57,464,109	13%
Failure to supervise or monitor case	657	232	35%	$323,775	$75,115,769	9%
Medication errors	338	103	30%	$178,534	$18,388,988	5%
Failure/delay in referral or consultation	217	94	44%	$259,992	$24,439,234	3%
Not performed	198	85	43%	$216,635	$18,413,992	3%
Failure to recognize a complication of treatment	187	56	30%	$233,956	$13,101,517	3%
Delay in performance	180	71	39%	$348,184	$24,721,067	3%
Failure to instruct/communicate with patient	110	27	25%	$183,329	$4,949,871	2%

Table 4-3. Closed Pediatric Malpractice Claims, 1985–2009, by Associated Personnel[5]

	Closed Claims	Paid Claims	% Paid to Closed	Average Indemnity	Total Indemnity
Other physician	2,706	744	27.40%	$302,518	$225,073,072
Nurse	535	197	36.82%	$297,017	$58,512,412
Consultant	475	162	34.11%	$387,538	$62,781,172
Resident/intern	352	126	35.80%	$413,282	$52,073,498
Emergency physicians	265	89	33.58%	$228,595	$20,344,964
Family members	185	42	22.70%	$243,172	$10,213,218
Other person or personnel	172	33	19.19%	$399,152	$13,172,000
Radiologist	165	56	33.94%	$277,340	$15,531,063
Other hospital personnel	158	67	42.41%	$89,534	$5,999,386
Patient	120	22	18.33%	$219,412	$4,827,074
Anesthesiologist	75	23	30.67%	$541,744	$12,460,120
Nurse practitioner	48	15	31.25%	$295,933	$4,439,000

duct on the part of the insured physician. Although only 6% of these claims result in an indemnity payment, the average payout is $339,853, the second highest average payout among the 10 most prevalent medical misadventures.

Often more than one defendant is named in the litigation. Table 4-3 identifies other associated personnel named in closed pediatric claims from the PIAA database of closed pediatric claims from 1985 to 2009. The most common category of associated personnel in closed pediatric malpractice claims is that of other physician, which accounts for 51% of all closed pediatric claims. The cases with the high-

est average payout ($541,744) are those in which anesthesiologists are named as associated personnel. Although residents are named in less than 7% of all pediatric claims, the average indemnity for those cases is $413,282.

Successful risk management requires the right attitude, knowledge, good communication skills and a commitment to the process.

The attitude includes an awareness of potential risk and liability, a disciplined approach to documentation, a desire for effective communication, and an appreciation of the effect other forces (eg, government regulation) have in affecting how health care is delivered.

The knowledge base for good risk management begins with a comprehensive understanding of the following: the relationship among the pediatrician, patient, and patient's family; informed consent (ie, parental permission for minor patients); consent by proxy and patient assent; and communication and documentation skills.

Each practice operation has its own vulnerabilities to liability. The next section denotes common malpractice risks associated with specific office procedures and suggests ways to reduce those risks. At best it is an overview of a generic pediatric office. These recommendations are intended to educate and in no way substitute for on-site risk management assessment or legal advice.

Risk Management Tour of the Pediatric Office

The pediatrician and administrator must work together to establish a plan to

- Identify potential patient care problems. New practices may need to rely on past experiences in other settings or the findings of colleagues in similar practices to determine "existing" problems. Often medical malpractice insurance companies conduct on-site risk audits and recommend specific loss prevention tips for practices.
- Equip and train staff to do their jobs (eg, orientation for new staff, continuing education for all employees, corrective action training for employees demonstrating deficiencies in problem areas).
- Establish criteria for patient care responsibility.
- Measure and monitor staff performance.
- Improve and audit medical record keeping.
- Investigate and resolve staff problems and patient complaints.
- Take corrective actions when appropriate.

- Encourage communication of potential patient safety concerns.
- Protect patients and employees by complying with federal and state health care regulations (eg, Occupational Safety & Health Administration [OSHA], Clinical Laboratory Improvement Amendments [CLIA], Health Insurance Portability and Accountability Act [HIPAA]).
- Inform patients of their rights and responsibilities in maintaining the therapeutic alliance among the parent, patient, and pediatrician.

Scheduling Appointments

A common source of patient dissatisfaction in a physician's office is the length of time the patient must wait after arriving for an appointment. When patients endure long waits, they perceive a lack of concern. The more dissatisfied patients become, the more likely they are to file malpractice claims should a problem arise. Efforts to prevent or at least minimize patient dissatisfaction begin with first contact between the patient and staff—usually a telephone call to schedule an appointment. Consider the following points when developing scheduling protocols:

- The receptionist's self-identification, demeanor, tone, and courtesy
- Whether the receptionist asks callers for permission before putting them on hold
- The average length of time a patient is left on hold
- The length of time between the call and the next available appointment (days, weeks, or months)
- The time spent in the reception area waiting to see the physician

Longer wait times are associated with greater patient dissatisfaction.[6] The following are some rules of thumb to minimize patient wait time:

- Consider reminder calls, usually on the day prior to the appointment, to encourage patients to arrive promptly.

- Allow enough time before and after seeing patients.
- Avoid overbooking.
- Schedule extra time for new patients, health supervision visits, and special procedures.
- Block time each day for walk-ins and emergencies. Fill these times no earlier than the evening before.
- Save room for "see today" visits on Fridays and Mondays and before and after long weekends.
- Inform patients of any delays in the appointment schedule and the cause for the delay.
- Call patients at home to advise them of any expected delays.
- Post a sign in the reception area to speak with the receptionist if the wait exceeds 20 minutes.
- Know your schedule and where you stand in relation to it throughout the day.
- Consider providing office hours on weekends and evenings for patient convenience and to help keep your patients from seeking nonurgent care at emergency facilities or retail-based clinics.

Documentation of appointment information is almost as critical as the progress note itself. Always document appointments using the following guidelines:

- Record missed or canceled appointments (and any known reasons) in the patient's medical record.
- Do not erase, obscure, or otherwise obliterate any appointment in the appointment book or electronic schedule.
- Document any attempts to reach the patient to reschedule a missed appointment. If circumstances warrant, send a certified letter with a return receipt.

Remember that the receptionist and front office staff are the first and last points of contact with the patient. Their professional demeanor, friendliness, courtesy, and efficiency (or lack thereof) leave lasting impressions. Monitor staff-patient interactions from time to time and use teachable moments to correct small problems before they escalate.

Tracking Laboratory Tests

The mismanagement of patients' test results is a subtle but potentially harmful error common to pediatric care. Failing to follow up on an abnormal laboratory or diagnostic test result can have serious consequences for a patient's health. If a patient's condition is undiagnosed because test results did not come back from the laboratory or were filed before the pediatrician could take action, there will be no good excuse to offer a jury should the pediatrician be sued. If the pediatrician believes a test or diagnostic procedure is important enough to justify the cost and patient inconvenience, it is important enough to follow up.

Tracking systems do not have to be elaborate or expensive. They just have to be effective. One method is to have staff

- List all tests ordered in a notebook by date.
- Flag clinically urgent or important tests.
- Check off entries as results come in and are forwarded for your review and initialing before filing in the medical record.
- At a set interval (eg, every 2 weeks) review the log for results that are past due.
- If test results are missing, contact the facility to see if the test was done.
- If the test was not done, contact the patient or parent to remind him or her to have the test done.
- Document all follow-up of missing result in the patient's medical record.

The tracking system that is right for your practice is the one that you will use. If a tracking system is too complicated or burdensome, it will not be effective. Having a system that is not used could be more damaging to the defense of a medical malpractice claim than not having one at all.

When the results of diagnostic tests are allowed to fall through the cracks, harmful delays in treatment or diagnosis can occur. As demands on pediatric offices continue to grow, mishandled test results could become a growing problem.

The 4 basic steps for managing test results are tracking tests until the results have been received, notifying patients of the results, documenting that the notification occurred, and making sure that patients with abnormal results receive the recommended follow-up care. The sample Laboratory/Diagnostic Test Tracking Log on page 63 reflects these important steps.

The AAP Periodic Survey of Fellows notes an improvement in the proportion of pediatricians who report routine documentation of medical reports (Table 4-4). In 1992, significantly fewer pediatricians reported documentation of each type of report. Unfortunately, the survey did not assess all 4 steps of tracking these reports.

Making and Managing Referrals

All referrals to other health care professionals (eg, specialists, subspecialists, mental health providers, dentists) should be documented in the medical record. For important or urgent referrals, the pediatrician should consider having the referral appointment made before the patient leaves the office. A follow-up system to make sure the patient makes and keeps the appointment is essential to good continuity. A designated individual in your office can be in charge of making and following up on referrals. A tickler file may be useful. This is a collection of date-labeled file folders organized in a way that allows time-sensitive documents to be filed according to the future date on which each document needs action. Each day, the folder of the current date is retrieved from the tickler file so that any documents within it may be acted on. Essentially, a tickler file provides a way to send a reminder to oneself in the future by tickling one's memory.

A reminder system of some kind can be used to check that appointments are made and referral reports have been received and reviewed by the referring physician. If no report has been received, contact the consultant (and document the contact) to ascertain whether the patient is getting the referred care needed.

If the pediatrician is the recipient of a referral from another provider, it is essential to document the referral, evaluate the patient, and communicate with the referring provider in a timely manner. An example of a Consultation Request and Report Form is on page 65.

Billing and Collections

Many malpractice claims are initiated in response to the manner in which collection efforts are made. A written collection policy ensures that all employ-

Table 4-4. Routine Documentation of Review of Medical Reports From Other Sources, 1992, 1996, 2001, and 2007[1]

		Percent of Pediatricians Reporting			
		1992	1996	2001	2007
		(n = 995)	(n = 762)	(n = 786)	(n = 667)
Review of reports from other sources are routinely documented (or initialed)					
	Laboratory reports	70.9[a]	88.4	89.4[b]	93.1[a,b]
	X-ray reports	68.1[a]	86.3	87.8	90.6[a]
	Consultant reports	67.3[a]	84.3	85.8[b]	89.2[a,b]
Hospital discharge summaries		64.1[a]	78.4	79.7	82.4[a]

[a]P<0.001, 2007 v 1992.
[b]P<0.05, 2007 v 2001.

ees know what the policy is and how to handle each billing and collection situation. It also reduces the likelihood of staff members being inconsistent or unfair in how billing problems are resolved. Issues to be addressed in billing and collections policies may include

- Informing patients before their first appointment about your fee and payment requirements, and the legal requirement of paying co-payments and deductibles.
- Setting up systems for identifying circumstances that may require special action (eg, patients experiencing financial hardship, patients expressing dissatisfaction with the quality of medical care or how requests for payment were communicated).
- Decisions about special arrangements for payment should take into consideration state law and contractual obligations.
  - The patient's past payment history.
  - The quality of care rendered.
  - The patient's satisfaction. Sometimes not paying a bill is the patient's way of telling you there is a problem with your office or your relationship with the patient. If the patient balks at paying a bill, ask why. If appropriate, work out an agreeable payment arrangement. If accommodation is not possible, consider whether the relationship should be terminated and follow steps outlined later in this chapter.
- Consider the cost of legal action versus how much money the patient owes. Obtain information from the appropriate small-claims court in your area. Be cautious about suing for small sums of money.
- Before initiating collection procedures, make sure you personally review the patient's medical record (even the first reminder phone call that a bill is overdue).

- Understand the patient's rights concerning privacy and the physician-patient relationship. (Do not send any medical information to a collection agency.)
- Be aware of the Fair Debt Collection Practices Act. (Periodically evaluate the collection agency's practices.)

Keeping a Safe Environment

Patients develop impressions of the kind of medical care they will receive when they view practice surroundings. If the surroundings are pleasant, clean, and convenient, patients will more likely view the physician as competent and providing quality care.

- To prevent patient injury, evaluate the facility to ensure easy access. All patient care areas should be checked, including the parking lot, to identify potential safety hazards.
- Provide comfortable office furnishings to allow patients and families to feel at ease. Check furnishings periodically to ensure that they are in good condition. Take steps to maintain cleanliness and good housekeeping. Messy or dirty offices create a negative impression and may transmit infections from patient to patient. The effect on the patient's perception of quality is significant.
- Have furnishings that meet patient needs in terms of safety, size, and comfort. Childproof your office. Furniture with sharp corners can be hazardous to cruising toddlers. Soft, low seating may be very comfortable for most patients but could be problematic for pregnant women. Cover electrical outlets. New building construction after 1992 must meet accessibility standards for offices covered by the Americans with Disabilities Act (ADA). Make sure your furniture placement and traffic patterns do not erode ADA guidelines for patients or parents with disabilities.

- Should you decide to have toys in the reception area, make sure they are safe for children of all ages, disinfected routinely, and checked regularly for broken pieces. Also have your staff watch for stray items (eg, toys, reading materials, jackets) in the walkways that might cause a visitor to trip or fall. The path from the door to the reception window or desk should not become an obstacle course. Remember, parents carrying infants, small children, and diaper bags may not be able to see the floor to navigate around clutter.
- Keep the room at a comfortable temperature and provide plenty of lighting.
- Floor surfaces should be level and kept dry. If mats are used at entrances to prevent snow and rain from being tracked into the building, check the mats periodically to ensure that they do no become a safety hazard.
- Maintain a lost-and-found department for patient convenience.

Maintaining Medical Equipment

Patients may be injured because of faulty or improper use of medical equipment. The practice administrator should institute a policy of regular maintenance and use of all equipment.

- Train all employees on the proper use of equipment. Document the training (date, content, time) and place it in each employee's personnel file. Conduct periodic retraining to keep employees skills sharp and up to date.
- Calibrate all equipment as recommended by the manufacturer. Follow all recommendations for ongoing quality assessment (eg, operational controls, preventive maintenance schedules). Periodically (at least annually) review maintenance and use policies.
- Should a patient or employee be injured by medical equipment in your office, some additional steps should be taken.

  – Report the incident to your professional liability insurance carrier. The loss-prevention manager should be able to advise you on how to respond to the injured person.
  – Do not tamper with medical equipment or attempt to repair it yourself.
  – In keeping with the focus on patient safety, you may wish to conduct an adverse event assessment to identify any systematic problems that may have contributed to the error.
  – *Do not document any assumptions about an equipment malfunction or improper usage in the patient's medical record.*

Preparing for Emergencies

- All medical offices should have a written protocol for handling a medical emergency and environmental disasters (eg, fires, tornadoes, earthquakes).
- Post emergency numbers such as ambulances, hospitals, and poison control next to all telephones.
- Require all staff to stay current on cardiopulmonary resuscitation.
- The office should have emergency equipment and medications. Medications should be labeled distinctly to avoid confusion. Information on pediatric dosages should be immediately available for checking and rechecking accurate administration.
- Staff should be trained in emergency procedures, and emergency drills should be conducted regularly. Records of the procedures should be accessible to staff. Training and drill documentation should be kept in a permanent storage site.

Guidelines for responding to emergencies and disasters can be obtained from OSHA (www.osha.gov).

Protecting Patient Confidentiality

Patient privacy regulations were changed extensively with the implementation of HIPAA. Resources to help pediatricians comply with HIPAA are available on the AAP *Practice Management Online* (http://practice.aap.org).

Communication between the patient and physician is confidential; safeguarding that confidentiality is critical to the physician-patient relationship. Patients have filed many lawsuits because of disclosure of confidential information. The privacy of patient health information is governed by a patchwork of federal, state, and common law. Recent efforts to establish federal privacy standards appear to offer only minimal requirements and allow states to create more stringent requirements. In pediatrics, the triad relationship among the patient, pediatrician, and parent (or legal guardian) tends to complicate confidentiality, particularly as the patient matures into adolescence and young adulthood. Confidentiality policies of the practice should be consistent with applicable state laws, especially as they relate to conditions and circumstances under which the adolescent patient is considered an emancipated minor. This confidentiality privilege extends to all members of the health care team.

- All personal data, medical notes, and billing information are confidential and may not be communicated to anyone without the patient's or parent's written consent. Certain medical conditions (eg, HIV status) may have specific disclosure requirements.
- Loose talk or office chatter that others overhear can be the basis for a defamation or invasion of privacy suit. Watch your voice volume; pay attention to who is nearby and the content of conversations.
- Do a *confidentiality audit* of your office. Test to see how easy overhearing conversation is, particularly from the front office. If necessary, install some soundproofing materials. Also make sure

your patient's medical and financial records are kept private. Use privacy screens on computer monitors and do not leave test results or other confidential information unattended at the fax machine or elsewhere.

- The mobility afforded by wireless phones makes it possible to conduct patient care conversations in public settings (eg, restaurants, airports) in which bystanders cannot help but overhear your comments. Do not allow convenience to override confidentiality.
- Train all new employees on their specific responsibilities in protecting patient confidentiality. Make sure all staff members understand that violation of a patient's privacy may result in disciplinary action up to and including termination of employment. Staff members should, at the time of hiring, sign a form pledging confidentiality of patient information; this form becomes a part of the personnel record.

Handling Patient Complaints

A patient may demonstrate dissatisfaction and intention to sue long before legal papers are served. A staff member may be the first to be aware of a patient complaint. No matter how incidental the complaint may seem, staff should be trained to listen and respond to patient concerns appropriately. A system for communicating patient problems to administrative supervisors and the patient's primary care physician should be in place to ensure that patterns and trends can be studied and redressed, whether these are problems shared by several patients or a patient with ongoing difficulties.

- Institute a formal complaint policy in the office. Use a report form and complaint log to track the occurrence and disposition of all patient complaints. Do not enter this information in the patient's medical record.
- Notify the physician of the complaint on the day it is received.

- Respond to the complaint quickly and follow up with the patient.

No practice is free from problems or complaints. It is the ability of the practice to attend to concerns (real or perceived) and respond quickly and appropriately that distinguishes good from adequate management. Such efforts can keep minor problems from festering into major problems and reduce the likelihood of litigation. Make sure your staff knows to separate the person from the problem; a tendency to label people as "whiners" or "troublemakers" can have a chilling effect on communication and decreases the ability of the practice to resolve difficulties and strive for improvement.

Terminating the Physician-Patient Relationship

Once a physician-patient relationship has been established, the physician is not free to terminate the relationship at will without formal, written notification in conformity with state law. The physician-patient relationship continues until it is ended by one of the following circumstances:

- The patient has no need for further care or is formally transferred to another provider.
- The patient terminates the relationship.
- The physician formally and legally terminates the relationship.

Failure to implement and document a formal termination process may constitute patient abandonment and bring about fines or legal action if the patient is harmed by the abandonment.

There may be circumstances in which it is deemed necessary to terminate the physician-patient relationship. Perhaps the patient is noncompliant (ie, does not follow the agreed-on course of treatment, fails to keep appointments, does not share fundamental health care principals such as the need for preventive medicine and immunizations). First,

attempt to assess the reason(s) for the noncompliance (eg, communication or language barriers, failure to understand the importance of the follow-up visit). If you believe that to continue treatment without consistent patient follow-through is likely to increase the chances of a complication or poor outcome, the wisest course of action may be to terminate the relationship. Perhaps the patient is unreasonably demanding, threatening, verbally abusive, or rude. Sometimes the physician and patient simply do not get along. Perhaps a patient may routinely fail to pay bills without offering an explanation or seeking to set up a payment plan. Any of those problems (and many others) may be sufficient reason to dismiss a patient from your practice.

If you do so, be sure to follow appropriate steps to minimize the chance of being sued for abandonment. Typically these include

- First, put the notice in writing, such as a letter addressed to the patient on your practice letterhead.
- The reason for dissolving the relationship may or may not be stated.
  - If it is for noncompliance, say so clearly in the letter.
  - If it is for personality conflict, an unpaid bill, or a reason not to be made public, it may be prudent to avoid stating the reason in writing.
- Agree to continue to provide treatment and access to services for a reasonable period, such as 30 to 90 days (depending on state law and contractual agreements—how much time you are required to give a patient to seek another health care professional varies in each state and may be stipulated in your contract with managed care organizations or third-party payers) to allow the patient sufficient time to secure a new physician.

- Offer to provide resources or recommendations to help the patient locate another physician of like specialty.
- Offer to send copies of medical records to the new physician on receiving a signed authorization from the patient to do so.
- Send the letter by certified mail, return receipt requested. Keep the receipt in the patient's file along with a copy of the letter.

Be aware that a physician *cannot* refuse to give a patient an appointment because the patient has not paid a bill without instituting a formal process to terminate the physician-patient relationship.

No patient should be dismissed from the practice for reasons protected under federal or state law (eg, religion, ethnicity, race, medical condition such as HIV status).

The physician-patient relationship is the foundation of medical law. On it rests the legal rights and obligations of patients and physicians. Contact your practice's legal advisor to make sure your termination process is legally sound and adequately protects you and your office staff. (See Sample Letter of Withdrawal on page 68.)

Safeguarding the Rights of the Patient

Pediatricians and office staff should be aware of all applicable rights afforded to patients.

- The right to choose the physician from which the patient wishes to receive medical care
- The right to say whether medical treatment will begin and to set limits on the care provided
- The right to know before the treatment begins what it will involve, what effects it will have on the patient and family, what the inherent dangers are, and what it will cost

Informed Consent to Treatment

Informed consent is not just a piece of paper. It is the communication, education, and interaction among the physician, parent, and patient about a proposed action by the physician, such as a proposed test or treatment. Failure to secure informed consent can result in severe legal consequences.

- Treating a patient without permission can be grounds for a civil or criminal battery charge and may be grounds for medical negligence, as well.
- Treating a patient with the patient's consent but failing to explain the inherent risks of a procedure could result in a charge of negligence.

Implied consent is reflected in the patient's actions such as having a prescription filled or accepting an injection.

Expressed consent is an oral or written acceptance of the treatment. Obtain the written form of expressed consent when the proposed treatment involves surgery or high-risk diagnostic or treatment procedures. Experimental drugs or procedures, typically offered as part of a research trial, require different informed consent documentation.

The legal principle of informed consent rests in the understanding that a mentally competent adult has control over his or her own body. Therefore, physicians must obtain the patient's or parent's informed consent before beginning medical treatment.

Informed consent will develop from the patient's understanding of the following factors:

- Nature, benefits, and risks of the proposed treatment or testing
- Nature, benefits, and risks of alternate treatment or testing
- Nature, benefits, and risks of no treatment or testing

Many states have established informed consent disclosure standards. These may be based on physician standard expectations (ie, what a reasonable physician in the community would disclose), reasonable patient standard (ie, what a reasonable patient would want disclosed), a hybrid of both, or mandated specific disclosures for specific treatments.

Physicians in states with statutory disclosure standards are well advised to tell patients everything a reasonable person would want to know about the intervention, ask questions to ascertain the patient's understanding of what was communicated, and note the patient's final decision and be sure the patient signs the appropriate statutory consent forms.

Informed Consent and the Minor Patient

The doctrine of informed consent takes a different form when the patient is a minor. In general, parents provide *informed permission* for diagnosis and treatment of children. As the child matures, a subtle shift occurs in which pediatricians secure parental permission for medical treatment along with the *assent of the child,* if appropriate. As the patient enters adolescence, the law recognizes specific circumstances in which the adolescent patient can consent to medical treatment without consent from the parent. The ability of minor patients to consent to medical care is an extremely complex area of law and often depends on unique circumstances (eg, whether the minor is considered emancipated) and the nature of the care being sought (eg, reproductive issue for adolescents). Careful attention to all applicable state law is essential to risk management in this area.

Medical offices may need to implement specific policies and procedures for documenting other issues related to informed consent for pediatric patients.

- *Consent by proxy*—when parents or legal guardians delegate the authority to grant permission to provide medical care to their minor children to a legally competent adult (eg, noncustodial parent, stepparent, nanny or au pair, grandparent)
- *Informed refusal*—when parents or legal guardians or their agents choose to forego necessary medical treatment (eg, immunizations, surgery)

Medical Record Keeping

Risk management experts recommend the following loss-prevention tips:

- Fasten all loose materials into the paper medical record.
- Ensure that all notes are legible.
- Clearly identify allergies in the medical record.
- Record patient name on every page in the medical record.
- Physicians should initial every entry in the medical record.
- Financial data should not be kept in the medical record.

An example of a medical record review sheet has been provided on page 67. It is prudent to make sure that the previously mentioned guidelines are being met by periodically checking several medical records.

A well-documented, legible, structured medical record is the physician's first line of defense in case of a malpractice suit. The medical record is a form of communication among health care professionals about the patient's condition. This documentation identifies the patient, supports the diagnosis, justifies the treatment, and documents the results of treatment.

Auditing the Quality of Record Content

Records are the heart of systematic patient care. Excellent record keeping is one of the most effective tools in patient care and in preventing or defending claims. Following are the key elements of good medical records:

Uniform Layout

Medical records should be uniform within the practice. An excellent way to structure medical records is to insert dividers for laboratory results, imaging reports, and progress notes; clearly document allergies; and use a problem list. In this format, the record is organized for easy scanning by all health care professionals who subsequently need to review it.

Assembled Securely

Secure all pages in each section of the record in chronologic order with fasteners to prevent pages from being lost. Sometimes outside auditors vigorously shake records to see if any poorly secured documents fall out.

Organized

Organize records for easy and accurate retrieval. Whatever system is used, it should be logical and clear to all staff members and physicians (eg, active versus inactive patients, color coding for chronic conditions or frequent diagnoses).

Timely

Note the date and time of the examination or contact. Note the date and time the entry was made. The greater the time lapse between the examination and entry, the less credible the medical record.

Conversations

Address and document patient or family worries or concerns in patient records. Record the source of the information if not the patient.

Important Instructions

Always document important warnings and instructions given to the patient. This can prevent misunderstandings between what you said and what the patient heard. Also, documenting instructions may help prove noncompliance. Juries tend to be less sympathetic toward noncompliant patients.

Informed Consent

To reinforce the signed consent form, always document that the information has been disclosed and whether any additional information was distributed (eg, patient education brochures).

Potential Complications

Document all possible complications. Failure to recognize a complication in time to prevent injury is a common basis for a lawsuit. Proving negligence is difficult if the record shows prior awareness that a complication might occur.

Releasing Medical Records

Make sure that the medical records release policies of the practice are up to date and followed.

Retaining Medical Records

Make sure that the policies and procedures of the practice for retaining medical records are up to date and followed.

Electronic health records may make adherence to many of these suggestions easier and more routine.

See Chapter 11 for a more detailed discussion of medical records.

Sample Forms and Letters

Sample forms for managing specific risks begin on the next page.

- Consent by Proxy for Nonurgent Pediatric Care
- Laboratory/Diagnostic Test Tracking Log
- Follow-up Appointment Log Sheet
- Consultation Request and Report Form
- Authorization Form: Transfer of Medical Records
- Medical Record Review Form
- Sample Letter of Withdrawal

(continued on page 69)

Consent by Proxy for Nonurgent Pediatric Care

For families who are ongoing patients of _____

(Health care facility)

I (we) appoint _____

(Name) (Address)

Driver's license number _____

Relationship to patient _____

(Describe relationship)

as my (our) proxy decision-maker for consenting to nonurgent medical care for my (our) children listed as follows. Be advised that protected patient health information may be shared with the proxy to facilitate informed decision-making.

Name: _____

Date of Birth: _____

Name: _____

Date of Birth: _____

Health care services/procedures for which the proxy is permitted to consent are as indicated below in the checked boxes (check all that apply):

☐ Immunizations ☐ Radiographs ☐ Blood tests ☐ Specialty appointments (referrals)

☐ Other (Please describe.) _____

Contact information

If the nature of the medical care is nonroutine, please try to contact me (us) about the health care of my (our) child(ren) at the following telephone number(s):

Parent's name: _____ Signature: _____

Daytime phone: _____ Date: _____

Evening phone: _____

Cell phone: _____

Parent's name: _____ Signature: _____

Daytime phone: _____ Date: _____

Evening phone: _____

Cell phone: _____

This form, which should not be considered a legal document without advice from a lawyer, may be used as a template for documenting consent by proxy for nonurgent pediatric care. This form should be reviewed to be consistent with state law (eg, proxies may not consent to immunizations in some states) and may be legally valid for only a specified time period.

Laboratory/Diagnostic Test Tracking Log

Date Ordered	Patient ID #	Patient DOB	Name of Laboratory/ Diagnostic Test	Date Results Received at Office	Date and Initial Results Reviewed by MD/DO	Date Results to Patient	Date Follow-up Scheduled (if Needed)

Follow-up Appointment Log Sheet

Date	Patient Name or ID #	Reason for Appointment	Estimated Follow- up Date	Date of Phone Call/ E-mail/Letter	Date of Follow-up Appointment

This entire form should be enlarged to make room for the information.

Consultation Request and Report Form

Today's Date:

Appointment Made for: Age:

Patient's Name:

To: Dr

From: Dr

Patient Location:

Type of Consultation Desired: ☐ Consultation Only

                                     ☐ Consultation and Follow Jointly

                                     ☐ Accept in Transfer

Referring Diagnosis:

Reason for Consultation:

Urgent _____ Within 1 Week _____ Not Urgent _____

Signature: Date: Time:

Consultation Report:

Authorization Form: Transfer of Medical Records

Date: _____

I, _____ authorize _____
(Please print parent's name here.)

Dr _____ to make available
(Fill in the name of the physician and practice.)

to Dr _____
(Insert full name, address, and telephone number of the new physician and practice.)

all records and reports relative to my child's case, including photographs and images.

Name of patient _____ Date of Birth _____
(Please print patient's name here.)

Signed _____ Date _____
(signature of parent or legal guardian)

Medical Record Review Form

Evaluation Criteria	Yes	No
Patient name and medical record number are on each page of record.		
Record is legible.		
Allergies and drug sensitivities are recorded in a prominent place in record.		
Advice given by telephone is recorded.		
Problem list is used to indicate significant surgical procedures and acute and chronic problems.		
Progress notes include chief complaint, clinical findings, diagnostic or medical impression, and studies ordered.		
Progress notes are dated and signed.		
Diagnostic reports are initialed or signed after review by physician.		
Errors entered in record are corrected by drawing a line through error, dating, and initialing.		
Record follows established page order and is in good repair.		

Sample Letter of Withdrawal

Denise Doctor, MD
ABC Pediatric Group
1111 First St, Suite 200
Hometown, ST 54321
444/555-6666

<Date>

<Inside address>

Dear <Patient's Name>:

I regret to inform you that I will no longer be able to provide medical care to your children. If you require medical care within the next 30 days, I will be available but will not be available to care for your children after <month, day, year>.

Please secure the care of another pediatrician. If you do not know another pediatrician, please contact your health plan or the American Academy of Pediatrics HealthyChildren.org "Find a Pediatrician" tool (www.aap.org/referral) to locate a pediatrician in your area. To assist you in continuing to receive medical care, I will make a copy of your children's medical records available to the new pediatrician you designate.

After you have chosen another pediatrician, please complete and return the enclosed Authorization Form: Transfer of Medical Records.

If you have any concerns about this transition or need my help, please call my office. Again, I will be available to you for the next 30 days. After that time, my office will not be in a position to serve you. I extend to you best wishes for your future health and happiness.

Sincerely,

Denise Doctor, MD

Summary

In today's environment of rapidly changing culture and an increasingly litigious society, pediatricians need to use every management tool available to have an effective risk management program. This requires the cooperation and commitment of everyone in the practice to adhere to the concepts of not only governmental regulation but also management principles to enhance patient safety, prevent medical errors, maintain quality care, and protect patient confidentiality. Judicious use of the information described in this chapter will help practitioners recognize risk exposure, determine the causes of risk, implement corrective actions, and monitor indicators of risk to determine if corrective actions are effective. Remember that a commitment to risk management also requires a willingness to learn new concepts, streamline procedures, reduce variability, and change behavior.

References

1. American Academy of Pediatrics. *Periodic Survey of Fellows #69: Experiences with Medical Liability: Executive Summary.* Elk Grove Village, IL: American Academy of Pediatrics; 2007. http://www.aap.org/research/periodicsurvey/PS69exsummedicalliability.pdf. Accessed April 21, 2011

2. Balsamo RR, Brown MD. Risk management. In: Sanbar SS, Firestone MH, eds. *Legal Medicine.* 6th ed. St. Louis, MO: Mosby; 2004:187–206

3. American Society for Healthcare Risk Management. *Certified Professional in Healthcare Risk Management (CPHRM) Prep Guide.* 4th ed. Chicago, IL: American Society for Healthcare Risk Management of the American Hospital Association; 2006

4. Hickson GB, Clayton E, Githens P, Sloan FA. Factors that prompted families to file malpractice claims following perinatal injuries. *JAMA.* 1992;267(10):1359–1363

5. Physician Insurers Association of America. *A Risk Management Review of Malpractice Claims—Pediatrics.* Rockville, MD: Physician Insurers Association of America; 2009

6. Anderson RT, Camacho FT, Balkrishnan R. Willing to wait? The influence of patient wait time on satisfaction with primary care. *BMC Health Serv Res.* 2007;7:31. http://www.ncbi.nlm.nih.gov/pmc/articles/PMC1810532/pdf/1472-6963-7-31.pdf. Accessed April 21, 2011

Resources

Malpractice insurance companies conduct risk management surveys for their insureds and sometimes offer premium discounts for participants.

Hospital risk managers may be willing to help practices implement risk management programs.

The AAP offers risk management seminars at its annual National Conference & Exhibition.

Topics covered in the monthly "Pediatricians and the Law" column of AAP News include risk management and loss prevention; these topics are also covered on the AAP *Practice Management Online* (http://practice.aap.org).

Health Insurance Portability and Accountability Act compliance resources are available for free on the Member Center of the AAP Web site (www.aap.org/moc/hipaa/index.cfm).

CHAPTER 5

Telephone and On-call Care

Andrew R. Hertz, MD, FAAP

- -

KEY CONCEPTS

- Risk Management Principles
- Patient Access and Call Processing
- After-hours Patient Calls
- Recording Phone Calls
- Physician-to-Physician Telephone Calls
- On-call Coverage
- Best Practices Checklist

Telephone care is a high-risk liability activity for a pediatric practice. The Physician Insurers Association of America (PIAA) database of closed malpractice claims contains 817 involving telephone medicine from 1985 to 2006. One third of these claims (272) resulted in a payout to the plaintiff and totaled more than $74 million. Pediatrics accounted for 12% of the claims but nearly 16% of the indemnity dollars. Furthermore, of the 4 primary care specialties representing three quarters of all telephone claims, pediatricians had the highest percentage of paid claims (41%). In contrast, the rate of payment for all pediatric claims in the PIAA database during that same period was 28%.[1]

There are several reasons pediatricians are vulnerable during telephone care encounters. Physicians cannot rely on their traditional senses of sight, sound, touch, and smell to assess the patient and caregiver's concern. Patient telephone care is a high-volume occurrence responsible for as much

as 30% of care provided to children in a primary pediatric care setting during office hours, as well as 80% of after-hours care.[2] For multiple reasons beyond the scope of this chapter, physicians are being forced into providing more complex non–face-to-face care to patients. Unlike other primary care physicians, pediatricians do not speak directly to the patient but usually must obtain a history from a third-party caregiver. Lastly, telephone care is often delegated to mid-level practitioners who may not be adequately trained in the subtleties of non–face-to-face care.

Educational efforts over the past few decades have resulted in improved pediatrician telephone encounter documentation during office hours (though no change in after-hours documentation) (Table 5-1). Improved risk management processes have been the aim of educational efforts by the American Academy of Pediatrics (AAP) and other professional societies, medical malpractice carriers, and hospitals.

The primary objective in telephone care must be to provide quality care in a cost-efficient manner without placing patients at risk This non–face-to-face care occurs during 2,000 to 3,000 annual telephone calls (10 to 15 per day) to the pediatrician.[3] Only through the diligent practice of basic risk management principles for telephone care can a physician best limit liability associated with this significant mode of patient care.

First and foremost in risk reduction is pediatricians understanding 3 important points about telephone triage. First, any medical advice provided by a physician or practice employee over the phone on which

TABLE 5. 1. Documentation of Telephone Contacts Among Pediatricians Providing Care in Office-Based Settings, 1992, 1996, 2001, and 2007 (Percent of Pediatricians Reporting)

	DURING OFFICE HOURS				AFTER HOURS	
	1992 (n = 946)	1996 (n = 629)	2001 (n = 752)	2007 (n = 635)	2001 (n = 708)	2007 (n = 596)
Practice keeps record of						
ALL telephone contacts	44.1[a]	62.0	68.0[b]	74.6[a,b]	53.2	54.5
SOME telephone contacts	41.3[a]	29.4	25.4	21.6[a]	34.3	34.2
NO telephone contacts	14.6[a]	8.6	6.6[c]	3.8[a,c]	12.4	11.2
For practices who record ALL or SOME telephone contacts, the following items are included in the telephone log:						
Patient's problem	95.7[a]	98.1	98.2	99.0[a]	97.9	96.8
Instructions or information given	85.8[a]	91.8	91.6[b]	95.3[a,b]	90.5[c]	94.2[c]
To whom the call was referred	78.6[a]	86.9	85.1	88.4[a]	79.5	81.1
Time of call	73.6[a]	84.3	83.6[c]	87.5[a,c]	84.4	86.4
Document physician returned the call	58.5[a]	69.3	71.8[b]	79.6[a,b]	67.1[b]	75.6[b]
Other[d]	0.3[a]	7.7	5.3	6.1[a]	4.7	6.8

[a]P<.01, 2007 v 1992.
[b]P<.01, 2007 v 2001.
[c]P<.05, 2007 v 2001.
[d]Includes patient/parent demographic information, chronic conditions, allergies, prescription information, pharmacy name and phone number, who took the call, co-signature of physician, other pertinent information.

the caller may reasonably rely establishes a physician-patient relationship and is considered medical practice. Second, regardless of who in the office provides telephone advice, physicians are accountable for that advice. Third, even physicians, generalists, and specialists providing telephone advice to another physician about a patient may be liable for that advice. This chapter will help to outline best practices to limit medical risk associated with all 3.

Case law has determined that telephone calls made merely to schedule an appointment with a health care professional do not by themselves establish a physician-patient relationship, provided no ongoing relationship exists and no medical advice was provided.[4]

Lawsuits about telephone triage usually involve failure to follow through on a physician's duty to treat (an abandonment of the patient), the provision of substandard telephone care, or the untimely provision of care. A duty to treat is established when a patient (or parent) calls a physician or the

physician's delegate, such as a nurse or covering on-call physician.

If an emergency exists, the physician or delegate must assess and advise. It is at the point when the practitioner begins to give advice that the physician of record becomes responsible for that patient encounter. To not provide complete advice or follow-up care could constitute patient abandonment. Failure of the telephone provider to complete a thorough, logical, and systemic evaluation of the patient's problem, resulting in a reasonable call disposition and administration of appropriate advice including follow-up plans, may be considered the provision of substandard care.

Once the duty to treat is established, the most common critical errors made in telephone care that have led to malpractice judgments include not obtaining enough information to recognize the seriousness of the problem, which subsequently results in harm to the patient, or not sufficiently documenting the telephone encounter to show that quality care was delivered. To remedy this, pediatricians or their delegates must take steps to ensure that a systematic, thorough assessment of the problem is conducted in a manner consistent with applicable standards of care (ie, using clinically based, pediatric-specific telephone triage and advice guidelines). Furthermore, these practices must be well documented for each telephone encounter.

Risk Management Principles

Physicians can manage the medicolegal risk associated with telephone calls through the use of careful call-processing procedures, delegation of calls to qualified clinical staff, and standardized telephone care guidelines and consistent documentation. There are 12 basic principles physicians should consider for their practices to reduce the risk associated with telephone calls. (See also "Best Practices Checklist" on pages 80–81.)

1. *Be accessible.* Do not have your staff create a roadblock between you and the phone. Create policies and procedures that indicate when staff should interrupt you for a phone call. If a caller perceives her concern to be urgent, treat it as such.

2. *Provide prompt and courteous service.* Patients should have rapid access to a live person. Monitor hold times in your office and adjust staff and the number of phone lines accordingly. Return calls within a reasonable time. Staff should explain to callers when to expect a call-back (eg, within 1 hour, at the end of the half day) and ask if this will be acceptable.

3. *Honor a patient's request to be seen.* The caller may not be able to adequately explain the concern in words. Even if a thorough telephone assessment does not deem a face-to-face encounter necessary, respect the caller's fears and accommodate them.

4. *Review the patient medical record.* As practices become engaged in the use of electronic health records (EHRs), every effort should be made to

have a patient's medical record accessible to all telephone care providers. Viewing the patient record helps ensure continuity of care, decreases redundant or inappropriate care, and decreases provision of inappropriate advice.

5. *Document all calls to some extent and selected calls thoroughly.* The extent to which any medical encounter is documented is always a balance between patient care and safety, efficiency, and liability. All calls should receive the minimum demographic documentation listed in Table 5-2 and clinical documentation listed in Table 5-3. Table 5-4 shows additional information about the conclusion of calls that should be documented. Standard telephone log forms with check boxes simplify this process. High-risk calls in which medication or care plans are significantly altered, the caller refuses to comply, or the caller's immediate health is in jeopardy warrant more detailed documentation. All telephone care documentation should be archived in a call log or the patient's chart. Changes in medical management or high–legal-risk calls should certainly be documented in the patient chart. As EHRs become commonplace in practice, all telephone encounters should be documented within the EHR.

6. *Do not end a conversation until the caller understands and agrees with the plan.* To reduce communication errors, always ascertain a caller's understanding of and agreement with the advice given. Callers also should always be instructed about the circumstances for which they should seek additional medical advice or care.

7. *Judiciously and reluctantly prescribe medications over the telephone.* Some states have laws prohibiting prescribing medication over the telephone without seeing the patient face-to-face. Know your state laws and act accordingly. If you choose to prescribe medications via the telephone, keep the following in mind: Prescribing medication to a patient for a new problem over the phone obviously is a high-risk endeavor.

The physician cannot rely on any of the many skills used during the physical examination to ensure correct diagnosis. If medication is prescribed, the dosage and any drug allergies certainly should be well documented. Nonphysician staff prescribing medications should only do so with very specific guidelines and standing orders about new and renewal medications and in compliance with state laws.

8. *Exclude nonclinical staff from providing telephone triage and advice.* It is generally accepted that nurses with appropriate training and support are considered appropriate providers of telephone triage and advice. Nonclinical or clerical staff should refrain from providing any medical advice except under the simplest and strictest guidelines. Even having nonclinical or clerical staff provide dosage information for acetaminophen would be problematic if the caller were the mother of a 3-week-old. Clerical staff should receive training on recognizing potentially urgent situations and how to manage them.

9. *Require all telephone care providers to use standard guidelines.* To ensure the delivery of high-quality telephone triage and advice by nonphysician clinical staff, use one of the readily available and proven pediatric telephone triage guideline books (see "Resources" on page 82). These books provide thorough triage, allow for rapid assessment and advice, and decrease the amount of required documentation.

Table 5-2. Demographic Documentation

Initials of nurse or physician performing triage
Date and time of initial call to office
Name of patient
Name of caller
Patient birth date and age
Caller telephone number
Time caller reached (if call returned) and time of all attempts

Table 5-3. Clinical Documentation

Reason for call (chief complaint)
Assessment of present illness history, significant past history, and drug allergies
Guideline used (optional for physician)
Reason for disposition (may be that all triage questions were negative) (optional for physician)
Disposition recommended

Table 5-4. Closure Documentation

Advice given
Caller's understanding of and agreement with plan (recommended)
Indications that the caller has been instructed as to under which circumstances to call back
Dosage and specifics of medication prescribed (over-the-counter or prescription)
Details of any follow-up calls

10. *Telephone care providers should have documented training and oversight.* Because the physician is ultimately responsible for all advice given, telephone triage should be delegated to the most qualified and best-trained staff member. These individuals should undergo specific training in the use of telephone triage guidelines, work within standard policies and procedures, and have continuous oversight and quality assurance initiatives.

11. *Maintain patient confidentiality.* Patient information should be given over the phone carefully. The information given may be sensitive and the person receiving the information may not be entitled to it. Immunization records may be harmless, but patient test results given to a noncustodial parent may cause major problems.

12. *Decrease patient telephone calls.* Encourage patients to use Web sites with medical and self-care information. This information may be found on your practice Web site; a local children's hospital site; the official AAP Web site for parents, HealthyChildren.org; or other similar sites that your practice recommends.

Patient Access and Call Processing

An essential aspect of any medical practice is efficient patient telephone access. In fact, 24-hour access and physician accessibility are key components of the National Committee for Quality Assurance Patient-Centered Medical Home certification requirements. However, physicians must minimize the inherent liability associated with this telephone access. The key principles of access apply to office-hours and after-hours calls.

Access should be prompt with minimal transfer and wait times prior to speaking with a live person. If recorded "hold" messages are used at any time, or if patients are asked to leave a message, the caller should be instructed that if the call concerns a potentially life-threatening emergency, emergency medical services should be contacted immediately.

When leaving a live or recorded message, a caller should be informed as to how long it may take for the call to be returned and instructed to call again or seek immediate medical care if the patient's condition worsens.

Nonclinical staff that often first answer telephone calls in the office and answering services are not qualified to give medical advice. However, these staff should have a basic list of urgent problems requiring immediate medical intervention or transfer of the call to a qualified medical practitioner. Many such lists of urgent issues exist and can be found in the resources recommended on page 82. Similarly, any patient requesting to urgently or immediately speak with a nurse or physician should have the request honored.

After-hours Patient Calls

Pediatricians in general practice receive, on average, 1,000 after-hours telephone calls each year (Table 5-5).[5] These calls have a significant effect on patient care and pediatrician medicolegal risk and lifestyle. When making decisions on how to manage after-hours calls, pediatricians need to consider patient safety, medicolegal risk, costs, patient satisfaction, physician practice styles, and physician satisfaction.

How Do Most Pediatricians Handle After-hours Calls?

One of the central tenets of the medical home concept is the "assurance that ambulatory and inpatient care for acute illnesses will be continuously available (24 hours a day, 7 days a week, 52 weeks a year)."[6] How pediatric practices maintain that continuity after hours varies widely. American Academy of Pediatrics Periodic Survey of Fellows #43, a mail-in survey conducted in 2000, focused on practice and personal characteristics of pediatricians. Of the 1,600 AAP Fellows surveyed, 52% participated in the study. The moderate response rate suggests that there should be caution in assuming these results can be generalized to all AAP Fellows. Results of this survey, in which pediatricians were asked about the types of telephone triage they provided during and after hours, are summarized in Table 5-6.[7]

Weighing Options

Pediatricians can choose to take their own after-hours calls, purchase service from a locally operated hospital-based nurse triage program, purchase service from a commercial nurse triage program, create their own nurse triage program for their practice, or a combination of these options.[8]

Table 5-5. Characteristics of After-hours Calls to Pediatric Offices[5]

Volume (Number of Calls)
- Average range from 900 to 1,800 calls per year—some variation by practice location, style
- Two to 4 calls per pediatrician per weeknight
- Four to 8 calls per pediatrician per weekend day/night
- Seasonal variation—2x calls in winter months

Timing (When They Occur)
- Forty-five percent: 5:00–10:00 pm weekdays
- Forty-five percent: 8:00 am–10:00 pm Saturdays/Sundays
- Ten percent: 10:00 pm–8:00 am 7 days per week

Table 5-6. After-hours Options[7]

Types of Telephone Triage Provided After Office Hours	% of Pediatricians Reporting[a]
• Voice mail directions to call 911 for an emergency or leave nonurgent recorded message	14
• Answering service/hospital switchboard (page physician on call)	64
• Centralized triage service with trained staff	11
• Centralized triage service with trained staff using written/computerized decision protocols	20

[a]Multiple responses were possible; therefore, does not total 100%.

Many pediatric practices use after-hours nurse triage services. These services are well accepted by parents and pediatricians, and some medical malpractice carriers have lowered premiums for physicians contracting with such services for after-hours calls. It is important to evaluate the quality of the call center before making a final decision on whether to use it. A report of the AAP Section on Telephone Care and Committee on Practice and Ambulatory Medicine details the critical success factors for pediatric call centers.[9]

After-hours nurse telephone triage services offer numerous advantages. Specially trained nurses undergo rigorous quality assurance programs. Their efficient use of standard guidelines ensure consistent care and outstanding documentation—excellent risk-reduction techniques. Their timely response to patient calls earns high patient satisfaction marks. These services can manage 75% to 80% of all after-hours calls, thereby preventing pediatrician burnout. Unfortunately, the services can be costly, ranging in price from $4 per call for locally operated services to $15 to $20 per call for commercial services.[10] In 1998 it was estimated that 25% of pediatricians used a locally operated, hospital-based nurse triage program after hours.[9] Regrettably, financial pressures have forced several

of these centers to close, requiring pediatricians to find other solutions for after-hours calls.

Most importantly, pediatricians should realize that even when off-site triage services are used, primary care physicians remain ultimately responsible for all triage and advice provided to their patients. That is why careful review and selection of triage services and guidelines cannot be overstated.

Juries in telephone malpractice cases have indicated that delegation of after-hours care to nurses is acceptable as long as they have been trained, have physician backup, and are regularly evaluated.[5] In a successful malpractice claim, the plaintiff must prove that the medical care fell below the standard and that this breach was the proximal cause of the patient's injury. The extensive documentation of well-run call centers is a strong legal defense should any claims involving after-hours telephone care arise.

Having the pediatrician answer evening, nighttime, and weekend calls is the cheapest option but offers none of the advantages of a nurse system. Like other physicians, pediatricians are notoriously poor at documenting telephone calls, especially when awakened in the middle of the night by the telephone. According to AAP Periodic Survey of Fellows #69, some improvement in the documentation of telephone calls during office hours has been seen. The percentage of pediatricians reporting keeping records of all telephone calls during office hours increased from 44% in 1992 to 68% in 2001 to 75% in 2007. However, in 2001, only 53%, and in 2007, 55% of pediatrician respondents reported keeping records of all after-hours telephone calls; the question was not asked in previous periodic surveys (see Table 5-1).[11] Very few residency programs teach physicians how to perform telephone triage. Sometimes pediatricians do not answer after-hours calls promptly, which can lead to increased legal risk and decreased patient satisfaction.

Recording Phone Calls

Although recording all telephone encounters may be helpful to the practice, it may not be legally useful or practical. In some jurisdictions, recorded telephone calls are not admissible unless the caller is specifically aware that the telephone conversation is being recorded. Some jurisdictions specifically bar recorded telephone encounters from being admissible in the defense of a medical negligence claim.[12] Given the high volume of telephone calls and long tails when caring for children, storing recordings or transcripts of telephone encounters may not be practical for most pediatric practices.

Physician-to-Physician Telephone Calls

A key requirement for any physician malpractice claim is that a physician-patient relationship existed between the plaintiff and defendant. If a telephone call involves an existing patient of yours or your practice, certainly a physician-patient relationship exists and your telephone care is subject to scrutiny. However, if you, or a delegate of yours, are speaking to a nonestablished patient directly, or if you are speaking to another physician about a patient who you are not in direct contact with at that time, the issue becomes hazier.

It has clearly been established that a nonclinical phone call to schedule an appointment or address administrative matters concerning a practice's relationship with its patients does not establish a physician-patient relationship.[4]

If you are an on-call, on-service, or assigned covering physician, and you speak directly to a patient who you have never seen before and may never see face-to-face, a physician-patient relationship is established once you take affirmative action with regard to care of the patient.[13] This affirmative action may take the form of providing advice, a diagnosis, treatment, or other similar actions over the phone.

A physician-to-physician telephone call can also be a source of liability because a physician-patient relationship can be established during these encounters. A physician-patient relationship can be established without direct audio relationship with a patient if another physician is acting directly on behalf of the patient. The key point here seems to be whether the telephone discussion is a formal responsibility of an on-call or on-service physician, or a professional conversation between 2 colleagues for which the consulted physician has no formal contractual or implied responsibility.

For example, a physician-patient relationship is not established if a community pediatrician making rounds on a newborn in the hospital discusses the newborn's condition with a respected colleague who also works in the community and not for the hospital. This type of conversation is seen as a casual and professional interaction that is part of the practice of medicine. Similarly, if the community pediatrician discusses the same newborn with a neonatologist who is not on service but happens to be walking to the parking lot with the community pediatrician, a *curbside consultation* exists and the neonatologist is likely not to be held accountable for his or her advice. However, if the community pediatrician requests to speak with the attending, on-call neonatologist and a subsequent conversation takes place resulting in the community physician following the neonatologist's advice, the telephoned neonatologist is considered to have established a physician-patient relationship and may be accountable for the advice.[13] An exception to this relationship is when the consulted physician refuses to offer advice or provide care to the patient based on a number of reasons, which may include the issue being beyond the expertise of the physician, or the consultant not feeling he or she has enough information at that time to render an opinion or provide advice.

Telephone calls between emergency department (ED) and on-call physicians clearly have been deemed to establish a physician-patient relationship, and the care provided during such calls can be subject to scrutiny. Specialists who are on call for a hospital ED establish a physician-patient relationship when they provide telephone consultation to an ED physician. Similarly, a general pediatrician who is contacted by an ED physician about that general pediatrician's own patient, about the patient of a physician for whom the pediatrician is covering, or in the pediatrician's role as the ED on-call pediatrician, establishes a physician-patient relationship if the pediatrician provides guidance to the ED physician.

In summary, formal telephone calls between 2 physicians during which a formal request is made for care advice from the on-call or on-service physician are felt to establish a physician-patient relationship and the contacted physicians, even if they never have a face-to-face encounter with the patient, are responsible for medical advice they provided during those calls.

All on-call physicians should document their telephone calls with consulting physicians, no matter how simple the question or how well they know the inquiring physician. Documentation should be similar to a physician-patient telephone call. It should be noted that although these physician-to-physician telephone calls cannot currently result in a billable encounter (only a liability encounter), many AAP sections are working on creating a process for billing for these telephone calls.

On-call Coverage

The AAP Periodic Survey of Fellows has tracked trends in medical liability for pediatricians since 1987. One consistent finding is that 50% of medical malpractice cases involved claimants who were not regular patients of the pediatrician they sued. Of those, 30% involved coverage situations.[11]

Some basic on-call risk-reduction rules follow, including the reasons why they are important[14]:

1. *All physicians in practice should have practice coverage arrangements for those times when they are unavailable.* Although coverage arrangements are especially important for solo practitioners, it is also important for physicians in group practice to understand their coverage arrangements with their associates. One of the advantages of working in a group practice is that it increases the physician denominator for sharing on-call duties. Coverage gets trickier when practices merge or share calls and different practice cultures must be blended. Constraints from managed care panels add another layer of complication to determining call schedules. Good planning and good communication are at the heart of seamless coverage. Physicians should try to share call coverage with other physicians with similar practice styles and patient care beliefs.

2. *All physicians in practice should have secondary coverage arrangements for those times when their primary coverage physicians are unavailable.*

3. *Covering physicians should be of the same medical specialty as treating or attending physicians when possible.* An important first step in making sure that your patients will have access to a comparable level of care during your absence is to have a physician with specialty training similar to yours as the covering physician. This may not be possible in all localities. In many medically underserved communities, it is not uncommon for family physicians to cover for pediatricians. Check with your medical malpractice insurance company to see if any special arrangements should be made before you leave town.

4. *Covering physicians should have privileges at the same hospitals as treating or attending physicians and should be credentialed by the same managed care organizations.* In the event that one of your patients may require hospitalization during your absence, you will want the physician covering for you to be able to treat the patient.

5. *Treating or attending physicians should ascertain whether covering physicians have professional liability insurance and the extent of that coverage.*

If the physician covering for you has no professional liability coverage or inadequate coverage, you may become the deeper pockets should something go wrong with one of your patients during your absence.

6. *Treating or attending physicians should provide covering physicians with information on patients with anticipated problems, and this should be documented in the patients' medical records.*

7. *All hospitalized patients of treating or attending physicians should be informed of coverage arrangements and, when possible, introduced to covering physicians.* Many practices address this eventuality during new-patient orientation. The patient receives a letter explaining that when you are unavailable, "Dr Doe" will be responsible for your care. If you are concerned about a particular patient with a complicated case, you may want to take the time to introduce that patient and his or her family to the covering physician as part of passing the baton to your colleague.

8. *Treating or attending physicians should advise hospitals and answering services of the dates of absence or unavailability.* Even the best coverage situation can be undermined if it is not activated by proper notification. Have a checklist of all entities that will need to be notified of your away status, and see that your staff notifies them and documents the notification.

9. *Covering physicians should advise treating or attending physicians about patients' course of treatment during the coverage period, and this should be documented.* This is the other side of passing the baton. When you return, the covering physician should provide you with a briefing of the patients treated during your absence. A telephone conversation can give you the heads-up you would need for a smooth reentry to your practice. Of course, the covering physician will need to furnish documentation of the care provided and interactions with patients. These items, including telephone interactions between the covering physician and your patients, should be added to patients' medical records.

10. *A coverage arrangement should contain an understanding as to which physician will bill the patient; treating or attending physicians should inform patients of this.* Likewise, inform your covering physician of any contractual agreements you have with managed care plans. Provide the substitute physician with guidelines on specific payment methods (eg, patient co-payments) or referral guidelines or restrictions (restricted panels) so that the covering physician can follow plan requirements that apply to a given patient. Remember, you are entrusting your patient relationship (your best protection from malpractice claims) to another physician. Do not let misunderstandings concerning billing or managed care referrals or authorizations between the covering physician and your patient erode your relationship with the patient. Have a written coverage arrangement between you and your substitute that spells out these responsibilities. This is an issue between you and the covering physician that should be settled before the first patient is seen by your substitute.

Does Billing Create Additional Liability?

If coverage is shared among independent physicians and each one bills patients directly for services provided when on call, will the absent physician be held responsible for the negligent acts of on-call physicians?

Usually not. Courts in most states have held that making physicians vicariously liable for a substitute's actions would discourage coverage arrangements and might diminish patient access to medical services when a patient's regular physician is unavailable. A state supreme court ruled that sharing calls did not constitute a joint venture because neither property nor labor were combined for profit and there were no shared rights of mutual control. As such, the plaintiff lacked evidence to prove that the attending physician controlled the on-call physician's clinical decision-making. It is uncertain how the court may have ruled had the physicians shared more than an on-call arrangement or had they not billed independently. However, you may be responsible for the actions of a covering physician if you select someone you have reason to believe is not competent or does not have the appropriate skills or training to care for your patients. Then you could be liable for putting your patients in harm's way. You may also be responsible for the covering physician's acts if a physician-employee relationship exists between you and the covering physician.

Best Practices Checklist

Following are best practices for management of telephone care in pediatric offices.

Staff

- Does the practice clearly define who gets what calls and in what time frames? For example,
    - Calls that must be immediately put through to the physician
    - Calls that the physician will return within a specific period (eg, 15 minutes, 1 hour)
    - Calls that the staff may handle
- Has the practice developed or purchased algorithms or standard guidelines containing questions and answers for staff to use when eliciting information from patients? Are they periodically reviewed and updated?
- Does the practice only allow licensed personnel with appropriate training and licensure to triage calls?
- Does the practice specifically prohibit personnel to render medical advice unless they are trained to do so?
- Does the practice identify high-volume times for calls and dedicate appropriate staff to triage calls to prevent delay with triage?
- If messages are left on an office voice mail, are they returned in a timely manner?

Documentation

- Is there a call triage template for staff to ensure that all required information is obtained?
    - If so, is this information maintained in the patient's medical record?
    - Even if no form or template is used, are all telephone calls documented in the patient's medical record?
- Is there a policy for providing staff with access to patient medical records while triaging calls?
- Is there a system for documenting and communicating all after-hours calls, whether received by the attending physician or someone else?

Confidentiality

- Does the patient's medical record accompany the telephone message for the physician's review whenever possible (particularly during office hours)?
- Does the practice make every effort not to leave confidential information on answering machines?
- Do staff maintain patient confidentiality by conversing with patients in private areas, out of the hearing range of other patients?
- Are physicians discrete in using cell phones when discussing patients? Remember, cell phones are not secure and it is easy for bystanders to overhear cell phone conversations when made in a public place.

Patient Safety

- Is there a stated policy that all telephone conversations are to end by encouraging patients to call back if their condition changes or if they do not receive a response from the physician in a predetermined period?
- Does the practice appear to always err on the side of having the patient visit the office for treatment?

Patient Satisfaction

- Do questions on patient satisfaction surveys elicit the amount of time patients are being left on hold or receive busy signals when calling the office?
- Are patients informed of the time frame in which they can expect to receive callbacks?
- Does the triage staff assess the caller's understanding of the communication and solicit unspoken concerns before closing the conversation?

Summary

Telephone care, including calls to patients and other physicians, and shared coverage arrangements are an integral part of the practice of pediatrics and are potential sources of malpractice claims. Telephone calls are considered a physician-patient encounter whether the call is taken by the physician, an employed nurse, or an outside call center. Organized procedures, protocols, training, supervision, careful communication, excellent documentation, and judicious delegation of patient telephone care can reduce the potential for claims in these areas but cannot eliminate them.

References

1. Physician Insurers Association of America, *Data Sharing Closed Malpractice Claims 1985-1999*. Rockville, MD: Physician Insurers Association of America; 2000

2. Bergman AB, Dassel SW, Wedgewood RJ. Time-motion study of practicing pediatricians. *Pediatrics.* 1966;38(2):254–263

3. Poole SR. Creating an after-hours telephone triage system for office practice. *Pediatr Ann.* 2001;30(5):268–273

4. *Weaver v University of Michigan Board of Regents,* 506 N.W. 2nd 264 (Mich Ct App 1993)

5. Poole SR. *The Complete Guide: Developing a Telephone Triage and Advice System for a Pediatric Office Practice During Office Hours and/or After Hours.* Elk Grove Village, IL: American Academy of Pediatrics; 2003

6. American Academy of Pediatrics Medical Home Initiatives for Children with Special Health Care Needs Project Advisory Committee. The medical home. *Pediatrics.* 2002;110(1):184–186

7. American Academy of Pediatrics Division of Health Policy Research. *Periodic Survey of Fellows #43: Characteristics of Pediatricians and Their Practices: the Socioeconomic Survey: Executive Summary.* Elk Grove Village, IL: American Academy of Pediatrics; 2000. http://www.aap.org/research/periodicsurvey/ps43aexs.htm. Accessed April 21, 2011

8. http://www.aap.org/sections/telecare/options.htm. Accessed May 26, 2011

9. American Academy of Pediatrics. *Strategies for Practice Management: A Report from the Provisional Section on Pediatric Telephone Care and the Committee on Practice and Ambulatory Medicine: Pediatric Call Centers and the Practice of Telephone Triage and Advice: Critical Success Factors. AAP News [insert].* 1998;14(11):10

10. Poole SR, Melzer SM. Computerized pediatric telephone triage and advice programs at children's hospitals: operating and financial characteristics. *Arch Pediatr Adolesc Med.* 1999;153(8):858–863

11. American Academy of Pediatrics Division of Health Policy Research. *Periodic Survey of Fellows #69: Experiences With Medical Liability.* Elk Grove Village, IL: American Academy of Pediatrics; 2007. http://www.aap.org/research/periodicsurvey/PS69exsummedicalliability.pdf. Accessed May 26, 2011

12. Wick W; Editorial Committee. Telephone contact and counseling. In: Sanbar SS, ed. *Legal Medicine.* 5th ed. St. Louis, MO: Mosby, Inc.; 2001:281–288

13. West JC. Medical malpractice: on-call status plus medical advice equals physician-patient relationship. Mead V. Legacy Health System No A130969 (Or. App. October 28, 2009). *J Health Risk Management.* 2010;30:44–45

14. Berger JE. Good call system, clear coverage plans cut holiday liability risk. *AAP News.* 1999;15(12):15

Resources

Schmitt BD. *Pediatric Telephone Protocols: Office Version.* 13th ed. Elk Grove Village, IL: American Academy of Pediatrics; 2011

Hertz AR. *Pediatric Nurse Telephone Triage: A Companion to Pediatric Telephone Protocols.* Elk Grove Village, IL: American Academy of Pediatrics; 2011

American Academy of Pediatrics Section on Telehealth Care

American Academy of Pediatrics members are welcome to join the Section on Telehealth Care to be connected to top-notch educational programs and practice tools. Contact the AAP Division of Pediatric Practice.

CHAPTER 6

Legal Issues Relating to E-mail, Web Sites, and Telemedicine

Gary N. McAbee, DO , JD, FAAP, and Jeffrey L. Brown, MD, FAAP

KEY CONCEPTS

- E-mail and the Law
- Basic Principles for E-mail Use
- Secure Messaging
- Establishing Internal Policies and Procedures
- Admissibility in Court
- Web Sites
- Telemedicine

Medical encounters that are not face-to-face, including e-mail, Web-based health education, and telemedicine consultation, have assumed an extremely important role in pediatric practice. The user-friendly technology of smartphones and other similar devices has created an environment in which transmission of data using these technologies now exceeds transmission by telephone. For many parents and patients, e-mail and text messaging have become their preferred method of communication. Studies have demonstrated that most parents believe that all pediatricians should use e-mail and many would choose a pediatrician who used e-mail.[1,2]

These technologies offer many advantages for busy pediatricians as well, including

- Avoiding the telephone-tag/missed-message problem common to many patient queries.
- Enhancing the physician-patient relationship by e-mail when it is used as an ancillary method to face-to-face contacts; it is especially useful for answering questions about well-child care and other nonurgent questions.
- Reaching teenaged and young adult patients who use text messaging, e-mail, and social networking sites to communicate with their peers and find comfort using that same technology to communicate with their physician. In contrast with telephone communication, the doctor's response to a patient's query is in written form, so it can be referenced at a time that is convenient for them.
- Providing attachments to the e-mail, which might include prewritten patient education materials and links to educational Web sites.
- Using specialized software so that e-mail can be used to notify patients about changes in office policy, remind them of missed visits and needed immunizations, schedule and confirm appointments, and provide other useful functions.

Easy availability and apparent simplicity may cause physicians to inadvertently ignore the large array of potential legal problems that may be associated with its use. Before using e-mail, text messaging, chat rooms, or interactive Internet sites to communicate with patients, risk management and security protocols should be established to protect the privacy and integrity of these communications and minimize liability. This chapter discusses some of the legal pitfalls associated with the use of e-mail and telemedicine and offers some strategies for preventing them.

E-mail and the Law

E-mail is part of telemedicine law and medical records law and is subject to many of the legal issues associated with telephone care.[3,4]

Along with texting, it is the fastest growing means of communication worldwide. The speed, ease, and low cost of e-mail have made it the communication vehicle of choice for many physicians and patients. Payment by third-party payers for e-mailed health care advice would make it more likely for this method to be incorporated into the communication patterns of health care professionals.

Congress has included e-mail within the definition of telemedicine. Thus, any telemedicine interaction between a patient and physician requires informed consent, not only because medical information might be obtained, transmitted, or stored during the consultation, but also because patients are engaging in a specific medical encounter. States may have special rules for informed consent involving telemedicine.

There is a common misconception that an e-mail sent from the physician's computer to the patient's computer is a private and exclusive communication between the 2 parties, as if they were in an examination room alone together. This perception is not accurate.

Potential Breaches of Privacy

Breaches of privacy can occur when an e-mail is

- Sent to the wrong address by the patient or pediatrician
- Left on the screen of an unattended computer where it can be seen by other parties
- Forwarded inappropriately or circulated by unauthorized personnel

- Obtained by a computer hacker and used for unauthorized purposes

All of these may also be a potential violation of the Health Insurance Portability and Accountability Act (HIPAA).

Establish a Physician-Patient Relationship

Typically, a physician-patient relationship that connotes a legal duty is established via a face-to-face encounter. Examples of a legal duty being established through a telephone call do exist, especially if the physician is an on-call physician.[5,6] A legal duty established through electronic means has not yet been extensively tested but is a potential legal issue that may evolve in the future.

Licensing Issues

Pediatricians should be aware of potential medical licensing issues, especially when their communications cross state lines. Because state law determines policy on licensure to practice medicine within state boundaries, pediatricians engaged in e-mail consultation, diagnosis, or treatment of patients in another state could risk violating state law. Moreover, these electronic visits with patients in another state may not meet the terms of professional liability coverage. It is unlikely that penalties would be incurred, but just staying in touch via e-mail with patients who are temporarily out of state (eg, at college) might potentially place physicians at risk for practicing beyond the limitations of their medical license and liability insurance.

Basic Principles for E-mail Use

Patients need to know in advance what the physician's policies are for using e-mailed communications. They should understand what kinds of questions are appropriate, how often e-mail is read, and when they can expect a reply. A series of disclaimers attached to your e-mailed communications will help to reduce errors, poor outcome, and the potential for medical malpractice, but disclaimers should not be construed as providing protection from liability.

Patient and Professional E-mail Should Not Be Commingled With Private E-mail

Just as you would not mix your personal letters with a consultation letter from a patient's cardiologist, a professional e-mail account and address that is different from personal e-mail should be used for patient communication. A professional account using encrypted transmission technology is the preferred method.

Unsecured E-mail Messages Should Be Labeled as Such

The popular commercial e-mail services use a variety of protocols that include Simple Mail Transfer Protocol (SMTP), Post Office Protocol (POP3), Internet Message Access Protocol (IMAP), and hypertext transfer protocol (http) (also called Web-based e-mail; not dedicated to e-mail use; used by some large servers, eg, Hotmail). These should not be considered secure and can be thought of as being similar to sending a fax transmission or a postcard. Although the use of nonsecure e-mail is discouraged, a disclaimer to patients should be used when professional e-mail is not encrypted. For example: "We make every effort to keep e-mailed communication with our patients confidential. However, e-mail sent to this address should not be considered secure. Sensitive information should be discussed with the physician in person or over the telephone."

Frequency of E-mail Retrieval Should Be Disclosed to the Patient

The almost instantaneous speed with which an e-mailed message is delivered suggests to the sender that it may be read just as quickly. This might result in a delay in treatment or communication, especially when the patient has an urgent problem. The patient should be warned in advance that you might not respond right away. For example: "E-mail messages may not be read every day. In most cases, we will respond within 1 business day of their receipt. If your e-mail concerns a medical or psychiatric emergency, dial 911 immediately. If it relates to an urgent problem, contact our office immediately by telephone at 555/555-5555."

Advise the Patient That E-mail Has Been Received

An automated reply that advises the patient that an e-mail has been received should be sent from your e-mail account.

E-mail Subject Line Should Not Disclose Sensitive Content

The subject line of the e-mail should be general in nature. A subject line that might be read by a casual bystander that says "Positive pregnancy test" would not be appropriate.

Prepare for the Possibility That E-mail Might Inadvertently Be Sent to the Wrong Party

Almost everyone who uses e-mail regularly has had the experience of sending a communication to the wrong e-mail address. This can happen for numerous reasons. The name might be part of a group mailing; it might have similar spelling to another person in your address book; or you might simply click the wrong screen button. A disclaimer attached to every mailing might help to lessen liability if confidential information is disclosed. The disclaimer should instruct the recipient of the following:

- This e-mail is privileged and confidential.
- It is intended only for the individual to whom it is addressed.
- Use of its contents or attachments by an unauthorized individual may be unlawful.

- If it has been received in error, the e-mail and any attachments should be deleted from the recipient's computer, and the sender should be notified immediately by return e-mail.

E-mailed Correspondence Should Become Part of the Patient's Permanent Medical Record

As with any correspondence received in postal mail from or about a patient, e-mailed correspondence should be filed electronically or printed to be placed in a patient's paper chart. It should include your comments and those of the patient. Some physicians create e-mail files on their computers in which to save the correspondence for quick reference.

Patients Should Be Advised That Each E-mail or a Summary of E-mail Consultations Will Be Incorporated Into the Patient's Permanent Medical Record

This can be particularly important in communications with adolescent patients, depending on state laws affecting adolescent confidentiality.

E-mail Should Not Be Forwarded or Carbon Copied to a Third Party Without the Patient's Consent

These rules for e-mail are similar to those for other forms of written communication.

Group E-mails Should List 1 Person's Name and the Others Should Receive Blind Copies

This is the best way to ensure the confidentiality of other addressees. One of the blind copies should also be addressed to the sender so that it can be referenced later.

Computer Hard Drives and Other Devices Used for E-mail Should Be Deleted Prior to Their Disposal

Patient information contained on computer hard drives and other electronic devices, such as mobile phones used for e-mail, should be deleted prior to their disposal just as paper files should be shredded prior to discarding them.

A Practical Note

Use of commercial comprehensive services created specifically for professional use will address many of the practical issues associated with sending e-mail correspondence to your patients. As a next-best solution, when nonsecure commercial e-mail services like Gmail, Hotmail, or Yahoo! are used for professional purposes, some of their standard features can be modified to create disclaimers. For example, the out-of-office reply feature can be used to send an automated and immediate receipt to the patient. It can be programmed to read: "This is an automated message to confirm that your e-mail has been received. Please be advised that e-mail sent to this address is not secure and may not be read every day. If your e-mail relates to a sensitive matter or an urgent problem…." Similarly, the signature feature of the e-mail account can be programmed to add a wrong-address disclaimer to your response automatically: "This message contains privileged information that is intended only for the person to whom it is addressed…." Another feature of most commercial e-mail services is one that can automatically send a copy of your sent e-mail to your saved mail or inbox folder for filing. Most services can also be programmed to notify you that your e-mail has been received or read by the recipient.

Secure Messaging

It is important to note the difference between conventional and Web-mediated secure messaging. Secure messaging reduces a number of the risks identified previously by offering capabilities such as *authentication of users* (requiring users to log on to the system and use a password), *encryption* (scrambling information so it cannot be read by anyone except those intended), *digital signatures,* and *an established list of patients* from whom messages will be accepted.

Establishing Internal Policies and Procedures

Prior to establishing e-mail communication with patients, internal policies and procedures should be established. There should be awareness of whether

- Applicable laws and standards, especially those regarding confidentiality, are being breached. Regarding adolescents, state laws relating to privacy, if stricter than HIPAA, are controlling.
- Contracts with payers or accreditation agency agreements specify additional standards for patient privacy for electronic communication.
- The professional liability insurance carrier covers electronic communications with patients as part of the standard contract.

Other Considerations

When establishing policies and procedures for the use of e-mail with patients, pediatricians should

- *Establish a rigorous information security infrastructure* that includes policies and procedures, training and awareness, and appropriate technology and architecture to protect health information against threats to security and integrity, unauthorized access, and repudiation (eg, acceptable approaches to encryption, authentication, and identification).
- *Be aware that e-mail is discoverable in legal proceedings.*

Admissibility in Court

In general, e-mail as part of the medical record is treated no differently than any other part of the paper or electronic health record (EHR). It is part of the business record and may be admitted as evidence in court as such. However, e-mail communication that is not part of the medical record or accounting records does face a problem of authentication. For example, it might not have been sent by the person whose name is on the e-mail, or it might have been altered after it was sent. The rules relating to admissibility of e-mail in court are evolving.[7]

Web Sites

Like the telephone, the Internet can be used to provide services that fall within the bounds of medical practice and constitute the initiation of physician-patient relationships. It is important that pediatricians be aware of their ethical and legal responsibilities, set clear parameters around relationships with patients, meet licensure requirements, and secure sufficient medical liability coverage.

Information-Only Web Sites

The pediatrician who provides only generic information to users, regardless of detail, is less likely to develop a physician-patient relationship from Web-based interactions alone. Such sites are comparable to publishing a printed health care newsletter, provided both are meant strictly for user education. In recent years, practice Web sites are being used with greater frequency for marketing purposes to attract new patients. Patients most likely to use them may be unhappy with their present care, have had changes to their health insurance, or are moving into a new location. The site might also be used to decrease informational phone calls that would normally be made to the office staff. For example, it might have postings about product recalls, vaccine availability during shortages, and prevalent infectious diseases present in the community.

If the practice Web site is updated regularly and contains accurate information, its use should create little liability for physicians. There are, however, some prudent rules that should be followed when establishing maintenance procedures for the site.

- One physician or other health care professional should be assigned to read and monitor the site at frequent intervals. Information does change, and it is essential that it be kept up to date. The last date that the information is reviewed should be documented.
- Posted information should not misrepresent practice policies and procedures.
- Physician biographies should contain accurate information.
- Services that are not currently being provided should not be advertised.
- Information on which patients might rely must be kept up to date and accurate (eg, insurance accepted by the practice, office hours, hospital affiliations, cross-coverage with outside medical groups).
- Links to other reference Web sites should carry a disclaimer that informs patients that you are not responsible for their content. Links to parenting magazines, medical reference sites, search engines, and even government Web sites like the Centers for Disease Control and Prevention should carry a disclaimer that might read: "These Internet links are being provided to our patients solely for convenience. The advice and information contained in them does not always conform to our professional opinions or to the advice that we might offer to an individual patient. Therefore, accessing these useful sites should not be used as a substitute for having a formal consultation with one of our physicians."

Patient-Specific Information Web Sites

Patient-specific information Web sites may be somewhat more targeted to the user, providing information addressing specific user questions. For example, if the parent of a child with recurrent otitis media asks a question about antibiotic choice, surgical treatment, or hearing loss, the Internet pediatrician may respond by providing very detailed information. The physician is likely to cross the line only if the information offered is tailored to the specific patient's symptoms and alleged medical history. Such a scenario strongly resembles the practice of medicine without adequate information.

Medical Dialogue Web Site

"Ask the pediatrician" sites offer patients, for a fee, feedback from a pediatrician based on information they provide. The prudent pediatrician will couch the online medical dialogue in cautious language such as, "Based on what you have told me, I believe…" and follow this statement with a disclaimer and a recommendation that the patient visit his or her pediatrician. Regardless of cautious language and disclaimers, however, "ask the pediatrician" sites move very close to physician-patient relationships and, at the very least, a duty to provide accurate, unbiased information exists.

With the appropriate warranties, it is somewhat less likely that a traditional relationship will be created, but warranties can falter if the information exchanged is too specific and authoritative. For instance, if a frequent online user is not following up with a treating physician, the online pediatrician has an ethical responsibility to help the user find traditional care.

Increasingly, patients and parents rely on the Internet for clinical health care information. Some ask their physicians to recommend Web sites, while others surf the Internet themselves. Either way, physicians should be aware of the risks involved and try to minimize them.

Some important considerations include

- Are you, the physician, writing the clinical content?
- If the clinical content is on a third-party site, do you review it regularly and have the opportunity to change the clinical information?
- How often are changes and updates made to clinical information on third-party sites? Are you notified when changes are made?
- Does the content conform to your specialty's standard of care?
- Are medical recommendations made? If so, is there a disclaimer to state that the recommendations do not constitute specific medical treatment or advice and are to be used for informational purposes only?
- Is your interactive Web site secure? Can you judge the validity of the authorship, accountability, and attribution of communications with users?
- Is the clinical practice or practitioners sponsored or in any way directly connected to commercial material? Is that connection disclosed to consumers?

Having high-quality clinical information readily accessible can be beneficial to a pediatrician and patients, but it must be provided responsibly. Limiting the degree of unintentional interaction, validating users' identities, and employing appropriate disclaimers can reduce some risk.

Physicians no longer are the primary source of information for patients. Health care professionals use Web sites to market services, educate consumers, and communicate with patients interactively. Although the law has not kept pace with these changes in medicine, e-visits are not free of liability risks; it is just harder to know what those risks are and how to manage them.

Telemedicine

Changes in health care legislation will hasten the speed with which physicians use electronic record keeping for patient encounters and other transmission of medical data. Recent Medicare and Medicaid payment incentives for EHRs may hasten the expansion of their use. In addition, many will have their office computers linked to system or hospital computers to receive x-ray images and inpatient and outpatient records from other practitioners. It will also be used for monitoring homebound patients or those in remote areas without immediate access to in-person care. Telemedicine can involve intrastate, interstate, and intercountry patient encounters, and the legal issues may differ. The Centers for Medicare & Medicaid Services (CMS) has proposed new rules addressing credentialing for physicians involved in telemedicine. These rules will soon be finalized, and physicians participating in telemedicine should review them.

Telemedicine can involve video encounters with a live patient or simply electronic conveyance of medical information from one site to another (eg, teleradiology, telepathology). The key legal issues in telemedicine are standard of care, quality of care, licensure, credentialing, malpractice and insurance coverage, liability and scope of practice, informed consent, regulatory and billing compliance, confidentiality, privacy, and exceptions for educational purposes.[8,9] The American Academy of Pediatrics Council on Clinical Information Technology and Committee on Medical Liability and Risk Management have a technical report on the pediatric applications of telemedicine.[10]

One important issue is jurisdictional; ie, where is the care being rendered? Does the technology transport the patient to the physician or the physician to the patient? If a medical malpractice action is initiated, which state will have jurisdiction, the one where the doctor is providing the service or the one where the patient is physically located?

Current thought is that the site of care is where the patient is located. However, if the encounter involves a patient and physician in different states, the issue of federal jurisdiction is raised depending on the alleged monetary damage amount. The issue of jurisdiction is even more complicated if the encounter takes place in different countries. If the only contact is physician-physician and the patient is not directly involved, most of the legal issues relating to telemedicine are unlikely to be applicable unless the physician's legal duty has already been established (eg, via contract).

Clearly, telemedicine requires a comprehensive legal analysis of contract, negligence, malpractice, privacy and confidentiality, and strict liability issues. Regarding confidentiality, HIPAA rules relating to adolescent confidentiality provide a minimum threshold but do not override state laws, which afford more protection than HIPAA.

Medical Licensure

Telemedicine is not bound by geography, but medical licensure is. Many states have passed laws on telemedicine medical licensure.[11] Some allow physicians to practice in another state as consultants. Some grant reciprocity and endorsement between states. Some provide limited scope licensing within a state. Beyond the licensure issue, if patients are seen via telemedicine equipment located in a hospital (most are), physicians also need to be credentialed and have privileges at that institution; the new CMS guidelines will be applicable to this issue. If the clinical encounter is for educational purposes and does not involve managing the health care of a specific patient, a licensing exception is likely. Similarly, a licensing exception is likely for out-of-state medical emergencies or natural disasters.

Medical Liability

As the application of telemedicine expands so, too, will medical liability exposure for the various health care entities involved. Therefore, full consideration should be given to the legal implications of telemedicine before pediatricians participate in telemedicine medical encounters, especially if state boundaries are crossed. It would be shortsighted for pediatricians to assume that the lack of existing case law means that liabilities for this mode of health care delivery do not exist.

The use of telemedicine is relatively new in pediatrics; therefore, malpractice claims resulting from its use are only beginning to be reported. From the 2010 risk management review of the Physician Insurers Association of America, a large organization of physician-owned or managed insurance companies, there were 3 claims filed for pediatric cases involving telemedicine between the years 1985 and 2009, with 1 paid for a total indemnity of $30,000.[12] Another recent survey of telemedicine malpractice notes that most reported cases involved physicians prescribing medication across state lines without previously examining the patient.[13]

The physician's exposure to liability from participating in telemedicine can be gauged by exploring how telemedicine affects the following: the physician-patient relationship, communication, consultant relationships with other health care professionals, direct and vicarious liability, malpractice insurance coverage, medical licensure, and integrated delivery systems.

The traditional medical negligence doctrine requires that the plaintiff (patient) prove that the defendant (physician) had a duty toward and implicit contract with the plaintiff as a result of an established physician-patient relationship. The plaintiff must then prove, generally by a preponderance of evidence, that the defendant breached this duty by failing to conform to the accepted standard of care and that as a direct result of the breach, the plaintiff sustained harm with ascertainable damages. Telemedicine challenges this doctrine, reconfiguring the physician-patient relationship and the duty that flows from that relationship.

Creating the Physician-Patient Relationship

To prove medical negligence the plaintiff must demonstrate that the physician had a duty to the plaintiff. This usually is based on the existence of the physician-patient relationship. In the traditional practice of medicine, this relationship occurs through face-to-face interaction. Many physicians think that without face-to-face interaction, there is no physician-patient relationship and, therefore, no duty. This is no longer true. The existence of the relationship rests on whether the services being provided fall within the scope of medical practice. Medical practice generally includes treating, prescribing, diagnosing, or offering patient-specific medical advice and information such as prognostic information.

Defining Roles and Communication Responsibilities

In any telemedicine encounter, it is critical that the referring physician know the identity and credentials of the consulting physician participating in the telemedicine encounter. It is also important that the referring physician spell out the responsibility of the consultant involved in the encounters, especially regarding follow-up care. Should the roles be confused over responsibilities in making a diagnosis or initiating treatment or follow-up care, the quality of care may be compromised.

In cases in which a referring physician seeks the advice of another physician for a diagnostic consultation, complete and accurate communication is needed. First, the primary care physician must communicate with the consulting physician via telemedicine about the patient's signs and symptoms as well as comprehensive background medical information. Second, the referring physician must inform the patient of the need for the referral and the factors on which the recommendation to use telemedicine is based. The patient or his or her custodial parent or legal guardian should be provided with sufficient information to consent to the referral, and the use of telemedicine may need to be specified. The referring physician should explain to the patient the role of the consulting physician in the encounter, how information will be shared, and the process for follow-up care. Third, the consulting physician should provide the referring physician with enough information to allow the referring physician the opportunity to accept the diagnosis based on the findings of the encounter and background information provided. Communication issues, most often lack of communication, often are problems that contribute to an adverse outcome that could potentially result in a malpractice action.

Consultant Liability

Telemedicine has only begun to generate case law, and existing case law does not provide substantial clues as to the potential liability of telemedicine consultations. A single encounter may conceivably involve several consultants that may communicate among themselves, with the primary physician, or with the patient.

Patient Abandonment

Once the physician-patient relationship has been established, care must be taken to ensure that the referring and consulting physicians fulfill their contract to care for the patient and that steps are taken to prevent patient abandonment. *Abandonment* refers to the deliberate, premature termination of the physician-patient relationship. A physician, whether acting as consultant via telemedicine or in any other capacity, has a duty of care if it has been determined that a physician-patient relationship exits. Because of this duty, it is incumbent on the consultant to ensure that the referring physician also has performed his or her duty to the patient. If the referring physician has failed in his or her duty, it is conceivable that the consultant can be held responsible for this omission as part of his or her duty.

Liability for Technology Failures

The liability for technology failures is apt to be shared among all involved parties. In the context of telemedicine, it is possible that a physician or other practitioners, lacking experience with the new technology or technique, may fail to use it in an optimal fashion or may even misread the pertinent data, information, or image because of unfamiliarity with the system capability or inadequate resolution. Such oversight may lead to liability for misuse. It is reasonable to view telemedicine as a tool that will require skill and practice for the individual physician to use it adeptly.

Telemedicine technologies may suffer intermittent failures or unreliability. Many telecommunications systems depend on satellites. A malfunctioning or broken satellite link would disrupt the telemedicine intervention. Jumbled signals may cause degradation of the image or lead to the misreading of pertinent medical data used in making a critical patient care decision. While safeguards and backup systems will be established to make telemedicine encounters less vulnerable to technologic glitches, no system can be made impervious to failure.

Site of Malpractice Actions

Like licensure, malpractice insurance is acquired and required only in the state in which the physician maintains his or her practice. If a physician crosses a state line to practice telemedicine, the physician must find out whether malpractice insurance covers out-of-state telemedicine encounters. Additional insurance may need to be purchased

for such activities. It is essential that physicians know the extent of their liability coverage. Moreover, physicians may find their insurance coverage inadequate if the remote state has malpractice laws that are less beneficial to physicians than the state in which they usually practice medicine.

Crossing state lines in telemedicine creates concern about jurisdictional issues should a malpractice claim occur. Malpractice laws vary from state to state. There is no clear guidance for where an injured party may bring an action against a physician in these cases. This could create an environment in which venue shopping or looking for the jurisdiction in which rewards could be most lucrative becomes a major concern. Malpractice involving interstate telemedicine could be referred to federal jurisdiction for remedy when parties are from different states and the amount of alleged monetary damages meets the minimum federal threshold.

Fraud and Abuse

There are other legal issues relating to fraud and abuse and telemedicine. These include potential violations of state and federal laws including antitrust laws, antikickback laws (eg, physician offers free Web site as an inducement to obtain patients), beneficiary inducement laws (eg, free coupons on a physician's Web site for medical services at a pharmacy on-site), and physician self-referral laws (Stark). These laws are complex and physicians should seek legal opinions to be assured that any e-health component of their practice is in conformity with these laws.

Summary

Nothing to date has indicated that the application of e-mail, Internet sites, or telemedicine in patient care is unusually hazardous. Admittedly, malpractice carriers may have to look at expanding their rating base to include additional considerations for physicians practicing telemedicine outside of the insurers' traditional geographic boundaries.

Non–face-to-face care will have an effect on referring physicians as well, as they may increase their risk when engaging in telemedicine with long-distance consultants. Because such activities will increase liability exposure for the carrier, insurers may impose limitations on coverage or not cover at all. Therefore, pediatricians need to review applicable laws and standards, licensures, liability, and payment for electronic services. There is little doubt that the use of telemedicine and other electronic visits will continue to grow, especially as applications increase and barriers decrease. Pediatricians will need to ensure that their liability protection is applicable and adequate for care rendered across state lines.

References

1. Anand SG, Feldman MJ, Geller DS, Bisbee A, Bauchner H. A content analysis of e-mail communication between primary care providers and parents. *Pediatrics.* 2005;115(5): 1283–1288. http://pediatrics.aappublications.org/content/ 115/5/1283.full.pdf+html. Accessed June 13, 2011

2. Larson J. The new world of physician-patient electronic communication. 2011. AMN Healthcare Web site. http://www.amnhealthcare.com/News/news-details. aspx?Id=36642. Accessed June 13, 2011

3. Buckner F. Electronic mail communication with patients. In: Sanbar SS, Firestone MH, eds. *Legal Medicine.* 6th ed. Philadelphia, PA: Mosby; 2004;417–423

4. Buckner F, King RC. Telemedicine. In: Sanbar SS, Firestone MH, eds. *Legal Medicine.* 6th ed. Philadelphia, PA: Mosby; 2004;424–431

5. *Mead v Legacy Health System,* 220 P3d 118 (Or App 2009)

6. *Dodd-Anderson v Stevens,* 905 F Supp 937 (D Kan 1995)

7. *Lorraine v Markel American Insurance Company,* 241 F R D 534 (D Md 2007)

8. Singh SN, Wachter RM. Perspectives on medical outsourcing and telemedicine—rough edges in a flat world? *N Engl J Med.* 2008;358(15):1622–1627

9. Clifton AD. Licensure, reimbursement and liability in telemedicine: an academic perspective. *Ann Health Law.* 2008;18:62–65

10. Spooner SA, Gotlieb EM, American Academy of Pediatrics Steering Committee on Clinical Information Technology, Committee on Medical Liability. Telemedicine: pediatric applications. *Pediatrics.* 2004;113(6):e639–e643. http:// pediatrics.aappublications.org/content/113/6/e639.full. pdf+html. Accessed June 13, 2011

11. Telemedicine licensing provisions by state. American College of Radiology Web site. http://www.acr.org/ SecondaryMainMenuCategories/ GR_Econ/ FeaturedCategories/state/state_issues/ TelemedicineLicensingProvisionsbyStateDoc8.aspx. Accessed June 13, 2011

12. Physicians Insurers Association of America. *A Risk Management Review of Malpractice Claims—Pediatrics.* Rockville, MD: Physician Insurers Association of America; 2010

13. Natoli CM. *Summary of Findings: Malpractice and Telemedicine.* Washington, DC: Center for Telehealth & e-Health Law; 2009. http://www.ctel.org. Accessed June 13, 2011

CHAPTER 7

Liability for Vaccine Administration

Jonathan M. Fanaroff, MD, JD, FAAP, and David Marcus, MD, FAAP

KEY CONCEPTS

- Vaccine Adverse Event Reporting System
- National Vaccine Injury Compensation Program
- Compensation That May Be Awarded
- Changes to the Vaccine Injury Table
- Vaccine Excise Tax
- Vaccine Administrator Responsibilities
- Filing a Claim With the National Vaccine Injury Compensation Program
- Informed Consent, Minors, and Mandatory Immunizations
- Parental Questioning/Refusal of Vaccines
- Immunization Administration Practices: Findings From the Periodic Survey of Fellows

Vaccines are one of the great success stories in public health. Smallpox, officially eradicated in 1980, would kill approximately 2 million people every year if it were still around today. Polio was responsible for paralyzing 1,000 children globally every single day. Despite the successes of vaccines, pediatricians face a vigorous anti-vaccination movement. Additionally, while an unqualified public health success, there are clearly individual risks to vaccines, and indeed some children are injured as a result of vaccination. Because disease prevention is a core mission in pediatrics, pediatricians need to be aware of the significant medicolegal issues surrounding vaccination, as well as important government programs designed to determine adverse events associated with vaccines and compensate patients who have been injured by vaccines.

Vaccine Adverse Event Reporting System

The Vaccine Adverse Event Reporting System (VAERS) is a post-marketing passive surveillance program for monitoring adverse events following vaccination. Jointly managed by the Centers for Disease Control and Prevention (CDC) and the Food and Drug Administration (FDA), VAERS encourages the reporting of any *clinically significant* adverse event that occurs after the administration of any US-licensed vaccine, even if it is unclear whether the vaccine caused the event. In addition, the National Vaccine Injury Compensation Program (VICP) requires health care professionals to report any event listed in the manufacturer's package insert as a *contraindication* to subsequent doses of the vaccine, or any event listed in the VAERS Table of Reportable Events Following Vaccination that occurs within the specified period after vaccination.

The Vaccine Adverse Event Reporting System is designed primarily to detect possible signals of adverse events associated with vaccines, which lead to additional scientific investigation to determine whether vaccines cause a given event or the event is simply coincidental to vaccination (eg, epidemiologic studies confirming the association between the original rhesus rotavirus vaccine [licensed in 1998] and intussusception were initially triggered by VAERS reports). Like all passive surveillance systems, VAERS depends on voluntary reporting and is therefore subject to limitations of underreporting, reporting bias, simultaneous administration of multiple-antigen vaccines, and lack of incidence rates in unvaccinated comparison groups to be compared with rates among vaccinees. While some events reported to VAERS are truly caused by vaccines, others may be related to an underlying disease or condition or to drugs being taken concurrently, or may occur by chance shortly after a vaccine was administered. The CDC and FDA take into account the complex factors mentioned previously, as well as others, when monitoring vaccine safety and analyzing VAERS reports. Only through accurate and complete reporting of postvaccination events can the VAERS database serve its intended safety function.

Since 1990, VAERS has received about 330,000 primary reports, covering all US-administered vaccines, approximately 89% of which describe mild events such as fever, local reactions, episodes of crying or mild irritability, and other less-serious experiences. The remaining 11% of reports reflect serious adverse events involving life-threatening conditions, hospitalization, permanent disability, or death, which may or may not have been truly caused by an immunization.

While anyone can report to VAERS, vaccine providers send in the majority of reports (44%), followed by vaccine manufacturers (20%) and vaccine recipients or their parents or guardians (8%); other specified sources (21%) and no source indicated (7%) account for the remainder. Vaccine recipients or their parents or guardians are encouraged to seek the help of their health care

professional in filling out the VAERS form. It should also be noted that VAERS and VICP are separate and distinct programs. Reporting to VAERS does not file a claim for compensation with the VICP. Information about VAERS, reporting forms, adverse event data, and a copy of the reportable events table can be obtained by calling 800/822-7967 or visiting http://vaers.hhs.gov. Making a report to VAERS is not limited to health care professionals; anyone, including parents, can report an adverse event to VAERS. While VAERS determines potential adverse events related to vaccines, the next section discusses VICP, the program designed to compensate patients who have been injured by vaccines.

National Vaccine Injury Compensation Program

The National Childhood Vaccine Injury Act of 1986[1] (NCVIA) established the VICP. The VICP, which went into effect in October 1988, is a no-fault alternative to the tort system designed to compensate individuals thought injured by childhood vaccines, whether administered in the private or public sector. Petitioners are required to file claims with the VICP before they are allowed to bring a civil suit. Rules of evidence, discovery, and other legal procedures are relaxed to accelerate the compensation process. Negligence on the part of the manufacturer or health care professional is removed from proceedings, thus the no-fault designation. Judgments (whether dismissing the claim or awarding compensation) must be expressly rejected by the petitioner prior to seeking other remedies, such as filing a civil suit against a vaccine manufacturer or vaccine provider. The NCVIA was enacted in part as a result of an exponential increase in lawsuits against manufacturers of whole-cell pertussis vaccines and the threat from these manufacturers of ceasing production of the vaccine.

Congress created the VICP in 1986 to provide financial compensation to individuals injured by childhood vaccines, as an alternative to traditional civil litigation. In principle, the program acknowledges that society has a responsibility for compensating persons injured by vaccines because for almost all vaccines, a prospective vaccinee not only derives individual protection from vaccine but also helps society by contributing to herd immunity. For eligible individuals, the VICP allows compensation for unreimbursed medical expenses, pain and suffering, and lost wages. In addition, attorneys' fees and costs are paid even if the claim is not compensated as long as the claim is brought on a good faith and reasonable basis. Newly licensed vaccines require congressional action for the excise tax to be applied. The secretary of the Department of Health and Human Services (HHS) then publishes this in the *Federal Register* as part of the rule-making (regulation) process. Once the new vaccine has been added to the VICP, an 8-year look-back period applies, starting from the effective date of the excise tax.

The Department of Justice, HHS, and Office of Special Masters, US Court of Federal Claims, administer the VICP jointly. Vaccines designated by the CDC for "routine administration to children" are covered by the program. Once covered, persons vaccinated under routine and permissive recommendations (eg, human papillomavirus [HPV] vaccine in males) are eligible for compensation.

The VICP includes vaccines against the following diseases: *Haemophilus influenzae* type b (Hib); diphtheria, tetanus, and pertussis (DTP, DTaP [acellular pertussis], DTP-Hib, Tdap, DT, Td, tetanus toxoids [TT]); measles, mumps, and rubella (MMR, MR, M, R); polio (inactivated poliovirus vaccine [IPV] and live oral poliovirus vaccine [OPV]); rotavirus; hepatitis B (HBV); hepatitis A (HAV); varicella-zoster virus (VZV); influenza (trivalent inactivated [TIV], live attenuated [LAIV]); meningococcus (MCV4, MPSV4); HPV; and pneumococcus (PCV7, PCV13), as well as any combination of these. Additional vaccines may be added in the future as they are developed and put into general use.

Note: Anyone receiving a covered vaccine, no matter what age, may be eligible to file a VICP claim or have a claim filed on their behalf. In fact, the majority of claims filed annually are on behalf of adult recipients.

A unique feature of the NCVIA was creation of the Vaccine Injury Table (VIT), which lists medical conditions and the interval of onset following receipt of a covered vaccine. Individuals may receive a legal presumption of vaccine causation if they can prove that an injury listed on the VIT occurred within the prescribed time frame and there is not greater proof of an alternative cause for their medical condition.

In contrast with the first decade of the program, in which the majority of claims alleged DTP vaccine VIT injuries, most claims filed now allege conditions not listed on the VIT—so-called *off-table* claims. This shift occurred, in part, because of the removal of residual seizure disorder and shock collapse under DTP vaccine on the VIT. More significant was the doubling of the number of vaccines on the VIT, most of them added without associated injuries because serious causally related adverse events were not linked to these new vaccines, and the licensure of acellular pertussis vaccines to replace DTP, which eliminated a significant percentage of claims filed annually. Off-table cases require proof of causation, which can be difficult given the fact that few serious adverse events have been shown to be caused by vaccines.

Over the program's 2 decades, the US Court of Appeals for the Federal Circuit has clarified the standard of causation, trying to strike a balance between science and compensating petitioners. Starting in 2005, the federal circuit began placing less reliance on the former, which led to more petitioners receiving compensation, many through settlements. In *Althen v Secretary of HHS,*[2] the federal circuit seemed to relax the causation standard it had previously articulated by putting forth the following 3 criteria for proving causation: a medical theory causally connecting the vaccination and the injury; a logical sequence of cause and effect showing that the vaccination was the reason for the injury; and a showing of proximate temporal relationship between vaccination and injury. The decision held that there is no requirement that petitioners provide scientific literature to support their theory of causation; medical opinion or medical records can suffice under the law. It further stated that "close calls regarding causation are resolved in favor of injured claimants." In *Capizzano v Secretary of HHS*,[3] the appeals court criticized the special master for inadequately considering the opinions of treating physicians, and held that treating physicians are likely to be in the best position to determine whether "a logical sequence of cause and effect show[s] that the vaccination was the reason for the injury."

More recent decisions by the circuit seem to reverse this trend and have placed more reliance on using science and scientific opinion in determining causation. One example is *Moberly v Secretary of HHS*.[4] Here the federal circuit found the special master deciding the case had correctly interpreted and applied the traditional tort *preponderance* standard, and the petitioner's argument for a more relaxed standard was not consistent with the NCVIA.

Compensation That May Be Awarded

Vaccine-Related Injury

- Reasonable compensation for past unreimbursed and future unreimbursable medical, custodial care, and rehabilitation costs
- A $250,000 cap for actual and projected pain and suffering and emotional distress

- Lost earnings
- Reasonable attorneys' fees and costs
- Deadline for filing: within 36 months after the first symptoms appeared

Vaccine-Related Death

- For the estate of the deceased, $250,000
- Reasonable attorneys' fees and costs
- Deadline for filing: within 24 months of death and within 48 months after the onset of the vaccine-related injury from which the death occurred

The VICP created 2 classes of claims with differing filing, adjudication, and award guidelines—those involving vaccinations given prior to October 1, 1988 (pre-1988), and those involving vaccinations administered on or after October 1, 1988 (post-1988). Pre-1988 or retrospective claims had to be filed by January 31, 1991, and all have been adjudicated. Table 7-1 shows VICP statistics through December 31, 2010.[5] It should be noted that starting in fiscal year (FY) 2002, the VICP began receiving large numbers of claims alleging MMR vaccine or mercury/thimerosal-related injury, especially as it relates to autism, resulting in a total of 957 filings versus an average of 171 claims filed annually over the previous decade.

The VICP is a critical component to the national immunization strategy. In its quarter-century of existence, the VICP has met its policy goals of establishing an accessible forum for individuals injured by childhood vaccines and ensuring vaccine supply and stabilizing vaccine costs. Furthermore, claims against vaccine manufacturers are significantly reduced, as compared with the litigation manufacturers faced at the inception of the VICP. Although claims against health care professionals are more difficult to track, there is no indication that their liability experience is any different from that of manufacturers. While it is true that a new wave of court cases alleging thimerosal injury from childhood vaccines emerged in 2001, few cases alleging vaccine-related injuries otherwise were filed outside the VICP in recent years. In fact, an unpublished survey by program staff of vaccine companies in 2011 found less than 2 dozen non-autism claims had been filed the previous 5 years for all VICP vaccines.[6]

In 1998, a study was published in *Lancet*[7] alleging that the combination MMR vaccine led to the development of autism. The findings were never confirmed or reproduced, and a British General Medical Council tribunal uncovered dishonesty and irresponsibility in the conduct of the research. The paper was fully retracted from the published record in February 2010.[7] In many ways, however, the damage was already done. Starting in 2001, thousands of claims were filed in a special process set up by the court known as the Omnibus Autism Proceeding (OAP).[8] Hearings on general causation alleging autism (or autism spectrum disorder) from a combination of MMR vaccine and mercury/thimerosal *(combined theory),* or from thimerosal-containing vaccines alone, were held in 2007 and

2008. Three test cases were chosen for each theory being alleged. In February 2009, 3 special masters issued decisions on general causation and 3 test cases under the combined theory. Each special master ruled in favor of the respondent (HHS), and the decisions were subsequently appealed and affirmed by the US Court of Federal Claims and the US Court of Appeals for the Federal Circuit. Similarly, in March 2010, special masters decided in favor of HHS on general causation and 3 test cases for the thimerosal theory. None of the test cases was appealed by petitioners. Petitioners chose not to introduce new evidence and pursue a third theory (ie, MMR vaccine alone) because the record in the combined theory hearing included a great deal of evidence on MMR vaccine alone. The court has now turned its attention to the thousands of remaining individual autism claims in which petitioners are determining whether to dismiss the petitions or continue on an individual basis. Those choosing the latter are required to file new theories of causation and evidentiary support not introduced in test cases or part of the OAP.[9]

Table 7-1. Vaccine Injury Compensation Program[5]

Petitions Filed			
Fiscal Year	**Pre-1988 Claims**	**Post-1988 Claims**	**Totals**
1988–2001	4,258	1,841	6,099
2002–2010	2	7,487	7,489
Totals	4,260	9,328	13,588[a]

Program Adjudications					
Fiscal Years	**Compensable**		**Dismissed**		**Claims**
	Pre-1988	**Post-1988**	**Pre-1988**	**Post-1988**	**Totals**
1988–2001	1,175	488	3,061	646	5,370
2002–2010	8	873[b]	5	1,516[b]	2,402[b]

Program Awards Paid[a]						
Fiscal Years	**Claims**	**Awards**	**Claims**	**Awards**	**Total**	**Total**
	Pre-1988	**(Millions)**	**Post-1988**	**(Millions)**	**Claims**	**Awards**
1989–2001	1,172	$833.1	491	$413	1,663	$1,246.1
2002–2010	12	$19.6	874	$768	886	$787.6
Totals	1,184	$852.7	1,365	$1,181	2,549	$2,033.7

As of March 3, 2011, 2,618 families and individuals have been compensated. Seventy-two percent were awards on behalf of children; 65% of awards paid from FY 2007 through FY 2010 were on behalf of adults.
[a]Since 2001, 5,634 of these claims have been autism related (ie, filed under the Omnibus Autism Proceeding).
[b]From 2002 to 2010, 786 autism claims filed under the Omnibus Autism Proceeding were dismissed, and 1 claim was compensated.

Additionally, in February 2011 the US Supreme Court ruled in the case of *Bruesewitz v Wyeth*[10] that the no-fault compensation program protects vaccine manufacturers against lawsuits over the vaccine's design, an area of law known as *product liability*. Hannah Bruesewitz developed seizures and permanent brain damage after receiving the DTP vaccine in 1993. After her VICP claim was dismissed by the US Court of Federal Claims, the Bruesewitz family sued Wyeth, the maker of the vaccine, alleging that defective design of the vaccine led to Hannah's injuries. By a 6 to 2 vote, the court held that the VICP "preempts all design-defect claims against vaccine manufacturers brought by plaintiffs seeking compensation for injury or death caused by a vaccine's side effects." This, in effect, should allay vaccine manufacturers' concerns about future potential liability for vaccine lawsuits and should help ensure a continued supply of vaccines.

Changes to the Vaccine Injury Table

By law, the VIT can be modified or amended by the secretary of HHS in consultation with the Advisory Commission on Childhood Vaccines and after opportunity for public comment. Such changes apply only to cases filed after the effective date of changes. Separate efforts by the VICP to modify the VIT and aids began with publication of the 2 congressionally mandated Institute of Medicine reviews of vaccine adverse events in 1991 and 1994, respectively. The first set of changes, effective March 10, 1995, involved adding chronic arthritis for rubella-containing vaccines and removing shock-collapse and residual seizure disorder for DTP vaccines. Clarifications were also made in the definitions of residual seizure disorder and encephalopathy in the qualification and aids to interpretation, which define VIT conditions.

The second set of changes to the VIT, which became effective March 24, 1997, involved adding Hib, HBV, and varicella vaccines to the VICP. By law, all vaccines recommended by the CDC for routine administration to children are eligible for VICP coverage as long as they are subject to an excise tax under federal law and the secretary of HHS has added them to the VICP. The other modifications included the addition of thrombocytopenia for measles-containing vaccines and brachial neuritis for tetanus-containing vaccines. Coverage of the 3 new vaccines, however, did not begin until Congress set an excise tax for the new vaccines effective August 7, 1997.

Since 1997, the VIT has been modified several times by rule making. The general category of rotavirus vaccines was added effective October 21, 1998, and pneumococcal conjugate vaccines were added effective December 18, 1999. Additionally, a final rule effective August 26, 2002, added intussusception as a listed injury to the VIT under a second category of rotavirus vaccines (ie, live, oral, rhesus-based), which was removed by the secretary after the deadline for filing claims had expired. However, as of the time of writing, there is no condition specified for the newest rotavirus vaccines now being administered.

As part of the 1997 rule making, a new category was added to facilitate the addition of new vaccines to the VIT. The last VIT box includes any new vaccines that have been recommended by the CDC for routine administration to children after publication by the secretary of HHS of a notice of coverage. Because of this category, 4 new vaccines have been added. As of December 1, 2004, HAV has been included, and as of July 1, 2005, TIV is now covered. Meningococcus (conjugate and polysaccharide) and HPV were added in February 2007. As rule making and public comment are necessary for vaccines to have separate listings in the VIT, HHS had begun the process in September 2010 with publication of a notice in the *Federal Register*.[11] The 4 vaccines were proposed for addition to the VIT with no associated injuries or conditions. The recent H1N1 influenza (swine flu) pandemic scare provides some insight into the limitations of the VICP. Shortly after the outbreak in 2009, there was a widespread distribution of the pandemic H1N1 influenza vaccine. This vaccine is not on the VIT, however, and therefore is *not* covered under the VICP. However, the same H1N1 influenza vaccine was incorporated as a component of the 2010–2011 seasonal TIV, which *is* covered by the VICP. The 2009 monovalent H1N1 vaccine is covered by a separate program in HHS—the Countermeasures Injury Compensation Program (CICP).

The CICP, part of the Public Readiness and Emergency Preparedness Act in 2005, provides compensation to certain persons who sustain serious physical injuries (or death) as a result of a covered countermeasure designated under a secretarial declaration.[12] The CICP, which began operation in 2010, covers the H1N1 influenza vaccine, certain antiviral medications, filter face masks, mechanical ventilators, and diagnostic devices. Other declarations cover vaccines, antimicrobials, antitoxins, drugs, diagnostics, or devices used to identify, prevent, or treat smallpox, anthrax, botulism, or radiation syndrome. Unlike the VICP, the CICP is an exclusively administrative program run by the HHS. Requests for benefits must be filed within 1 year of the administration or use of the covered countermeasure that caused the injury, and must satisfy the requirements for a condition listed on a countermeasures injury table or prove that a covered countermeasure caused a specific injury. Under the CICP, the secretary must rely on compelling, valid, and reliable medical and scientific evidence to add injuries to an injury table or to determine that a countermeasure caused a specific injury. As of January 2011, 423 requests had been filed with the CICP, nearly all alleging injury from the 2009–2010 H1N1 pandemic influenza vaccine. The remaining 2% involved antiviral drugs, a respiratory protective device, anthrax vaccine, and smallpox vaccine.[13] More information about the CICP can be found at www.hrsa.gov/countermeasurescomp.

Vaccine Excise Tax

The Vaccine Injury Compensation Trust Fund provides funding for vaccine-related injuries or deaths from vaccines administered on or after October 1, 1988. It is currently funded by an excise tax of $0.75 imposed on each dose of covered vaccine for each disease to be prevented. For example, vaccines designed to protect against 3 diseases (eg, DTaP, MMR) are taxed at $2.25; vaccines to protect against 2 diseases (eg, Td, DT) are $1.50; and vaccines against a single disease (eg, IPV, TT, R) are $0.75. These revisions went into effect on August 6, 1997. Vaccine providers pay the excise tax when purchasing vaccine antigens from manufacturers.

Vaccine Administrator Responsibilities

Under the VICP, vaccine administrators are required to discuss risk communication, distribute approved handouts, and document key aspects of the vaccination process.

Informing Patients and Parents About Vaccines

Parents and patients should be informed about the benefits and risks of preventive and therapeutic procedures, including immunization. Patients, parents, or legal guardians should be informed about benefits to be derived from vaccines in preventing disease in individuals and the community, and about risks of those vaccines. Questions should be encouraged so that the information is understood.

The NCVIA included specific requirements for notifying *all* patients and parents about vaccine benefits and risks. Note that the NCVIA does not require parental consent but uses the term *legal representative,* defined as a parent or other individual who is qualified under state law to consent to immunization of a minor. Thus, state law is controlling in deciding who may give consent for vaccines.

This legislation, as subsequently amended, mandates that a CDC Vaccine Information Statement (VIS) be provided each time a vaccine covered under the VICP is administered (as indicated by the VIT), whether the vaccine is administered by a public or private physician and regardless of funding source.

Copies of current VISs can be obtained from state and local health departments, the CDC, the American Academy of Pediatrics (AAP), and vaccine manufacturers or by calling the CDC (800/232-4636). Those with Internet access can download copies from www.cdc.gov/vaccines/pubs/vis/default.htm. They are also available on the Immunization Action Coalition Web site, www.immunize.org, and the AAP Immunization Web site, www.aap.org/immunization. Vaccine Information Statements are available in English, Spanish, Chinese, and numerous other languages.

Pediatricians need to ensure that the VIS provided is the current version by noting the version date shown on the front page. Current version dates can be checked by calling the CDC or accessing the CDC VIS Web site.

Required Documentation

The NCVIA requires physicians administering VICP-covered vaccines to record the date of administration, vaccine manufacturer, lot number, and name and business address of provider in the patient's medical record. In addition, the CDC has issued instructions requiring physicians to record the VIS version date *and* the date the VIS is given (Table 7-2). The AAP Vaccine Administration Record has been updated to capture this information (see Resources on page 110).

Vaccines purchased under a CDC contract carry the same record-keeping requirements regardless of whether the vaccine is VICP covered. Although VIS distribution and vaccine record-keeping requirements do not apply to non–VICP-covered, privately purchased vaccines, the AAP recommends using VISs and following the same record-keeping practices with these vaccines. The AAP also recommends recording the site, route of administration, and vaccine expiration date after administering *any* vaccine.[14]

Parental Signatures

The VIS no longer includes space for parents' or patients' signatures to indicate that they have read and understood the material, although the physician has the option to obtain a signature. (Pediatricians should check state medical consent laws to determine whether state law requires a signature prior to vaccination.) Whether a signature is obtained, the physicians should document in the chart that the VIS has been provided and discussed with the parent, legal representative, or patient.

Table 7-2. Guidance in Using Vaccine Information Statements[14]

Distribution	Documentation in the Patient's Medical Record
Must be provided each time a VICP-covered vaccine is administered.[a]	Vaccine manufacturer, lot number, and date of administration[a]
Given to parent, legal representative, or patient (non-minor) to keep.[a]	Name and business address of the provider administering the vaccine[a]
Must be the current version.[b]	VIS version date and date it is provided[b]
Can provide (not substitute) other materials, written or audiovisual, as necessary.[c]	Site (eg, deltoid area), route of administration (eg, intramuscular), and expiration date of the vaccine[c]

Abbreviations: VICP, National Vaccine Injury Compensation Program; VIS, Vaccine Information Statement;
[a]Required under the National Childhood Vaccine Injury Act.
[b]Required under Centers for Disease Control and Prevention instructions implementing the National Childhood Vaccine Injury Act.
[c]Recommended by the American Academy of Pediatrics.

Filing a Claim With the National Vaccine Injury Compensation Program

In the event a parent decides to file a claim with the VICP, the pediatrician may be asked to assist in the process. While not required, it is generally advisable for the family to seek the assistance of a lawyer in filing the claim. Indeed, as long as requirements are followed, the VICP will actually pay attorneys' fees and other legal costs even if the claim is ultimately denied.

The NCVIA specifies certain medical records that must be provided with petitions filed under the VICP. However, the VICP has set forth in greater detail materials needed to complete the medical review of each claim. If relevant records on this list are not provided with the petition, the medical review, and therefore processing of the claim, may be delayed.

The following medical records should accompany the petition filed with the court and secretary:

1. Prenatal and birth records
   - Mother's prenatal record
   - Delivery record
   - Birth certificate
   - Newborn hospital record including physicians'/nurses' notes and radiology/laboratory results
2. Medical records prior to vaccination
   - Vaccination record (including lot number and manufacturer, if available)
   - Clinic notes (such as well-baby visits)
   - Private physician visits
   - Growth charts and laboratory/radiology results
3. Post-injury hospital/emergency treatment records
   - Admission/discharge summaries
   - History and physical examination records
   - Progress notes including physicians'/nurses' notes
   - Medication records
   - Laboratory/radiology/electroencephalogram (EEG) results
   - Flow sheets (respiratory care/treatments)
4. Post-injury outpatient records
   - History and physical examination records
   - Progress notes (including physicians'/nurses' notes)
   - Medication records
   - Laboratory/radiology/EEG results
   - Clinic notes
   - All evaluations
5. Vaccine Adverse Event Reporting System form (if submitted)
6. Long-term records
   - School records
   - Consultation reports and evaluations
   - Psychologic or educational assessments
   - Therapeutic treatment/progress records
7. Death records (when applicable)
   - Death certificate
   - Autopsy report (if done)
   - Autopsy slides

Note that numbers 1 and 6 may be omitted for adult compensation claims.

One key component of the VICP is to ensure that patients and parents are informed of the risks and benefits of each vaccine that the child is about to receive. The next section takes a closer look at the requirements of informed consent.

Informed Consent, Minors, and Mandatory Immunizations

Generally, a minor cannot give consent to his or her own medical treatment regardless of the minor's actual mental capacity to give informed consent. A physician is thus required to obtain consent from a parent or legal guardian before performing a medical or surgical test, procedure, or treatment on a minor. However, case law and legislative action have resulted in several exceptions to the parental consent requirement (eg, emergency treatment, emancipated minor, treatment for sexual assault, sexually transmitted infections [STIs], drug abuse, alcohol dependency). Some states attempt to balance the rights of the minor and the parent by requiring parental notification of medical tests or treatments consented to by minors.

Parental consent for immunizations is standard practice in 43 states. Most states (34) require separate consent for each injection when more than 1 injection is required to complete a vaccination but only for a limited number of medical procedures. Nine states allow adolescents to self-consent for HBV in STI and family planning clinics as part of the exemption for minors' receipt of sexual health services. Most states require consent for vaccination services provided to adolescents.[15] Pediatricians should be aware that the VIS is a minimum threshold used for informed consent but may not satisfy the requirement of informed consent as a sole document.

All states have immunization laws for school or child care entry, although all states allow exemptions for medical contraindications. Forty-eight states allow exemptions for religious objections, while 21 states allow exemptions for philosophical objections.[16] While some would debate the logic of requiring informed consent for legally mandated immunizations, open dialogue of risk communication is at the heart of the NCVIA. For this reason, just handing out a VIS by itself is not considered adequate informed consent. There should be a process and a dialogue.

In general, the public has been very accepting of immunization laws because it believes that these laws have contributed to disease control in our country. Vaccine laws date back to the 1870s when smallpox vaccine was first used. Even at that time, there was opposition to vaccination and when use of the vaccine decreased, causing a resurgence of smallpox, many states passed laws requiring vaccination. These laws were supported by the 1905 Supreme Court case *Jacobson v Massachusetts.*[17]

Henning Jacobson refused to receive the smallpox vaccination despite a city board of health order to do so. The Supreme Court upheld the government's right to pass and enforce mandatory vaccination laws, noting that "there are manifold restraints to which every person is necessarily subject for the common good." State immunization laws support the priority of vaccines and reinforce their importance.

Most parents accept vaccination of their children and realize the health benefits that it affords. There are still many parents, however, who question or refuse to consent for one or all vaccines for their children. In these cases, it is essential that the refusal is truly informed.

Parental Questioning/Refusal of Vaccines

Why do some parents question the necessity of recommended vaccines? Several explanations are possible. Today's parents have no personal memory of many of the diseases now preventable through vaccination. Certain immunizations prevent diseases that are now so rare that parents may not have heard of the disease (eg, Hib meningitis). In the face of low disease burdens, the rates of local and systemic adverse events, causally or temporally related to vaccination, appear more common than the diseases themselves. Parents may have particular difficulty distinguishing between reports of temporally related adverse events versus causally related adverse events. With millions of children vaccinated each year multiple times, a number of serious adverse events would be expected to follow vaccination, based on coincidence alone. Warnings from the media, on the Internet, and by vaccine activists alleging that immunizations are dangerous and may lead to autism, seizures, diabetes, or a number of other disorders are disturbing to parents and can contribute to delay or refusal of vaccine administration. That vaccines are required for all children prior to child care or school entry greatly disturbs some parents because they feel that their right to make decisions for their children has been taken away.

Exemptions

School and child care immunization laws have had a remarkable effect on vaccine-preventable diseases in the United States. Enforcement of laws through the exclusion of unvaccinated children from school or child care settings is a critical factor in ensuring success. At this time all states have allowed medical exemptions; 48 states have religious exemptions and 21 states now allow for philosophical or personal belief exemptions.[16] Between 1991 and 2004, the mean rate of religious exemptions did not change. However, exemptions for personal or philosophical beliefs increased from 0.99% to 2.54%.[18] This does not reflect the true incidence in different areas of the country. All over the United States, there are clusters of non-immunized children with rates as high as 26.9%.[19] Not surprisingly, enacting personal belief exemption laws and leniency in granting those exemptions are associated with higher nonmedical exemption rates and increased incidence of pertussis.

However, one study found that children aged 3 to 18 years, who had exemptions from vaccination, were 22 times more likely to acquire measles and nearly 6 times more likely to acquire pertussis than immunized children.[19] Moreover, annual incidence rates of measles and pertussis among vaccinated children aged 3 to 18 years were significantly associated with frequency of those who were exempt in that county, with relative risks of 1.6 and 1.9, respectively. The critical issue becomes whether some parents should be allowed to place other people's children at increased risk for disease by refusing immunizations for their own children. Few issues have raised as much controversy, pitting the duty of society to protect healthy children in conflict with the right of families to make health decisions for their children. The resulting polarized debate has led to consumer efforts in more than a dozen states to rescind mandates or provide philosophical exemptions.

Not surprisingly, declining immunization can lead to outbreaks of disease with related morbidity and mortality. In 2008, an unvaccinated 7-year-old with undiagnosed measles infection returning from Switzerland caused the largest outbreak of disease in San Diego, CA, since 1991. A CDC study showed significant rates of under-vaccination in public charter and private schools, as well as public schools in higher socioeconomic areas.[20] Thus, measles outbreaks can occur in clusters of unvaccinated children even with high community immunization rates. Fortunately, there were no deaths, which was not the case in an outbreak of Hib disease in Minnesota later that year.[21] Five cases of Hib, including 1 that resulted in death, occurred in children younger than 5 years. This was the largest number of Hib cases in children younger than 5 years in Minnesota since 1992. Three of the 5 cases occurred in unimmunized children.

So far, recent efforts to rescind vaccine mandates or provide philosophical exemptions have mostly failed because of active intervention by the AAP and its state chapters, the Immunization Action Coalition, the Pediatric Infectious Diseases Society, and others.

Physician Response

Pediatricians are very influential in helping parents decide whether to immunize their child. Some physicians choose to sever the relationship with parents who refuse to vaccinate, but this is not supported by the AAP. As noted in the AAP clinical report, "Responding to Parental Refusals of Immunization of Children," "Physician concerns about liability should be addressed by good documentation of the discussion of the benefits of immunization and the risks associated with remaining unimmunized. Physicians also may wish to consider having the parents sign a refusal waiver…. In general, pediatricians should avoid discharging patients from their practices solely because a parent refuses to immunize his or her child. However, when a substantial level of distrust develops, significant differences in the philosophy of care emerge, or poor quality of communication persists, the pediatrician may encourage the family to find another physician or practice. Although pediatricians have the option of terminating the physician-patient relationship, they cannot do so without giving sufficient advance notice to the patient or custodial parent or legal guardian to permit another health care professional to be secured. Such decisions should be unusual and generally made only after attempts have been made to work with the family."[22]

By being compassionate and understanding, the physician can still help guide parental decisions and in some cases allay fears that lead to parental refusal. A study by Smith et al[23] showed that parents were almost twice as likely to trust in vaccine safety when they were educated and supported by their health care practitioner.

Informed Refusal

When a patient refuses to allow a certain procedure to be performed, it is critical that the physician adequately inform the patient of the risks of not undergoing the procedure. *Truman v Thomas*[24] stemmed from the physician's failure to inform the patient of the risks of not consenting to a recommended procedure (in that case, a Papanicolaou test). The Supreme Court of California found that "a jury could reasonably conclude that Dr. Thomas had a duty to inform Mrs. Truman of the danger of refusing the test because it was not reasonable for Dr. Thomas to assume that Mrs. Truman appreciated the potentially fatal consequences of her conduct." Other courts have ruled similarly relating to other procedures and testing. Physicians should attempt to determine the patient's rationale for refusal, fully inform the patient of the possible

consequences of refusal, and document these conversations in the medical record.

If a parent refuses a recommended immunization for her child and the child later develops the disease, an issue of professional liability might arise. Therefore, it is in the interest of the pediatrician to document parental refusal to permit vaccination. The documentation should note that the parent was informed why the immunization was recommended, risks and benefits of immunization, and possible consequences of not allowing the vaccine to be administered. The process of completing the Refusal to Vaccinate form with the family can be part of educating the parent(s) about the importance of immunization and afford an opportunity for further dialogue on the topic. It may be advisable to document the patient educational brochures and literature provided to the parent, as well.

A sample Refusal to Vaccinate form can be found on the AAP Web site[25] and on the next page. At a minimum, a release statement should have parents acknowledge that

- These vaccines are recommended by their physician and by advisory groups like the AAP and CDC.
- Their child is significantly more likely to become infected with the illness if not adequately immunized against it.
- Infected children may develop complications from the illness that include permanent neurologic impairment, death, and cancer.
- Infected children may transmit their illness to others, who then may develop its complications.
- Parents may request immunizations for the child at a later time.
- They have read VISs for these vaccines and have been provided with an opportunity to ask questions.

Because informed consent procedures are now codified in many state statutes, the pediatrician should have a legal advisor or professional

Refusal to Vaccinate

Child's Name _____ Child's ID# _____

Parent's/Guardian's Name _____

My child's doctor/nurse, _____, has advised me that my child (named above) should receive the following vaccines:

Recommended		**Declined**
☐	Hepatitis B vaccine	☐
☐	Diphtheria, tetanus, acellular pertussis (DTaP or Tdap) vaccine	☐
☐	Diphtheria tetanus (DT or Td) vaccine	☐
☐	*Haemophilus influenzae* type b (Hib) vaccine	☐
☐	Pneumococcal conjugate or polysaccharide vaccine	☐
☐	Inactivated poliovirus (IPV) vaccine	☐
☐	Measles-mumps-rubella (MMR) vaccine	☐
☐	Varicella (chickenpox) vaccine	☐
☐	Influenza (flu) vaccine	☐
☐	Meningococcal conjugate or polysaccharide vaccine	☐
☐	Hepatitis A vaccine	☐
☐	Rotavirus vaccine	☐
☐	Human papillomavirus vaccine	☐
☐	Other _____	☐

I have read the Vaccine Information Statement from the Centers for Disease Control and Prevention explaining the vaccine(s) and the disease(s) it prevents. I have had the opportunity to discuss this with my child's doctor or nurse, who has answered all of my questions regarding the recommended vaccine(s). I understand the following:

- The **purpose** of and the need for the recommended vaccine(s).
- The **risks and benefits** of the recommended vaccine(s).
- If my child does not receive the vaccine(s) according to the medically accepted schedule, **the consequences** may include
  - Contracting the illness the vaccine should prevent (The outcomes of these illnesses may include one or more of the following: certain types of cancer, pneumonia, illness requiring hospitalization, death, brain damage, paralysis, meningitis, seizures, and deafness. Other severe and permanent effects from these vaccine-preventable diseases are possible as well.)
  - Transmitting the disease to others
  - Requiring my child to stay out of child care or school during disease outbreaks
- My child's doctor or nurse, the American Academy of Pediatrics, the American Academy of Family Physicians, and the Centers for Disease Control and Prevention all strongly recommend that the vaccine(s) be given according to recommendations.

Nevertheless, I have decided at this time to decline or defer the vaccine(s) recommended for my child, as indicated above, by checking the appropriate box under the column titled "Declined."

I know that failure to follow the recommendations about vaccination may endanger the health or life of my child and others with whom my child might come into contact.

I know that I may readdress this issue with my child's doctor or nurse at any time and that I may change my mind and accept vaccination for my child anytime in the future.

I acknowledge that I have read this document in its entirety and fully understand it.

Parent/Guardian Signature _____ Date _____

Witness _____ Date _____

I have had the opportunity to rediscuss my decision not to vaccinate my child and still decline the recommended immunizations.

Parent's initials _____ Date _____ Parent's initials _____ Date _____

Parent's initials _____ Date _____ Parent's initials _____ Date _____

This form may be duplicated **or changed** to suit your needs and your patients' needs. The American Academy of Pediatrics does not review or endorse any modification made to this document and in no event shall the AAP be liable for any such changes.

HE0342   Copyright © 2002   9-80/Rev0708

American Academy of Pediatrics

DEDICATED TO THE HEALTH OF ALL CHILDREN™

liability insurer review the sample form to ensure its appropriateness for use in that practice setting. This step will provide maximum legal protection for the pediatrician against the patient or parents.

Should Parents Be Immunized in the Pediatric Office?

In an effort to increase protection of infants and children from vaccine-preventable diseases, some pediatric offices have begun to offer immunizations to parents. This strategy is known as *cocooning*.[26] Though there are no liability cases recorded, the practice of parental vaccination raises a number of medicolegal issues. First, pediatricians generally do not care for adults and thus may not be able to adequately assess contraindications, obtain informed consent, and deal with adverse reactions such as anaphylaxis. Second, administering a vaccine creates a physician-patient relationship between the pediatrician and the adult. This may create exposure for other illnesses, injuries, or problems unrelated to the administration of the vaccine. Vaccine Injury Compensation Program liability protections apply to adults, as do the record-keeping requirements and distribution of VISs done for children. It is known that many medical liability insurance policies do not cover pediatricians for administering vaccines to adults. Accordingly, it is essential for pediatricians to discuss liability coverage issues with their malpractice insurer before offering adult immunization. Then there is the issue of appropriate record keeping. As with any other patient, records need to be kept, including consent as well as the vaccines that were given. There are also the issues of payment as well as communicating with the adult patient's medical home. In summary, while immunizing adults in the pediatric office will increase access and improve protection for parent and child, such programs must be initiated only after a thorough consideration of the financial and medicolegal issues involved. The pediatrician should at least document the recommendation for adult immuni-

zation in the vulnerable child's medical record if she does not administer the vaccine to adults.

Immunization Administration Practices: Findings From the Periodic Survey of Fellows

Throughout this chapter there has been a focus on potential liability related to vaccines as well as programs designed to improve vaccine safety and ensure a stable vaccine supply. Advice has been given on potential ways to minimize liability with respect to vaccination. It is equally important to determine how pediatricians administer vaccines in actual practice. In 2007, the AAP Committee on Medical Liability and Risk Management initiated a survey to explore pediatricians' practices on the provision and documentation of vaccine risk and benefit information. The survey was randomly sent to 1,605 active US AAP members. After 7 mailings there were 912 completed questionnaires, for a response rate of 56.8%. The analysis was further limited to the 716 pediatricians (78% of all respondents) who provide direct patient care *and* offer age-appropriate immunizations to all or some of the children in their practice. The results were then compared to prior surveys from 1990 and 2001. More information on the Periodic Survey of Fellows is available at www.aap.org/research/periodicsurvey. Key findings are as follows[27]:

- In 2007, as in 2001, about half of pediatricians verbally discussed the risks and benefits of recommended vaccines with every dose administered; slightly more than one fourth did so at only the first dose, and about one fifth did so only sometimes. Fewer than 3% said they never discussed the risks and benefits of a vaccine.
- The proportion of pediatricians in 2007 who said they distribute VISs or other written information at every dose of vaccine increased from that reported in 2001 (*P*<.001). Seven of 10 pediatricians in 2007 (compared with about 6 of 10 in 2001) reported distributing vaccine

information with every dose of each vaccine; in 2007, about one fifth (compared with one fourth in 2001) did so with the first dose only.

- In 2007, about two thirds of pediatricians said they documented the provision of VISs at every dose of each recommended vaccine, up from about 55% so reporting in 2001 ($P<.01$); in both survey years, about 11% said they do so at the first dose only.

- There was no change across survey years in the proportion of pediatricians who said they document parent's verbal consent for vaccines in the patient's record. More than one third of pediatricians in 2007 and 2001 said they document the parent's verbal consent for vaccines in the patient's record with each dose of each vaccine; about one fifth sometimes do so, while more than 4 of 10 pediatricians said they never document verbal consent.

- The proportion of pediatricians who reported they obtained the parent's signature as evidence of consent at every dose of each type of vaccine decreased from about 7 out of 10 pediatricians in 2001 to 6 out of 10 in 2007 ($P<.01$). About one fourth of pediatricians in 2007 (compared with about one fifth in 2001) said they never obtain the parent's signature as consent for recommended vaccines.

- There has been little change across years in the way pediatricians report handling parental refusal for a vaccine. About 96% in 2007 and 2001 reported always making an attempt to educate parents about the importance and safety of the immunization (not asked in 1990); about 96% in all 3 years said they always document refusal in the patient's record; and three fourths in all years always documented the provision of vaccine risk and benefit information. Only about 5% of pediatricians in 2007 and 2001 said if parents continue to refuse after educational efforts, they would always refuse to continue to be that patient's doctor (not asked in 1990).

However, the proportion of pediatricians who reported they always obtain a parent's signature as evidence of having received information and refusal increased over survey years, from 20% in 1990 and 24% in 2001 to 37% in 2007 ($P<.001$).

References

1. National Childhood Vaccine Injury Act of 1986, Pub L No. 99-660
2. *Althen v Secretary of Department of Health & Human Services,* 418 F3d 1274 (Fed Cir 2005)
3. *Capizzano v Secretary of Department of Health & Human Services,* 440 F3d 1317 (Fed Cir 2006)
4. *Moberly v Secretary of Department of Health & Human Services,* 592 F3d 1315, 1321 (Fed Cir 2010)
5. Monthly Statistics Report—12/31/2010. Rockville, MD: Division of Vaccine Injury Compensation, Health Resources and Services Administration
6. Unpublished survey of vaccine companies. Rockville, MD: Division of Vaccine Injury Compensation, Health Resources and Services Administration
7. Retraction—ileal-lymphoid-nodular hyperplasia, non-specific colitis, and pervasive development disorder in children. *Lancet.* 2010;375(9713):445
8. Autism Decisions and Background Information. US Court of Federal Claims Web site. http://www.uscfc.uscourts.gov/node/5026. Accessed June 17, 2011
9. Re: Claims for Vaccine Injuries Resulting in Autism Spectrum Disorder or a Similar Neurodevelopmental Disorder v Secretary of Health & Human Services. US Court of Federal Claims Web site. http://www.uscfc.uscourts.gov/sites/default/files/autism/Autism%20Update%201%2012%2011.pdf. Accessed June 17, 2011
10. *Bruesewitz v Wyeth,* No. 09-152 (US February 22, 2011)
11. Health Resources and Services Administration. National Vaccine Injury Compensation Program: revisions to the Vaccine Injury Table. *Fed Regist.* 2010;75(176):55503–55507
12. Pub L No. 109-148, Division C (42 USC §§247d-6d—247d-6e) (2005)
13. Health Resources and Services Administration. Countermeasures Injury Compensation Program Web site. http://www.hrsa.gov/gethealthcare/conditions/countermeasurescomp. Accessed June 17, 2011
14. American Academy of Pediatrics. Informing patients and parents. In: Pickering LK, Baker CJ, Kimberlin DW, Long SS, eds. *Red Book: 2009 Report of the Committee on Infectious Diseases.* 28th ed. Elk Grove Village, IL: American Academy of Pediatrics; 2009:5–8

15. English A, Shaw FE, McCauley MM, Fishbein DB, Working Group on Legislation, Vaccination, and Adolescent Health. Legal basis of consent for health care and vaccination for adolescents. *Pediatrics.* 2008;121(Suppl 1):S85–S87. http://pediatrics.aappublications.org/content/121/Supplement_1/S85.full.pdf+html. Accessed June 17, 2011

16. States with Religious and Philosophical Exemptions from School Immunization Requirements. National Conference of State Legislatures Web site. http://www.ncsl.org/default.aspx?tabid=14376. Accessed June 17, 2011

17. *Jacobson v Massachusetts,* 197 US 11 (1905)

18. Omer SB, Pan WK, Halsey NA, et al. Nonmedical exemptions to school immunization requirements: secular trends and association of state policies with pertussis incidence. *JAMA.* 2006;296(14):1757–1763. http://jama.ama-assn.org/content/296/14/1757.full.pdf+html. Accessed June 17, 2011

19. Felkin DR, Lezotte DC, Hamman RF, Salmon DA, Chin RT, Hoffman RE. Individual and community risks of measles and pertussis associated with personal exemptions to immunization. *JAMA.* 2000;284(24):3145–3150. http://jama.ama-assn.org/content/284/24/3145.full.pdf+html. Accessed June 17, 2011

20. Sugerman DE, Barskey AE, Delea MG, et al. Measles outbreak in a highly vaccinated population, San Diego, 2008: role of the intentionally undervaccinated. *Pediatrics.* 2010;125(4):747–755. http://pediatrics.aappublications.org/content/125/4/747.full.pdf+html. Accessed June 17, 2011

21. Centers for Disease Control and Prevention. Invasive *Haemophilus influenzae* type B disease in five young children—Minnesota, 2008. *MMWR Morb Mortal Wkly Rep.* 2009;58(3):58–60. http://www.cdc.gov/mmwr/preview/mmwrhtml/mm5803a4.htm. Accessed June 17, 2011

22. Diekema DS, American Academy of Pediatrics Committee on Bioethics. Responding to parental refusal of immunization of children. *Pediatrics.* 2005;115(5):1428–1431. http://pediatrics.aappublications.org/content/115/5/1428.full.pdf+html. Accessed June 17, 2011

23. Smith PJ, Kennedy AM, Wooten K, Gust DA, Pickering LK. Association between health care providers' influence on parents who have concerns about vaccine safety and vaccination coverage. *Pediatrics.* 2006;118(5):e1287–e1292. http://pediatrics.aappublications.org/content/118/5/e1287.full.pdf+html. Accessed June 17, 2011

24. *Truman v Thomas,* 611 P2d 902 (Cal 1980)

25. Documenting Parental Refusal to Have Their Children Vaccinated: Informed Refusal Form. American Academy of Pediatrics Web site. http://www.aap.org/immunization/pediatricians/pdf/RefusalToVaccinate.pdf. Accessed July 14, 2011

26. Walter EB, Allred N, Rowe-West B, Chmielewski K, Kretsinger K, Dolor RJ. Cocooning infants: Tdap immunizations for new parents in the pediatric office. *Acad Pediatr.* 2009;9(5):344–347

27. American Academy of Pediatrics. *Periodic Survey of Fellows #69: Experiences with Medical Liability: Executive Summary.* Elk Grove Village, IL: American Academy of Pediatrics; 2007. http://www.aap.org/research/periodicsurvey/PS69exsummedicalliability.pdf. Accessed June 17, 2011

Resources

American Academy of Pediatrics *Red Book Online* (www.aapredbook.org)

American Academy of Pediatrics Immunization (www.aap.org/immunization)

Vaccine Education Center at the Children's Hospital of Philadelphia (www.vaccine.chop.edu)

Centers for Disease Control and Prevention Vaccines & Immunizations (www.cdc.gov/vaccines)

Centers for Disease Control and Prevention Vaccine Information Statements (www.cdc.gov/vaccines/pubs/vis/default.htm)

American Academy of Pediatrics Vaccine Administration Record (https://www.nfaap.org/netforum/eweb/DynamicPage.aspx?webcode=aapbks_productdetail&key=fed9941b-3413-4727-a09a-a6863ac19518)

American Academy of Pediatrics Committee on Bioethics. Informed consent, parental permission, and assent in pediatric practice. *Pediatrics.* 1995;95(2):314–317

National Vaccine Injury Compensation Program (www.hrsa.gov/vaccinecompensation)

Newborn Care

Jay P. Goldsmith, MD, FAAP

Care of the newborn is an integral part of the practice of pediatrics. For the general pediatrician, the newborn is the cornerstone of building a practice; for the neonatologist, the newborn is the focus of practice. Every newborn who is seriously ill has the potential for a poor outcome, which is the underlying factor in most medical malpractice actions. Over the past 4 decades, remarkable advances in newborn care have led to markedly improved outcomes for neonates with a variety of acquired critical illnesses and congenital anomalies. These advances, along with others in medicine, have raised public expectation for the outcome from medical treatment to sometimes unrealistic levels. With increased expectations has come an increase in the number of malpractice actions in situations in which the outcome is not optimal. This chapter will review liability issues related to newborn care and suggest approaches to reduce the risk of being sued.

Communications Issues

The basis for many malpractice actions arises from problems related to poor communication. As all physicians know, an important aspect of the art of medicine is effective communication with patients and family members. To communicate effectively, physicians must take into account a number of factors, including severity and complexity of the newborn's illness, educational sophistication of the parents, sociocultural factors, and emotions sur-rounding the situation. Communication must be tailored in each situation to meet the family's needs. In the case of a newborn, factors unique to this period increase the possibility that communication may break down or be less than optimal.

The expectation for a healthy, "perfect" baby has never been higher. When circumstances are otherwise, the importance of effective communica-tion with parents and family members becomes paramount. In these situations, parents and pedia-tricians are frequently dealing with an unexpected situation, such as preterm delivery, birth of a depressed neonate in need of resuscitation, a newborn with a congenital anomaly, or a normal newborn who subsequently develops an acute ill-ness. These situations challenge pediatricians to maintain technical skills in resuscitation and emer-gency care, provide appropriate care for the new-born, and communicate effectively with the family. Dealing with the unexpected is emotionally taxing for parents and professionally challenging for phy-sicians. This type of situation presents significant opportunity for misunderstanding or miscom-munication. Pediatricians must review the situation thoughtfully and thoroughly with parents and other family members. Care should be taken to present information in language that is understandable and nontechnical. Questions should be dealt with in a forthright manner and physicians should not withhold information that may be relevant to the situation at hand. In some circumstances, it may be appropriate to defer answering questions, par-ticularly when information needed to provide an accurate answer may be lacking. Care must also be taken to present parents and family members the expected outcome as well as a realistic picture of potential complications that could occur. While it is not appropriate to raise fears of death or disability unnecessarily, if these are significant possibilities, parents should be informed to allow the develop-ment of realistic expectations. Hickson et al noted in a study of 127 families who had filed malpractice

claims following perinatal injuries that dissatisfac-tion with physician-patient communication was part of the reason that prompted the suit. Families believed that physicians attempted to mislead them (48%), withheld information (32%), or did not warn them about long-term neurodevelopmental problems (70%).[1]

Communication among multiple physicians car-ing for newborns who are ill raises additional chal-lenges. The delivery of a normal newborn typically involves at least 2 physicians, the obstetrician and pediatrician, both of whom will be communicating with the family. When a neonate is born prema-turely or with a malformation, or is acutely ill, other physicians may be consulted to assist with evalua-tion and treatment. While this is necessary to pro-vide optimal care, it does present communication challenges that can cause the parents to become confused or have misunderstandings. These situa-tions require close communication among the involved physicians. Reality often dictates that several physicians will be communicating with the family. When this is the case, care must be taken to ensure that information presented to the family is consistent to prevent confusion and unnecessary anxiety. This requires that all physicians involved in the newborn's care have a clear understanding of what each is communicating to the family. Consistency is key to prevent miscommunication that may become the focal point for a malpractice action. In summary, consistent, understandable communication is essential for optimal patient care and for parents to be adequately informed with realistic expectations. Such expectations will not eliminate but may reduce the possibility of a malpractice suit.

Communication among all physicians caring for the same patient is important for patient safety. This communication may be verbal or written (in the medical record) or through an intermediary such as a nurse. Situations of cross coverage (eg, in-hospital physician to primary care pediatrician, transfer of care responsibility to pediatric medical or surgical specialists) are often vulnerable to communication gaps. Gaps in adequacy of follow-up on emerging or existing problems can occur when an initiating physician does not make sure that the following physician is aware of the need for careful follow-up. This has become more problematic with the fragmentation of care imposed by requirements of managed care networks, such as the use of approved laboratories, formularies, and follow-up protocols. Failure of communication during handoffs of patients among physicians has become one of the most frequent causes of untoward outcomes and subsequent litigation. Documentation of verbal communication as well as written transfer notes are keys to preventing these lawsuits.

Prenatal Visit

Many pediatricians offer parents a prenatal visit to discuss delivery room and newborn care issues. The American Academy of Pediatrics (AAP) endorsed the prenatal visit in 1996 and published policy statements in 2001 and 2009 (Table 8-1).[2] This visit is an excellent opportunity for parents and pediatricians to become acquainted prior to the delivery and to review parental concerns and questions about newborn care. More importantly, it is an opportunity to begin to build the relationship between the physician and parents. In the event that there are postnatal complications, this prior familiarity between physician and parents should facilitate communication and lessen the stress associated with an unexpected situation. While routine prenatal visits have not been shown to reduce the risk of litigation, such visits may help facilitate communication when an unexpected situation arises.

Table 8-1. Objectives of the Prenatal Visit[2]

1. Establish a relationship between the physician and parent.
2. Gather basic information.
3. Provide information and advice.
4. Build parenting skills for mothers and fathers.
5. Identify high-risk situations, including family history of genetic abnormalities.

Delivery Room Care

The transition from an in utero existence to the outside world is the first critical step for all newborns. In most cases, this transition is successful and uneventful. In a few cases, the transition is complicated and the newborn requires resuscitative measures in the delivery room. Currently, accepted guidelines recommend that all deliveries be attended by individuals trained in and capable of initiating neonatal resuscitation.[3] Pediatricians, obstetricians, and hospital administrative staff must work together to establish criteria for the education, training, and experience required for individuals who attend deliveries to provide neonatal resuscitation. *Those individuals trained in neonatal resuscitation must be available at the hospital to attend deliveries 24 hours a day, 365 days a year.* These criteria should also outline the qualifications of individuals attending high-risk deliveries, such as those complicated by fetal distress, meconium-stained amniotic fluid, or prematurity. Once established, such criteria must be strictly followed. Failure to do so may open the door for litigation in situations resulting in a poor outcome. (See Resources on page 128.)

The involvement of pediatricians in litigation addressing the resuscitation of an asphyxiated or very premature newborn is becoming more frequent. Claims of substandard care include failure to effectively intubate or ventilate the newborn and failure to recognize and treat hypovolemia or shock, hypoglycemia, acidosis, and sepsis. Pediatricians who attend deliveries or are on call for newborn emergencies should maintain their technical and cognitive skills in this discipline. Periodic review of resuscitation skills with a programmed course does not ensure competency; other practice sessions with the neonatal team or high-fidelity simulator may be necessary to maintain necessary skills. Methods to determine the correct placement of an endotracheal tube, such as use of a carbon dioxide detector, should be routine in the performance of tracheal intubation.[4]

Normal Newborn Nursery

The care of the normal newborn is usually straightforward, but there are several issues that warrant discussion relative to reducing the risk of litigation. Patient care in the newborn nursery should be guided by policies and procedures based on accepted professional standards. Typically, such policies and procedures are developed by a multidisciplinary committee using published guidelines. Pediatricians play an integral role in developing nursery policies and procedures, serving on and frequently chairing the hospital committee that oversees this process. Policies and procedures must be practical and conform to accepted professional standards. *Guidelines for Perinatal Care,* a joint publication of the American Congress of Obstetricians and Gynecologists (ACOG) and AAP, is the most widely used reference of perinatal care.[3] Other useful references include the AAP *Red Book*[5] and *Pediatric Clinical Practice Guidelines & Policies.*[6] These publications reflect the consensus of a group of experts and may be used by attorneys to establish the standard of care in a malpractice action. It follows that care provided in accordance with such guidance provides for stronger defense in the event of a bad outcome. Given this, it is important in situations in which significant deviation from published guidelines is warranted that the pediatrician document the rationale thoroughly in the medical record. Failure to do so can make it difficult to defend a malpractice case. Moreover, ignorance

of the guideline is not a reasonable defense. Pediatricians must keep abreast of changing guidelines through AAP publications, and review and appropriately incorporate new guidelines into patient management and nursery policies and procedures.

Hyperbilirubinemia in the Healthy Term Newborn

Hyperbilirubinemia in the healthy term newborn represents one of the most common conditions encountered in the first week after birth, affecting approximately 60% of neonates born in the United States. Few issues in neonatal medicine have generated such long-standing controversy as the possible adverse consequences of neonatal jaundice and when to begin treatment. Under certain circumstances, bilirubin may be toxic to the central nervous system (ie, bilirubin-induced neurologic dysfunction) and may cause neurologic impairment even in healthy term newborns. The incidence of this complication is approximately 1 in 100,000 newborns and despite efforts to screen for and prevent high levels of hyperbilirubinemia, not all cases of kernicterus are preventable.

There are no simple solutions to the management of newborns with jaundice. Continuing uncertainties about the relationship between serum bilirubin levels and brain damage, as well as differences in patient populations and practice settings, contribute to variations in the management of hyperbilirubinemia. The trend toward earlier postpartum discharge from the hospital in recent years further complicates the management of jaundiced newborns because bilirubin levels peak after discharge and this places additional responsibilities on parents or guardians to recognize and respond to developing jaundice or clinical signs.

The AAP has developed recommendations to aid in the evaluation and treatment of the healthy term and late preterm newborn with hyperbilirubinemia.[7,8] In these guidelines, the AAP has attempted to describe a range of acceptable practices, recognizing that adequate data are not available from the scientific literature to provide more precise recommendations.

Pediatricians should become very familiar with these AAP recommendations. The potential risk to the central nervous system secondary to hyperbilirubinemia should be discussed with parents before hospital discharge. However, care should be taken to not frighten parents about this frequent sign (jaundice), which rarely becomes dangerous. Especially when an early discharge is anticipated, the first follow-up appointment for every newborn should be discussed with the parents, documented in the medical record, and planned according to risk, including the risk of hyperbilirubinemia, which may be determined by plotting a discharge bilirubin level on an hour-specific nomogram. (See Resources on page 128.)

Newborn Genetic Screening

Genetic diseases are an important group of disorders in the neonatal setting. All 50 states require newborn screening (NBS) for metabolic diseases. Specifics of the screening process, however, vary from state to state.[9] Individual state guidelines mandate the requirements for NBS, and such guidelines will determine local nursery policies related to screening. Pediatricians must be knowledgeable about NBS requirements in the state where they practice and be certain that nursery policies reflect state standards.

Pediatricians sometimes feel pushed and pulled in opposite directions by state-mandated tests, which are typically based on cost-effectiveness, political considerations, and limited financial resources in young families. Treating physicians should view state-mandated testing as a minimal standard; it is sometimes appropriate to do more, regardless of whether the state requires it or the insurer pays for it. Should the family decline to have recommended tests done despite risk communication, it would be

prudent to obtain an informed refusal. Physicians also should take the time to document this in the patient's medical record with references to why the test was recommended and the importance of early screening and detection (eg, is treatment available, are there genetic ramifications, does it influence prognosis?).

Confirmation of positive NBS test results is always necessary. Moreover, a positive test result may not necessarily demand treatment. As Brosco et al[10] point out, universal NBS has entered a new era of promise and controversy. With the use of tandem mass spectroscopy, states have substantially increased the number of conditions included in mandatory NBS programs. This expansion has mostly followed recommendations from an expert panel commissioned by the Maternal and Child Health Bureau, which proposed mandated screening for a core group of 29 conditions and suggested that 25 additional conditions be reported to families, although accepted treatments are not yet available. The Presidential Commission for the Study of Bioethical Issues criticized the recommendations, arguing that mandated NBS should be restricted to conditions that have availability of treatment accepted as effective and are accessible to patients. Brosco and colleagues cite the many children with histidinemia who were treated with low-histidine diets before it was recognized that such treatment was not effective (although it appears it was not harmful).[10] Additionally, NBS programs should not preclude the pediatrician's assessment of clinical symptoms at any age. Some disorders (eg, galactosemia, maple syrup urine disease) may become symptomatic before the availability of the NBS results and may warrant specific testing when clinically suspected. Furthermore, although NBS tests are designed to detect neonates with metabolic illnesses, certain tests may also identify carriers (ie, heterozygotes) or individuals with variants who may be clinically asymptomatic. Such information is important for the family because of the identification of *carrier couples.* This can have an effect on future pregnancies and other family members. Thus, the pediatrician needs to be aware of this aspect of NBS and provide appropriate counseling or referral for such families.

False-negative test results may occur for a variety of reasons. Pediatricians should be knowledgeable about procedures used in their state programs and be aware of those groups of newborns likely to be missed through screening (ie, those born prematurely, those who have received blood transfusions, those born out of state or out of country, and those who underwent testing too early). Under such circumstances, follow-up testing may be required for certain neonates even if NBS results are negative. Unfortunately, most states do not report negative results directly to the pediatrician, particularly if the pediatrician is not the physician of record during the newborn's neonatal stay. All reports are sent to the hospital of birth and not necessarily to the physician, making transfer of such information highly variable from state to state and institution to institution. Some states have developed a direct electronic system whereby these results may be easily obtained by the pediatrician; however, in many instances, a direct and easily accessible system is not currently in place and may require time-consuming efforts on the part of the pediatrician and office staff to obtain a hard copy of NBS results. Active involvement of local AAP state chapters in working with state NBS programs to facilitate the prompt and direct transfer of information to the pediatrician has been recommended. Increased litigation risk for missing genetic screening or not following up on the results of screenings are associated with babies transported from the hospital of birth to a referral center, those who see a different pediatrician than the one who attended to their care in the hospital, and those who were not screened because of early blood transfusion. The pediatrician at the first outpatient visit should attempt to ascertain whether appropriate screenings have been done and review the results, if available. It is important to document NBS results in the medical record.

With tremendous advances in biotechnology, an increasing number of diseases are shown to have a genetic basis. Many of these diseases will manifest at birth or within the first several months of life. The implications for pediatricians are several and important. The pediatrician usually will be the first physician to encounter a newborn with a genetic disorder. Given this, pediatricians must recognize the clinical findings of common genetic disorders and consider a genetic disorder in a newborn with suggestive or unusual findings. Such findings usually require a detailed family history, specialized diagnostic testing, or referral to a center with expertise in evaluation of genetic disorders. Some parents may delay an evaluation by a geneticist for fear of learning they are responsible for or have contributed to their baby's disease. When appropriate, parents should be counseled about the potential for a genetic disease even before the genetic evaluation. This counseling should be documented.

In many circumstances, the suspicion or diagnosis of a genetic disorder will have implications for future pregnancies for parents and possibly other family members. In such circumstances, referral of the family to a genetic counselor or geneticist is warranted to educate parents and family members about reproductive risks and options. Failure to refer when appropriate to do so puts the pediatrician at significant legal risk. When a genetic disease is suspected or diagnosed, referral for counseling is always a good risk management strategy.[9]

See Figure 8-1 for the NBS test sign-off process.

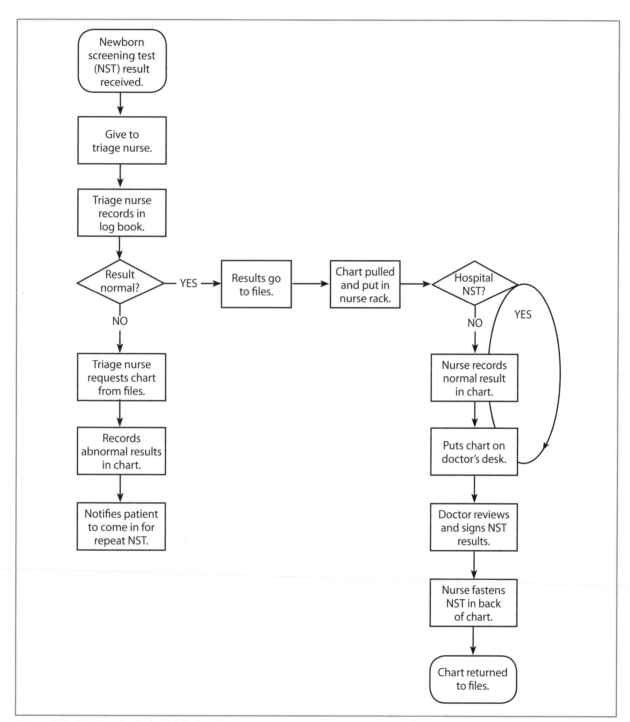

Figure 8-1. Continuous Cycle Risk Reduction

Source: *Health Information Management: Medical Records Process in Group Practice.* Englewood, CO: Center for Research in Ambulatory Health Care Administration; 1997

Group B Streptococcus Testing

Intrapartum infection of the newborn with group B streptococcus (GBS) remains a major perinatal problem. Intrapartum antimicrobial treatment of the mother has been shown to significantly reduce the incidence and severity of neonatal infection. The most recent protocol for the screening and treatment of mothers and newborns for GBS, promulgated by the Centers for Disease Control and Prevention (CDC) in 2010, recommends universal prenatal screening for colonization in all pregnant women at 35 to 37 weeks' gestation.[11] This new algorithm also provides for the management of mothers with threatened preterm delivery and newborns exposed to intrapartum antibiotic prophylaxis (Figure 8-2).

Health care professionals are urged to adopt the CDC recommendations. Furthermore, because this is still an evolving strategy, constant attention to revisions by ACOG, the AAP, and the CDC is urged.[11] The pediatrician should be reminded that universal screening for GBS has a certain incidence of false-negative test results, and mothers may be infected *after* the screen is performed at 35 to 37 weeks' gestation. Moreover, GBS may have high levels of resistance to certain antibiotics given to penicillin-allergic mothers. Therefore, newborns who manifest nonspecific signs of sepsis, even with a history of a negative maternal GBS screening result, should be evaluated and treated appropriately.

Maternal HIV Testing and Initiation of Breastfeeding

HIV infects 13% to 39% of neonates born to mothers who are seropositive. Early diagnosis and treatment has been shown to improve outcome and, importantly, recent advances in maternal chemoprophylaxis with zidovudine have significantly reduced the rates of vertical transmission from mother to baby. Failure to treat a mother who is seropositive and whose baby develops infection would be hard to defend. Routine testing of all pregnant women has been recommended, although this requires maternal consent. If the mother has been offered screening and declines, this should be documented in the newborn's medical record.

Because HIV may be transmitted in the cellular and cell-free fractions of human milk, breastfeeding and breast milk donation are contraindicated in mothers who are HIV seropositive. Mothers with HIV should be counseled accordingly.

Practitioners should be aware that many states have specific confidentiality laws related to HIV testing and disease. To protect from a lawsuit for breach of confidentiality, a specific consent form may be needed prior to testing or disclosure of HIV information.

Hepatitis B Immunizations

Universal immunization against hepatitis B is now advised. The AAP has developed a recommended schedule for hepatitis B virus immunoprophylaxis of newborns, which is based on maternal screening.[12] Administration of the vaccines requires compliance with National Vaccine Injury Compensation Program requirements (see Chapter 7). This includes risk communication and provision of the appropriate Vaccine Information Statements and required documentation.[13] All vaccine administrators are mandated by law to document in each patient's medical record the identity, manufacturer, date of administration, and lot number of certain specified vaccines, including most vaccines recommended for children. Although such data are essential for surveillance and studies of vaccine safety, efficacy, and coverage, these records often are incomplete and inaccurate.

If a parent does not consent to having a newborn immunized, documentation that the vaccine was offered and the risks of refusing the vaccine were

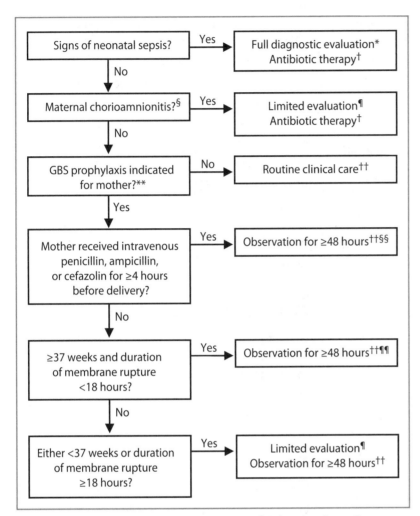

Figure 8-2. Algorithm for Secondary Prevention of Early-onset Group B Streptococcal Disease Among Newborns[11]

* Full diagnostic evaluation includes a blood culture, a complete blood count (CBC) including white blood cell differential and platelet counts, chest radiograph (if respiratory abnormalities are present), and lumbar puncture (if patient is stable enough to tolerate procedure and sepsis is suspected).

† Antibiotic therapy should be directed toward the most common causes of neonatal sepsis, including intravenous ampicillin for GBS and coverage for other organisms (including Escherichia coli and other gram-negative pathogens) and should take into account local antibiotic resistance patterns.

§ Consultation with obstetric providers is important to determine the level of clinical suspicion for chorioamnionitis. Chorioamnionitis is diagnosed clinically and some of the signs are nonspecific.

¶ Limited evaluation includes blood culture (at birth) and CBC with differential and platelets (at birth and/or at 6–12 hours of life).

** See table 3 for indications for intrapartum GBS prophylaxis.

†† If signs of sepsis develop, a full diagnostic evaluation should be conducted and antibiotic therapy initiated.

§§ If ≥37 weeks' gestation, observation may occur at home after 24 hours if other discharge criteria have been met, access to medical care is readily available, and a person who is able to comply fully with instructions for home observation will be present. If any of these conditions is not met, the infant should be observed in the hospital for at least 48 hours and until discharge criteria are achieved.

¶¶ Some experts recommend a CBC with differential and platelets at age 6–12 hours.

discussed should be noted in the medical record. Some states recognize a religious objection; some, a philosophical objection. Having a parent sign an informed refusal form available from the AAP should be considered.

Missed Diagnoses in the Neonatal Period

Significant diagnoses that are missed in the early neonatal period may expose the pediatrician to litigation for failure to diagnose. Examples of the most common lawsuits in this area are failure to diagnose developmental dysplasia of the hip (DDH), craniosynostosis, congenital heart disease, herpes infection, congenital cataracts, retinoblastoma, hearing loss, and seizures after intracranial hemorrhage or hypoxic-ischemic brain injury. Many of these problems have minimal or nonspecific clinical signs in the nursery or manifest symptoms after the baby is discharged. Some of these diagnoses may be discovered by appropriate screening examinations such as hearing screening, appropriate hip examination, and indirect ophthalmoscopy for red reflex. Babies with misshapen heads may commonly have positional skull deformities from intrauterine constraint or positional dolichocephaly. However, careful examination and possibly computerized tomography may be necessary to rule out craniosynostosis.[14] The most important aspect of defending these lawsuits is appropriate documentation of newborn examinations by the attending pediatrician. One risk management technique is to flag charts of newborns with risk factors so they can be assessed for the specific disorder at every outpatient visit if needed.

Initial Screening for Developmental Dysplasia of the HIP

Failure to diagnose DDH frequently leads to a claim of medical negligence, as the earlier the condition is diagnosed and the sooner treatment is initiated, the more favorable the outcome generally

is. More recent data suggest that the number of lawsuits related to DDH is decreasing. Pediatricians should be familiar with the clinical practice guideline and thoroughly document the presence of risk factors, performance of screening examinations, and physical findings (ie, presence of Barlow syndrome or Ortolani sign) that warrant referral to an orthopedic specialist.[15] Those with equivocal findings (eg, asymmetric thigh or buttock creases, apparent or true leg-length discrepancy, limited hip abduction) require a follow-up examination in 2 to 4 weeks and potentially an ultrasonography examination or orthopedic referral.

Maternal Serology for Syphilis

No newborn should leave the hospital without determination of the syphilis serologic status of the mother. Results of maternal serologic tests and treatment, if given, should be recorded in the neonate's medical record or be made available to the neonate's pediatrician.[5]

Discharge of Normal Newborn

Economic and social pressures in the 1980s and early 1990s have altered traditional approaches to childbirth in the United States. Discharging prior to 48 hours of life significantly truncates the period of observation previously afforded the newborn and removes the patient from the hospital setting at a time when several potentially dangerous clinical entities manifest themselves. The hospital stay of the mother and her healthy term newborn should be long enough to allow identification of early problems and ensure that the family is capable of caring for the newborn after discharge.

Although it remains controversial as to whether discharge prior to 48 hours places newborns at a greater risk, institutions must develop specific protocols and define criteria that must be met before early discharge can be considered. Protocols must take into account the availability of community resources and medical follow-up for the newborn.

Recently the AAP Committee on Fetus and Newborn published recommendations for minimum criteria that should be met before discharge of a healthy term newborn.[16] Safe transport of the healthy newborn should be discussed, including options for ensuring that car seats are safely installed, and guidelines for newborn transport are reviewed in the AAP policy statement, "Safe Transportation of Newborns at Hospital Discharge."[17]

In addition to the neonate meeting medical criteria, the mother must have a clear understanding of potential problems and how to seek medical care should they arise. All of these discussions and factors should be carefully documented in the medical record.

Critical Illness, Referral, and Transport

Quality care for high-risk newborns can best be provided by coordinating efforts of the primary care pediatrician and neonatologist. This ideally occurs in the newborn period, during the critical care and convalescing periods, and through the time of discharge. The AAP manual *Guidelines for Perinatal Care,* 6th Edition, offers guidance for the primary care pediatrician involved in providing neonatal care and discusses his or her individual and shared responsibilities, roles, and relationships with the neonatologist and neonatal intensive care unit (NICU).[3] Documentation of communication between physicians (written and verbal exchanges) is essential in these transfer of care situations.

Only 1 of 6 hospitals in the United States has NICU capabilities. Most deliveries take place in hospitals without these units. While most of these deliveries result in healthy term babies, situations can arise that necessitate management of critical illness and referral to a NICU. Examples of these situations include a high-risk delivery occurring before the mother can be transferred to a perinatal center,

delivery of a neonate who experiences intrapartum complications, or delivery of a neonate with serious illness apparent at birth or arising during the nursery stay. In each of these circumstances, the pediatrician will need to provide initial stabilization measures and then make a decision to manage the neonate locally or refer to a NICU. If the decision made is to manage the newborn locally, the pediatrician must be certain that the facility and staff are adequate to provide appropriate care for the newborn. This level of care must be ensured through all shifts, 24 hours per day, and on weekends. Often staffing or ancillary capabilities in smaller hospitals are inadequate during certain shifts and can lead to unforeseen problems. Failure to refer when it is clearly indicated can constitute grounds for a malpractice action in the event of a bad outcome.

In some circumstances, pediatricians may seek consultation with a neonatologist about management or transfer. It is important to document such consultations in the medical record. If the decision is made to transfer the patient to a NICU, arrangements must be made for safe transport of the newborn. Such decisions should be made in consultation with the accepting physician and an appropriate, mutually agreeable mode of transport. The options available typically include transport by staff from the local hospital or by a specialized transport team from the accepting center. In the former circumstance, the pediatrician must ensure that the neonate will receive appropriate monitoring and care en route, taking into account severity of illness and potential for complications during transport. When a specialized transport team is used, care should be guided by accepted standards and policies.[18] When transferring out of state, physicians must be diligent in ensuring that the transporting unit, whether it be ambulance or helicopter, is appropriately licensed. Emergency Medical Treatment and Active Labor rules may or may not be applicable depending on specific circumstances.

Neonatal Intensive Care Issues

The past 40 years have seen remarkable advances in the care of newborns. Neonates that previously would have died from complications related to preterm birth, congenital anomalies, or other critical illnesses now routinely survive with good long-term outcomes. However, the potential for poor outcomes in neonatal units is still significant and probably higher than any other setting in which pediatricians practice. In spite of this risk of poor outcome, the incidence of medical malpractice suits arising from care in the NICU is relatively infrequent. The relatively low incidence of litigation resulting from NICU care appears to result from involvement of the family in their baby's care (ie, family-centered care), efforts to keep parents well informed, and the perception that the risk of morbidity or mortality is significant in this setting, all of which contribute to creating realistic expectations. Nevertheless, this environment remains one with significant risks for outcomes that offer the potential for litigation. Several issues deserve careful consideration to reduce the risk of a malpractice suit related to care delivered in the NICU.

One of the more frequent areas of litigation is associated with the development of retinopathy of prematurity (ROP) in very low birth weight infants. Claimed breaches include the administration of excessive oxygen, inadequate monitoring of oxygen tension or saturation, or the failure to perform timely screening for the detection of threshold disease, which would lead to the potential for laser photocoagulation to prevent or ameliorate poor visual outcome. The AAP has published a protocol for ROP screening that creates a requirement that at-risk preterm newborns be examined at proper times to detect changes of ROP before they become permanently destructive. This statement presents the attributes on which an effective program for detecting and treating ROP could be based, including the timing of initial examination and subsequent reexamination intervals.[19]

The remarkable improvement in neonatal mortality has come from the result of better understanding of the pathophysiology of neonatal medicine and the implementation of new treatment modalities such as administration of exogenous surfactant, high-frequency ventilation, extracorporeal membrane oxygenation (ECMO), inhaled nitric oxide, and hypothermic neuroprotection following perinatal asphyxia. Some of these treatment modalities have potential serious short- or long-term complications. Occasionally, potential long-term complications are unknown, such as the ligation of the right common carotid artery that has to be performed in some patients undergoing ECMO. Centers providing treatment with potentially serious complications or unknown long-term effects should have strict written protocols under which those treatments are provided. Any variation of the protocol could be considered experimental and applied only under an experimental protocol after careful review by the human research committee of the hospital. Treatments are to be carefully explained to parents or legal guardians at a level that will enable them to understand. Possible barriers, such as language or culture, are to be identified. Consent forms that explain in detail the treatment and possible complications are to be signed by parents. Appropriate interpreters are to be available to help parents in this process.[20]

General experience has shown that iatrogenic problems are a common reason for a malpractice action related to neonatal intensive care. Caring for the extremely low birth weight neonate is a clinical situation particularly fraught with risks for adverse outcomes, both iatrogenic and disease derived. Given the complexity of care in this setting, the occurrence of adverse outcomes is not unexpected. Neonatal intensive care involves complex technology, drug therapy, numerous procedures, and a team of caregivers working together to provide highly sophisticated care. The potential for errors in calculation, communication, and performance of procedures is significant and requires vigilance on the part of all caregivers to keep errors at a minimum. Appropriate policies and procedures must be developed within an institution to standardize care practices, thereby lessening the opportunity for error to occur. When an adverse event occurs, the facts surrounding the event must be quickly analyzed, documented, and reported to the hospital's risk management department. The circumstances also must be communicated to the family. No attempt should be make to obscure or discount what has occurred when communicating with the family. Efforts to do so frequently only serve to inflame an already volatile situation and can make defense of a malpractice case more difficult. Many of these cases, if handled appropriately, can be settled before trial and without naming a physician in the settlement.

As part of patient safety standards, the Joint Commission requires hospitals to inform patients and their families of outcomes of care, including unanticipated outcomes. The requirement has the stated goal of improving "patient outcomes by respecting each patient's rights and conducting business relationships with patients and the public in an ethical manner."[21]

Another issue that affects malpractice risk in the NICU relates to the use of advanced practice registered nurses (APRNs) and physician extenders. While not unique to the neonatal setting, these individuals are used to a greater degree and often practice with a greater degree of autonomy in this setting than in other pediatric settings. As in other situations in which physicians serve in a supervisory role, responsibility ultimately falls on the physician in the event of a less-than-favorable outcome. This type of liability, known as *vicarious liability,* can result in a physician being named in a malpractice suit even though the event in question resulted from the actions of another individual. With this in mind, there are several issues that must be carefully addressed when using APRNs and physician extenders in the nursery setting.[22]

First, appropriate credentialing must be carried out, including verification of training, licensure, and clear definition of scope of practice. The latter is a critical issue; scope of practice must be clearly delineated and strictly followed. This includes the level of independent action and decision-making that is acceptable, in the NICU and outside the hospital during transports. The APRN should be certified by a nationally recognized organization and should maintain that certification. Regulations vary from state to state on licensure requirements and laws governing scope of practice for nurse practitioners. Collaborative practice agreements between the nurse practitioner and supervising physicians should also define the scope of practice and be acceptable to the signatories.

Deviation from the scope of practice opens the door for a host of problems in the event of a poor outcome. Clearly delineating these issues is an excellent risk management exercise that can prevent situations from arising that may put physicians and physician extenders at risk.

Neonatal Procedures

The practice of neonatal medicine includes the performance of invasive procedures including intubation, umbilical vessel catheterization, lumbar punctures, chest tube placement, central catheter placement, circumcision, and ligation of skin tags and accessory digits. Performance of procedures in the nursery involves the same issues faced in other patient care settings. First, appropriate policies and procedures reflecting current scientific knowledge and professional standards must be developed and adopted. Informed consent should be obtained, particularly for elective procedures such as circumcision, ligation of accessory digits, and administration of immunizations. Procedures should be performed by individuals credentialed to do so. Time-outs prior to the initiation of the procedure to appropriately identify the correct patient, correct site, and correct procedure should be performed in the nursery as they are in the operating room. In situations in which residents, students, or other individuals are learning to perform a procedure, appropriate supervision must be provided. Adequate documentation must be included in the medical record, including indications and any complications. Untoward outcomes should be reviewed and appropriate steps taken to improve practice outcomes. Following these steps is essential for good patient care and risk management.

Emerging areas of patient safety concern in the NICU are soft tissue damage, serious extremity damage, nerve injuries from intravascular infusions or umbilical vessel catheters, and medication errors. More research is needed to understand and prevent these injuries.

Discharge After Neonatal Intensive Care

Newborns who have had a complex neonatal course requiring intensive care are at risk for numerous problems following discharge. It is imperative that basic criteria be met before sending such newborns home.

Guidelines for discharging newborns after neonatal intensive care have been addressed by the AAP with a recent revision in 2008.[23] In addition to medical criteria (including specialized testing where indicated, immunization, and arranging for equipment or medications), there should be a home care plan with input from all appropriate disciplines. All low birth weight and premature neonates need to have appropriate car seat evaluations prior to discharge. Neonates born prematurely should have a period of observation in a car safety seat, preferably their own, before hospital discharge. These newborns need to be observed for oxygen desaturation, apnea, or bradycardia. Study should be performed by hospital staff trained in positioning neonates properly in car safety seats and in detecting apnea, bradycardia, and oxygen desaturation. The newborn should be positioned in optimal restraint and

the car seat placed at the angle approved for use in the vehicle. Test for a minimum of 90 to 120 minutes or duration of travel, whichever is longer. If the newborn fails this test, further interventions should be followed as per AAP policy.[24]

An assessment of family and home environmental readiness needs to be accomplished as well as that of the community and health care system. All arrangements for follow-up should be made in advance; primary care physicians should be notified and apprised of the newborn's course and condition; and an appointment should be scheduled. Parents also should understand how to seek emergency care should a problem arise prior to the first appointment with the primary care pediatrician. All of this should be carefully recorded in the neonate's medical record.

Neurological Injury Compensation Act Programs

Currently, 2 states, Virginia and Florida, have established programs to provide financial compensation for neonates who suffer neurologic sequelae from birth-related complications.[25-27] The impetus for both states to establish these programs was a crisis in the availability of malpractice insurance coverage for physicians providing obstetric care. These programs offer an alternative avenue for compensation in situations in which a newborn suffers significant neurologic morbidity from birth-related complications such as asphyxia and trauma. Previously, many of these cases ended up in the tort system, frequently with large indemnities, even when there was no breech of the standard of care. By offering an alternative avenue to litigation, this no-fault approach provides compensation in situations in which there is devastating neurologic injury and avoids the expense and personal toll resulting from a malpractice action. Families who seek and accept settlement from these programs can receive compensation and avoid the complexities of a lawsuit but forfeit their right to pursue compensation through the tort system. Both state programs require that the claimant be a term newborn and the injury occur during the intrapartum period.

Two decades after their establishment, the Virginia and Florida birth injury programs remain as the only experiments in American malpractice law. Even in these states, the majority of birth injury cases are still adjudicated through the standard court systems. It is not surprising that these models have failed to inspire similar programs in other states, despite widespread dissatisfaction with the current medical malpractice system. Failure to launch programs in other states likely reflects a mix of political, legal, and sociologic factors. Though successful in some ways, the programs have not been problem free. In Virginia, financial strains have periodically overshadowed all other dimensions of program performance, although the program's Web site notes actuarial studies reporting that the program will be fiscally sound for the next 20 to 25 years. (See http://vabirthinjury.com.) In Florida, qualification for inclusion in the program has been difficult for applicants to achieve.

The centerpieces of the birth injury programs and the design features that differentiate them most clearly from their tort counterparts are non-negligence compensation criteria and the way in which non-adversarial processes are used to incorporate expert opinion into the determination of eligibility. These principles are essential to the development of other state or federal malpractice reforms.

Neurologic Impairment in Newborns

Neurologic impairment in newborns continues to be a leading cause of malpractice claims. The Physician Insurers Association of America (PIAA) has studied common medical risk factors in pregnancy and childbirth and their relationship to subsequent liability actions. The study was conducted

first in 1987 and repeated in 1998 for its loss-prevention value to help physicians managing newborns recognize critical factors in identifying newborns who are neurologically impaired at an early stage.[28]

In reviewing a separate report of all closed malpractice claims submitted to the PIAA data-sharing program, neurologic impairment is the second most expensive condition in terms of indemnity. According to the closed claims studied from 1985 to 2009, more than 28.45% of all claims involving this condition result in an indemnity payment to the claimant, compared with 27.9% for all closed pediatric claims during the same period. The average pediatric indemnity payment reported was $271,784 per claim during the same period. The average indemnity payment for pediatricians for closed claims from 1985 to 2009 involving this condition was $443,804.[29]

The AAP and ACOG have jointly published a report on the causation of newborn brain pathology. The report, *Neonatal Encephalopathy and Cerebral Palsy: Defining the Pathogenesis and Pathophysiology,*[30] presents evidence-based information about the causes of neonatal encephalopathy and cerebral palsy and to what extent any such outcomes can be averted by the state of science and medicine. A new ACOG/AAP task force is presently revising this monograph. Current information, especially in the areas of neuroimaging and placental pathology, are expected to be included in this updated report due in 2012. The cause of fetal and neonatal neurologic injury has long been an area of debate and controversy in medical liability cases. This report can be used to provide evidence that most brain abnormalities do not usually result from an isolated intrapartum hypoxic event but rather are prenatal in origin. Several government and non-profit agencies have endorsed the report, including the National Institute of Child Health & Human Development, March of Dimes, and CDC. Pediatricians are often added to malpractice suits against obstetricians involving alleged intrapartum brain-injured babies for failure to perform adequate resuscitation and failure to recognize and treat seizures, hypotension, hypoglycemia, and other postnatal consequences of perinatal asphyxia or trauma. The recent success of whole-body and head-cooling hypothermic neuroprotection protocols in reducing morbidity and mortality when asphyxiated newborns are treated prior to 6 hours of age may also make the pediatrician responsible for early referral to a center capable of performing cooling. Care should be taken when called on to care for a depressed newborn to follow standard resuscitation guidelines and carefully observe and treat for possible post-asphyxial sequelae.[3,4]

Moreover, pediatricians should be reminded that our explanations to parents about the condition of their baby may stimulate litigation against our obstetric colleagues. While it has never been safer to have a baby in the United States, it has never been more dangerous to be an obstetrician. In a recent survey, 76% of obstetricians in the United States reported having faced litigation at some point in their careers—most often for having allegedly caused cerebral palsy.[31] The median award for medical negligence in childbirth cases is $2.3 million. Consequently, obstetricians pay some of the highest premiums for malpractice insurance—up to $200,000 per year in some states. Often, once the discovery process has begun in a malpractice case against an obstetrician for birth injury, other parties are named, including pediatricians for failure to resuscitate properly or recognize the severity of the newborn's problem.

In summary, newborn care is a challenge area for the pediatrician from medical and risk management perspectives. Attention to the issues outlined in this chapter should lessen the possibility that pediatricians will be named in a suit or sued successfully.

References

1. Hickson GB, Clayton EW, Githens PB, Sloan FA. Factors that prompted families to file medical malpractice claims following perinatal injuries. *JAMA.* 1992;267(10):1359–1363

2. Cohen GJ, American Academy of Pediatrics Committee on Psychosocial Aspects of Child and Family Health. The prenatal visit. *Pediatrics.* 2009;124(4):1227–1232. http://pediatrics.aappublications.org/cgi/reprint/124/4/1227. Accessed April 27, 2011

3. American Academy of Pediatrics, American College of Obstetricians and Gynecologists. *Guidelines for Perinatal Care.* 6th ed. Washington, DC: American College of Obstetricians and Gynecologists; 2007

4. Kattwinkel J, Bloom RS, eds. *Textbook of Neonatal Resuscitation.* 5th ed. Elk Grove Village, IL: American Academy of Pediatrics; 2006

5. Pickering LK, ed. *Red Book: 2009 Report of the Committee on Infectious Diseases.* 28th ed. Elk Grove Village, IL: American Academy of Pediatrics; 2009

6. American Academy of Pediatrics. *Pediatric Clinical Practice Guidelines & Policies: A Compendium of Evidence-Based Research for Pediatric Practice.* 10th ed. Elk Grove Village, IL: American Academy of Pediatrics; 2010

7. American Academy of Pediatrics Subcommittee on Hyperbilirubinemia. Management of hyperbilirubinemia in the newborn infant 35 or more weeks of gestation. *Pediatrics.* 2004;114(1):297–316. http://pediatrics.aappublications.org/cgi/reprint/114/1/297. Accessed April 27, 2011

8. Maisels MJ, Bhutani VK, Bogen D, Newman TB, Stark AR, Watchko JF. Hyperbilirubinemia in the newborn infant ≥35 weeks' gestation: an update with clarifications. *Pediatrics.* 2009;124(4):1193–1198. http://pediatrics.aappublications.org/cgi/reprint/124/4/1193. Accessed April 27, 2011

9. American Academy of Pediatrics Newborn Screening Authoring Committee. Newborn screening expands: recommendations for pediatricians and medical homes—implications for the system. *Pediatrics.* 2008;121(1):192–217. http://pediatrics.aappublications.org/cgi/reprint/121/1/192. Accessed April 27, 2011

10. Brosco JP, Sanders LM, Dharia R, Guez G, Feudtner C. The lure of treatment: expanded newborn screening and the curious case of histidinemia. *Pediatrics.* 2010;125(3):417–419. http://pediatrics.aappublications.org/cgi/reprint/125/3/417. Accessed April 27, 2011

11. Verani JR, McGee L, Schrag SJ, Centers for Disease Control and Prevention. Prevention of perinatal group B streptococcal disease—revised guidelines from CDC, 2010. *MMWR Recomm Rep.* 2010;59(RR-10):1–36. http://www.cdc.gov/mmwr/pdf/rr/rr5910.pdf. Accessed April 27, 2011.

12. American Academy of Pediatrics Committee on Infectious Diseases. Recommended childhood and adolescent immunization schedules—United States, 2010. *Pediatrics.* 2010;125(1):195–196

13. Centers for Disease Control and Prevention. National Childhood Vaccine Injury Act: requirements for permanent vaccination records and for reporting of selected events after vaccination. *MMWR Morb Mortal Wkly Rep.* 1988;37(13):197–200

14. Persing J, James H, Swanson J, Kattwinkel J, American Academy of Pediatrics Committee on Practice and Ambulatory Medicine, Section on Plastic Surgery, Section on Neurological Surgery. Prevention and management of positional skull deformities in infants. *Pediatrics.* 2003;112(1):199–202

15. American Academy of Pediatrics Committee on Quality Improvement, Subcommittee on Developmental Dysplasia of the Hip. Clinical practice guideline: early detection of developmental dysplasia of the hip. *Pediatrics.* 2000;105(4):896–905

16. American Academy of Pediatrics Committee on Fetus and Newborn. Hospital stay for healthy term newborns. *Pediatrics.* 2010;125(2):405–409. http://pediatrics. aappublications.org/cgi/reprint/125/2/405. Accessed April 27, 2011

17. American Academy of Pediatrics Committee on Injury and Poison Prevention. Safe transportation of newborns at hospital discharge. *Pediatrics.* 1999;104(4):986–987

18. American Academy of Pediatrics Section on Transport Medicine, Task Force on Interhospital Transport. *Guidelines for Air and Ground Transport of Neonatal and Pediatric Patients.* 3rd ed. Elk Grove Village, IL: American Academy of Pediatrics; 2007

19. American Academy of Pediatrics Section on Ophthalmology, American Academy of Ophthalmology, American Association for Pediatric Ophthalmology and Strabismus. Screening examination of premature infants for retinopathy of prematurity. *Pediatrics.* 2006;117(2):572–576. http://pediatrics.aappublications.org/cgi/reprint/117/2/572. Accessed April 27, 2011

20. Enforcement of Title VI of the Civil Rights Act of 1964—National Origin Discrimination Against Persons with Limited English Proficiency. *Fed Regist.* 2000;65(159):50123–50125

21. Joint Commission on Accreditation of Healthcare Organizations. Patient rights and organization ethics. In. *2001 Comprehensive Accreditation Manual for Hospitals: The Official Handbook.* Oakbrook Terrace, IL: Joint Commission on Accreditation of Healthcare Organizations; 2001:RI-1

22. American Academy of Pediatrics Committee on Fetus and Newborn. Advanced practice in neonatal nursing. *Pediatrics.* 2009;123(6):1606–1607. http://pediatrics. aappublications.org/cgi/reprint/123/6/1606. Accessed April 27, 2011

23. American Academy of Pediatrics Committee on Fetus and Newborn. Hospital discharge of the high-risk neonate. *Pediatrics.* 2008;122(5):1119–1126. http://pediatrics. aappublications.org/cgi/reprint/122/5/1119. Accessed April 27, 2011

24. Bull MJ, Engle WA, American Academy of Pediatrics Committee on Injury, Violence, and Poison Prevention, Committee on Fetus and Newborn. Safe transportation of preterm and low birth weight infants at hospital discharge. *Pediatrics.* 2009;123(5):1424–1429. http://pediatrics. aappublications.org/cgi/reprint/123/5/1424. Accessed April 27, 2011

25. Virginia Birth-Related Neurological Injury Compensation Act, 1987. §28.2–5000

26. Florida Birth-Related Neurological Injury Compensation Act, 1989. §766.303

27. Siegal G, Mello MM, Studdert DM. Adjudicating severe birth injury claims in Florida and Virginia: the experience of a landmark experiment in personal injury compensation. *Am J Law Med.* 2008;34(4):493–537

28. Physician Insurers Association of America. *Neurologic Impairment in Newborns: A Malpractice Claim Study.* Rockville, MD: Physician Insurers Association of America; 1998

29. Physician Insurers Association of American. *Risk Management Review—Pediatrics.* Rockville, MD: Physician Insurers Association of America; 2010

30. American College of Obstetricians and Gynecologists, American Academy of Pediatrics. *Neonatal Encephalopathy and Cerebral Palsy: Defining the Pathogenesis and Pathophysiology.* Washington, DC: American College of Obstetricians and Gynecologists; 2003

31. MacLennan A, Nelson KB, Hankins G, Speer M. Who will deliver our grandchildren? Implications of cerebral palsy litigation. *JAMA.* 2005;294(13):1688–1690

Resources

Management of Hyperbilirubinemia: Bhutani Nomogram

Nomogram for designation of risk in well newborns 36 weeks' or more gestation with birth weight greater than or equal to 2,000 g, or 35 weeks' or more gestational age and birth weight of greater than or equal to 2,500 g, based on the hour-specific serum bilirubin values (Bhutani VK, Johnson L, Sivieri EM. Predictive ability of a predischarge hour-specific serum bilirubin for subsequent significant hyperbilirubinemia in healthy term and near-term newborns. *Pediatrics*. 1999;103[1]: 6–14)

Neonatal Resuscitation Program™ - Reference Chart

! The most important and effective action in neonatal resuscitation is ventilation of the baby's lungs.

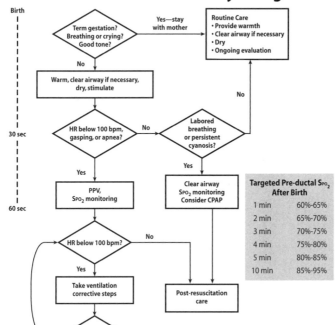

Birth

Term gestation? Breathing or crying? Good tone? → Yes—stay with mother → Routine Care
- Provide warmth
- Clear airway if necessary
- Dry
- Ongoing evaluation

No ↓

Warm, clear airway if necessary, dry, stimulate

30 sec

HR below 100 bpm, gasping, or apnea? → No → Labored breathing or persistent cyanosis? → No

Yes ↓ / Yes ↓

60 sec

PPV, SPO₂ monitoring

Clear airway SPO₂ monitoring Consider CPAP

HR below 100 bpm? → No

Yes ↓

Take ventilation corrective steps → Post-resuscitation care

HR below 60 bpm? → No

Yes ↓

Consider intubation Chest compressions Coordinate with PPV

Take ventilation corrective steps *Intubate if no chest rise!* → HR below 60 bpm?

Yes ↓

IV epinephrine

Consider:
- Hypovolemia
- Pneumothorax

Targeted Pre-ductal SPO₂ After Birth

1 min	60%-65%
2 min	65%-70%
3 min	70%-75%
4 min	75%-80%
5 min	80%-85%
10 min	85%-95%

A Airway
- Put baby's head in "sniffing" position
- Suction mouth, then nose
- Suction trachea if meconium-stained and NOT vigorous

B Breathing
- PPV for apnea, gasping, or pulse <100 bpm
- Ventilate at rate of 40 to 60 breaths/minute
- Listen for rising heart rate, audible breath sounds
- Look for slight chest movement with each breath
- Use CO_2 detector after intubation
- Attach a pulse oximeter

C Circulation
- Start compressions if HR is <60 after 30 seconds of effective PPV
- Give (3 compressions: 1 breath) every 2 seconds
- Compress one-third of the anterior-posterior diameter of the chest

D Drugs
- Give epinephrine if HR is <60 after 30 seconds of compressions and ventilation
- Caution: epinephrine dosage is different for ET and IV routes

Corrective Steps

M	Mask adjustment.
R	Reposition airway.
S	Suction mouth and nose.
O	Open mouth.
P	Pressure increase.
A	Airway alternative.

Endotracheal Intubation

Gestational Age (weeks)	Weight (kg)	ET Tube Size (ID, mm)	Depth of Insertion* (cm from upper lip)
<28	<1.0	2.5	6-7
28-34	1.0-2.0	3.0	7-8
34-38	2.0-3.0	3.5	8-9
>38	>3.0	3.5-4.0	9-10

*Depth of Insertion (cm) = 6 + weight (in kg)

Medications Used During or Following Resuscitation of the Newborn

Medication	Dosage/Route*	Concentration	Wt (kg)	Total IV Volume (mL)	Precautions
Epinephrine	IV (UVC preferred route) 0.01-0.03 mg/kg Higher IV doses not recommended Endotracheal 0.05-0.1 mg/kg	1:10,000	1 2 3 4	0.1-0.3 0.2-0.6 0.3-0.9 0.4-1.2	Give rapidly. Repeat every 3 to 5 minutes if HR <60 with chest compressions.
Volume expanders Isotonic crystalloid (normal saline) or blood	10 mL/kg IV		1 2 3 4	10 20 30 40	Indicated for shock. Give over 5 to 10 minutes. Reassess after each bolus.

*Note: Endotracheal dose may not result in effective plasma concentration of drug, so vascular access should be established as soon as possible. Drugs given endotracheally require higher dosing than when given IV.

DEDICATED TO THE HEALTH OF ALL CHILDREN™

ISBN 978-1-58110-502-5

©2011 American Academy of Pediatrics and American Heart Association
Supported in part by Fisher & Paykel Healthcare

NRP304

The recommendations in this publication do not indicate an exclusive course of treatment or serve as a standard of medical care. Variations, taking into account individual circumstances, may be appropriate.

CHAPTER 9

Adolescent Health Care

William M. McDonnell, MD, JD, FAAP

KEY CONCEPTS

- Informed Consent for Adolescents
- Informed Consent Exceptions for Particular Types of Care
- Emancipated Minors
- Mature Minor Doctrine
- Minors Requiring Emergency Care
- Right to Refuse Care
- Assent
- Confidentiality Principles
- Professional Ethics and Organizational Policies
- Financial Responsibility
- Substance Abuse
- Suicide

Physiologically, anatomically, and psychologically, adolescents are neither big children nor little adults, yet they have a number of characteristics in common with both. These characteristics produce legal complexities unique to the care of adolescent patients. Perhaps the most obvious of these legal challenges involves issues of informed consent to receive medical care. A fundamental principle of American law is that parents must provide informed consent prior to medical treatment of their children. By definition, adolescents are not of legal majority and lack the legal ability possessed by adult patients to provide such consent. Nonetheless, adolescents frequently seek care in numerous situations and for various conditions in which obtaining informed consent from a parent or legal guardian might be awkward, inconvenient, detrimental, or even impossible. In addition, adolescents may engage in medically and socially risky behaviors that present confidentiality and psychosocial implications for them and their pediatricians that are rarely encountered in the care of younger children. Pediatricians should be aware of the often complex legal issues involved in the care of adolescents to best care for these patients and to protect themselves from potential legal pitfalls.

Informed Consent for Adolescents

To protect individuals' autonomy and prevent unwanted bodily contact, physicians must obtain the agreement (ie, consent) of the patient prior to any physical contact. It is well established in American law that "Every human being of adult years and sound mind has a right to determine what shall be done with his own body."[1] Unlike competent adults, however, minor children lack the legal authority to provide informed consent for medical care. Instead, parents have the right and authority to make decisions about medical treatment for their minor children. Therefore, parents of adolescent children generally should be consulted for permission to evaluate and treat the child. The legal age of majority, after which an individual has legal rights as an adult to provide or refuse consent for treatment, is governed by state law. Although the vast majority of states set 18 years as the age of majority, a few use 19 or 21. Despite the general rule that adolescents younger than the age of majority cannot consent to medical care, a number of legal exceptions to the rule allow treatment of adolescents in certain circumstances without the approval or knowledge of a parent or legal guardian.

Informed Consent Exceptions for Particular Types of Care

All states have enacted laws that allow minors to provide their own informed consent related to particular types of care. It is well established that minors are more likely to seek care for certain conditions when they are able to do so independent of parental involvement.[2] To advance public policy goals of encouraging adolescents to seek treatment for these conditions, states have designated specific care for which minors may consent. Although these exceptions to the general rule of parental informed consent are very state-specific, some of the types of care most commonly addressed by state laws include treatment for sexually transmitted infections (STIs), reproductive health (including contraception, prenatal care, and abortion), mental health, and substance abuse.[3]

Emancipated Minors

The determination of whether a minor is emancipated is state law specific. Under most states' laws, emancipation is not determined based on a single criterion but rather involves an assessment of such factors as whether the minor is married, employed in a full-time job in the military, or living independently. When classified as *emancipated,* minors are adults according to laws relating to consent. These emancipated minors are permitted to provide (or refuse) informed consent as adults. When a patient has been legally emancipated, he should be treated by the physician as an adult. The patient has the same rights as any adult to provide or refuse

informed consent. In these situations, the emancipated minor's parents have no legal control over the adolescent's health care. Pregnancy and parenthood are not typically criteria for emancipation. Accordingly, the situation may arise in which an adolescent mother may provide consent for her child's care but not for her own. Nevertheless, minors who are parents will often meet other criteria for emancipation.

Mature Minor Doctrine

Some state courts have applied the *mature minor doctrine* in certain circumstances. Under this legal principle, older children who demonstrate a clear understanding of medical risks and benefits have been permitted to provide or refuse their own consent for medical care.[4] This designation of a mature minor may be applied based on common law principles or state statutes but needs to be adjudicated by a court on a case-by-case basis. Factors that are considered include age, maturity, reasoning ability, intellectual capacity, and comprehension of the health issue. The principles typically apply to adolescents older than 14 years. Although physicians generally have no discretion in attributing mature minor status to a minor, in some cases in which physicians provided necessary and appropriate care to adolescents, courts later supported the physicians by declaring the adolescent to be a mature minor and have thus declined to impose liability for failure to obtain adequate informed consent.[5] Nevertheless, a patient is not a mature minor until a court so designates, and pediatricians should never assume that mature minor status will apply until so ordered by a court.

Minors Requiring Emergency Care

Most states have adopted the *emergency exception* to informed consent. Rather than overriding the requirement for informed consent, the emergency exception allows the physician to infer consent under particular conditions as set forth in state law.

In most states, these conditions include a serious threat to life or health; a need for urgent intervention; circumstances under which reasonable parents would have given consent if they were able; no available option existing for obtaining actual informed consent; and the health care professional having no reason to believe that the patient's legal guardian would refuse consent.[6] However, the fact that the proposed treatment may be medically advisable or may become essential at some future time is not sufficient to allow treatment under this exception.[7] When a pediatrician believes that a patient's emergency condition meets the criteria for this informed consent exception under state law, the pediatrician should make and document an effort to contact the minor patient's parents or legal guardians, document the facts and circumstances that necessitated the emergency care, and provide care up to the point at which the emergency condition is stabilized.

Right to Refuse Care

The legal competence to consent to medical care is coincident with the ability to refuse to consent to care. Within limits, the law permits parents to make decisions concerning the care, custody, and control of their children, including consent to medical treatment.[8] Therefore, parents have considerable latitude in deciding to refuse consent for care. As discussed previously, informed consent is necessary before treatment can proceed, and the physician who treats a minor child despite parental refusal, in the absence of one of the specific consent exceptions, faces civil and possibly criminal liability.[9] Similarly, emancipated and mature minors legally function as adults, may consent to their own care, and may also choose to refuse care. The physician who disregards the refusal of these legally competent patients also faces potential civil and criminal liability, unless the treatment is specifically authorized by a court.

The US Supreme Court has held that "parents are free to become martyrs themselves. But it does not follow that they are free in identical circumstances to make martyrs of their children."[10] Thus, in some instances a parent's refusal to provide consent for treatment for the non-emancipated minor may rise to the level of medical neglect or child abuse. All states have enacted some form of mandatory reporting law for abuse and neglect of children. In cases in which refusal would reasonably be interpreted as medical neglect, the physician is obligated to report the situation to appropriate child protective services or law enforcement. State agencies and courts have the authority to override parental refusals and to provide consent for medical care on the adolescent minor's behalf. Pediatricians should be aware that it is the state authority, not the physician, that makes the decision to overrule parental refusal and provides the necessary consent.[11] Physicians reporting their suspicions of medical neglect may be immune from liability as long as they do so in good faith. However, if they deliberately or recklessly misrepresent facts or medical risks to state authorities to convince those authorities to intervene, physicians risk liability.[12]

The law clearly recognizes that refusal of medical treatment, even when that treatment is necessary to preserve life, is not necessarily inappropriate.[13,14] The federal Patient Self-Determination Act requires hospitals, hospices, and other health care institutions to inform patients or their legal guardians about their rights under their state's laws to refuse or accept medical care.[15] This law does not require physicians to inform patients of these rights during clinic visits in the office setting, but these visits might nonetheless be an appropriate setting to conduct these discussions. Some state medical societies have developed materials on patient self-determination or health care power of attorney to aid the pediatrician in educating patients and parents on their options.[16]

Assent

Although the right to give and refuse consent for care is usually restricted to competent adults, the ethical (and sometimes legal) principle of *assent* allows the non-emancipated minor some degree of autonomy over health care decisions. When medical care is provided in the context of medical research, federal regulations require that minors must agree to the treatment when they have the capacity, based on age, maturity, and psychological state, to understand the implications of their decision.[17] On the other hand, assent generally lacks the force of law outside of the research setting. Instead, ethical principles dictate that pediatricians should give serious consideration to each patient's developing capacities for participating in decision-making. Nevertheless, because non-emancipated minors in most circumstances lack ultimate decision-making authority, the degree to which assent is sought must depend on the legal guardian's willingness to incorporate that assent into the consent decision. No one should solicit a patient's views without intending to weigh them seriously. In situations in which the patient will have to receive medical care despite her objection, the patient should be told that fact and should not be deceived.[18]

Confidentiality Principles

The care of adolescents can often present challenges related to confidentiality. As with informed consent, general rules of confidentiality apply to adolescents, but a number of legal exceptions alter the application of those general rules to these patients. One of the most important and well-established obligations owed by a health care professional to a patient is the protection of confidential medical information.[19] It is well established that adolescents are more likely to seek care and obtain follow-up care when they are assured of confidentiality. State and federal legal principles protect the confidentiality of health care services, communications between patients and health care professionals, and resulting medical records. As a general matter, the legal duty of confidentiality extends only to competent adults, and parents who provide informed consent for care of their children are entitled to full disclosure about the child's medical care. However, special applications of these general rules to adolescents may affect the way pediatricians communicate with adolescents and their parents.

State Confidentiality Laws

Because the special needs of adolescents sometimes conflict with general informed consent rules, many states allow minors who are not emancipated to provide their own informed consent for particular classes of treatment. Minors who are sexually active, pregnant, or infected with an STI, and those who abuse drugs or alcohol or suffer from emotional or psychological problems, might avoid seeking care if they must involve their parents. As corollaries to these special informed consent rules, state laws also often provide confidentiality to adolescents receiving care under these special informed consent rules. Many of these laws specify that when an adolescent minor consents to care, the care must be confidential and disclosure may only occur with the agreement of the minor.[20] Some state laws expressly permit discretionary disclosure of specific types of confidential information to a parent without a minor's consent.[21] These laws override rules against breach of physician-patient confidentiality. Some state-specific rules also direct that physicians must breach confidentiality in certain circumstances, such as in abortion cases[22] or when necessary to protect the life or safety of third parties.[23] State laws vary widely in this area, and physicians should be aware of their local laws.

Additional state law legal principles also protect the confidentiality of medical information. These include medical record statutes, the physician-patient privilege, professional licensing laws, and the constitutional right of privacy (in some state constitutions). Although these laws generally do not have provisions specific to adolescents, most apply to adolescents' care. These laws vary in terms of whose permission is required to disclose protected information.

Finally, all states have adopted mandatory reporting requirements related to child abuse and neglect. When a pediatrician has a reasonable suspicion of child abuse or neglect, this information must generally be provided to law enforcement or child protective services, regardless of other confidentiality concerns. Consensual sexual activity between unmarried adolescents and noncustodial adults may present physicians with troubling confidentiality and reporting issues. All states have criminalized such activity via statutory rape laws. However, there is wide variety among states regarding whether physician reporting of such activity is mandatory or even permissible.[24] Because of the complexities of state-specific laws in this area, physicians who treat adolescent patients should familiarize themselves with child protection laws in their state related to adolescent-adult sexual behavior.

Federal Confidentiality Laws

A number of federal laws affect the confidentiality of adolescents' medical treatment and records. Privacy regulations promulgated under the Health Insurance Portability and Accountability Act (HIPAA)[25,26] are perhaps the most often implicated and referenced. However, federal laws related to family planning service programs and to drug and alcohol treatment programs may also be important.

In 1996, the US Congress enacted HIPAA to address health insurance reform, administrative simplification, and patient confidentiality. Pursuant to the law, the US Department of Health and Human Services issued the final HIPAA privacy rule in 2002. This rule imposes strict confidentiality requirements on *covered entities,* which include health plans, health care clearinghouses, and health care professionals. Although states are permitted to enact even more stringent confidentiality rules,

covered entities must at a minimum meet the confidentiality requirements of HIPAA.

The HIPAA privacy rule specifically limits physicians' use and disclosure of patient information. However, these protections do not generally prohibit the disclosure of minors' health information to parents. The HIPAA rule specifically designates parents and legal guardians as the "personal representatives" of minors and allows these personal representatives access to health information and minors' medical records.[26] However, the HIPAA rule also expressly recognizes that some state laws (including case law) do protect minors' health information from parental access, and the rule specifically incorporates those state law rules.[26] As an additional protection for minors' confidentiality, the HIPAA rule states that if there is no applicable state law about the rights of parents to access the protected health information of their children, the physician may provide or deny parental access to the records, as long as the decision is made by a licensed health care professional, in the exercise of professional judgment.[26] Although the HIPAA privacy rule seems to add little to minors' privacy from their parents, it does preserve protections provided by state laws. The Department of Health and Human Services has declared, "The HIPAA privacy rule defers to state and other law in the area of parents and minors, [and] the Department assumes that the current practices of health care providers with respect to access by parents and confidentiality of minor's records…can continue under the privacy rule."[26]

Although HIPAA may add little to adolescents' privacy from their parents, it does protect their health information from disclosure to other people. In general, the HIPAA privacy rule prevents health care professionals from using and disclosing health information without patients' (and their personal representatives') consent. Even inadvertent breaches of the rule from administrative carelessness violate the rule and can result in punishment. To protect against improper disclosures, HIPAA requires that providers seek written consent for most disclosures, implement certain administrative policies and safeguards to prevent improper disclosures, limit access to patient information to those personnel who need it, and provide HIPAA training to all personnel who deal with confidential patient information.[26] In 2009, Congress passed the Health Information Technology for Economic and Clinical Health (HITECH) Act,[27] which amended HIPAA to provide additional privacy protections for patient health information that is electronically transmitted. Violations of HIPAA and HITECH carry substantial potential civil and criminal liabilities for pediatricians. A complete description of all HIPAA and HITECH requirements is beyond the scope of this chapter, and pediatricians are strongly encouraged to consult with local counsel to establish HIPAA- and HITECH-compliant office procedures and to address any specific HIPAA issues that may arise.

Another area in which federal laws may directly affect confidentiality issues for adolescent health care is reproductive health care. The federal government provides grants for voluntary family planning services through the Family Planning program, Title X of the Public Health Service Act.[28] These grants fund contraceptive services and related preventive health services, such as infertility services; natural family planning methods; special services to adolescents; adolescent abstinence counseling; breast and cervical cancer screening and prevention; and STIs and HIV prevention education, counseling, and testing.[29] Services provided to adolescents under Title X funding must be provided on a confidential basis.[29] Although the law requires that "to the extent practical" providers under Title X should encourage family involvement,[30] neither parent notification nor consent is required.

Because treatment for drug and alcohol abuse may carry particular stigma, and breaches of confidentiality may be particularly damaging to patients needing these services, the federal government has established a distinct set of privacy rules related to substance abuse programs. Under the Federal Drug and Alcohol Confidentiality Law, any individual or entity that provides alcohol or drug abuse diagnosis, treatment, or referral for treatment or prevention, and that receives federal funds in any form (including holding Internal Revenue Service tax-exempt status), must follow this specific confidentiality law.[31] School-based programs are specifically included. When state law permits a minor to consent for substance abuse treatment, this federal law prohibits disclosure of the nature, or even the fact, of such treatment, unless the minor provides written consent for disclosure. If state law requires parental consent for treatment, the provider should decline to provide care until the parent provides consent but cannot notify the parent that the minor is seeking this care unless the minor gives written consent for the notification, or if the program director determines that the minor lacks the capacity to make a rational choice about parental notification.

Professional Ethics and Organization Policies

The principles embodied in state and federal laws that provide protection for the privacy of adolescents and confidentiality for care they receive are consistent with and supported by the policies and codes of ethics of numerous professional health care organizations, including the American Academy of Pediatrics (AAP). Numerous AAP policies[32–39] address issues of importance for adolescents and support their right to confidential care. The AAP stresses that adolescents need to know that health professionals will provide them with the best possible care and counseling if they choose to seek treatment. This includes encouraging adolescent patients to include their parents in their health care decisions, even if state law does not mandate parental notification.

Financial Responsibility

Courts have noted that costs for medical care properly provided to minors, whether by parental consent or one of the proper exceptions to the parental consent requirement, must be borne by the parent.[11] On the other hand, an emancipated adolescent is legally an adult, responsible for his own financial obligations, and the emancipated minor's parent will not be held financially responsible for medical costs.[40] A more controversial and unclear situation is one in which an non-emancipated minor legally consents for care under one of the state law exceptions, but communication of the treatment to the parents is necessary to obtain payment. Although state laws vary on the acceptability of notification in the form of billing, notifying parents in this fashion, when the care would otherwise be deemed confidential, may constitute an improper breach of confidentiality. For example, the Federal Drug and Alcohol Confidentiality Law regulations specifically prohibit this practice, stating that prohibitions against parental notification apply to "any disclosure of patient identifying information to the parent or guardian of a minor patient for the purpose of obtaining financial reimbursement."[31]

Substance Abuse

Substance abuse is widely recognized as one of the most serious and frequent health and social challenges facing adolescents.[35] The complex balance of the adolescent's interests, parental interests, and societal interests often generate difficult ethical and legal issues in this area. Legal questions about informed consent and confidentiality may be the most common.

As with other forms of medical evaluation and treatment, medical care for substance abuse must be preceded by valid informed consent. As discussed previously, adolescents generally lack the legal authority to provide valid informed consent for treatment. Because adolescents might be un-likely to seek needed care for substance abuse if parental involvement were required, most states have enacted laws that specifically authorize adolescents to provide informed consent for this treatment.[3] Additionally, most of these states also require that physicians maintain confidentiality about such treatment, even from the adolescent's parent or legal guardian.

Adolescent substance abuse may be the most commonly missed pediatric diagnosis. The AAP has encouraged pediatricians to screen for this condition[35] and has provided specific guidance on alcohol,[32] tobacco,[41] marijuana,[42] and inhalant[43] use, as well as indications for management and referral of patients.[44] The US Supreme Court has ruled that random drug testing of adolescents in school, as a condition of participation in extracurricular activities, is not unconstitutional.[45] Even under this ruling, however, drug testing is to be conducted with the consent of the adolescent as a condition of school activities. The very different situation of a parental request to involuntarily test an adolescent for the presence of drugs in blood or urine raises additional legal questions. As a practical matter, such a request may interfere with a pediatrician's attempt to work with the patient to overcome the problem. The AAP has opined that "involuntary testing is not appropriate in adolescents with decisional capacity—even with parental consent."[33] Complex and varied state laws may render such involuntary testing a violation of state confidentiality, informed consent, and privacy laws. Therefore, unless properly authorized and directed by law enforcement or the courts, pediatricians should decline to conduct involuntary substance abuse testing of adolescents.

Suicide

Suicide and suicide attempts are common among adolescents.[46] The evaluation and treatment of adolescents who have attempted suicide may raise a number of issues, including standard of care, informed consent, and confidentiality. Although no specific tests exist for identifying a suicidal individual, a number of risk factors have been identified.[46] Pediatricians should be aware of these risk factors and recommended management.

As with substance abuse, most states have enacted laws that permit adolescents to provide consent for treatment for mental health issues.[3] Such laws also generally convey a confidentiality right to the adolescent patient. Within the limits of these confidentiality laws, pediatricians should encourage adolescent patients to involve parents in their care.

Summary

The law recognizes that many situations involving adolescent patients differ from those involving younger or older patients. As a result, exceptions and variations to the usual rules of consent and confidentiality are common in this area of practice. Therefore, it is important for the pediatrician to be knowledgeable about laws that apply to adolescent care.

References

1. *Schloendorff v Society of New York Hospital*, 211 NY 125, 105 NE 92 (1914)

2. Reddy DM, Fleming R, Swain C. Effect of mandatory parental notification on adolescent girls' use of sexual health care services. *JAMA.* 2002;288(6):710–714. http://jama.ama-assn.org/content/288/6/710.full.pdf+html. Accessed May 9, 2011

3. Boonstra H, Nash E. Minors and the right to consent to health care. *The Guttmacher Report on Public Policy.* 2000;4–8. http://www.guttmacher.org/pubs/tgr/03/4/gr030404.pdf. Accessed May 9, 2011

4. McGuire AL, Bruce CR. Keeping children's secrets: confidentiality in the physician-patient relationship. *Houst J Health Law Policy.* 2008;8:315–333

5. Sigman GS, O'Connor C. Exploration for physicians of the mature minor doctrine. *J Pediatr.* 1991;119(4):520–525

6. *Shine v Vega*, 709 NE2d 58 (Mass 1999)

7. *Tabor v Scobee*, 254 SW2d 474 (Ky 1951)

8. *Troxel v Granville*, 530 US 57 (2000)

9. McDonnell WM. Between a rock and a hard place: when parents refuse treatment for their children in the ED. *ED Legal Letter.* 2008;19(1):6–8

10. *Prince v Massachusetts,* 321 US 158 (1944)

11. *Schmidt v Mutual Hospital Services, Inc.,* 832 NE2d 977 (Ind App 2005)

12. *Mueller v Auker,* 576 F3d 979 (9th Cir 2009)

13. *Cruzan v Director, Missouri Department of Health,* 497 US 261 (1990)

14. *Bouvia v Superior Court,* 179 Cal App3d 1127 (1986)

15. Patient Self Determination Act 1990, Pub L No. 101–508, codified at 42 USC 1395cc(a)

16. California Medical Association. *New Advance Health Care Directive Kit.* Sacramento, CA: California Medical Association; 2011

17. Requirements for permission by parents or guardians and for assent by children. 45 CFR §46.408

18. American Academy of Pediatrics Committee on Bioethics. Informed consent, parental permission, and assent in pediatric practice. *Pediatrics.* 1995;95(2):314–317

19. Confidentiality and disclosure in the physician-patient relationship. In: Furrow BR, Greaney TL, Johnson SH, Jost TS, Schwartz RL. *Health Law Cases, Materials and Problems.* 6th ed. St. Paul, MN: Thomson/West; 2008:289–326

20. *S.C. v Guardian ad litem,* 845 So2d 953 (Fla 4th DCA 2003)

21. Mont. Code Ann. § 41-1-403 (1995)

22. Tex. Fam. Code Ann. § 33.002

23. *Tarasoff v Regents of the University of California,* 551 P2d 334 (Cal 1976)

24. Madison AB, Feldman-Winter L, Finkel M, McAbee GN. Commentary: consensual adolescent sexual activity with adult partners—conflict between confidentiality and physician reporting requirements under child abuse laws. *Pediatrics.* 2001;107(2):e16

25. Health Insurance Portability and Accountability Act of 1996, Pub L No 104–191

26. US Department of Health and Human Services. Standards for privacy of individually identifiable health information. Final rule. *Fed Regist.* 2002;67(157):53181–53273, 45 CFR §§160.101 et seq. and §§164.102 et seq

27. Health Information Technology for Economic and Clinical Health Act, Title XIII of Division A and Title IV of Division B of the American Recovery and Reinvestment Act of 2009, Pub L No 111–5

28. Public Health Service Act (Title X), Family Planning Program. Pub L No 91-572, codified at 42 USC §§300–300a-6

29. US Department of Health and Human Services. Family planning. Office of Population Affairs Web site. http://www.hhs.gov/opa/familyplanning/index.html. Accessed May 18, 2011

30. Omnibus Budget Reconciliation Act of 1981, Pub L No. 97-35, §931(b)(1), 95 Stat. 570, codified at 42 USC §300(a)

31. Statutory Authority for Confidentiality of Drug Abuse Patient Records. 42 CFR 2.1 et seq

32. Kokotailo PK, American Academy of Pediatrics Committee on Substance Abuse. Alcohol use by youth and adolescents: a pediatric concern. *Pediatrics.* 2010;125(5):1078–1087

33. American Academy of Pediatrics Committee on Substance Abuse. Testing for drugs of abuse in children and adolescents. *Pediatrics.* 1996;98(2):305–307

34. Knight JR, Mears CJ, American Academy of Pediatrics Committee on Substance Abuse, Council on School Health. Testing for drugs of abuse in children and adolescents: addendum—testing in schools and at home. *Pediatrics.* 2007;119(3):627–630. http://pediatrics.aappublications.org/cgi/reprint/119/3/627. Accessed May 9, 2011

35. Kulig JW, American Academy of Pediatrics Committee on Substance Abuse. Tobacco, alcohol, and other drugs: the role of the pediatrician in prevention, identification, and management of substance abuse. *Pediatrics.* 2005;115(3):816–821. http://pediatrics.aappublications.org/cgi/reprint/115/3/816. Accessed May 9, 2011

36. Klein JD, American Academy of Pediatrics Committee on Adolescence. Adolescent pregnancy: current trends and issues. *Pediatrics.* 2005;116(1):281–286

37. Kaufman M, American Academy of Pediatrics Committee on Adolescence. Care of the adolescent sexual assault victim. *Pediatrics.* 2008;122(2):462–470

38. Blythe MJ, Diaz A, American Academy of Pediatrics Committee on Adolescence. Contraception and adolescents. *Pediatrics.* 2007;120(5):1135–1148. http://pediatrics.aappublications.org/cgi/reprint/120/5/1135. Accessed May 9, 2011

39. American Academy of Pediatrics Committee on Adolescence. The adolescent's right to confidential care when considering abortion. *Pediatrics.* 1996;97(5):746–751

40. *Accent Service Company v Ebsen,* 306 NW2d 575 (Neb 1981)

41. American Academy of Pediatrics Committee on Environmental Health, Committee on Substance Abuse, Committee on Adolescence, Committee on Native American Child Health. Tobacco use: a pediatric disease. *Pediatrics.* 2009;124(5):1474–1487. http://pediatrics.aappublications.org/cgi/reprint/124/5/1474. Accessed May 9, 2011

42. Heyman RB, Anglin TM, Copperman SM, American Academy of Pediatrics Committee on Substance Abuse. Marijuana: a continuing concern for pediatricians. *Pediatrics.* 1999;104(4):982–985

43. Williams JF, Storck M, American Academy of Pediatrics Committee on Substance Abuse, Committee on Native American Child Health. Inhalant abuse. *Pediatrics.* 2007;119(5):1009–1017. http://pediatrics.aappublications.org/cgi/reprint/119/5/1009. Accessed May 9, 2011

44. American Academy of Pediatrics Committee on Substance Abuse. Indications for management and referral of patients involved in substance abuse. *Pediatrics.* 2000;106(1):143–148

45. *Board of Education v Earls,* 536 US 822 (2002)

46. Shain BN, American Academy of Pediatrics Committee on Adolescence, American Academy of Child and Adolescent Psychiatry. Suicide and suicide attempts in adolescents. *Pediatrics.* 2007;120(3):669–676. http://pediatrics.aappublications.org/cgi/reprint/120/3/669. Accessed May 9, 2011

CHAPTER 10

Pediatric Emergency Medicine

William M. McDonnell, MD, JD, FAAP

- -

KEY CONCEPTS

- Emergency Medical Treatment and Labor Act
- Unique Risks
- Medical Records
- Consent for Treatment
- Informed Refusal
- Child Protection
- Coordinating Care
- Nonurgent Care
- Adolescent Assault Victims
- Death of a Child
- Physicians' Liability During Disasters

One of the more common sources of medically related lawsuits is emergency department (ED) encounters. The pediatric ED is a high-pressure, high-volume area of the hospital where physicians often treat children and adolescents who are seriously ill and injured. This environment, which often requires rapid clinical decision-making and involves frequent interruptions, may contribute to adverse outcomes and medical errors.[1–3] Patients and parents in the ED setting may be more likely to be upset by their illnesses, long waiting times, seemingly bureaucratic registration systems, and crowded, uncomfortable waiting areas. The visit with the ED physician may seem impersonal and

brief. With no preexisting physician-patient relationship, it may be difficult for the ED pediatrician to establish a rapport with the family. Under these circumstances, the family may be more likely to be dissatisfied with the care provided and more likely to blame (and sue) the physician for any adverse outcome.[4] More than 4,300 claims of negligence in the care of children were closed against emergency physicians and pediatric emergency physicians from 1985 to 2008, and more than $225 million was paid. Payment was made for 26% of these claims, and the average indemnity for a paid claim against an emergency physician during this period was $199,000.[5]

Emergency Medical Treatment and Labor Act

One of the most relevant and important legal principles for physicians providing care in the emergency department is the Emergency Medical Treatment and Labor Act (EMTALA).[6] Although EMTALA specifies emergency evaluation and treatment with some particularity, and provides substantial penalties for violations, pediatricians of all practice types tend to be unaware of the law and its requirements.[7] The act broadly applies to physicians who encounter patients with emergency medical conditions in the hospital, including ED physicians, physicians on call to the ED, and even physicians who work in areas of the hospital outside of the ED but encounter patients seeking emergency care (eg, the grandparent who suffers chest pain while visiting an inpatient grandchild on the pediatric floor). The act extends to hospital-owned urgent care centers and the physicians who work in them, even when urgent care centers are located away from the main hospital campus.

Physicians historically retained the choice of whether to enter into a physician-patient relationship and provide care to any particular person, but the US Congress eliminated the optional nature of emergency care by passing EMTALA in 1985. To "deal with the problem of patients being turned away from emergency rooms for non-medical reasons,"[8] and specifically because Congress was "concerned about the increasing number of reports that hospital emergency rooms are refusing to accept or treat patients with emergency conditions if the patient does not have medical insurance,"[9] EMTALA requires physicians to properly evaluate every patient and stabilize all emergency medical conditions regardless of the patient's ability (or intention) to pay. Physicians are required to follow appropriate procedures when transferring patients from the ED, and physicians who are on call to the ED must respond in a timely fashion. Violations of the law can be punished by substantial monetary penalties or possible exclusion from Medicare and Medicaid. Additionally, hospitals face potential personal injury damages under EMTALA. As discussed later in this chapter, plaintiffs may also bring separate legal claims, distinct from EMTALA claims, against hospitals and physicians for medical malpractice.

At the core of EMTALA obligations is the requirement that hospital EDs provide an "appropriate" medical screening examination (MSE) to all persons who come to any location on the hospital campus requesting examination or treatment for a possible emergency condition.[10] The MSE must be provided by a physician or other medical person designated by the hospital's rules or bylaws, and must be sufficient to reasonably determine under the circumstances whether an emergency medical condition exists.[11] Not all MSEs need be equally

extensive. Depending on the nature of the patient's complaint and presenting condition, an appropriate MSE may require laboratory, radiologic, or other diagnostic testing, or specialty consultation. On the other hand, some minor complaints might require no more than a brief history, vital signs, and a limited physical examination.[12] The MSE may not be delayed to inquire about payment or insurance status. An emergency condition is a medical condition with acute symptoms (including pain) sufficiently severe such that lack of immediate medical treatment could reasonably result in serious jeopardy to the health of the person, serious impairment to bodily function, or serious dysfunction of an organ or body part.[6]

If the MSE reveals an emergency condition, the hospital and treating physician must stabilize the condition, to the extent that they are able, prior to discharge or transfer. An emergency condition is considered to be stabilized if all necessary medical treatment has been provided to ensure that material deterioration of the condition is not likely to result from discharge or transfer. The services of an on-call physician specialist may be required to stabilize a patient. The Emergency Medical Treatment and Labor Act specifically applies to on-call physicians, and if the on-call physician does not come to the ED within a reasonable period, leading to the patient's deterioration or transfer to another facility, the on-call physician is subject to EMTALA liability.

In some cases, hospitals may lack resources and expertise to stabilize a particular emergency condition. In such cases, the patient may be transferred to another facility prior to stabilization if all of the following are true: the patient requests the transfer in writing or the physician certifies in writing that the medical benefits of appropriate treatment at another facility outweigh the risks of the transfer; the accepting facility agrees to accept the patient; the transferring facility sends all relevant medical records; and the transferring facility sends the patient with appropriate personnel and equipment.[6] A receiving facility with specialized capabilities needed by the patient and not available at the transferring facility must agree to accept the transfer and to treat the patient if it has available space and qualified personnel.

The potential penalties for EMTALA violations are substantial. Each violation of EMTALA carries a civil penalty of up to $50,000. Physicians should be aware that investigators may determine that multiple, distinct violations have occurred in a single patient encounter, leading to monetary penalties far in excess of $50,000. For example, when a patient is discharged without discovery of an emergency condition, the hospital may have violated the MSE, stabilization, and appropriate transfer requirements (discharge constitutes a transfer under EMTALA). Physicians and hospitals found to have violated EMTALA may also be excluded from participation in Medicare, Medicaid, and other government health care financing programs. Although violations that pose an immediate and serious risk to public safety will be placed on the so-called fast track to termination through a 23-day process, any unresolved EMTALA violation can result in termination through the more deliberate 90-day process.[13] Finally, patients may sue hospitals (but not individual physicians) to recover personal injury damages arising from EMTALA violations.

Although EMTALA was initially enacted to prevent discrimination against patients who lack financial resources to pay for their care, it is the actions of the physician that meet or fail to meet EMTALA requirements that will determine liability. It is not necessary to show improper motives by the physician to find an EMTALA violation.[14] Ignorance of the law is not protective. In 1990, Congress amended the law to allow enforcement actions even when physicians and hospitals are unaware of their own violations of EMTALA.

Claims for medical malpractice arise under state law and vary from state to state. As a federal law, EMTALA does not take the place of or limit any malpractice claim under state law. Instead, it offers another, sometimes easier way for a plaintiff to make a claim for damages. An EMTALA claim may be more favorable to a plaintiff by avoiding state law limitations on damages or other substantive or procedural barriers under state law.[15,16]

When treating children in the hospital environment, physicians should treat all patients without regard to their ability to pay or the method of payment. In the ED, all patients should be given an examination appropriate for their complaint and presenting condition, including diagnostic studies and specialty consultations when medically indicated. Pediatricians and pediatric subspecialists who provide on-call coverage to hospital EDs must respond promptly to requests for consultation from the ED physician. Pediatric subspecialists who practice in units that provide specialized care to children should accept requests for transfer from other facilities when patients need the special service and the unit has capacity to treat them.

Unique Risks

Practice in the ED setting presents particular legal risks to physicians. Emergency departments have experienced a steady increase in the volume and acuity of patient visits.[17] Even with increased attention to patient safety, the care of children in the ED is especially prone to error and subsequent litigation.[18] Medical errors and adverse outcomes are more likely to occur with children treated in the ED on weekends or holidays, or at night.[19] Children brought for care at these times may be more likely to be seriously ill; the risk of crowding is higher; and patients are more likely to leave the ED without being fully evaluated and treated.[20,21] Physicians should be aware that malpractice lawsuits are sometimes brought in cases with poor outcomes, even if the medical care was entirely appropriate.

Allegations of diagnostic error account for about half of the medical malpractice lawsuits involving care of children in the ED.[20] Additional cases are commonly premised on allegations of improper performance of a procedure, failure to properly supervise staff, failure to perform an indicated procedure, and improper delay in treatment.[20] Medical diagnoses commonly associated with pediatric ED malpractice claims include meningitis, neurologically impaired newborns, and pneumonia in lawsuits involving children younger than 2 years; fracture, meningitis, and appendicitis in lawsuits involving children from 3 to 11 years of age; and fractures, appendicitis, and testicular torsion in lawsuits involving children from 12 to 17 years of age.[20,22]

Meningitis, appendicitis, and numerous other pediatric conditions can be medically and legally risky in the ED setting. Pediatricians in the ED should take particular caution to provide the most appropriate care when these conditions are suspected. Physicians should recall that under EMTALA, discharging a patient from the ED who has an unstable emergency medical condition constitutes an improper transfer, risking medical malpractice and EMTALA claims. Lack of an established and continuing patient relationship may pose increased liability risks. Emergency department physicians may substantially lessen this risk by encouraging and facilitating primary care follow-up and communicating with the primary care practitioner when feasible and appropriate.[23]

Medical Records

State laws require that ED pediatricians, like all physicians, document their findings appropriately in the medical record. Careful documentation is not only a compliance requirement, but it is also an important risk management measure. Medical malpractice cases are considered complex litigation, commonly taking more than 2 years, and sometimes as long as 5 years, to go to trial.[24]

Pediatricians may not remember the details of a patient encounter when litigation arises months or even years later, and the medical record may provide the only reliable source of information. The medical record can be invaluable to the defense of a malpractice action if it is well documented and contemporaneous with the events of the case. On the other hand, carelessly worded entries can be harmful to the pediatrician and a powerful tool for the plaintiff's attorney.[25]

Records should be legible and concise but complete enough to substantiate the care that was provided. The history should contain all important information relevant to the chief complaint. Such relevant information may include home medications, activity levels, and how well the child was eating or drinking. The physical examination must include all important findings, including vital signs. Important positive and negative findings should be documented. The child's general appearance, state of hydration, and level of activity will often be important. Injuries should be described with pictures or diagrams when appropriate. Notes should be dated and timed and should document any specialist consultations. If laboratory tests or radiographs were obtained, results should be recorded or referenced to another location in the medical record. Serial physical examinations should also be documented, including improvements in the patient's condition, and if the child was well appearing at the time of discharge, this should be reflected in the note.

With limited options for continuity of care, discharge instructions are particularly important. Instructions for home care, recommendations for follow-up treatment and reevaluations, and return instructions should be carefully noted. Communications with the patient's primary care practitioner about follow-up arrangements should be described in the record.[23] Clear, preprinted handout instructions may be very useful but should always be explained verbally as well, and oral communication should be documented in the record. The parent should be asked to sign the medical record, indicating that he or she understands the discharge instructions.

In the medical record, the physician should avoid all but the most widely accepted abbreviations and avoid insensitive terms such as FLK (funny-looking kid) in the records. Such coded comments in the medical record will not remain hidden in any subsequent litigation. Inflammatory statements should be left out of the record. Nursing and physician notes should be consistent. If errors in the record are discovered, they should be corrected with a single line (dated and initialed) that does not hide the error, and the accurate information then added.

Consent for Treatment

Informed consent rules present particular challenges in the ED. The general principles of informed consent apply in the ED as they do in all US health care settings. To protect individuals' autonomy and unwanted bodily contact, physicians must obtain the agreement of the patient prior to any physical contact. It is well established in American law that "Every human being of adult years and sound mind has a right to determine what shall be done with his own body."[26] Unlike competent adults, however, minor children lack the legal authority to provide informed consent for medical care. Instead, parents have the right and authority to make decisions about medical treatment for their minor children.[27] Therefore, parents accompanying their children to the ED should be consulted for permission to evaluate and treat the child. Updates about risks, benefits, and alternatives should be regularly provided. It is well established that parents may sue for the failure to obtain consent prior to treatment of their children.[28] Recent state supreme court decisions suggest that this legal claim for failure to obtain informed consent may be expanding, finding that plaintiffs may recover on informed consent claims even when the medical care was appropriate.[29,30]

Pediatricians' informed consent obligations become more complex when children are seen without a parent or legal guardian present. When an accompanying teacher, sibling, or neighbor does not have the authority to give consent for treatment, reasonable efforts should be made to contact the legal guardian. This effort and telephone consent for treatment, if obtained, should be obtained over a permit line and recorded in the medical record.

However, the unique characteristics of emergency care have led to some special informed consent rules in the ED setting. The Emergency Medical Treatment and Labor Act requires that hospitals and physicians provide an appropriate MSE and any necessary stabilizing treatment to every patient who presents to the ED and for whom treatment is requested. The law allows anyone, even a bystander, to request treatment on the child's behalf, and even the obvious presence of signs or symptoms of an emergency condition will be sufficient to imply a request for treatment. Therefore, ED physicians are legally obligated to evaluate and stabilize pediatric patients with potential emergency conditions, even if no legal guardian is available to provide consent. On the other hand, if the patient has no emergency condition or the emergency condition has been stabilized, EMTALA requirements and authority are concluded, and informed consent must be obtained prior to any further treatment.[31]

In addition to EMTALA, a number of state law principles limit informed consent rules in the ED, and in some circumstances allow for treatment without express parental consent. Most states have adopted the *emergency exception* to informed consent. Rather than overriding the requirement for informed consent, the emergency exception allows the physician to infer consent under particular conditions as set forth in state law. In most states, these conditions include a serious threat to life or health; a need for urgent intervention; circumstances under which reasonable parents would have given consent if they were able (an objective standard);

no available option existing for obtaining actual informed consent; and the health care provider having no reason to believe that this particular patient's legal guardian would refuse consent (a subjective standard; eg, a previously expressed religious objection to a particular treatment, which might not be thought objectionable to a reasonable parent, would nonetheless prevent the use of this exception).[32] If the patient's condition does not immediately require urgent intervention, the fact that the proposed treatment may be medically advisable or may become essential at some future time is not sufficient to allow treatment under this exception.[33] Pediatricians who work in the ED should be aware of their own states' specific rules in this area.

Another area in which state laws make certain exceptions to the informed consent rules is for *emancipated minors*. Each state has its own rules for adolescents who meet specific criteria such as marriage, military service, and independent living to be classified as emancipated and therefore adults in the eyes of law. These emancipated minors are permitted to provide (or refuse) informed consent as adults. When patients have been legally emancipated, they should be treated by the physician as adults, with the same rights and responsibilities of providing informed consent.

Some state laws also allow minors who are not emancipated to provide their own informed consent for particular classes of treatment such as reproductive health, sexually transmitted infections (STIs), substance abuse, and mental health. Minors who are sexually active, pregnant, or infected with an STI, and those who abuse drugs or alcohol or suffer from emotional or psychological problems, may avoid seeking care if they must involve their parents. Recognizing this, many states explicitly authorize minors to provide consent for care for one or more of these conditions.[34,35] State laws vary widely in this area, and physicians should be aware of their local laws.

Finally, some states' courts have applied the *mature minor doctrine* in certain circumstances. Under this legal principle, older children who demonstrate a clear understanding of medical risks and benefits have been permitted to provide or refuse their own consent for medical care.[36] This designation of a mature minor may be applied based on case law precedents or particular state laws,[36] but in either event it is applied by judges, not physicians, and is done on a case-by-case basis. Pediatricians should never assume that mature minor status will apply until so ordered by a court.

Informed Refusal

Parents in the ED sometimes refuse to allow pediatricians to give recommended treatment to their children. Within limits, the law permits parents to make decisions concerning the care, custody, and control of their children, including medical treatment.[37] Therefore, parents have considerable latitude in deciding to refuse consent for care. As discussed previously, informed consent is necessary before treatment can proceed, and the physician who treats a minor child despite parental refusal, in the absence of one of the specific consent exceptions, faces civil and possibly criminal liability.[27]

The most effective means of overcoming the legal risks associated with treatment without informed consent is to obtain that needed consent. When a parent refuses recommended care for the child in the ED, physicians should explore what the parent objects to and the reasons for that objection. Simple miscommunications and misunderstandings may be the most common sources of refusals. Within the limits of patient privacy and confidentiality rules such as HIPAA, the pediatrician may find it helpful to involve other physicians in the ED, the patient's primary care practitioner, or other family members in the discussion.[38,39]

In some instances, a parent's refusal to provide consent for treatment may rise to the level of medical neglect or child abuse. All states have enacted some form of mandatory reporting law for abuse and neglect of children. In cases in which the consent refusal would reasonably be interpreted as medical neglect, the physician is obligated to report the situation to appropriate child protective services or law enforcement. State agencies and courts have the authority to override parent refusals and to provide consent for medical care on the child's behalf. Pediatricians should be aware that it is the state authority, not the physician, who makes the decision to overrule parent refusal and provide the necessary consent.[40] Some states specifically grant physicians, hospital administrators, or other medical personnel temporary authority to hold a pediatric patient in the ED against the parent's wishes until the physician or hospital personnel can communicate with state authorities. This authority varies widely among states, and physicians should be aware of their own state laws. Physicians reporting their suspicions of medical neglect are usually immunized from liability, so long as they do so in good faith. However, if they deliberately or recklessly misrepresent facts or medical risks to state authorities to convince those authorities to intervene, physicians risk liability.[41]

When parents refuse recommended treatment but such refusal is a reasonable choice that does not rise to the level of medical neglect, the physician should carefully document the options, risks, and benefits that were discussed, and the parents' choice. The physician should also document why or why not such refusal of recommended care amounted to medical neglect, and why or why not this led the physician to contact child welfare authorities.

Child Protection

In all states, physicians in the ED have reporting obligations when the physician has a reasonable suspicion of child abuse. State laws vary widely, but many allow a physician or hospital to detain a child against parental wishes to leave the facility when child abuse is suspected, until law enforcement or child welfare authorities can be contacted. Physicians are cautioned that their legal authority in this area is very state specific, and what may be specifically authorized behavior in some states may constitute illegal imprisonment in others. Individual state rules in this area should be thoroughly explored before the situation arises.

Coordinating Care

Pediatric patients are sometimes referred to the ED by private pediatricians who plan to examine and treat them in the ED. The Emergency Medical Treatment and Labor Act allows the hospital to provide MSEs for a patient by any health care professional specifically authorized by the hospital. However, any significant delay in evaluation and stabilizing care should not be permitted. The presumption should be that any patient arriving at the ED will be seen by the ED physician. If care in the ED is to be conducted by or transferred to a private pediatrician, this arrangement should be discussed by both physicians and carefully documented in the medical record.[23]

Good communication with referring pediatricians may also be beneficial when the referring pediatrician will not be managing the child in the ED. The private pediatrician should not expect to call in orders by telephone for the ED physician. The American College of Emergency Physicians has noted that orders for ED patients that are dictated by a physician from outside the ED can adversely affect the quality of medical care that patients receive and create legal liability for physicians.[42] Rather, the ED physician must examine the child prior to treatment. If a disagreement about management or the need for admission cannot be settled over the phone, the private pediatrician may come to the hospital to take over care of the child.

Parents often bring a child to the ED seeking a second opinion or additional care that they believe was improperly denied by their pediatrician. These patients should be treated just as any other patient by the ED staff, with an appropriate screening examination and any necessary stabilizing care. Good communication with the private pediatrician is important. The ED staff should ask parents if they wish to have the private pediatrician informed of the ED visit and explain the value of this communication. Communication between the ED physician and primary care pediatrician facilitates clear responsibilities for follow-up care.[23]

Nonurgent Care

Historically, managed care organizations (MCOs) often requested that EDs obtain approval for ED care of MCO patients prior to evaluation and treatment in the ED. Through this pre-approval process, MCOs sought to reduce ED care for non-emergent conditions. However, EMTALA clearly requires that EDs treat all patients in the same fashion, regardless of insurance status. All patients must receive a screening evaluation and any necessary stabilizing care, regardless of their insurer and of the insurer's approval or disapproval of the visit.[12] This EMTALA obligation extends to every patient seeking treatment in the ED for any medical condition.[12]

In recent years, states have widely adopted laws that require insurers to provide coverage of ED care in all cases in which a "prudent layperson" would have thought that the child had an emergency condition.[43] Although some have speculated that these prudent layperson laws and EMTALA together have contributed to ED overcrowding for nonurgent care, research suggests that hospital inpatient capacity, critical care resources, and lack of adequate primary care resources are the primary contributors to ED crowding.[17,44–46] The American Academy of Pediatrics has recognized that "surprisingly, this saturation of emergency services is not primarily a result of excessive, inappropriate use of the ED by those with non-emergent problems. It is

a by-product of increasing numbers of patients with serious illnesses or injuries requiring hospital and/or intensive care unit admission."[17]

Adolescent Assault Victims

Health care professionals for children and adolescents have a responsibility to find the best possible means to treat victims of violence, with the goal of promoting healing and reducing the risk of future adverse outcomes. Achieving this goal will require a comprehensive understanding of the consequences of violent injury for adolescents and integrated care plans that involve a range of disciplines and care settings. A stepwise approach to the treatment of adolescent victims of violence is often helpful. Health care professionals can build on current knowledge of violence epidemiology, adolescent development and psychology, trauma care, rehabilitation, and community involvement to treat patients ever more systematically and successfully. Careful evaluation of how victims of violence respond to treatment may help determine what works best and how treatment may be further improved.[47] From a legal standpoint, violent assaults against adolescents, particularly when conducted by adult perpetrators, will often meet the definition of child abuse in most states. Therefore, physicians caring for these patients will usually have an obligation to report such incidents to law enforcement authorities or child welfare officials. With respect to "consensual" sexual relations between an adolescent and an adult, there is wide variation and often ambiguous language in state laws that may impose on physicians a legal obligation to report the sexual activity.[48] A clear understanding of relevant state laws is essential.

Death of a Child

Although the death of a child in the ED may be a relatively uncommon event, a substantial portion of child deaths occur in hospital EDs or on arrival at EDs.[49] Such deaths impose a number of ethical and legal obligations on physicians. A team-oriented approach may be most effective in addressing the myriad social, emotional, and legal issues surrounding the child's death.[50] The team may include a range of professionals, such as emergency medical technicians and paramedics, social workers, child life workers, mental health professionals, the family's religious or spiritual leader, nurses, and physicians.

In most jurisdictions, the sudden and unexpected death of a child occurring in the field or ED is considered a medical examiner's case requiring an autopsy. These legal requirements must be explained to the family. Although health care professionals and family members may understandably wish to continue diagnostic efforts to determine the cause of death or remove medical devices to "clean up" the body, physicians should be aware of state medical examiner laws that often will prohibit any further interventions after death is pronounced, including removal of lines or tubes or obtaining any biological specimens. Nonetheless, the ED team can be sensitive and supportive by cleaning the resuscitation area, covering disfiguring injuries and wounds as much as possible with clean sheets, and carefully explaining the purpose of indwelling tubes or lines.[50]

Emergency departments should have written policies and procedures with accompanying checklists to be instituted in the event of a child's death. Such policies and checklists will help ED staff comply with state law requirements addressing medical examiner notification, requests for organ and tissue donation, and preservation of potential evidence. Emergency departments may choose to include bereavement support services in these policies and checklists, such as clergy notification, notification of primary care physician, funeral information, support group information, and memorial services including casts of handprints or footprints and locks of hair. As with any other ED encounter, documentation remains important. The physician

should ensure an accurate and detailed medical record that includes details of any resuscitation or other treatment, notation of the time of death, the child's history and circumstances leading to the death, the physical examination including vital signs on arrival, notation of any diagnostic study results, and communications with parents or guardians, medical examiner, primary care provider, child protective services, and law enforcement.

Pediatricians' Liability During Disasters

Disasters—unforeseen and often sudden events that cause great damage, destruction, and human suffering—may be natural (eg, earthquakes, hurricanes, tornadoes, floods) or artificial (eg, fire, mass-transportation incidents, environmental toxins, civil unrest).[51] Pediatricians not only play a crucial role in disaster planning but may also provide desperately needed triage and treatment services following a disaster. They may be called on to respond to treat victims at the scene, at casualty collection points, at hospitals (where they may not have privileges), or at shelters. Such care may be regulated by a number of laws and rules and may present unique potential legal liabilities.

Medical malpractice exposure may be a significant risk. Most malpractice insurance coverage is limited to the physician's usual scope of practice and practice setting.[52] Although precise coverage limits will depend on the particular malpractice insurance policy, policies may not cover medical activity for a disaster in another state. Many policies do not cover out-of-office care or the expanded scope of practice that may be required during a disaster. One alternate source of liability protection may be state Good Samaritan laws. All states have adopted some variation of these laws, designed to encourage prompt and voluntary emergency care by removing the threat of liability. Pediatricians should be aware that Good Samaritan protections usually cover only voluntary acts as opposed to paid services or services that are legally required. Therefore, any payment for services, including meals and lodging, will generally void the legal protections of these laws. There is wide variation in these state laws, and pediatricians would be wise to consult with legal counsel in advance about their own laws.[53]

Another potential protection for physicians treating victims in the aftermath of a disaster is immunity provided by governmental entities. When providers practice under the auspices of an official disaster agency, such as the Federal Emergency Management Agency, the Department of Health and Human Services, a local emergency medical services authority, or other recognized governmental body, governmental immunity may protect against claims of medical negligence. Physicians who decide to provide care through one of these governmental agencies should expressly inquire about legal protections provided by these agencies.

Conclusion

A combination of clinical, psychosocial, communication, and legal features of the ED make it a potentially high-risk legal environment for pediatricians. A modest investment of time and effort by pediatricians toward learning about the most relevant federal and state laws, including rules addressing emergency treatment obligations, informed consent, confidentiality, and reporting obligations, may substantially reduce potential legal risks.

References

1. Westbrook JI, Coiera E, Dunsmuir WT, et al. The impact of interruptions on clinical task completion. *Qual Saf Health Care.* 2010;19(4):284–289

2. Williams BG, Hlaing T, Aaland MO. Ten-year retrospective study of delayed diagnosis of injury in pediatric trauma patients at a level II trauma center. *Pediatr Emerg Care.* 2009;25(8):489–493

3. Larose G, Bailey B, Lebel D. Quality of orders for medication in the resuscitation room of a pediatric emergency department. *Pediatr Emerg Care.* 2008;24(9):609–614

4. Hickson GB, Clayton EW, Githens PB, Sloan FA. Factors that prompted families to file medical malpractice claims following perinatal injuries. *JAMA.* 1992;267(10):1359–1363

5. Physician Insurers Association of America. *Risk Management Review of Malpractice Claims—Pediatrics.* Rockville, MD: Physician Insurers Association of America; 2008

6. Emergency Medical Treatment and Labor Act, Pub L No. 99-272, Title IX, Section 97

7. McDonnell WM, Roosevelt GE, Bothner JP. Deficits in EMTALA knowledge among pediatric physicians. *Pediatr Emerg Care.* 2006;22(8):555–561

8. *Bryan v Rectors and Visitors of the University of Virginia,* 95 F3d 349 (4th Cir 1996)

9. *Correa v Hospital San Francisco,* 69 F3d 1184, 1189 (1st Cir 1995)

10. McDonnell WM. Clearing the fog (a bit): the 2003 EMTALA regulations and their implications for pediatric emergency departments. *Pediatr Emerg Care.* 2004;20(8):536–539

11. *Baber v Hospital Corporation of America,* 977 F2d 872 (4th Cir 1992)

12. US Department of Health and Human Services, Centers for Medicare and Medicaid Services. Medicare program; clarifying policies related to the responsibilities of Medicare-participating hospitals in treating individuals with emergency medical conditions. Final rule. *Fed Regist.* 2003;68(174):53222–53264

13. US Department of Health and Human Services, Centers for Medicare and Medicaid Services. Appendix V—interpretive guidelines—responsibilities of Medicare participating hospitals in emergency cases. In: *State Operations Manual.* 2010. http://www.cms.gov/manuals/Downloads/som107ap_v_emerg.pdf. Accessed May 5, 2011

14. *Roberts v Galen of Virginia, Inc.,* 525 US 249 (1999)

15. *Romar v Fresno Community Hospital and Medical Center,* 583 F Supp 2d 1197 (ED Cal. 2008)

16. *Cooper v Gulf Breeze Hospital, Inc.,* 839 F Supp 1538 (ND Fla 1993)

17. American Academy of Pediatrics Committee on Pediatric Emergency Medicine. Overcrowding crisis in our nation's emergency departments: is our safety net unraveling? *Pediatrics.* 2004;114(3):878–888. http://pediatrics.aappublications.org/cgi/reprint/114/3/878. Accessed May 4, 2011

18. Krug SE, Frush K, American Academy of Pediatrics Committee on Pediatric Emergency Medicine. Patient safety in the pediatric emergency care setting. *Pediatrics.* 2007;120(6):1367–1375. http://pediatrics.aappublications.org/cgi/reprint/120/6/1367. Accessed May 4, 2011

19. Kozer E, Scolnik D, Macpherson A, et al. Variables associated with medication errors in pediatric emergency medicine. *Pediatrics.* 2002;110(4):737–742. http://pediatrics. aappublications.org/cgi/reprint/110/4/737. Accessed May 4, 2011

20. Selbst SM, Friedman MJ, Singh SB. Epidemiology and etiology of malpractice lawsuits involving children in US emergency departments and urgent care centers. *Pediatr Emerg Care.* 2005;21(3):165–169

21. Cross KP, Cammack VH, Calhoun AW, et al. Premature departure from the pediatric emergency department: a cohort analysis of process- and patient-related factors. *Pediatr Emerg Care.* 2010;26(5):349–356

22. McAbee GN, Donn SM, Mendelson RA, McDonnell WM, Gonzalez JL, Ake JK. Medical diagnoses commonly associated with pediatric malpractice lawsuits in the United States. *Pediatrics.* 2008;122(6):e1282–e1286. http://pediatrics.aappublications.org/cgi/reprint/122/6/e1282. Accessed May 4, 2011

23. Selbst SM. Communication between ED physician, pediatrician can head off malpractice suits. *AAP News.* 2008;29(10):26

24. Legislative Subcommittee to Study Medical Malpractice. *Legislative Counsel Bureau Bulletin No. 03-9.* 2003. http://www.leg.state.nv.us/Division/Research/Publications/InterimReports/2003/Bulletin03-09.pdf. Accessed May 6, 2011

25. Donn SM. Medical record can be invaluable in malpractice case. *AAP News.* 2004;25(7):12

26. *Schloendorff v Society of New York Hospital,* 211 NY 125, 105 NE 92 (1914)

27. McDonnell WM. Between a rock and a hard place: when parents refuse treatment for their children in the ED. *ED Legal Letter.* 2008;19(1):6–8

28. Veilleux DR. Medical practitioner's liability for treatment given a child without parent's consent. *Am Law Rep.* 1989;67:511–534

29. *Bubb v Brusky,* 768 NW2d 903 (Wis 2009)

30. *McQuitty v Spangler,* 976 A2d 1020 (Md 2009)

31. American Academy of Pediatrics Committee on Pediatric Emergency Medicine. Consent for emergency medical services for children and adolescents. *Pediatrics.* 2003;111(3):703–706. http://pediatrics.aappublications.org/cgi/reprint/111/3/703. Accessed May 4, 2011

32. *Shine v Vega,* 709 NE2d 58 (Mass 1999)

33. *Tabor v Scobee,* 254 SW2d 474 (Ky 1951)

34. Boonstra H, Nash E. Minors and the right to consent to health care. *The Guttmacher Report on Public Policy.* 2000:4–8. http://www.guttmacher.org/pubs/tgr/03/4/gr030404.pdf. Accessed May 9, 2011

35. Guttmacher Institute. An overview of minors' consent law. *Guttmacher Institute State Policies in Brief.* 2011. http://www.guttmacher.org/statecenter/spibs/spib_OMCL.pdf. Accessed May 9, 2011

36. McGuire AL, Bruce CR. Keeping children's secrets: confidentiality in the physician-patient relationship. *Houst J Health Law Policy.* 2008;8:315–333. http://www.law.uh.edu/hjhlp/Issues/Vol_82/McGuire.pdf. Accessed May 9, 2011

37. *Troxel v Granville,* 530 US 57 (2000)

38. O'Malley PJ, Brown K, Krug SE, American Academy of Pediatrics Committee on Pediatric Emergency Medicine. Patient- and family-centered care of children in the emergency department. *Pediatrics.* 2008;122(2):e511–e521 http://pediatrics.aappublications.org/cgi/reprint/122/2/e511. Accessed May 4, 2011

39. Roberts JR. InFocus: lack of liability protections with standard AMA forms. *Emerg Med News.* 2010;32(6):12–15

40. *Schmidt v Mutual Hospital Services, Inc.,* 832 NE2d 977 (Ind App 2005)

41. *Mueller v Auker,* 576 F3rd 979 (9th Cir 2009)

42. American College of Emergency Physicians. Policy statement: telephone orders in the emergency department. 2008. http://www.acep.org/practres.aspx?id=29696. Accessed May 9, 2011

43. McDonnell WM, Guenther E, Larsen LF, Schunk J. The reimbursement gap: providing and paying for pediatric procedural sedation in the emergency department. *Pediatr Emerg Care.* 2009;25(11):797–802

44. McCabe JB. Emergency department overcrowding: a national crisis. *Acad Med.* 2001;76(7):672–674

45. Forster AJ, Stiell I, Wells G, Lee AJ, van Walraven C. The effect of hospital occupancy on emergency department length of stay and patient disposition. *Acad Emerg Med.* 2003;10(2):127–133

46. Rathlev NK, Chessare J, Olshaker J, et al. Time series analysis of variables associated with daily mean emergency department length of stay. *Ann Emerg Med.* 2007;49(3):265–271

47. Krug SE, Tuggle DW, American Academy of Pediatrics Section on Orthopaedics, Committee on Pediatric Emergency Medicine, Section on Critical Care, Section on Surgery, Section on Transport Medicine, Committee on Pediatric Emergency Medicine, Pediatric Orthopaedic Society of North America. Management of pediatric trauma. *Pediatrics.* 2008;121(4):849–854. http://pediatrics.aappublications.org/cgi/reprint/121/4/849. Accessed May 4, 2011

48. Madison AB, Feldman-Winter L, Finkel M, McAbee GN. Commentary: consensual adolescent sexual activity with adult partners—conflict between confidentiality and physician reporting requirements under child abuse laws. *Pediatrics.* 2001;107(2):e16

49. Patterns of childhood death in America. In: Field MJ, Behrman RE, eds. *When Children Die: Improving Palliative and End-of-Life Care for Children and Their Families.* Washington, DC: National Academy Press; 2003:41–71

50. Knapp J, Mulligan-Smith D, American Academy of Pediatrics Committee on Pediatric Emergency Medicine. Death of a child in the emergency department. *Pediatrics.* 2005;115(5):1432–1437. http://pediatrics.aappublications. org/cgi/reprint/115/5/1432. Accessed May 4, 2011

51. Markenson D, Reynolds S, American Academy of Pediatrics Committee on Pediatric Emergency Medicine, Task Force on Terrorism. The pediatrician and disaster preparedness. *Pediatrics.* 2006;117(2):e340–e362

52. American Academy of Pediatrics Committee on Pediatric Emergency Medicine, Committee on Medical Liability, Task Force on Terrorism. The pediatrician and disaster preparedness. *Pediatrics.* 2006;117(2):560–565. http:// pediatrics.aappublications.org/cgi/reprint/117/2/560. Accessed May 4, 2011

53. Rosenbaum S, Harty MB, Sheer J. State laws extending comprehensive legal liability protections for professional health-care volunteers during public health emergencies. *Public Health Rep.* 2008;123(2):238–241. http://www.ncbi. nlm.nih.gov/pmc/articles/PMC2239336/pdf/phr123000238. Accessed May 4, 2011

CHAPTER 11

Documenting Pediatric Care

Steven M. Donn, MD, FAAP

KEY CONCEPTS

- What Constitutes a Medical Record?
- Retention of Medical Records
- Fraud and Abuse
- Defending Potential Malpractice Claims
- Improving Documentation Skills
- Safeguarding Confidentiality
- Release of Records
- Documentation Guidelines
- Electronic Health Record Systems
- Ground Rules for Consistent Record Keeping

A complete, accurate, and objective medical record is an excellent foundation for defense against allegations of negligence, improper treatment, or omission in care. An incomplete record enables a plaintiff's attorney to challenge the physician's testimony and may encourage the attorney to pursue a medically defensible malpractice case.

Physicians should record all data they will need for the continuing care of the patient. Usual entries include past history, social situation, family history, caregiver, medications, allergies, present complaints, clinical findings and impressions, radiology reports, recommended treatment and follow-up, and anything else the physician considers to be of clinical

significance. In malpractice litigation the absence of sufficiently detailed chart entries usually reflects adversely on the physician.

What Constitutes a Medical Record?

Historically, the definition of a legal medical or health record seemed straightforward. Simply stated, it was the contents of the paper chart. Patients had limited interest in or access to the information contained in their record. With the advent of various electronic media, the Internet, and the consumer's enhanced role in compiling health records, the definition of the legal health record (LHR) became more complex. Recognizing these changes, the American Health Information Management Association (AHIMA) formed a special task force of members from provider settings and law practices, information technology vendors, and information systems consultants to develop guidelines to assist organizations in defining their health records for legal applications.[1,2]

There is no one-size-fits-all definition of the LHR because laws and regulations governing the content vary by practice setting and state. However, there are common principles to be followed in creating a definition. The LHR is the documentation of the health care services provided to an individual in any aspect of health care delivery by a health care provider or organization. The LHR is individually identifiable data, in any medium, collected and directly used to document health care or health status. The term includes records of care in any health-related setting used by health care professionals while providing patient care services, for reviewing patient data, or for documenting observations, actions, or instructions. Some types of documentation that comprise the LHR may physically exist in separate and multiple paper-based or electronic media.

Examples of documentation found in the LHR include

- Advance directives
- Anesthesia records
- Care plan
- Consent for treatment forms
- Consultation reports
- Discharge instructions and summary
- E-mail containing physician-patient or physician-physician communication
- Emergency department record
- Functional status assessment
- Graphic records
- Immunization record
- Intake/output records
- Medication orders
- Medication profile
- Multidisciplinary progress notes/documentation
- Nursing assessment
- Operative and procedure reports
- Orders for diagnostic tests and diagnostic study results (eg, laboratory, radiology)
- Patient-submitted documentation
- Pathology reports
- Practice guidelines or protocols/clinical pathways that imbed patient data
- Problem list
- Records of history and physical examination
- Respiratory, physical, speech, and occupational therapy records
- Selected waveforms for special documentation purposes
- Telephone consultations
- Telephone orders

Administrative Data

Administrative data are not considered part of the LHR (eg, in response to a subpoena for the medical record). Nonetheless, they should be given the same level of confidentiality as the LHR. Administrative data are patient-identifiable data used for administrative, regulatory, health care operation, and payment (financial) purposes.

Examples of administrative data include

- Assurance or utilization management
- Authorization forms for release of information
- Birth and death certificates
- Correspondence concerning requests for records
- Event history/audit trails
- Patient-identifiable claim
- Patient-identifiable data reviewed for quality
- Patient identifiers (eg, medical record number, biometrics)
- Protocols/clinical pathways, practice guidelines, relevant medical articles, and other knowledge sources that do not imbed patient data

Retention of Medical Records

Failure to maintain and retain medical records has ramifications to billing fraud and abuse, malpractice defense, professional misconduct, and even criminal prosecution. Federal law, state law, and regulatory requirements govern the appropriate length of time to retain patient medical records. The duration may be addressed in contractual arrangement between the physician and payers. If records are purchased as the result of the sale of a practice, the length of retention may be specified in the terms of the purchase agreement.

Federal Requirements

Many of the federal requirements for retaining medical records are based on health conditions or government agencies (eg, Occupational Safety and Health Administration, vaccines, termination of pregnancy) that may be relevant to specific information contained in the patient medical record.

State Requirements

The majority of states have specific retention requirements that should be used to establish a facility's retention policy. In the absence of specific state requirements for record retention, physicians should keep health information for at least the period specified by the state's statutes of limitations related to medical malpractice lawsuits or for a sufficient length of time to prove compliance with laws, regulations, and prevailing standards. If the patient was a minor, the physician should retain health information until the patient reaches the age of majority (as defined by state law) plus the period of the statute of limitations, unless otherwise provided by state law. A longer retention period is prudent because the statute may not begin until the potential plaintiff learns of the causal relationship between an injury and the care received. In some states, the toll starts on the alleged incident or event that caused the injury; in other states, it starts when the injury or problem is discovered. Because of unique circumstances surrounding informed consent in pediatric-aged patients, physician liability may extend beyond the statute of limitation for minors.

Fraud and Abuse

Because patient records and billing information are essential for health care fraud and abuse investigations, health care professionals should ensure that their staff know and follow all relevant retention requirements. Compliance programs should establish written policies to address the retention of specific types of documentation including clinical and medical records, health records, claims records, and compliance policies. Compliance documentation should address the practice's procedures that have been established to protect the integrity of the compliance process. Examples of compliance

documentation include employee training documentation, reports from hotlines, results of internal investigations, results of auditing and monitoring, modifications to the compliance program, and self-disclosures. The federal government has a multiplicity of laws in its anti–fraud-and-abuse arsenal. These and comparable state statutes can extend the retention period of medical and financial records. For instance, under the False Claims Act,[3] claims may be brought up to 6 years after the incident; however, on occasion, the time has been extended to 3 years after the date when the facts material to the right of action are known or reasonably should have been known but in no event more than 10 years after the date of violation (31 USC §3731[b][2]). The 2009 amendments to the Civil False Claims Act expands the scope of liability for physicians (31 USC §3731[b][1]). For instance, the False Claims Act no longer requires proof that the physician intended to defraud the government. In addition, courts have held that health care providers have a duty to familiarize themselves with *all requirements* of the law for reimbursement (Re: Cardiac Devices Qui Tam Litigation, 221 FRD 318 [D. Conn 2004]). The documentation should be retained according to applicable federal and state regulations and laws, and must be maintained for a sufficient length of time to ensure their availability to prove compliance. These added complexities reinforce a practice's need for legal advice in determining and implementing its specific record-retention policies.

Defending Potential Malpractice Claims

The medical record is the single most important piece of evidence in resolving medical malpractice allegations because it supplies "the moment of truth." Many medical liability experts favor keeping all patient records permanently simply because without the record it is nearly impossible to defend a malpractice case. Although fees for long-term storage and security are expensive, they are outweighed by the value of being able to defend potential malpractice cases. If forever is not an option, ask a legal advisor or professional liability carrier for advice on how long to keep inactive records and how to do so.

Unless state or federal law requires longer periods, the AHIMA recommends that specific patient health information be retained for established minimum periods (Table 11-1). State mental health laws may have different rules relating to the retention of psychiatric records. In particular, AHIMA stresses that medical records for minors be held until the patient achieves the age of majority plus the state's statute of limitations as determined by state law. This is because failure of a legally authorized representative to litigate a possible malpractice action on

behalf of a minor does not waive the minor's right to sue (within the adult statute of limitations) when the minor reaches the age of majority.

Not only are medical records essential to successfully defending a malpractice claim, problems with patient records can be the basis for legal action against a physician or institution. Other claims that may have been related to inadequacies in medical record documentation are listed in Table 11-2. Failure to document consent for treatment can lead to allegations of negligence based on inadequate informed consent or civil or criminal battery. Not properly recording physician-to-physician communication can contribute to medical errors. Health care facilities must comply with many layers of regulatory requirements. Anyone who has dealt with regulatory oversight groups will tell you

Table 11-1. American Health Information Management Association Recommended Retention Standards[2]

Health Information	Recommended Retention Period
Diagnostic images (eg, radiograph)	5 years
Disease index	10 years
Fetal heart monitor records	10 years after the newborn reaches the age of majority
Master patient/person index	Permanently
Operative index	10 years
Patient health/medical records (adults)	10 years after the most recent encounter
Patient health/medical records (minors)	Age of majority plus statute of limitations
Physician index	10 years
Register of births	Permanently
Register of deaths	Permanently
Register of surgical procedures	Permanently

Table 11-2. Closed Malpractice Claims Against Pediatricians (1985–2009): Selected Claims by Associated Medical and Legal Issues[4]

Issue	Total Claims	Closed Claims	Paid Claims	% Paid to Closed	Paid Total Indemnity	Average Indemnity
Problems with records	217	203	120	59%	$26,624,395	$221,870
Consent issues, breach of contract or warranty	157	137	37	27%	$2,194,450	$59,309
Communication between providers	161	144	58	40%	$24,160,441	$416,559
Billing and collection	41	41	4	10%	$177,500	$44,375
Failure to conform with regulation/statute/rule	40	40	9	23%	$4,814,972	$534,997
Assault and battery	26	25	13	52%	$413,891	$31,838
Breach of confidentiality	28	26	0	0	$0	$0

that doing the right thing without documenting what was done, by whom, and how often, is simply inadequate.

Improving Documentation Skills

Knowing how to document care concisely and carefully is as important as being able to locate the medical record. Risk managers have suggested some pointers (and a clever acronym) to help physicians improve their documentation skills.[5] OLFACTORY is an acronym for making the medical record more defensible. It is used in teaching risk-reduction strategies to physicians, particularly those strategies related to improving communication in the medical record.

O = Original
L = Legible
F = Factual
A = Accurate
C = Consistent
T = Timely
O = Objective
R = Rational
Y = Yours

Original

Do not alter existing documentation or withhold elements of a medical record once a claim emerges. In most states, alteration of a medical record is a criminal offense and may result in suspension or loss of medical license. In addition, it makes defense of a medical malpractice action extremely difficult. Even minor record alterations can greatly harm credibility. Errors and unrelated comments in medical records can be explained and defended, but alterations cannot. If you are named in a claim and the medical record has problems, immediately indicate them to your defense attorney. Never destroy or rewrite and replace a prior record. Periodically, a physician defendant fails to heed this age-old advice. The plaintiff's attorney may already have a copy of the records and the changes

are immediately obvious. Once an entry is made into a medical record, it should not be deleted. Erasures or correction fluid should never be used in patient records. You may amend the record at a later date if it is determined that the original entry is incorrect. For such edits, draw a single line through the incorrect word or phrase. It should be clearly marked, dated, and initialed by the author, but the original entry should remain legible. Instead of changing a previous note, consider writing a new one. However, these modifications only should be done if the new or amended information has direct bearing on subsequent patient care. If it is clearly being done for defensive purposes, your motives for amending the records may be questioned and may compromise the credibility of your records.

When releasing medical records, follow applicable laws and send a photocopy or summary of the record. Keep the original record. State laws relating to release of certain medical information (eg, HIV status) should be assessed, as different rules relating to consent to disclosure may apply.

Legible

Illegible records are unclear and may compromise the quality of care. It is not enough for the writer to know what the notation means; the record is needed for communicating with other physician and clinical staff. Illegible record keeping has been found to be a violation of the physician's duty to the patient and suggests a willingness to endanger the patient. Records that are sloppy can make the writer appear careless or unprofessional. The use of unauthorized abbreviations, acronyms, or unusual expressions is often interpreted as obscuring medical information. Illegibility increases the potential for medical errors, especially with medications and dosages.

Factual

Records should be as concrete and concise as possible. Quality is usually preferred over quantity, but do not write too little. Documentation should be pertinent to medical care. Limit descriptions to what happened. Do not use the record to explain, rationalize, or argue your case. Medical complications, mishaps, or unusual occurrences should be documented in the patient record (eg, "8 month old infant fell 3 feet from examination table to carpeted floor"). This should be done even if an incident report has been filed because the incident report may not be available for patient care and is usually not available in litigation to prove that follow-up care was adequate.

Do not use the patient chart to question the quality or appropriateness of previous care. Medical records often reflect differing diagnoses and treatment recommendations among multiple caregivers. However, oral or written criticism of previous health care contributes nothing to the patient's needs and may open the door to litigation. Patients may take casual remarks critical of prior care quite seriously, possibly destroying their relationships with previous caregivers or you. Because all pertinent facts about prior care are rarely available, caution is advised in making judgments and comments if you disagree with a past or current caregiver. Likewise, basing your opinion of prior care solely on the patient's report of prior circumstances may not reflect changes in signs or symptoms over time. In addition, the patient's perceptions and recollections may be inaccurately or incompletely reported. If, after all of the information is considered, you do judge your patient's prior care to have been flawed, a factual summary of clinical events and honest answering of patient inquiries is advised.

Accurately and objectively document a new patient's condition at the time you assume care. This, combined with a thorough review of prior treatment records, should keep the record straight without pointing fingers or blaming others if prior care is problematic. Remarks or record entries critical of prior care may prompt patients to consider litigation, even when no negligence occurred.

Specialists should avoid sending consultation notes that state, "Dictated but not read," and generalists should consider not accepting such reports. Also, never allow anything to be placed in the medical record until it has been reviewed, dated, and signed.

Accurate

Avoid words or expressions that are vague or may have more than one meaning. Do not use noncommittal terms that could be interpreted as being defensive. Omit premature conclusions. Precise descriptions of physician findings are preferable to subjective or unsubstantiated comments. Differentiate between direct observations and information reported by the patient. Diagrams or line drawings that clearly identify findings (eg, lesions, injuries) help avoid misinterpretation. Pertinent positive and negative clinical findings should be documented

Consistent

In litigation, medical records are scrutinized carefully. Use of a style of chart entry (eg, Subjective, Objective, Assessment, Plan; checklists, documentation prompts) can improve the effectiveness of the record, ease or speed the process of retrieving significant information, better organize the medical record, and provide clear alerts (eg, allergies, medication charting). Document all clinical findings that are essential to a diagnosis or patient care. Document the clinical findings that are customarily recorded in similar situations. When a record varies in degree of detail or type of information recorded from one entry to the next, it could have misleading implications about what was examined or done for the patient.

Timely

Record the date and time on all entries in the medical record. Notes should be contemporaneous. Label added information as *addendum* and indicate when (and why) it was entered. For each office visit, a progress note should give a pertinent chronologic report of the patient's course and reflect any change in condition and results of treatment. Each page (eg, notes, laboratory and radiology reports) of the patient medical record should include the patient's name (identification number) and the complete date (month/day/year). Entries in the margin or inserted between lines should be avoided. In litigation, such notes suggest that the entry was added to the chart after the fact with the intent to falsify the record. Late dictation should be so noted if dictated long after a complication occurs.

Objective, Rational

Under the Health Insurance Portability and Accountability Act (HIPAA), patients are ensured the right to access their medical records. Patients may be sensitive to notes they view as disrespectful or prejudicial. Socioeconomic information about the patient or family should only be noted if it is relevant to patient care. Obviously, derogatory or discriminatory remarks about the patient have no place in the medical record.

Address disagreements or conflicts with other physicians, nursing staff, or administration through the appropriate chain of command, not in the medical record. If you disagree with a clinical conclusion, read other practitioners' notes and reread your prior notes. Review radiology and other special study reports, even if you have already read the films or seen the test data. If you must document a different diagnosis or recommended treatment, factually state your opinion and rationale. Avoid presenting subjective statements about prior treatment or poor outcomes as facts. Use quotation marks to indicate patient's or family's impressions (eg, "cerebral palsy from a birth injury").

Regardless of the writer's intention, the words listed in Table 11-3 can be interpreted as indicating substandard performance or allocating blame.

Another pitfall in documentation is the use of superlative modifiers. These adjectives broaden or restrict a term's definition. Medical records often are replete with inappropriate superlative modifiers, such as *severe, profound, excessive,* or *prolonged.* Certain modifiers should be avoided when describing treatment modalities, such as *urgent, STAT,* or *emergent.* Modifiers add little purpose in the provision of health care, but they have considerable jury appeal in the hands of a skilled attorney. In complex medical situations, it is difficult for a lay jury to separate the specific medical meaning from its own general understanding of words such as *severe, massive, deep,* or *excessive.*

Malpractice claims have sometimes identified the fact that critical reports, notes, and consultations pointing to a different available diagnostic or treatment path were overlooked or not addressed by the

Table 11-3. Examples of Words Not to Be Used in Patient Charts

Substandard Performance	Deserving of Blame
Aberrant	Accidental
Bad	Blame
Defective	Careless
Excessive	Confused
Faulty	Erroneous
Inadequate	Error
Incorrect	Fault
Insufficient	Foolish
Miserable	Inadvertent
Mishandled	Misadventure
Poor	Mistake
Problem	Mix-up
Sloppy	Negligent
Substandard	Regret
Undesirable	Regretful
Unnecessary	Sorry
Unsatisfactory	Terrible
Wrong	Unfortunate

attending physician. Medical records should document a thought process.

Patient complaints about the quality of care or threats to sue may be briefly documented in the patient record. However, these notations should be brief, nonjudgmental, and appropriately framed in patient care context. Do not describe the parent's threats as demanding, vindictive, unreasonable, or malicious. A better approach is to write, "Parent's dissatisfaction may create problems with future cooperation and compliance." By noting legal threats like this, the record may be used to establish a starting point for the statutory limitations period and may reveal a litigious tendency of the patient's family. Moreover, the notation is there because it has direct implications on continued medical care. Never use the medical record to speculate whether you think a parent or patient will sue. To do so, absent an actual threat, only suggests that you believe there is a basis for a lawsuit.

Yours

Write your own note. Do not merely countersign notes written by someone else. Avoid cutting and pasting if using electronic record keeping. It is generally understood that while the record belongs to the physician, the information belongs to the patient. Because the medical record is confidential, you, the physician, are responsible for safeguarding information in the record. It should remain secure and not be made public.

Safeguarding Confidentiality

Communication between patient and physician is confidential; safeguarding confidentiality is critical to the physician-patient relationship. It is not uncommon for patients to file lawsuits because of breach of confidential information; however, the plaintiff must demonstrate compensable injury from the breach. In pediatrics, the triad relationship among the patient, pediatrician, and parent or legal guardian tends to complicate confidentiality, partic-

ularly as the patient matures into adolescence and young adulthood. Your practice's confidentiality policies should be consistent with applicable state laws, especially as they relate to conditions and circumstances under which the adolescent patient is considered an emancipated minor. This confidentiality privilege extends to all members of the health care team. Federal privacy rules have been promulgated by the Department of Health and Human Services, requiring most health care facilities to upgrade their policies and procedures to meet these standards. The Health Insurance Portability and Accountability Act provides a minimal threshold of privacy but does not override a state law that affords a higher level of protection of confidentiality.

- All personal data, medical notes, and billing information are confidential and may not be communicated to anyone without the patient's written consent.
- Loose talk (ie, office chatter) that others overhear can be the basis for a defamation or invasion of privacy suit. Watch your voice volume; minimize conversations in corridors, elevators, and other sites where you may be unaware of the presence of others.
- Do a confidentiality audit of your office. Test to see how easy it is to overhear conversations (eg, can people in the reception area hear conversations in the front office, telephone triage staff). Solutions can be training staff to minimize discussions about individual patients, installing soundproofing materials, and putting privacy screens on computer monitors.
- Avoid discussing a patient's medical care on a wireless phone with the patient or anyone else. Police scanners and radios may pick up these conversations unbeknownst to the callers. The mobility afforded by these devices makes it possible to conduct patient care conversations in public settings (eg, restaurants, airports) in which bystanders cannot help but overhear

your comments. Do not allow convenience to override confidentiality.

- Train all new employees on specific responsibilities in protecting patient confidentiality. Make sure all staff members understand that violation of a patient's privacy may result in disciplinary action up to and including termination of employment.

Release of Records

State disclosure law can be obtained from many sources. Methods of obtaining state disclosure law information include

- Many state medical associations publish books on the release of patient health information. These books often contain copies of state law and address the issue of who may consent.
- Your state's hospital association may publish a book on informed consent that lists who may consent and may cover release of health information. To inquire, call your state hospital association.
- You may want to ask your legal counsel or malpractice insurance carrier to provide you with copies of applicable state disclosure and consent law.

Documentation Guidelines

Do

- Document all clinical findings, including pertinent positive and negative findings, that are essential to a diagnosis or patient care.
- Document clinical findings that are customarily recorded in similar situations.
- Document the reason for your conclusion or action if it is not obvious. Your note should reflect a thought process.
- Describe the extent of the physical examination.
- Document the possible complications that are being considered.

- Describe factors present that can interfere with reliable evaluation.
- Be complete. Any lists written in the records should be complete or contain a general inclusive statement.
- Complete all boxes, blanks, or checklists in medical record forms. If forms are based on clinical guidelines or recommendations, reference this in a footnote on the form. Update forms as appropriate. Failure to complete a form will be interpreted as failing to do the task or procedure.
- Document sources of information if other than the patient.
- Summarize any worries or concerns expressed by the patient or family.
- Carefully document medical complications, mishaps, or unusual occurrences in the records.
- Legal threats and complaints about the quality of care may be briefly documented in the patient's record in a nonjudgmental manner.
- Document informed consent, or consent by proxy if applicable, for medical testing or treatment as required by law.
- Document important warnings given to the patient.
- Always document evidence of patient noncompliance and reasons, if known.
- Document informed refusals.
- Make sure your documentation practices meet the Centers for Medicare & Medicaid Services guidelines for evaluation and management services.
- Use terms that reasonably reflect what happened.
- Document the reasons and rationale if you choose not to accept the recommendations of a consultant or colleague.

Do Not

- Document negative findings that are not customarily recorded in similar situations.
- Forget to document every patient-related telephone call (especially those after hours or repeated).
- Misrepresent the facts.
- Refer to risk-prevention activities as such in the medical record.
- Record information that may have legal implications but no value to patient care in the patient's chart (eg, the patient has sued another physician, the injury may result in loss of income or other damages).
- Refer to incident or variance reports having been filed. Doing so may make them discoverable.

Do Not Alter the Medical Record

- Once an entry is made into medical record, it should not be deleted for any reason.
- The physician may edit the record if, at a later date, it is determined that the original entry is incorrect or circumstances have changed.
- Such edits should be clearly marked, dated, and initialed by the author (original entry should remain legible).
- With an electronic health record (EHR), changes are easier to make, and by using audit trails and electronic signatures, the original note and correction may be made evident (but the changes may be more difficult to discern).

Electronic Health Record Systems

Electronic health record systems originally designed for use in adult care are now frequently used in child care. The following outlines special features necessary for an EHR system to support health care for children. Features of practice management services (eg, billing, accounts receivable, scheduling, payroll), however, are beyond the scope of this section.

An essential function of a pediatric EHR system is to facilitate care that is accessible, family-centered, continuous, comprehensive, coordinated, compassionate, and culturally effective—the *medical home.* The purpose of EHR systems is to compile and centralize all pertinent information related to a child's medical (and relevant nonmedical) care so as to ensure that optimal pediatric care is provided. In doing so, EHR systems have the capacity to improve the quality of care that children receive from their primary care practitioner as well as from ancillary health care professionals.

National and international organizations are defining standards for recording, storage, and transmission of patient data. The exceptional diversity of current hardware and software requires implementation of standards for data definition and interchange so that systems can interact. Federal and state legislation requires the adoption of standards for transmission of health information in electronic form.[6] The *International Classification of Diseases, Ninth Revision, Clinical Modification* provides a well-known, standardized terminology for recording information about diagnoses, but it has proven inadequate to represent detailed information about clinical observations (eg, there is no classification to represent the common finding of fussiness in young infants). Commercial vendors sometimes do not recognize the special needs of pediatric practice. Some vendors offer systems specifically for the care of children, but providers must recognize certain caveats, such as wrong templates (eg, a 1-year-old who is oriented as to time, place, and person); unauthorized access to the EHR; too much information; and paying attention to the EHR rather than to patient's or parent's facial and body cues.

General attributes of computer-based patient records described by the Institute of Medicine are all vital for pediatric records. These include problem lists, measurement and recording of health status and functional level, statements about the logical basis for all diagnoses and conclusions, linkage with all of a patient's clinical records across settings and periods, assurance of confidentiality, widespread accessibility, selective retrieval and formatting, linkage to local and remote knowledge sources, decision support, structured data collection using a defined vocabulary, aiding evaluation of quality and costs of care, and flexibility and expandability to meet evolving practice needs. The American Academy of Pediatrics (AAP) issued a clinical report to make vendors and standards organizations aware of special issues in pediatric practice for software design and to provide pediatricians with a set of requirements or desirable features to use when evaluating EHR systems.[7] These include

Data Representation

- *Growth data.* Attention to the special significance of children's growth in pediatric practice is essential for any pediatric EHR system. Recording, graphic display, and special calculations of growth patterns are critical functions. The ability to calculate, display, and compare a child's growth percentiles and body mass index with normal ranges is vital. Because normal growth ranges vary among ethnic and geographic groups, the ability to use different ranges for different patients may be important in some practice settings. Head circumference, an important measurement used almost exclusively for pediatric patients, should be a part of growth metrics. Because small changes in growth may be important to small patients (eg, a few gram weight gain in a premature neonate), systems should be able to store data on a small enough scale to represent these changes.

- *Patient identifier.* A universal patient identifier is a desirable but as yet unachieved goal. Any system that is ultimately implemented to assign such identifiers will need to provide for assignment immediately at the time of birth (or even before birth for prenatal procedures performed on a fetus). Electronic health record systems may need to accommodate temporary

(ie, changing) data in this key field, including certain identifying data associated with a patient change in the perinatal period. For example, newborns are often named with their mother's surname or full name (eg, "Infant Boy Smith," "Boy Jane Jones") at the time of birth, and this is changed in the first few days of life. Flexibility of search criteria to allow for changing identification data is desirable in pediatric systems. Systems should be able to maintain a record of multiple names used by a patient.

- *Special terminology and information.* Special terminology is used in pediatric care. Electronic health record systems need to include common pediatric terms (a pediatric lexicon) used to describe pediatric preventive health care (eg, developmental milestones, educational progress, anticipatory guidance) and physical findings (eg, weak cry, bulging fontanelle, umbilical granuloma). Currently, standard lexicons are incomplete with respect to pediatric care; system designers will need to provide supplementary nomenclature or allow users to augment supplied lexicons in ways that preserve the value of standard vocabularies and adequately represent pediatric concepts.

- *Age-based normal ranges.* Normal ranges for vital signs and other physiologic parameters change with a child's age. Pediatric EHR systems should allow the user to easily compare a patient's vital signs with age-based normal ranges. The same is true for laboratory values, but normal ranges for adults are usually supplied by the reference laboratory and not the EHR; the EHR should be able to accept normative values provided by the reference laboratory. Systems that allow users to alter normal ranges to represent specific ethnic or geographic populations are desirable.

- *Time of birth.* The time of a child's birth is important in calculating exact age in the first days of life and should not be omitted from EHR systems.

Data Processing

- *Prescribing of medications.* Prescribing of medications for pediatric patients is based on the age and weight or body surface area of the child. Prescription tools that supply standard recommended adult doses and do not include pediatric dose calculation functions are unlikely to be useful in the care of infants and children and may be misleading or potentially dangerous in the pediatric context. Functions that facilitate calculation of drug doses based on available data are essential for pediatric care. Decision-support tools supplied to assist in selecting medications and preventing errors should include pediatric-specific data.

- *Immunizations.* Efficient recording (data input) and effective display of immunization data are essential. Mechanisms for immunization decision support (eg, deficiency alerts) that include easy updating as recommendations change should be included.[7] For effective interaction with immunization registries, the ability to flexibly format immunization data and support electronic data interchange with registries is vital. Because physicians who treat infants and children are asked to provide data about immunization completeness in multiple formats, flexibility in a system's ability to provide immunization reports is highly desirable. Features that support reminder systems to prevent missed immunizations would also be desirable; these reminder systems can take the form of messages sent to parents, flags for physicians during acute care, or other forms.

- *Special parent documentation requirements.* Parents may ask to review or append chart information. State and federal regulations (ie, HIPAA privacy regulations) dictate procedures and limitations of parental appendixes to a child's chart. Systems should also support the generation and maintenance of summary reports for parents and other health care professionals about children with special health care needs.

- *Reporting.* The ability to easily customize reports to match mandated formats (eg, school or camp physicals, reports to school nurses) would be particularly valuable to practitioners of child health.

System Design

- Special privacy issues
  - *Adolescent privacy.* Privacy laws addressing adolescents' medical information (especially sexual and mental health and behavior issues) vary from state to state. Electronic health record systems must be able to respond to these privacy needs by allowing restriction of access to this information according to laws and policies.
  - *Genetic information.* Electronic health record systems must provide protection of information on a patient's genetic information, including newborn metabolic screening results. This protection must extend to those who are genetically unrelated to their parents (eg, those born after donor embryo procedures).
  - *Guardianship data.* A child's legal guardian may be different from that child's biological parents; EHR systems should be able to reflect this.
  - *Adoption issues.* Electronic health record systems must be able to represent relationships in families involving adopted children. If the child is not aware of adoptive status, this should be noted.
  - *Foster care.* Physicians often are asked to evaluate children in foster care. Systems should support reporting requirements of social service agencies in these cases and protect the privacy of these patients after changes in a child's foster care status.
  - *Abuse and neglect.* State laws vary concerning the use of data in cases of abuse and neglect. Systems need to be able to protect data in ways consistent with these laws.

- *Financial responsibility data.* Sometimes, a parent or guardian is not the financially responsible person. Systems should allow enough flexibility in a patient's medical record to allow identification of this distinct role.

- *Pediatric work settings.* Data entry (documentation) tools must work in busy pediatric settings. For example, speech interfaces may be impractical in noisy environments. Computers in examination rooms with curious children may also present special challenges for system design.

- *Family member links.* Electronic health record systems should be able to maintain links to records of other family members (who may have different surnames). Because an interaction with 1 family member often triggers an encounter with another family member (typically a sibling), EHR systems should support easy movement among records of children within the same family.

- *Registry links.* Electronic health record systems should promote links to newborn screening systems at the hospital, state, or national level so as to ensure optimal communication, including timely notification and follow-up.

- *Consideration of national policies.* The AAP has published policies that may affect the design and use of EHR systems. These policies should be considered in the design of software systems for use in pediatric health care.

Ground Rules for Consistent Record Keeping

Rule 1: Patient Records Must Contain Customary Information

- A signature or the name of the physician is on every entry.
- The date and time are on every entry.
- For dictated records, the date of dictation is on every entry.

- A follow-up plan or a return visit is documented for every office or outpatient encounter.
- Initials or electronic signatures are on diagnostic test results and consultation reports after reading or viewing them.
- Initials or electronic signatures and review dates are on entries of supervised personnel.
- Patient's identification is on every page.

Rule 2: Patient Records Must Contain Sufficient Medical Background Information

- Personal biographical information is documented.
- Allergies and medication reactions are prominently displayed.
- Past medical history is documented.
- Family history is documented.
- Substance abuse history, including tobacco, alcohol, and drugs, is documented.
- Immunization record is documented.
- Use of over-the-counter and prescription medication and herbal or natural products is documented.

Rule 3: Patient Records Must Contain Current Medical History and Findings

- Pertinent history relating to the current problem is documented.
- Pertinent physical examination findings relating to the current problem are documented.
- Completed problem list is documented if applicable.

Rule 4: Document Patient Care Actions

- Appropriate diagnostic studies were ordered.
- Appropriate consultations were requested.
- Appropriate preventive services were offered.
- Adequate communications between consultants and primary care physicians are shown.
- Informed consent disclosures are documented.

Rule 5: Patient Records Must Show Consistency Between Findings and Conclusions and Between Conclusions and Actions

- Problems from prior visits are being addressed.
- Diagnostic studies were ordered when indicated by findings or conclusions.
- Conclusions are consistent with findings.
- Actions are consistent with conclusions.
- Use of consultants is consistent with conclusions.

Rule 6: If There Are Practice Guidelines That May Apply, Patient Records Must Be Consistent With Them and Should Demonstrate Awareness of Them

- Records are consistent with any applicable clinical practice guidelines.

Rule 7: From a Liability Standpoint, Whenever You Are Writing in a Medical Record, Pretend That the Phrase, "Dear Mr/Ms Attorney," Is Written at the Top (Someday, That Is Who May Be Reading It)

References

1. Rhodes HB, Larson JC. *Practice Brief: Release of Information: Laws and Regulations.* Chicago, IL: American Health Information Management Association; 1999
2. Fletcher DM, Rhodes HB. *Practice Brief: Retention of Health Information (Updated).* Chicago, IL: American Health Information Management Association; 2002
3. False Claims Act, 31 USC 3729
4. Physician Insurers Association of America. *A Risk Management Review of Malpractice Claims—Pediatrics.* Rockville, MD: Physician Insurers Association of America; 2010
5. Gafner R. *Streetwise! Practical Risk Management for Practicing Physicians.* Houston, TX: Medical Risk Management, Inc.; 1995:69–81
6. Health Insurance Portability and Accountability Act of 1996
7. Spooner SA, American Academy of Pediatrics Council on Clinical Information Technology. Special requirements of electronic health record systems in pediatrics. *Pediatrics.* 2007;119(3):631–637

Resources

Pediatric Visit Documentation Forms for well-child visits are available on the AAP Online Bookstore (www.aap.org/bookstore).

Resources for HIPAA compliance for pediatricians are available to AAP members on the Member Center of the AAP Web site (www.aap.org/moc).

CHAPTER 12

Medical Liability Experiences of Pediatricians

Parul Divya Parikh, MPH, and Jay P. Goldsmith, MD, FAAP

KEY CONCEPTS

- Closed Pediatric Malpractice Claims
- Trends Among American Academy of Pediatrics Members
- Risk Management Pointers

The American Academy of Pediatrics (AAP) Committee on Medical Liability and Risk Management studies closed malpractice claims against pediatricians periodically to identify common risk areas and factors associated with indemnity payments. These analyses also reveal how pediatricians' medical liability experiences compare with those of other specialists.

Closed Pediatric Malpractice Claims

One of the best sources of information on closed malpractice claims is the Physician Insurers Association of America (PIAA). Since 1985, this organization of malpractice insurers, many of them physician owned or operated, has pooled and codified data from its member companies on closed malpractice claims. The compiled data on pediatricians are then compared with that of all physician specialties to observe differences, if any, of this specialty group from the population of all specialties. The PIAA member companies insure approximately 60% of all practicing physicians in the United States.

Pediatricians Compared With Other Physicians

The PIAA provides overall statistics covering the number of claims reported and dollars paid for each specialty. The analysis encompasses all PIAA closed malpractice claims against pediatricians from 1985 to 2009 and a separate analysis of claims closed in 2009.

From 1985 to 2009, the total indemnity paid on behalf of pediatricians was approximately $544 million (for 7,186 closed claims). Of the 28 specialties included in the PIAA database, pediatrics ranks 10th in the number of claims reported and eighth highest in terms of total amount of moneys paid for settlements or awards for malpractice actions (Table 12-1).

Most pediatric malpractice claims are closed with no payout to the plaintiff. According to PIAA data, only 27.9% of malpractice claims against pediatricians are closed with indemnity payments, compared with 29.47% for the average of all physicians. The specialty with the highest percentage of paid-to-closed claims is dentistry, with 44.65% incurring a payment. The specialty with the lowest percentage of paid-to-closed claims is cardiovascular diseases (nonsurgical), with only 18.5%.

On the other hand, the cumulative average indemnity for pediatrics is 27.8% higher than the average paid for all physicians between 1985 and 2009

Table 12-1. Comparative Claim Payment Analysis

Malpractice Claims Closed Between 1985 and 2009 by Specialty[1]						
Specialty Group	Closed Claims	Paid Claims	% Paid to Closed	Total Indemnity	Average Indemnity	Largest Payment
Anesthesiology	9,536	3,054	32.03	$700,392,192	$229,336	$5,048,678
Cardiovascular and Thoracic Surgery	7,498	1,766	23.55	$396,988,303	$224,795	$5,005,000
Cardiovascular Diseases (nonsurgical)	4,735	876	18.5	$218,678,876	$249,633	$1,950,000
Dentists	916	409	44.65	$17,397,358	$42,536	$1,000,000
Dermatology	2,815	818	29.06	$115,208,979	$140,842	$3,000,000
Emergency Medicine	4,636	1,196	25.8	$243,271,318	$203,404	$2,000,000
Gastroenterology	2,676	496	18.54	$109,659,521	$221,088	$2,900,000
General and Family Practice	28,231	8,989	31.84	$1,487,973,668	$165,533	$4,089,414
General Surgery	25,623	8,771	34.23	$1,654,243,079	$188,604	$3,116,180
Gynecology	2,928	886	30.26	$141,473,705	$159,677	$2,000,000
Internal Medicine	33,747	8,461	25.07	$1,844,275,990	$217,974	$12,000,000
Neurology (nonsurgical)	3,956	868	21.94	$279,287,658	$321,760	$5,000,000
Neurosurgery	5,794	1,646	28.41	$532,031,130	$323,227	$5,600,000
Obstetric and Gynecologic Surgery	33,510	11,768	35.12	$3,372,306,313	$286,566	$13,000,000
Ophthalmology	7,120	2,037	28.61	$377,383,385	$185,264	$3,550,000
Oral Surgery	68	23	33.82	$564,083	$24,525	$133,500
Orthopedic Surgery	23,111	6,753	29.22	$1,144,155,740	$169,429	$3,000,000
Other Nonsurgical Specialties	2,582	606	23.47	$125,292,955	$206,754	$8,749,980
Otorhinolaryngology	4,146	1,322	31.89	$281,612,813	$213,020	$4,199,329
Paraprofessional	463	119	25.7	$25,070,053	$210,673	$1,322,290
Pathology	1,732	494	28.52	$124,101,295	$251,217	$2,700,000
Pediatrics	**7,186**	**2,005**	**27.9**	**$544,926,823**	**$271,784**	**$5,250,000**
Plastic Surgery	9,071	2,392	26.37	$286,903,489	$119,943	$2,000,000
Psychiatry	2,395	479	20	$76,503,198	$159,714	$2,375,000
Radiation Therapy	2,409	685	28.44	$202,384,071	$295,451	$2,700,000
Radiology	14,103	4,119	29.21	$864,737,771	$209,939	$3,125,000
Resident/Intern	135	44	32.59	$2,689,932	$61,135	$200,000
Urologic Surgery	5,951	1,742	29.27	$321,778,143	$184,718	$3,200,000
ALL GROUPS	247,073	72,824	29.47	$15,491,291,841	$212,722	$13,000,000

($271,784 versus $212,722). When ranked by the highest to lowest average indemnity paid per specialty, pediatrics is fifth (Table 12-2).

Companies participating in the PIAA data-sharing system reported 214 pediatric claims closed in 2009, of which only 65 (30.37%) resulted in an indemnity payment. Total indemnity paid for these claims amounted to approximately $20 million. The average indemnity paid for a pediatric claim in 2009 was $316,521, compared with $523,201 in 2004. This 2009 average indemnity for pediatricians ($316,521) was 2.59% less than the overall indemnity paid for all physician specialties ($324,969). In 2009, the median payment for pediatric claims was $200,000, which is the same as the overall median of paid claims for all physicians. The largest single pediatric payment reported in 2009 was $1.3 million. Among claims against all specialists closed in 2009, the largest single case payment reported was $4.5 million for a neurosurgery claim.

The 30.37% of pediatric paid-to-closed claims in 2009 increased slightly from 29.96% a decade before. This percentage of pediatric paid-to-closed claims was higher than the percentage for all physician specialty groups—29.05% of all claims closed in 2009 resulted in a payment.

Trend Analysis of Claims by Year Cased Closed

Another good way to examine closed claims is to take 3 points in time and compare various aspects of the claims closed during each of those identified years (Table 12-3).

While the decline in number of claims closed appears to be something to celebrate, it is not. This number simply reflects the number of claims closed in a given year, which often has more to do with the resolution process (eg, settlement, trial, other). It does not mean that fewer claims were lodged against pediatricians in 2009 than in 2004 or 1999. A most interesting finding in this analysis is the

sharp increase (in 2004) and decline (in 2009) in the average indemnity paid on behalf of pediatricians. These findings are consistent with the medical liability crisis that occurred around 2002 to 2006 and has eased in recent years.

There is some good news. Pediatric claims were a relatively small percentage of claims reported to the

Table 12-2. Physician Insurers Association of America Average Indemnity Payment Closed Malpractice Claims—Highest to Lowest[1]

Specialty	Claims Closed 1985–2009
Neurosurgery	$323,227
Neurology (nonsurgical)	$321,760
Radiation Therapy	$295,451
Obstetric and Gynecologic Surgery	$286,566
Pediatrics	**$271,784**
Pathology	$251,217
Cardiovascular Diseases (nonsurgical)	$249,633
Anesthesiology	$229,336
Cardiovascular and Thoracic Surgery	$224,795
Gastroenterology	$221,088
Internal Medicine	$217,974
Otorhinolaryngology	$213,020
Paraprofessional	$210,673
Radiology	$209,939
Other Nonsurgical Specialties	$206,754
Emergency Medicine	$203,404
General Surgery	$188,604
Ophthalmology	$185,264
Urologic Surgery	$184,718
Orthopedic Surgery	$169,429
General and Family Practice	$165,533
Psychiatry	$159,714
Gynecology	$159,677
Dermatology	$140,842
Plastic Surgery	$119,943
Resident/Intern	$61,135
Dentists	$42,536
Oral Surgery	$24,525
ALL GROUPS	$212,722

Table 12-3. Closed Pediatric Claims Indemnity Payments, Selected Years[1]

	1999	2004	2009
Number of closed claims	227	278	214
Number of paid claims	68	56	65
Percent paid to closed	29.96	20.14	30.37
Average indemnity, pediatrics	$242,270	$460,970	$316,521
Average indemnity, all specialties	$252,642	$324,834	$324,969

PIAA in 2009; only 2.5% of claims and 2.6% of indemnity dollars were attributable to pediatric claims.

Legal Defense Expenses

More than $10.6 million was reported in defense payments for the 214 pediatric claims closed in 2009. It is worth noting that almost two thirds of this expenditure covered defense expenses in claims in which no indemnity was paid. However, over a decade, the cost of legal defense per case in all closed pediatric cases almost doubled, increasing from an average of $25,659 in 1999 to $49,686 in 2009.

Table 12-4 depicts the cost of defense expenses at 5-year intervals and compares overall defense expenses for pediatricians in those cases in which an indemnity (settlement or award) was paid.

Table 12-4. Legal Defense Expenses for Closed Pediatric Claims, Selected Years[1]

	1999	2004	2009
Expenses paid, all claims	$5,824,519	$8,578,911	$10,632,722
Average expenses paid	$25,659	$30,859	$49,686
Expenses paid, paid claims	$2,514,772	$4,105,340	$5,992,755
Average expense paid	$36,982	$73,310	$92,196
Expenses paid, no indemnity	$3,309,747	$4,473,571	$4,639,967
Average expense paid	$20,816	$20,151	$31,141

Even in those cases in which no indemnity payment was made on behalf of the pediatrician, the average defense expense was $31,141 in 2009. The average defense expense for 2009 was nearly triple that amount if an indemnity was paid ($92,196).

Pediatricians need to be sure that their insurance policies include legal defense costs in their indemnification payments. If there is a deductible for defense costs, the insured physician should be sure it is reasonable. Otherwise the insured physician could end up paying some of the defense costs out of pocket.

Primary Allegations

An important risk management strategy is to identify the most prevalent medical misadventures among closed malpractice claims against pediatricians (Table 12-5). Medical misadventures are the primary allegations of medical negligence cited in these claims.

Among claims paid from 1985 to 2009, 35% were for diagnostic errors. This is the most prevalent alleged medical misadventure in pediatric claims. Among claims involving diagnostic error, meningitis was the most prevalent condition that was incorrectly diagnosed by pediatricians. Appendicitis, specified non-teratogenic anomalies, pneumonia, and the brain-damaged baby rounded out the top 5 patient conditions resulting in litigation under the diagnostic error allegation.

Although not in the top 5 most frequent medical misadventures in claims against pediatricians, delay in performance (used by PIAA to describe claims

Table 12-5. Claims by the Most Prevalent Medical Misadventure—Pediatric Claims Closed 1985 to 2009[1]

Medical Misadventure	Closed Claims	Paid Claims	% Paid Claims	Total Indemnity	Average Indemnity
Errors in diagnosis	2,328	812	35	$226,917,718	$279,455
No medical misadventure	1,545	101	6.5	$34,325,159	$339,853
Improper performance	926	265	29	$57,464,109	$216,846
Failure to supervise/monitor case	657	232	35	$75,115,769	$323,775
Medication errors	338	103	30	$18,388,988	$178,534
Failure/delay in referral/consultation	217	94	43	$244,39,234	$259,992
Not performed	198	85	43	$18,413,992	$216,635
Failure to recognize complication	187	56	30	$13,101,517	$233,956
Delay in performance	180	71	39	$24,721,067	$348,184
Performed when not indicated or contraindicated	110	27	25	$4,949,871	$183,329

Table 12-6. Pediatric Claims by Most Prevalent Patient Condition, in Decreasing Order of Total Number of Closed Claims[1]

1985–2009	2009 Only
Newborn with brain damage	Viral infection in conditions classified elsewhere
Meningitis	Circumcision, ritual or routine
Routine infant or child health check	Developmental delay in child (eg, reading, speech)
Respiratory problems in newborn	Routine infant or child health check
Pneumonia	Newborn with brain damage
Appendicitis	Meningitis
Specified non-teratogenic anomalies	Birth trauma
Premature newborn	Birth
Congenital anomaly of genital organs	Congenital anomaly of genital organs
Birth	Malignant neoplasm of the brain

in which the physician defers testing or treatment of a patient) was the *most expensive* misadventure (ie, that with the highest average indemnity [$348,184]). The misadventure with the highest percentage of paid claims to closed claims was failure/delay in referral/consultation (43%). It is interesting to note that no medical misadventure (discussed on page 170) is ranked second among indemnity payments for medical misadventures. Only 6.5% of those cases resulted in indemnity payments. The patient condition most often associated with no medical misadventure was the baby with brain damage, with $6,095,432 in total indemnity payments (1985–2009) resulting in an average indemnity payment of $761,929 per case.

Patient Conditions

An analysis of closed claims by patient condition is important for many reasons (Table 12-6). These cases can indicate areas in which additional risk management may be warranted. Pediatricians may also want to pursue continuing medical education for these patient conditions.

From 1985 to 2009, the most prevalent patient condition for which claims were filed against pediatricians was neurologic impairment of a newborn—more than 8% of claims paid were for this condition alone. However, the second most prevalent condition, meningitis, resulted in a higher percentage of paid claims (44%) and a higher average indemnity. Seven of the top 10 conditions resulting in paid claims concerned conditions at or around the time of birth.

Medical Procedures

It often is helpful to examine closed claims by the medical procedure performed in the incident that led to the malpractice allegation (Table 12-7). This can be useful to practitioners in assessing liability risks associated with specific procedures. Primary care pediatrician activities are more cognitive than procedure oriented, compared with other specialists, so it is not surprising that the most common procedures in pediatric claims are diagnostic interviews, consultations, and general physical examinations. However, prescribing medications remains a common activity associated with claims and is receiving considerable attention from patient safety advocates.

Other Medicolegal Issues

The PIAA uses the term *no medical misadventure* to denote those claims with no identifiable medical mishap. These may include frivolous claims (ie, those without any misconduct or medical error

on the part of the insured physician) or claims that have no basis for medical negligence but are felt to have some legal merit under an associated medicolegal issue. The PIAA database further codifies these claims by their related medicolegal issue.

Vicarious liability, problems with patient records, consent issues, breach of contract or warranty, and communication between providers are some examples of these associated medicolegal issues (Table 12-8). The fourth most prevalent allegation against the pediatrician within this category involves problems with medical records. Although these accounted for only 6% of the associated medicolegal issues against pediatricians between 1985 and 2009, litigation involving patient record problems resulted in an indemnity payment in 60% of the claims, with an average indemnity of $230,338. This result confirms the importance of adequate medical record documentation and appropriate retention policies for pediatric medical records. Moreover, as pediatricians and hospitals rapidly shift to electronic health records (EHRs), this area should be watched carefully for additional medicolegal risks.[1]

Table 12-7. Pediatric Claims by Most Prevalent Procedures Performed, in Decreasing Order of Total Number of Closed Claims[1]

1985–2009	2009 Only
Diagnostic interview, evaluation, or consultation	General physician examination
General physical examination	Diagnostic interview, evaluation, or consultation
Prescription of medication	Prescription of medication
No care rendered	Miscellaneous manual examination
Injections and vaccinations	Injections and vaccinations
Miscellaneous nonoperative procedures	No care rendered
Miscellaneous manual examination	Cesarean deliveries
Respiratory therapy	Miscellaneous nonoperative procedures
Advice given to patient without treatment rendered	Circumcision
Cardiopulmonary resuscitation	Diagnostic procedures involving cardiac and circulatory functions

Table 12-8. Associated Issues Ranked by Average Indemnity Payment—Closed Pediatrics Claims, 1985 to 2009[1]

Other	$258,659
None	$342,446
Vicarious liability	$203,416
Problems with records	$230,338
Problems with patient history, examination	$426,109
Communication between providers	$397,767
Consent issues, breach of contract, warranty	$59,309
Lack of adequate facilities or equipment	$349,239
Premature discharge from institution	$430,131
Equipment malfunction or utilization problem	$467,636
Punitive damages	$294,760
X-ray error	$294,628
Abandonment	$185,322
Billing and collection	$44,375
Improper conduct by physician	$54,788
Failure to conform with regulations/statute/rule	$534,997
Laboratory error	$213,198
Assault and battery	$31,838
Unnecessary treatment	$384,375
Pharmacy error	$67,580
Res ipsa loquitur—self-evident	$125,000
Unnecessary treatment	$384,375
Comorbid conditions affecting care	$61,897
Surgical/medical device	$284,167
Complementary or alternative medications	$358,333
Third-party claimant	$226,250
Managed care referral problem	$400,000
Aseptic technique	$312,500
Telemedicine	$30,000

Malpractice claims often involve more than one person in the treatment that led to allegations of negligence. In 76% of the closed claims against pediatricians, associated personnel were involved in the case. Most often the associated personnel were other physicians. Table 12-9 lists the 5 most common personnel identified in closed claims against pediatricians.

It is interesting to note that many of the closed claims involving associated personnel with the highest average indemnity are not among the most frequent (Table 12-10). The exception is claims involving residents or interns.

Trends Among American Academy of Pediatrics Members

Since 1987, the AAP Division of Health Services Research has monitored the medical liability experience of pediatricians at various intervals (1987, 1990, 1992, 1995, 2001, and 2007) via the AAP Periodic Survey of Fellows (Table 12-11).

Table 12-9. Associated Personnel—Closed Pediatric Claims, 1985 to 2009[1]

Associated Personnel	Closed Claims	Paid Claims	% Paid to Close	Average Indemnity
Other physician	2,706	744	27.49	$302,518
Nurse	535	197	36.82	$297,017
Resident/Intern	352	126	35.80	$413,282
Consultant	475	162	34.11	$387,538
Emergency physician	265	89	33.58	$228,595

Table 12-10. Most Expensive Average Indemnity, Associated Personnel—Closed Pediatric Claims, 1985 to 2009[1]

Associated Personnel	Closed Claims	Paid Claims	% Paid to Close	Average Indemnity
Anesthesiologist	75	23	30.67	$541,744
Nurse anesthetist	21	8	38.10	$447,327
Nurse midwife	19	4	21.05	$432,002
Resident/Intern	352	126	35.80	$413,282

Table 12-11. Pediatrician and Malpractice Characteristics Among American Academy of Pediatrics Members[2]

	(% of pediatricians reporting)					
	1987	1990	1992[a]	1995[a]	2001[a]	2007[a]
Percent of pediatricians who have had a claim or suit brought against them (including claims during residency)[b]	26.9	29.3	30.4	29.9	28.4	31.5
Percent of pediatricians who have had a claim or suit brought against them (excluding claims during residency)	NA	27.9	29.5	28.2	25.5	28.2
Mean number of years in practice (for those sued)[c]	17.6	18.0	18.6	18.6	20.2	23.8
Among male pediatricians[d]					22.1	25.4
Among female pediatricians[d]					16.3	20.6
Mean number of years in practice (for those not sued)[c]	13.8	14.2	11.4	11.1	11.3	13.5
Among male pediatricians[d]					13.5	17.2
Among female pediatricians[e]					9.5	10.9
Percent of pediatricians who have had a claim or suit brought against them employed						
Full-time	NA	NA	95.3	94.7	96.0	93.5
Part-time	NA	NA	4.7	5.3	4.0	6.5
Mean number of times sued[e]	1.6	1.6	1.6	1.6	1.7	1.5
Mean number of months before suit was filed[d]	30.2	37.9	33.0	35.4	27.2	32.4
Percent of males sued[f,g]	29.9	34.9	35.8	35.8	34.5	38.8
Percent of females sued[f]	18.1	16.0	17.8	16.8	16.3	18.4
Percent of pediatricians who were party to a claim or suit for malpractice while a resident	NA	9.5	8.4	9.7	8.7	8.5

Abbreviation: NA, not asked.
[a]1992, 1995, 2001, and 2007 data exclude residents and all claims that occurred during residency unless otherwise noted.
[b]$P<.05$, 2007 vs 1987.
[c]Difference in mean number of years in practice between those who were sued and those who were not sued was significant ($P<.01$) for the years 1987, 1990, 1992, 1995, 2001, and 2007.
[d]$P<.01$, 2007 vs 2001.
[e]$P<.05$, 2007 vs 2001.
[f]Difference between percent of male versus female pediatricians sued was significant ($P<.01$) for all years.
[g]$P<.01$, 2007 vs 1987.

According to the most recent findings, the following aspects of medical liability have not changed:

- Approximately 3 of 10 pediatricians reported being sued at least once for malpractice (including residency training) at each point when surveys were taken.
- The percentage of pediatricians party to a claim or suit for care provided during residency training has remained less than 10% since first measured in 1990.
- There has been no change from 2001 to 2007 in the proportion of pediatricians who have had claims or suits brought against them during residency or post-residency, and little change in the characteristics of those who were sued.

The percent of pediatricians who have had a claim or suit brought against them (excluding claims during residency) is 28.2%. This percentage has remained fairly constant since the AAP started measuring it in 1987. The number of times sued per pediatrician has decreased slightly from 1.7 in 2001 to 1.5 in 2007 (P<.05).

Other specialties are not so fortunate. Nearly 91% of obstetricians-gynecologists indicated they had experienced at least one liability claim filed against them during their professional careers, with an average of 2.69 claims per physician. Of those who reported claims at some point during their career, nearly 42.8% reported at least 1 claim filed against them was a result of care rendered during their residency training.[3]

Time between occurrence and suit being filed has shown some fluctuation. Since 1987, it had been more than 30 months, but in 2001, this period fell to 27 months. The time interval between the alleged incident and the malpractice claim being filed increased in 2007 to 32.4 months (P<.01).

Outcomes of Recent Claims

As shown in Table 12-12, in 2007 compared with 2001, significantly more pediatricians reported their most recent claim or suit was dropped by the plaintiff (45.8% versus 33%, P<.01). About one third of pediatricians in both survey years said their most recent claim or suit was settled out of court (34.7% versus 36.2%, not significant) and similar proportions in both years report the plaintiff lost (8% versus 9% of all claims, not significant) or won (1.8% versus 2.7% of all claims, NS). Fewer pediatricians in 2007 said their most recent claim or suit is still in progress (9.8% versus 19% in 2001, P<.01). Regardless of the outcome of the most recent claim or suit, about 6 of 10 pediatricians in 2007 and 2001 said they were not pressured by their insurance carrier or employer to settle the suit of out of court.

Table 12-12. Outcome of Most Recent Claim or Suit by Year Among American Academy of Pediatrics Members[2]

	(% of pediatricians reporting)					
	1987	1990	1992[a]	1995[a]	2001[a]	2007[a]
Plaintiff won	1.9	0	2.0	1.5	2.7	1.8
Out-of-court settlement	36.7	31.2	29.4	30.5	36.2	34.7
Most recent claim or suit still in process[b,c]	24.9	29.3	22.4	20.2	19.0	9.8
Plaintiff dropped claim or suit[b,d]	35.9	29.8	35.1	37.0	33.0	45.8
Plaintiff lost[c]	0.5	9.8	11.0	10.7	9.0	8.0

[a]1992, 1995, and 2001 data exclude residents and all claims that occurred during residency.
[b]P<.01, 2007 vs 2001.
[c]P<.001, 2007 vs 1987.
[d]P<.05, 2007 vs 1987.

Table 12-13. Amount of Out-of-Court Settlements or Suits Lost in Court, 1987–1992; Amount Paid by Malpractice Insurance Carrier, 1995, 2001, and 2007, Among American Academy of Pediatrics Members[2a]

$	(% of pediatricians reporting)					
	1987	**1990**	**1992[b]**	**1995[b]**	**2001[b]**	**2007[b]**
0–115,000	70.7	71.7	70.8	73.4	63.6	53.8
115,001–400,000	18.4	13.8	20.2	16.0	20.4	30.0
400,001–1,200,000	10.7	15.6	5.6	10.6	15.0	13.8
3,000,000–7,500,000	–	–	–	–	1.4	2.6
TOTAL	99.8[c]	100.1[c]	100.0	100.0	100.3[c]	100.2

[a]Note change in wording of questions between years.
[b]1992, 1995, 2001, and 2007 data exclude residents and all claims that occurred during residency.
[c]Percents do not sum to 100 because of rounding error.

In all survey years, most claims or suits reported by pediatricians were settled or paid for less than $115,001. However indemnity payments in the $3 million to $7.5 million category nearly doubled from 2001 to 2007 (Table 12-13).

Characteristics of Patient Claimants and Site of Claim

Counter to some myths that most suits arise from uninsured patients, the majority of pediatricians in 2007 and 2001 reported that patients filing claims or suits had private health insurance (57% versus 64%, not signficant). In 2007, 40% of surveyed pediatricians, compared with 28% in 2001, said that patients filing claims were covered by pubic health insurance (P<.01), and 3% versus 9% reported these patients had no health insurance (P<.05).

Consistent with past survey years, the majority of pediatricians in 2007 (59%) said the patient filing the most recent claim or suit was not a regular patient. About 3 of 10 pediatricians who reported a claim by a non-regular patient said it involved a coverage situation.

In all survey years, most pediatricians said the hospital was the site of the alleged malpractice. However, fewer pediatricians in 2007 than in 2001 reported the hospital as the site (52% versus 64%, P<.01). Thus, pediatricians should be vigilant about the malpractice risk associated with a scenario

involving a hospitalized patient of another practice whom they are covering on call, or a patient of their own practice not seen on a regular basis.

In all survey years, the largest proportion of pediatricians who have had a claim brought against them said the hospital was also named in their most recent claim or suit (Table 12-14). While the proportion naming the hospital as a claimant in 2007 has remained about the same as in 2001, there has been a significant decline from that reported in 1987 (51.5% versus 61.2%, P<.05).

The next largest proportion said other pediatricians and other physicians were also named in the suit. There is no statistical difference between 2007 and 2001 in the proportion; however, there has been a significant decline from 1987 in the proportion naming another pediatrician (36.7% versus 60%, P<.01) and nonphysician medical staff (11.8% versus 22.6%, P<.01).

While the Periodic Survey of Fellows findings do not shed much light on increases in malpractice costs—to do so would require a methodology that is sensitive to geographic markets—the findings seem to reaffirm that premium increases have more to do with market forces in the insurance industry and the need for lasting tort reforms than any change in pediatric behavior resulting in more frequent or severe claims.

Table 12-14. Others Named in Claim or Suit Among American Academy of Pediatrics Members[2]

	(% of pediatricians reporting)					
	1987	**1990**	**1992[a]**	**1995[a]**	**2001[a]**	**2007[a]**
No one else named	9.0	10.2	14.5	12.6	10.2	12.7
Hospital[b]	61.2	64.9	51.8	52.4	56.2	51.5
Other pediatrician(s)[c]	60.0	51.0	46.5	49.4	43.8	36.7
Other physician(s)	51.0	46.9	46.2	44.2	44.7	46.3
Nonphysician medical staff[c]	22.6	10.8	14.5	15.6	15.5	11.8
Manufacturer	7.2	4.1	4.6	3.7	1.8	3.9
Managed care organization	NA	NA	NA	4.5	5.8	5.7
Other	6.8	6.7	8.2	4.9	8.4	10.5
Among pediatricians naming multiple responses						
1 other named in claim or suit				38.4	35.2	40.5
2 others named in claim or suit				32.3	40.3	35.5
3 others named in claim or suit				21.0	20.9	18.5
4 others named in claim or suit				7.4	3.1	5.0
5 others named in claim or suit				0.9	0.5	1.0

Not statistically significant, 2007 versus 2001.

Note: Multiple responses were possible.

[a]1992, 1995, 2001, and 2007 data exclude current residents and all claims that occurred during residency.

[b]$P<.05$, 2007 vs 1987.

[c]$P<.01$, 2007 vs 1987.

American Academy of Pediatrics Periodic Survey of Fellows #69 was mailed to a random sample of 1,605 active US members of the AAP from March to August 2007, with a response rate of 56.8%. For more information on Periodic Survey of Fellows #69, visit www.aap.org/research/periodicsurvey.

Risk Management Pointers

1. Pediatricians are not as likely to be sued (or sued more than once) as other specialists, but when pediatric claims involve an indemnity payment, it tends to be significantly higher than most other specialties.

2. Total indemnities against pediatricians appear to be increasing. You may want to have your insurer give you a breakdown of pediatric claims in your state or region to see if this is true in your locality. If it is, you may want to compare the limits of your policy against regional pediatric indemnities to see if additional coverage is needed.

3. The average cost to defend a pediatric malpractice case increased from $25,659 in 1999 to $49,686 in 2009. Find out if your insurance policy has a deductible and if it adequately covers legal defense expenses as well as indemnity.

4. Even if the quality of medical care provided is good, pediatricians may be liable for an array of other medicolegal issues. If you are not familiar with these risks, contact your insurer to request further information on the issues listed in Table 12-8.

5. Problems with medical records can be the basis of legal actions against physicians. Without good documentation, it is very difficult to defend a claim and claims are much more likely to result in indemnity payments. Conduct a spot test of your medical record documentation. As EHRs become more common in office and hospital settings, you should become familiar with the specific program in use and learn about the medicolegal risks associated with EHRs.

6. Sign up for a risk management or loss-prevention course specifically geared toward pediatric ambulatory care. Many insurers will offer a discount premium to physicians who participate in such courses.

References

1. Physician Insurers Association of America. *A Risk Management Review of Malpractice Claims—Pediatrics.* Rockville, MD: Physician Insurers Association of America; 2010

2. American Academy of Pediatrics. *Periodic Survey of Fellows #69: Experiences With Medical Liability: Executive Summary.* Elk Grove Village, IL: American Academy of Pediatrics; 2007. http://www.aap.org/research/periodicsurvey/ PS69exsummedicalliability.pdf. Accessed April 28, 2011

3. Kane CK. American Medical Association policy research perspectives. Medical liability claim frequency: a 2007–2008 snapshot of physicians. http://www.ama-assn.org/resources/ doc/health-policy/prp-201001-claim-freq.pdf. Accessed July 12, 2011

CHAPTER 13

Coping With Malpractice Litigation Stress

Robert A. Mendelson, MD, FAAP

KEY CONCEPTS

- Common Reactions to Being Sued
- A Stressful Life Event
- Understanding Physician Personality Traits
- Coping Strategies
- Counteracting the Stressor
- Accepting the Outcome and Moving On
- Supporting Colleagues Who Are Being Sued

For some physicians, being the target of a malpractice claim is devastating. The well-known fact that one third of pediatricians will become a defendant in a medical malpractice lawsuit at some time during their careers has little relevance until they experience a serious negative outcome or are actually served with a summons. When these events occur, for most physicians, life is changed in ways previously unimagined. *Malpractice litigation syndrome* was identified by Chicago psychiatrist Sara Charles, MD, in the mid-1980s.[1]

Despite significant efforts to change tort law for medical malpractice, major reform of the system is still needed in many states. In an environment complicated by changes in practice patterns that dramatically affect the control clinicians possess over their work, physicians remain legally and morally responsible for their decision-making. When a poor outcome occurs, an accusation of malpractice remains the primary means of assigning fault and thereby obtaining the goal of the tort—compensation.

Common Reactions to Being Sued

Every lawsuit is unique. For pediatricians, the inherent vulnerability of their patients is central. Any bad outcome is a tragedy. When it involves a child, it is especially so. That pediatricians have a special parental feeling for children obviously plays a role in their specialty choice. When they oversee a bad outcome that will affect the rest of the child's life, it is singularly painful. A lawsuit makes it even more so.

When sued, most physicians are hurt and angered. This anger arises in large part from the attack on our sense of honor. Honor has many faces, but in this case, it is that sense of personal integrity and principled uprightness of character that most physicians, and in fact most people, cherish. It resides in the core of our being and the threat of its loss is one of the most devastating experiences humans can incur. A public charge of malpractice accuses us of having failed in our responsibility, of being incompetent, and of lacking care and concern for our patient. Such an accusation injures the core of our being and therefore our self-esteem. There are few injuries sustained by dedicated physicians that are more painful.[2]

Although many people suggest that an allegation of malpractice should not be taken personally, most physicians consider it a direct assault on their personal and professional integrity. The common assumption held not only by the public but also by some physicians is that being sued means that you are a "bad doctor."

However, recently, the threat of being sued has become an inescapable reality for all who practice medicine. Good physicians, even the best physicians, are frequent targets of malpractice suits. Regardless of the eventual legal outcome of the allegation, most physicians tend to perceive litigation as a stressful life event that results, at least temporarily, in considerable emotional distress that affects not only the physician but also the physician's family. Such a response is normal and to a large extent, unavoidable. It is, in fact, a function of being human.

A Stressful Life Event

Most physicians feel that litigation, similar to divorce or the death of a loved one, is a stressful life event. More than 90% acknowledge periods of emotional disequilibrium, especially during periods of heightened stress such as deposition or trial. One third of physicians experience symptoms of depression such as insomnia, loss of energy, feelings of hopelessness, and in some instances, suicidal ideation. Headache, gastrointestinal symptoms, inner tension, frustration, anger, and anxiety all can occur.[3] Consultation with your personal physician—not self-medication—is indicated whenever symptoms persist or interfere with your ordinary functioning. Taking an active approach to stress management early on is highly advisable and can help buffer the harmful effects of chronic stress. Emotional reactions to being sued occur whether the suit is the first one experienced or the latest in a series of allegations. Each suit has its own life history that stems from the nature of the injury, the physician's perception of the events that gave rise

to the suit, related or unrelated circumstances in the physician's personal or professional life, and the nature of the relationship between the patient and physician.

In some cases, because of the triviality of the alleged injury and the physician's short-term relationship with the patient, the major source of stress may lie in the frustration and inconvenience the suit causes. In other cases, a suit may be filed on behalf of a long-term patient who had a poor outcome or died, for which the doctor may or may not feel responsible. Each of these situations is unique, will generate specific reactions, and requires different coping strategies.

Understanding Physician Personality Traits

To understand some of these reactions, it is important to be aware of the commonly shared personality characteristics of physicians.

Physicians' obsessive-compulsive personality traits are very helpful to the physician and patient. They stimulate physicians to be careful, responsible, conscientious, and prepared to consider a wide range of diagnostic possibilities and treatment options. Physicians also tend to have high expectations of themselves and are consequently self-critical.

When a physician is sued, however, these same personality traits generate self-doubt, self-scrutiny, feelings of guilt and shame, and often self-condemnation. Often the event that generated the suit already has been a source of sleepless nights and self-accusations, even in instances in which the physician performed with the highest level of competence. To be legally accused of negligence for such an event is enormously disturbing.

Coping Strategies

Although you may ordinarily cope well with stress, do not be surprised if initially you do not have the energy to take your daily run or exercise. It may take some weeks after the complaint before you resume your usual schedule. Most importantly, you need to talk with someone—your lawyer, spouse, or mental health professional. You need to increase your feelings of control over your practice and repair your feelings of self-esteem; become familiar with the legal process and the stress associated with it; if needed, rearrange aspects of your practice and if possible, avoid situations that increase stress; research the clinical issues involved in the claim; observe your emotional and physical reactions and how you are relating to others; schedule leisure activities; and play an active role in the defense of your case. If you happen to be a codefendant, it may be more useful to work together in your mutual defense than to work against one another. Lastly, because the complaint suggests that you are incompetent and a "bad doctor," you need to restore your feelings of being a good physician to be a good and successful defendant.

When formally charged with malpractice, most physicians feel stunned and often deny the event. As the reality and degree of accusations are accepted and the initial reaction diminishes, the physician generally begins to experience a range of symptoms principally characterized by anger and depression. The development of these symptoms signals a period of emotional disequilibrium that may disappear within weeks. However, occasionally symptoms persist for a longer period, diminish and recur periodically, or last until the resolution of the suit or longer.[4]

By its very nature, litigation is a lengthy and unpredictable process. Consequently, symptoms may recur whenever the lawsuit demands the physician's attention. For example, a week or two following the delivery of the complaint and after consultation with a lawyer and liability insurer, emotional equilibrium may return. A call many months later to schedule the first deposition may cause the whole spectrum of symptoms to reemerge. This pattern may occur repeatedly over a number of years, depending on the degree of the physician's in-

volvement with the case up to and including the time of trial.

For those physicians who feel they performed competently in the event in question, becoming a defendant involves a mobilization of healthy and constructive anger. For those who feel they were negligent or contributed in some fashion to the injury claimed by the patient, or those who are ambivalent about their role, the process of litigation is much more difficult. These latter reactions must be discussed in detail with legal counsel.

Counteracting the Stressor

Litigation stress has many facets. Finding the right coping strategy depends on identifying the underlying stressor at work and taking appropriate action. These are not stages; not every physician is equally vulnerable to each stressor.

Unpredictability

After being served with a suit, the physician's name can be dropped from the complaint within months, or the physician may still be waiting for trial 5 or 6 years later, no matter the merits of the case.

The manner by which lawyers proceed, rules of law, delays, testimony of experts, judge, and if the case goes to trial, jury all contribute to the inherently unpredictable nature of the litigation process. This generates feelings of frustration and anxiety.

Suggested coping strategies include

- Recognize that the legal process is unpredictable in terms of its rules, lawyers, judges, juries, and outcomes.
- Take appropriate steps to keep informed about the process so you can anticipate possibilities.
- Ask your attorney to explain points of law and what you can anticipate throughout the process.
- Spend the time and put in the effort to educate your lawyer on all aspects, medical and otherwise, of the lawsuit. Help make your lawyer become an expert in your case.

Loss of Control

When faced with a stressful situation, the average physician tends to address the problem to regain control of the situation and reduce the feeling of discomfort engendered by stress.[5] Litigation, however, draws the physicians into the legal environment. The lawyer, in offering reassurances, often tells the physician not to worry. "Just do what I tell you." Few words stimulate greater anxiety. They tend to erode rather than support the physician's characteristic mode of functioning and result in feelings of dependence and powerlessness, which in turn generate greater anxiety.

Suggested coping mechanisms include

- Examine your ordinary office and practice procedures and make changes where indicated.
- Examine your use of time and initiate changes that help you feel more in control (eg, shorten office hours, lengthen patient visits, schedule more leisure time).
- Consult with your personal and professional financial advisor. It may be unpleasant, but planning for your future can reduce anxiety and feelings of helplessness.
- Participate in loss-prevention education programs through your liability insurer, specialty society, or medical association.
- Get involved in your local American Academy of Pediatrics chapter or other volunteer organizations.

Meaning of the Event

This probably sounds preachy, but try to find some meaning in the event. Pain can be a great teacher of life's most difficult lessons.[6] Searching for meaning in the event, however painful and difficult, may provide insights and lessons over time.

- Reflect on your feelings of competence and take whatever measures necessary to solidify them.
- Reflect on the meaning of your profession and career and plan accordingly.

- Examine how this event affects your relationship with patients, especially if the plaintiff was a long-standing patient or acquaintance. Work to neutralize negative feelings.

Means of Coping

Looking on your past and monitoring your current behavior can help you employ many different coping tools.

- Look back on your life history. What coping mechanisms have helped you in the past? Use them now and modify them if they stop being effective.
- Reflect on your past difficulties, claim your triumphs, and learn from your failures.
- Self-observation is critical. If somatic symptoms develop that do not readily diminish, consult your physician. A mental health specialist could be very helpful if persistent emotional symptoms or alcohol or drug abuse develop.
- Build more or better use leisure time—active sports, work-free vacations, and more family time are helpful diversions.
- Make necessary changes in your practice. Restructure to make it less anxiety provoking and more manageable.
- Do your best to consider the process as a business decision rather than taking it personally. Remember, medicine is a calling. Medicine is a noble profession, but medicine is also a business. People in business get sued.
- If needed, seek professional help in the form of counseling or medication.

Social Support

Recognize that most physicians need to share their reaction to the experience, but this can be unwise. Check with your attorney before discussing the case with anyone other than your spouse. Although your colleagues and coworkers often are part of your social support system and willing to hear you out, be prudent. Do not confide in those who have been involved in the case or who may be called as witnesses. One of the first questions a plaintiff attorney asks the defendant is whether he or she has discussed the case with anyone. If the answer is yes, subpoenas will likely be sent to those with whom you have discussed the case. Remember that discussions with your attorney are privileged, and in many states conversations with your physician or mental health professional are privileged as well. Many organized support groups have confidentiality policies among the participants—an important consideration. Moreover, these pledges usually are respected by the court system. State medical societies or malpractice insurers often have formal litigation support groups facilitated by legal or health care experts. Consult with your attorney before participating in any of these support groups just to make sure that these discussions will not be discoverable under the laws of your state.

Accepting the Outcome and Moving On

The majority of cases filed against physicians nationwide result in no payment to the plaintiff. They are not settled and are usually withdrawn or dismissed. According to the Physician Insurers Association of America, 72% of the medical malpractice claims filed against pediatricians from 1985 to 2009 were resolved without any payment to the plaintiff.[7] If you settle, you need to include your family as well as your legal counsel in your decision-making.[8] Of the few physicians who go to trial, most win. They often feel they have been exposed to an unnecessary period of enormous stress. They may feel more wary but also more competent and more open to risk management suggestions. Many physicians who lose feel isolated from the medical community and lacking in support from their peers. Although an awkward situation, the loss of a malpractice case often represents a need for compensation by the plaintiff rather than a judgment of medical competence and, in most cases, these physicians need the support and

encouragement of their immediate medical community.[9]

Most physicians cope with litigation effectively, especially if they prepare themselves psychologically, maintain competence, obtain carefully selected emotional support during the process, and implement interventions that enhance their control over their practice. If the angry and negative feelings and attitudes persist after the suit is over and the physician feels that nothing positive was gained from the experience, professional counseling may be beneficial to aid the recovery process and help the physician return to a normal practice and lifestyle, older but certainly wiser.

Supporting Colleagues Who Are Being Sued

If you have a colleague who is being sued, be supportive by expressing sympathy and asking what you can do to help. Be on the alert for signs of withdrawal, depression, substance use and abuse, or other symptoms that would suggest the need for professional help. If you feel it is appropriate, encourage your colleague to seek professional help and personal support. If you do not feel that professional help is indicated, be there to offer the personal support that is so important in this situation.

Summary

- Acknowledge the feelings associated with getting sued.
- Learn more about litigation stress and how to cope with it.
- Find out about support groups, such as those offered by your professional liability insurance carrier or local medical society, and consider availing yourself of these resources.
- Learn about the legal process and your role in it.

- Remember that a lawsuit is not a personal attack but a common part of medical practice. It's one of the costs of doing business in medicine.
- Avoid discussing case details, which may be subject to discovery. Conversations with spouses are protected if done in private.
- Be active. Participate in activities outside medicine to help avoid dwelling on litigation issues.
- Be supportive of colleagues who may be struggling with litigation stress.

References

1. Charles SC. Malpractice litigation and its impact on physicians. *Curr Psychiatr Ther.* 1986;23:173–180
2. Dodge AM, Fitzer SF. *When Good Doctors Get Sued: A Guide for Physicians Involved in Malpractice Lawsuits.* Wilsonville, OR: BookPartners; 2001
3. Charles SC. Coping with a medical malpractice suit. *West J Med.* 2001;174(1):55–58. http://www.ncbi.nlm.nih.gov/pmc/articles/PMC1071237/pdf/wjm17400055. Accessed May 3, 2011
4. Martello J. Trials, settlements, and arbitration. The defendant's perspective. *Clin Plast Surg.* 1999;26(1):97–101
5. American College of Obstetricians and Gynecologists Committee on Professional Liability. Coping with the stress of malpractice litigation. ACOG Committee Opinion No. 406. *Obstet Gynecol.* 2008;111(5):1257–1258
6. Charles SC, Frisch PR. *Adverse Events, Stress, and Litigation: A Physician's Guide.* New York, NY: Oxford University Press; 2005
7. Physician Insurers Association of America. *Risk Management Review—Pediatrics.* Rockville, MD: Physician Insurers Association of America; 2010
8. Charles S. Personal insight, preparation key to coping with litigation stress. *AAP News.* 2000;16(5):14
9. American College of Obstetricians and Gynecologists. *Professional Liability and Risk Management: An Essential Guide for Obstetrician/Gynecologists.* 2nd ed. Washington DC: American College of Obstetricians and Gynecologists; 2008

Resources

The Physician Litigation Stress Resource Center is a central clearinghouse and resource for physicians and other health care professionals who are interested in the stress associated with medical malpractice litigation and in the changing climate of malpractice litigation. This site provides lists of articles and books in medical and popular literature as well as lists of links to other sites that may offer support to physicians. Visit www.physicianlitigationstress.org.

Charles SC, Frisch PR. *Adverse Events, Stress, and Litigation: A Physician's Guide.* New York, NY: Oxford University Press; 2005

James JM, Davis WE. *Physician's Survival Guide to Litigation Stress: Understanding, Managing and Transcending a Malpractice Crisis.* Lafayette, CA: Physician Health Publications; 2007

CHAPTER 14

Testifying as an Expert Witness

Gary N. McAbee, DO, JD, FAAP, and the American Academy of Pediatrics Committee on Medical Liability and Risk Management

T he medical expert witness is at the core of a medical malpractice lawsuit. Except for a few cases involving a legal principle such as res ipsa loquitur ("the thing speaks for itself"; eg, a surgical sponge left inside a patient), an expert is typically required for a malpractice case to proceed through the legal system. The purpose of the medical expert is to assist the triers of facts (ie, jury or judge) in understanding the scientific issues so they can arrive at a fair and equitable result. In fact, an expert may even be needed before a malpractice lawsuit can be filed. In approximately half of the states, a plaintiff's attorney must file a certificate or affidavit of merit attesting to the fact that the expert has reviewed the medical records and opined that negligence has occurred. Thus, it is essential that an expert's testimony be fair, objective, unbiased, accurate, and honest.

The expert witness process has been criticized from many perspectives. Although many have written about the widespread existence of improper expert testimony,[1] there is surprisingly little data that assess the prevalence and degree of it.[2] Improper medical testimony exists in various forms. There is the obvious problem of an expert giving inaccurate or frankly dishonest testimony about credentials or experience. More commonly, the problem is when the expert embellishes or distorts the facts of the case, or proposes a theory that few would agree with. Although some of these issues are obviously improper, additional information needs to

be available about the expert process on a continual basis so that honest, competent practitioners are encouraged to effectively participate in the legal process. For instance, a recent survey found that only 25% of pediatric residents had exposure to the medical expert process during their residency training.[3]

Oversight has been difficult, especially at the point of the certificate or affidavit of merit. Oversight at this early time in the process may be critical because approximately two thirds of lawsuits are eventually dropped, withdrawn, or dismissed without any money being paid out.[4,5] Nevertheless, costs in defending these lawsuits (including expert witness costs) have reached $49,686 in 2009 for cases involving pediatrics (compared with $92,196 for cases that have eventually resulted in payment).[6] The US Government Accountability Office reported that between 1985 and 1998, more than 60% of medical malpractice cases were dropped without payment, at a cost of $3 billion spent on defending meritless claims and $4.5 billion spent on claims not deemed meritless but closed without any payment being made. Also, improper testimony may remain hidden if the case is settled and not published.

The American Academy of Pediatrics has been instrumental in devising various strategies to improve the expert witness process at the state and federal levels. The following policy statement,

"Expert Witness Participation in Civil and Criminal Proceedings," updated and revised in 2009, provides guidance to practitioners who participate in the medical expert witness process. The policy asserts that the best strategies for improving the quality of medical expert testimony involve strengthening the expert's qualifications for serving as a medical expert (which has been included in some recent state tort reforms), educating pediatricians about standards for experts and their testimony, and providing specific guidelines for expert conduct throughout the legal process.

References

1. Huber PW. *Galileo's Revenge: Junk Science in the Courtroom.* New York, NY: Basic Books; 1991
2. Safran A, Skydell B, Ropper S. Expert witness testimony in neurology: Massachusetts experience 1980-1990. *Neurol Chron.* 1992;2(7):1–6
3. Donn SM, Caspary G, McAbee G. Medico-legal education of pediatric residents: are we doing better? Pub No. 580514. Presented at Annual Pediatric Academic Societies Meeting; May 3–6, 2008; Honolulu, HI
4. Carroll AE, Buddenbaum JL. Malpractice claims involving pediatricians: epidemiology and etiology. *Pediatrics.* 2007;120(1):10–17
5. American Medical Association. *Physician Practice Information Survey.* Chicago, IL: American Medical Association; 2010
6. Physicians Insurers Association of America. *25 Years (1985-2010) Risk Management Review—Pediatrics.* Rockville, MD: Physician Insurers Association of America; 2010

Organizational Principles to Guide and Define the Child
Health Care System and/or Improve the Health of all Children

Policy Statement—Expert Witness Participation in Civil and Criminal Proceedings

abstract

The interests of the public and both the medical and legal professions are best served when scientifically sound and unbiased expert witness testimony is readily available in civil and criminal proceedings. As members of the medical community, patient advocates, and private citizens, pediatricians have ethical and professional obligations to assist in the administration of justice. The American Academy of Pediatrics believes that the adoption of the recommendations outlined in this statement will improve the quality of medical expert witness testimony in legal proceedings and, thereby, increase the probability of achieving outcomes that are fair, honest, and equitable. Strategies for enforcing guidance and promoting oversight of expert witnesses are proposed. *Pediatrics* 2009;124:428–438

BACKGROUND

The American Academy of Pediatrics (AAP) first articulated policy on appropriate medical expert witness testimony in 1989 and was among the first medical specialty societies to do so.[1] The statement was revised in 1994[2] to incorporate additional provisions on expert witness testimony guidelines from the Council of Medical Specialty Societies.[3] A 2002 revision outlined responsible practices that physicians should follow to safeguard their objectivity in preparing and presenting expert witness testimony. Key legal concepts were explained, and the role of the expert witness in the litigation process (pretrial and trial) was described.[4] This latest AAP iteration expands the requirements and qualifications for experts testifying in civil and criminal cases, the latter primarily relating to cases involving alleged child abuse and/or neglect. The importance of expert witness testimony in the process of determining civil liability, child safety, or criminal culpability and its unique significance in pediatric cases are also stressed. Recent efforts to improve the quality of medical expert witness testimony are described. The known strengths or weaknesses of these programs are noted. Enforcement of policy recommendations are sought for the first time.

WHAT IS EXPERT TESTIMONY?

The expert witness plays an essential role under the US system of jurisprudence. Courts rely on expert witness testimony in most civil and criminal cases to explain scientific matters that may or may not be understood by jurors and judges. Standards of admissibility of expert witness testimony vary depending on state and federal rules of proce-

CONTRIBUTORS:
COMMITTEE ON MEDICAL LIABILITY AND RISK MANAGEMENT

KEY WORDS
expert witness, legal and ethical standards, oversight, peer review

ABBREVIATIONS
AAP—American Academy of Pediatrics
FRE—Federal Rule of Evidence

This document is copyrighted and is property of the American Academy of Pediatrics and its Board of Directors. All authors have filed conflict-of-interest statements with the American Academy of Pediatrics. Any conflicts have been resolved through a process approved by the Board of Directors. The American Academy of Pediatrics has neither solicited nor accepted any commercial involvement in the development of the content of this publication.

www.pediatrics.org/cgi/doi/10.1542/peds.2009-1132

doi:10.1542/peds.2009-1132

All policy statements from the American Academy of Pediatrics automatically expire 5 years after publication unless reaffirmed, revised, or retired at or before that time.

PEDIATRICS (ISSN Numbers: Print, 0031-4005; Online, 1098-4275).

Copyright © 2009 by the American Academy of Pediatrics

dure and evidence. Although most state laws conform to both the Federal Rules of Procedure and Federal Rules of Evidence (FRE),[5] some do not. The same testimony from a given expert witness, therefore, might be admissible in some state courts but not in federal court, and vice versa. FRE 702 authorizes a judge to admit expert testimony into evidence if it assists the jury or the judge to "understand the evidence or to determine a fact in issue." FRE 703 permits a qualified expert to give testimony based on data of others, provided that the data are of the kind customarily used by the expert's peers. FRE 704 permits an expert to opine on the ultimate factual issue.

In a malpractice case, testimony of an expert witness differs from that of other witnesses. "Witnesses of fact" (those testifying because they have personal knowledge of the incident or are persons involved in the lawsuit) typically restrict their testimony to the facts of the case at issue. The expert witness is given more latitude. The expert witness is allowed to compare the applicable standards of care with the facts of the case and interpret whether the evidence indicates a deviation from the standards of care. Without the expert's explanation of the range of acceptable treatment modalities within the standard of care and interpretation of medical facts, juries may not have the technical expertise needed to distinguish malpractice (an adverse event caused by negligent or "bad" care) from maloccurrence (an unavoidable adverse event or "bad outcome").[6] An expert must be qualified. Although the rules vary among jurisdictions about whether the expert must be of the same specialty as the defendant, the expert, nevertheless, must demonstrate to the judge sufficient knowledge and expertise about the issue to qualify as an expert.

LEGAL AND ETHICAL STANDARDS OF TESTIMONY

The judge acts as the gatekeeper in deciding the qualifications of the expert as well as the relevance and reliability of the testimony. The 2 main standards used by judges in determining relevance and reliability are referred to as the Daubert and Frye standards.[7,8] The Daubert standard (expanded in later cases known as Joiner[9] and Kumho[10]) was established by the US Supreme Court in the 1993 case *Daubert v Merrell Dow Pharmaceuticals Inc*. This standard is used in federal courts and has been adopted by many states for use in state courts. Under the *Daubert* decision, a judge will act as the gatekeeper for expert testimony in determining whether the opinion is both relevant and reliable. The judge can, but is not required to, assess testimony according to 4 guidelines in determining whether it is reliable: (1) whether the expert's theory or technique can be (or has been) tested; (2) whether the theory or technique has been subjected to peer review or publication; (3) the known or potential error rate of the theory; and (4) whether there is general acceptance in the relevant scientific community. The latter "general-acceptance" standard is at the core of the Frye standard of expert testimony established more than 80 years ago.[8] The Frye standard is still used in some states. Other states use a hybrid of the Daubert and Frye standards. Under the Daubert standard, trial judges are to focus on the reasoning or scientific validity of the methodology, not the conclusion of the methodology. Once the judge permits expert testimony to be admitted into evidence, it is the role of the jury to determine the "weight" (or importance) of the testimony. The *Daubert* court noted that challenges to questionable testimony are to be con-

tested via cross-examination and the presentation of contrary evidence.[7]

The effect of the *Daubert* decision in reducing "junk science" from being admitted into evidence continues to be debated.[11] Yet, it seems to have benefited, rather than harmed, the process.[12] The importance of standards for admissibility of expert testimony at the trial level is underscored by the fact that appellate courts can only consider an "abuse-of-discretion" standard in reviewing a trial judge's decision to admit or exclude expert testimony (ie, defers to the trial judge's rulings unless overtly erroneous).[9] Critics have voiced concern over judicial discretionary power in admitting experts simply because some judges may lack the requisite scientific or medical background to interpret potentially complex medical issues.[13]

Attorneys may request experts to state that their testimony is being given "within a reasonable degree of medical certainty." This rubric is not universally defined and has been interpreted differently by the courts.[14,15] Also, it is not a standard required in all jurisdictions.[16] Ideally, expert witnesses should be unbiased conveyers of information. The pivotal factor in the medical tort process is the integrity of the expert witness testimony. It should be reliable, objective, and accurate and provide a truthful analysis of the standard of care. Regrettably, not all medical experts testify within these boundaries.[17] The medical community has long been aware that not all experts testify within scientific standards and ethical guidelines.[17,18] However, more research is needed to determine how invasive improper expert testimony is in the legal process. In a study of expert witnesses in lawsuits against neurologists over a 10-year period, significant errors of fact or interpretation and incorrect statements were noted to be common.[19] One study of characteristics of expert witnesses in neurologic birth injury cases noted that a small group of physicians provided a disproportionate percentage of expert testimony in cases and that there may be suboptimal expertise and possible bias in testimony.[20]

WHAT IS MEDICAL MALPRACTICE?

Medical malpractice law is based on concepts drawn from tort and contract law. It is commonly understood as liabilities arising from the delivery of medical care. Causes of action can be based on negligence, insufficient informed consent, intentional misconduct, breach of a contract (ie, guaranteeing a specific therapeutic result), defamation, divulgence of confidential information, or failure to prevent foreseeable injuries to third parties. Medical negligence is the predominant theory of liability in medical malpractice actions.

According to *Black's Law Dictionary*,[21] negligence is defined as "the failure to exercise the standard of care that a reasonably prudent person would have exercised in a similar situation." To establish negligence, the plaintiff must prove all of the following elements: (1) the existence of the physician's duty to the plaintiff, usually based on the existence of the physician-patient relationship; (2) the applicable standard of care and its violation (ie, breach of the duty); (3) damages (a compensable injury); and (4) a legally causal connection between the violation of the standard of care and the injury. In a medical malpractice case, experts may be asked to provide an opinion about 1 or all of these elements of a malpractice case. Experts should not testify about all of these elements if they are not within their area of expertise (eg, it may not be appropriate for a pediatrician to testify about whether a cesarean delivery

should have been performed to prevent a brachial plexus injury).

Besides negligence, a medical malpractice lawsuit may also include an allegation of insufficient informed consent. Informed consent includes a discussion with a noncoerced patient or parent who has decision-making capacity. The discussion should include the benefits versus the risks of proposed and alternative tests or treatments and the option of no treatment. When insufficient informed consent is an aspect of the case, the expert should be familiar with the standards of informed consent in the particular state involved. There are 2 main standards of providing informed consent that have been implemented by either judicial decision or statute: the "reasonable-patient" standard versus the "reasonable-physician" standard (also known as "community" or "professional" standard).[22] In the former standard, the physician must disclose the treatments and risks that a reasonable patient/person would want disclosed (at trial, typically decided by the jury but may require expert testimony). In the latter standard, the physician must disclose the treatments and risks that a reasonable physician would disclose to the patient (at trial, typically requires expert testimony). In some circumstances in some jurisdictions, failure to obtain informed consent can result in a claim of "battery" (intentional, unauthorized touching of a person).[22,23]

HOW ARE STANDARDS OF CARE DETERMINED?

In the law of negligence, the standard of care is generally thought of as "that degree of care which a reasonably prudent person should exercise in same or similar circumstances."[21] If the defendant's conduct falls outside the standards, then he or she may be found liable for any damages that re-

sulted from this conduct. In medical negligence disputes, the defendant's medical decision-making and practice are compared with the applicable standard of care. Generally, this is understood to be "that reasonable and ordinary care, skill, and diligence as physicians and surgeons in good standing in the same general line of practice, ordinarily have and exercise in like cases."[21] Many courts have held that the increased specialization of medicine and establishment of national board certification is more significant than geographic differences in establishing the standard of care. These courts contend that board-certified medical or surgical specialists should adhere to standards of their respective specialty boards (ie, a national standard). However, this recognition of specialty-based standards has critics, because it does not account for rural and other underserved communities or access to specialized health care facilities.[24] Thus, some jurisdictions continue to use a "locality" standard in which the physician is held to the standards of like physicians in the community.[24] Some states require out-of-state experts to demonstrate that they have familiarity with the "local" standard of care.

WAS THE STANDARD OF CARE BREACHED?

In medical liability cases, the role of the expert witness is often to establish standards of care applicable to the case at issue. The expert may also be asked to opine about any deviation from acceptable standards. When care has been deemed "substandard," the expert witness may be asked to opine whether that deviation from the standard of care could have been the proximate (ie, legal) cause of the patient's alleged injury. Because courts and juries depend on medical experts to make medical standards understandable, the testimony should be clear, coherent, and consistent with the standards applicable at the time of the incident. Although experts may testify as to what they think the most appropriate standard of care was at the time of occurrence, they should know and consider alternative acceptable standards. These alternatives may be raised during direct testimony or under cross-examination. Expert witnesses should not consider new evidence, guidelines, or studies that were not available to the treating physicians at the time of the occurrence. Expert witnesses should not define the standard so narrowly that it only encompasses their opinion on the standard of care to the exclusion of other acceptable treatment options available at the time of the incident.

MEDICAL ERRORS VERSUS NEGLIGENCE

The Institute of Medicine's sentinel report on medical errors, *To Err Is Human: Building a Safer Health System*,[25] provides a helpful framework for understanding the many factors involved in medical interventions and how their permutations can affect patient outcome. Whenever a medical intervention is undertaken, several outcomes can occur—the patient's condition can improve, stay the same, or deteriorate. These same outcomes are possible even when the medical treatment is performed properly. A negative outcome alone is not sufficient to indicate professional negligence. It is essential that the trier of the case (either jury or judge) understand that negligence cannot be inferred solely from an unexpected result, a bad result, failure to cure, failure to recover, or any other circumstance that shows merely a lack of success.

BURDEN OF PROOF

In a medical malpractice case, the plaintiff bears the burden of proof and must convince a jury by a "preponder-ance of the evidence" that its theory of the case is more probably true than alternative theories. A "preponderance of the evidence" means more than 50% likely. Thus, jurors in a medical malpractice case must be persuaded that the evidence presented by the plaintiff is more plausible than any counterargument offered by the defendant.[26] The plaintiff and defense attorneys will present their respective experts, each side hoping their witnesses will appear more knowledgeable, objective, and credible than their counterparts. In a criminal case, the prosecutor bears the burden of proof, and the guilt must be proven by the much higher standard of "beyond a reasonable doubt."

PRETRIAL ROLE OF EXPERT TESTIMONY

In medical malpractice, expert witness testimony may be used to evaluate the merits of a malpractice claim before filing legal action. Some states have enacted laws that require that a competent medical professional in the same area of expertise as the defendant review the claim and be willing to testify that the standard of care was breached.[27] This may require a filing of an affidavit or certificate of merit that malpractice has occurred. Some states have deemed this system unconstitutional, claiming that legitimate plaintiffs may be denied access to the legal system solely on procedural, rather than substantive, grounds.[28]

Some states use review panels to pre-screen medical malpractice cases. These panels typically consist of a physician, attorney, and lay representative. However, state laws that govern the timing and process for review panels can vary. Depending on the state, the review can take place before or after the claim has been filed. Review-panel findings can be binding or nonbinding. The opinion of the review panel may or may not be admissible should the matter proceed to litigation. The continuing future role of these panels has been questioned.[29]

Those who are seeking regulation of expert witness testimony have noted that the expert opinions provided during this early stage of the legal process are subject to even less scrutiny and accountability than testimony provided later. Critics believe that the lack of oversight of experts during the pretrial reviews allows too many nonmeritorious cases to proceed, thereby defeating the purpose of having pretrial reviews.[30]

EXPERT REPORTS AND DEPOSITION

The purpose of "discovery" is to identify all the facts related to the case. Discovery is applicable to both fact witnesses and expert witnesses. The deposition of key fact witnesses is a very important facet of the discovery process in malpractice cases. A deposition is a witness's recorded testimony, given under oath, while being questioned by attorneys for the parties in the case. Throughout the deposition process, attorneys gather information on what fact witnesses will say and assess the relative effectiveness of their testimony as well as their demeanor (eg, clarity, believability, arrogance, sincerity). Crucial decisions in determining the next phase of the case (eg, seeking a settlement, going to trial, moving for dismissal/summary judgment) are often based on the strength of the testimony. Experts can also be deposed. Rather than through depositions, written reports of the experts are typically shared between the 2 parties before trial. However, some states may not require disclosure of the identity of the expert or even disclosure of the report. Most medical malpractice lawsuits that are resolved in favor of the plaintiff are typically settled during or at the conclusion of the discovery phase.[31]

UNIQUE FACTORS IN PEDIATRIC CASES

In theory, expert witness testimony from the plaintiff and the defense should give the jury enough of a technical understanding of the medical care provided and its appropriateness to determine if the preponderance of the evidence proves the defendant liable for the plaintiff's injury. In cases that reach trial, some authorities note that jurors can generally be effective in assessing expert testimony.[32] However, other aspects of the proceedings may unduly influence triers of the case. This is particularly true in cases that involve children. Because people tend to have a natural sympathy for children, the focus of the trial has the potential to become the plaintiff rather than the evidence. A jury might be influenced by the needs of, for example, a family with a neurologically impaired infant or a ventilator-dependent teenager.

Patients who experience long-term consequences of injuries attributable to medical negligence should be appropriately and promptly compensated. However, using malpractice awards to compensate patients for adverse outcomes not caused by medical negligence is not the intent of the system. Whether society at large should provide more assistance to families faced with such tragic circumstances is a policy decision. Wanting to assist the families of children with disabilities or injuries regardless of whether the physician committed any medical error may seem altruistic to the jury, but in fact, it is an inappropriate outcome. To prevent unjust results, objective expert witness testimony is needed.

CRIMINAL CASES

Pediatricians often serve as experts in civil child protection cases (in which custody of children may be at issue) and in criminal cases of alleged child abuse and neglect. The new subspecialty of "child abuse pediatrics" approved by the AAP and the American Board of Pediatrics sets high standards for professional competence and conduct in this area. Pediatricians who are not board certified in child abuse pediatrics may still be called to testify in cases of abuse and neglect if they have special knowledge and experience that qualifies them to explain medical issues to the court, both as experts and as fact witnesses. Pediatricians who are inexperienced in evaluating children suspected of abuse or neglect should be cautious of providing an expert opinion because of the devastating outcome of a wrongful conviction based on inaccurate testimony. This is a high-risk area for expert testimony, and even experienced professionals have been engaged in controversy.[33] If a general pediatrician feels uncomfortable in testifying in these cases, consultation with subspecialists in child abuse pediatrics should be strongly considered.

IMPROVING THE QUALITY OF EXPERT TESTIMONY

Various branches of organized medicine and some state medical licensure boards have implemented programs to help curb unscientific expert witness testimony. Strategies for regulating expert witness testimony generally fall under the principles of education, prevention, peer review, and sanctioning.

Education

Continuing medical education about the expert witness process is needed at all levels of pediatric experience.[34]

The 2006 AAP graduating resident survey revealed that only 25% of residents reported that their training program provided adequate education on the expert witness process.[35] Educational programs at both the national and state levels are critical for this effort. One strategy for effective programs is to use false or unscientific testimony from closed cases for teaching purposes in continuing medical education venues. This strategy is particularly effective when biased or false testimony played an important role in the outcome of the case. It illustrates the power of expert witness testimony in malpractice litigation and can be an excellent teaching technique to present acceptable and optimal treatment modalities that should have been introduced by the experts.

Prevention

Despite the critical importance of the expert witness, no uniform standards on credentialing of experts currently exist. One specialty society has initiated a process to certify experts.[36] Imposing eligibility restrictions on those who provide expert witness testimony might be a way to prevent irresponsible testimony. By 2006, approximately 22 states had measures requiring minimum qualifying standards for physician experts.[37] Some states have proposed or enacted legislation or regulations that tighten the qualifications for medical experts to more closely match those of the defendant physician (eg, geographic factors, specialty training, certification, percentage of time spent on direct patient care, etc).[38,39]

Other preventive measures decrease financial incentives for serving as an expert witness, which is especially applicable to witnesses who travel extensively to provide expert services ("itinerant" witnesses). Examples include recommending caps on the percentage of annual revenue that a medical expert can derive from testimony fees or establishing fee schedules for expert witness testimony that are based on a set hourly rate (determined to be reasonable or comparable to other medical consulting services). The medical profession has deemed it unethical for expert witnesses to base their fees for testifying contingent on the outcome of the case.[40–42] Other suggestions for preventing itinerant experts include the sponsoring by medical specialty societies of expert scientific panels and court-appointed medical experts (permitted under FRE 706). A few medical societies have proposed that, for physicians to serve as experts in malpractice cases, they are required to join their medical society (even those from out-of-state). Thus, all experts testifying in that state would be potentially subject to disciplinary action of the local medical organization. Some states require an expert to hold a medical license in that state. Some states consider expert testimony as part of the "practice of medicine," with possible sanctioning by the licensing board for improper testimony.[43] The American Medical Association House of Delegates has discussed a series of resolutions aimed at curtailing improper testimony by physicians and in 1998 adopted the position that the provision of expert witness testimony should be considered the practice of medicine and should be subject to peer review.[44] Adopting this approach not only makes medical licensure a requirement for providing expert witness testimony but also puts physicians on notice about potential actions against their medical license for giving false, biased, or unscientific testimony. Because licensing

boards already function as disciplinary bodies, they may be an appropriate setting for judging the appropriateness of physician conduct, which can include expert testimony.[45] However, not all courts have agreed that medical expert witness testimony is engaging in the practice of medicine.[46]

Peer Review

Specialty medical organizations have established programs in which a panel of peers will review and critique the content of expert witness testimony.[47–50] Sometimes, the testimony and the peer analysis, along with commentary, are published in scientific journals. Some specialty societies, such as the American Association of Neurologic Surgeons (www.aans.org/about/membership/professional_conduct10_06.pdf), maintain libraries of expert witness testimony that are accessible by legal counsel of their members. There are obstacles to an effective peer-review process, including costs, time, and possibility of lawsuits against peer reviewers.[51–53] Any oversight process must be fair and objective and ensure due process. Peer review has lead to sanctioning of experts.

Sanctioning

The most aggressive method of curbing irresponsible testimony is to discipline physicians whose expert opinions are deemed to be biased, inaccurate, incomplete, or unscientific. Disciplinary actions can even result in the physician being expelled from membership in professional organizations. Such actions have been upheld by the appellate courts.[54]

There have been lawsuits against expert witnesses for alleged improper testimony. Historically, the principle of witness immunity has shielded experts from legal reprisal that is based

on the nature of their testimony.[55,56] To bring greater accountability to expert witness testimony in malpractice cases, some legal authorities have sought to have a distinction drawn between expert witnesses and witnesses of fact relating to immunity.[55] These critics postulate that because experts testify voluntarily and receive significant compensation for their services, general witness immunity should not apply to them. Various courts have responded differently to this concept.

Additional proposals that may affect or improve the expert witness system include mediation and arbitration[57,58]; specialized health courts[59]; an internal dispute-resolution process within the hospital[60]; standardizing and regulating expert medical case review, analysis, and testimony[61]; adopting a "data-based standard of care in allegations of medical negligence"[62]; use of third-party experts[63]; and encouraging academic institutions to be accountable for the testimony of their faculty members.[64] At least 1 federal judge has suggested that judges may be more willing to use third-party experts if the experts were more easily accessible and their fairness and impartiality could be ensured by professional oversight and discipline.[65]

Because of the increasing complexity and uncertainty surrounding the issue of expert testimony by physicians, the medical community must proceed cautiously. Although courts have upheld the right of specialty organizations to discipline a member for improper testimony, any disciplinary process is fraught with risks and must be fair and objective and ensure due process. An expert witness disciplinary program that is too aggressive may be seen as organized medicine's discouragement of physicians from testifying. Some courts have been punitive about efforts to quash potential experts from testifying.[66] The physician community will need to remain firmly committed to reviewing and sanctioning false statements by medical experts for both the defense and the plaintiff or prosecutor. It has been suggested that fear of sanctions could dissuade physicians from fulfilling their civic and professional duty to participate as experts in legal processes. One concern is that a decrease in the number of physicians willing to provide expert witness testimony may be associated with greater reliance on "professional" witnesses. Beyond the considerable legal risks, disciplinary programs are labor intensive and may be expensive to implement and maintain. Because disciplinary programs can be beyond what a state or local organization can shoulder, specialty societies are often urged to provide this service for their members on a nationwide basis.[47,67] Continual attempts to improve the expert witness process should affect the delivery of future medical care by reducing the number of lawsuits and litigation costs and ensuring adequate physician supply in those specialties with high exposure to malpractice lawsuits.[68]

RECOMMENDATIONS

The AAP recognizes that physicians have the professional, ethical, and legal duty to assist in the legal process when medical issues are involved. Physicians who serve as expert witnesses have an obligation to present complete, accurate, and unbiased information to assist the triers of facts to understand the scientific issues so that they can arrive at a fair and equitable result. At this time, the best strategies for improving the quality of medical expert witness testimony must include strengthening the qualifications for serving as a medical expert, educating pediatricians about standards for experts, and providing more specific guidelines for physician con-

duct throughout the legal process. To that end, the following recommendations are offered.

Advocacy and Education

The AAP believes that the establishment of certain minimal qualifications for physicians who serve as expert witnesses will improve the quality of testimony and promote just and equitable verdicts. Therefore, the AAP supports the following efforts.

1. Implement the recommendations of this statement through legislative or regulatory reform of expert witness testimony (eg, establish minimal qualifications for expert witnesses).

2. Educate pediatricians (during residency training and through continuing medical education) and provide them with the skills and knowledge base needed for them to provide objective, scientific, and ethical expert witness testimony in legal proceedings.

3. Implement additional specialized education as well as oversight safeguards for experts participating in the criminal law process because of heightened concerns for convictions based on inaccurate expert testimony in criminal cases.

4. Aid in the establishment of expert panels to study, standardize, and disseminate elements of expert testimony that have been inadequately addressed (eg, define "within a reasonable degree of medical certainty," establish the role of evidence-based medicine in expert opinions, opine whether expert testimony should be considered "the practice of medicine").

Relevant Qualifications

Physicians should limit their participation as medical experts to cases in which they have genuine expertise. The following qualifications must be

met (and verified) to demonstrate relevant education, certification, and experience.

1. Physician expert witnesses must hold a current, valid, and unrestricted medical license in the state in which they practice medicine.

2. Physician expert witnesses should be certified by the relevant board recognized by the American Board of Medical Specialties or a board recognized by the American Osteopathic Association or by a board with equivalent standards. Alternatively, the expert should be capable of demonstrating sufficient training or clinical experience in the clinical area at issue to be qualified and accepted as an expert by the relevant specialty board(s).

3. Physician expert witnesses must have been actively engaged in clinical practice in the medical specialty or area of medicine about which they testify, including knowledge of or experience in performing the skills and practices at issue to the lawsuit. Alternatively, the expert should be able to demonstrate updated competence in the profession within a reasonable time period contiguous to the alleged act. Evidence of updated competence could include medical student or resident teaching, relevant publications, or research.

4. Unless retired from clinical practice, most of the expert's professional time should not be devoted to expert witness work. If retired, the physician should render expert opinions on cases that occurred at the time he or she was in active practice.

5. Physician expert witnesses should not give false, misleading, or misrepresentative details about their qualifications.

Standards of Testimony

Physician expert witnesses should take all necessary steps to provide thorough, fair, objective, and impartial review of the medical facts. To meet that obligation, physicians who agree to testify as experts in medical malpractice cases should conduct themselves as follows.

1. Regardless of the source of the request for testimony (plaintiff or defendant), physician expert witnesses should lend their knowledge, experience, and best judgment to all relevant facts of the case.

2. Physician expert witnesses should take necessary steps to ensure that they have access to all documents used to establish the facts of the case and the circumstances surrounding the occurrence. If all medical records are unavailable for review, experts should consider recusing themselves from serving in an expert capacity.

3. Physician expert witnesses should not exclude relevant information for any reason and certainly not to create a perspective that favors the plaintiff or the defendant.

4. The physician expert should be comfortable with his or her testimony regardless of whether it is to be used by the plaintiff or defendant.

Standards of Care

The physician expert witness should be familiar with the medical standards of care at the time of the incident at issue. A physician who is unfamiliar with the medical standards would not meet the recommended qualifications of an expert.

1. Before testifying, the physician expert witness should thoroughly review and understand the current concepts and practices related to that standard as well as the concepts and practices related to that standard at the time of the incident that led to the lawsuit.

2. The testimony presented should reflect generally accepted standards within the specialty or area of practice about which the physician expert witness is testifying, including those held by a significant minority.

3. When a variety of acceptable treatment modalities exist, this should be stated candidly and clearly.

4. In states where the standard of practice is based on the "locality rule," the physician expert witness must be knowledgeable about local practice and procedure at the time of the incident at issue.

5. Expert witness testimony should not condemn performance that clearly falls within generally accepted practice standards or condone performance that clearly falls outside accepted practice standards.

6. An expert should respect the privacy and confidentiality of the process as required by law.

Assessing Breach of Care and Proximal Cause

Physician expert witnesses must exercise care in assessing the relationship between the breach in the standard of care and the patient's condition, because deviation from a practice standard may not be the cause of the patient outcome at issue. Thus, physician expert witnesses should base distinctions between medical malpractice and medical maloccurrence on science, not on unique theories of causation that would not be deemed reliable according to the Daubert, Frye, or other applicable standards.

Ensuring That Testimony Is Proper

Physician expert witnesses:

1. Must take all necessary precautions to ensure that the expert work is relevant, reliable, honest, unbiased and based on sound scientific principles.

2. Know that transcripts of depositions and courtroom testimony are public records and may be reviewed by others outside the courtroom.

Ethical Business Practices

The business practices (eg, marketing, contractual agreements, and payment for services) associated with the provision of expert witness testimony must be conducive to remaining nonpartisan and objective throughout the legal proceedings.

1. Contractual agreements between physician expert witnesses and attorneys should be structured in a way that promotes fairness, accuracy, completeness, and objectivity.

2. Compensation for expert witness work should be reasonable and commensurate with the time and effort involved and prevailing market value.

3. Compensation for expert witness work must not be contingent on the outcome of the case.

COMMITTEE ON MEDICAL LIABILITY AND RISK MANAGEMENT, 2007–2008
*Gary N. McAbee, DO, JD, Chairperson
Jeffrey L. Brown, MD
Steven M. Donn, MD
Jose L. Gonzalez, MD, JD, MSEd
David Marcus, MD
William M. McDonnell, MD, JD
Robert A. Mendelson, MD
Charles H. Deitschel Jr, MD, Immediate Past Chairperson

LIAISONS

Lisa M. Hollier, MD – *American College of Obstetricians and Gynecologists*

CONSULTANTS

C. Morrison Farish, MD
Holly Myers, JD
Sally L. Reynolds, MD

STAFF

Julie Kersten Ake

*Lead author

REFERENCES

1. American Academy of Pediatrics, Committee on Medical Liability. Guidelines for expert witness testimony. *Pediatrics.* 1989;83(2):312–313

2. American Academy of Pediatrics, Committee on Medical Liability. Guidelines for expert witness testimony in medical liability cases. *Pediatrics.* 1994;94(5):755–756

3. Council of Medical Specialty Societies. *Statement on Qualifications and Guidelines for the Physician Expert Witness.* Lake Bluff, IL: Council of Medical Specialty Societies; 1989

4. American Academy of Pediatrics, Committee on Medical Liability. Guidelines for expert witness testimony in medical malpractice litigation [published correction appears in *Pediatrics.* 2002; 110(3):651]. *Pediatrics.* 2002;109(5):974–979

5. Legal Information Institute. Federal rules of evidence [2006]. Available at: www.law.cornell.edu/rules/fre/rules.htm. Accessed March 7, 2008

6. Localio AR, Lawthers AG, Brennan TA, et al. Relation between malpractice claims and adverse events due to negligence: results of the Harvard Medical Practice Study III. *N Engl J Med.* 1991; 325(4):245–251

7. *Daubert v Merrell Dow Pharmaceuticals Inc,* 509 US 579 (1993)

8. *Frye v United States,* 293 F 1013 (DC Cir 1923)

9. *General Electric Co v Joiner,* 522 US 136 (1997)

10. *Kumho Tire Co Ltd v Carmichael,* 526 US 137 (1999)

11. Kassirer JP, Cecil JS. Inconsistency in evidentiary standards for medical testimony: disorder in the courts. *JAMA.* 2002;288(11):1382–1387

12. Cecil JS. Ten years of judicial gatekeeping under *Daubert. Am J Public Health.* 2005;95(S1): S74–S80

13. Gatowski SI, Dobbin SA, Richardson JT, Ginsburg GP, Merlino ML, Dahir V. Asking the gatekeepers: a national survey of judges on judging expert evidence in a post-*Daubert* world. *Law Hum Behav.* 2001;25(5):433–458

14. *Cf Nunez v Wilson,* 507 P 2d 939 (1973)

15. *Matott v Ward,* 48 NY2d 455 (1979)

16. Hassman PE. Admissibility of expert medical testimony as to future consequences of injury as affected by expression in terms of probability or possibility. 75 ALR 3d 9:24 (1977)

17. Brent RL. The irresponsible expert witness: a failure of biomedical graduate education and professional accountability. *Pediatrics.* 1982;70(5):754–762

18. Weintraub MI. Expert witness testimony: a time for self-regulation? *J Child Neurol.* 1995;10(3): 256–259

19. Safran A, Skydell B, Ropper S. Expert witness testimony in neurology: Massachusetts experience 1980–1990. *Neurol Chron.* 1992;2(7):1–6

20. Kesselheim AS, Studdert PM. Characteristics of physicians who frequently act as expert witnesses in neurologic birth injury litigation. *Obstet Gynecol.* 2006;108(2):273–279

21. Garner BA, ed. *Black's Law Dictionary.* 8th ed. Eagen, MN: Thomson-West Publishing Co; 2004

22. Merz JF. An empirical analysis of the medical informed consent doctorine [sic]: search for a "standard" of disclosure. Available at: www.piercelaw.edu/risk/vol2/winter/merz.htm. Accessed February 28, 2008

23. *Meyers v Epstein.* 282 F Supp 2d 151 (SDNY 2003)

24. Lewis MH, Gohagan JK, Merenstein DJ. The locality rule and the physician's dilemma: local medical practices vs the national standard of care. *JAMA.* 2007;297(23):2633–2637

25. Institute of Medicine, Committee on Quality of Health Care in America. *To Err Is Human: Building a Safer Health System.* Kohn LT, Corrigan JM, Donaldson MS, eds. Washington, DC: National Academies Press; 2000

26. Mackauf SH. Neurologic malpractice: the perspective of a patient's lawyer. *Neurol Clin.* 1999;17(2): 345–353

27. Lobe TE. *Medical Malpractice: A Physician's Guide.* New York, NY: McGraw-Hill Inc; 1995

28. *Zeier v Zimmer Inc,* 152 P3d 861 (Okla 2006)

29. Kaufman NL. The demise of medical malpractice screening panels and alternative solutions based on trust and honesty. *J Leg Med.* 2007;28(2):247–262

30. McAbee GN, Freeman JM. Expert medical testimony: responsibilities of medical societies. *Neurology.* 2005;65(2):337

31. Fadjo D, Bucciarelli RL. Peer review of the expert witness: an opportunity to improve our medical liability system. *J Child Neurol.* 1995;10(5):403–404

32. Vidmer N. Expert evidence, the adversary system, and the jury. *Am J Public Health*. 2005;95(suppl 1):S137–S143

33. Marcovitch H. Some relief for expert witnesses. *Arch Dis Child*. 2007;92(2):102–103

34. McAbee GN, Deitschel C, Berger J; American Academy of Pediatrics, Committee on Medical Liability and Risk Management. Pediatric medicolegal education in the 21st century. *Pediatrics*. 2006; 117(5):1790–1792

35. Donn SM. Medicolegal issues get short shrift in pediatric residency training. *AAP News*. 2006; 27(7):16

36. American Society of General Surgeons. Education: ASGS expert witness certification program. Available at: www.theasgs.org/education/expwit.html. Accessed February 28, 2008

37. Kesselheim AS, Studdert DM. Role of professional organizations in regulating physician expert witness testimony. *JAMA*. 2007;298(24):2907–2909

38. Gomez JCB. Silencing the hired guns: ensuring honesty in medical expert testimony through state legislation. *J Leg Med*. 2005;26(3):385–399

39. Kansas Stat Ann 60–3412 (2005)

40. American Medical Association, Council on Ethical and Judicial Affairs. E-6.01: contingent physician fees. *Code of Medical Ethics*. Chicago, IL: American Medical Association; 1994. Available at: www. ama-assn.org/ama1/pub/upload/mm/Code_of_Med_Eth/opinion/opinion601.html. Accessed March 7, 2008

41. American Medical Association, Council on Ethical and Judicial Affairs. E-8.04: consultation. *Code of Medical Ethics*. Chicago, IL: American Medical Association; 1996. Available at: www.ama-assn.org/ ama1/pub/upload/mm/Code_of_Med_Eth/opinion/opinion804.html. Accessed March 7, 2008

42. American Medical Association, Council on Ethical and Judicial Affairs. E-9.07: medical testimony. *Code of Medical Ethics*. Chicago, IL: American Medical Association; 2004. Available at: www.ama-assn.org/ama1/pub/upload/mm/Code_of_Med_Eth/opinion/opinion907.html. Accessed March 7, 2008

43. *Joseph v District of Columbia Board of Medicine*, 587 A2d 1085 (DC 1991)

44. American Medical Association. *Expert Witness Testimony: Policy H-265.993*. Chicago, IL: American Medical Association; 1998 [reaffirmed 2000]. Available at: https://www.aapl.org/ AMA_expert_witness.htm. Accessed March 7, 2008

45. Turner JA. Going after the "hired guns": is improper expert witness testimony unprofessional conduct or the negligent practice of medicine? *Pepperdine Law Rev*. 2006;33(2):275–310

46. *Board of Registration for the Healing Arts v Levine*, 808 SW 2d 440 (Mo App WD 1991)

47. Milunsky A. Lies, damned lies, and medical experts: the abrogation of responsibility by specialty organizations and a call for action. *J Child Neurol*. 2003;18(6):413–419

48. American Association of Neurological Surgeons. Professional conduct: witness testimony. *AANS Bull*. 2006;15(2):3–4. Available at: www.aans.org/bulletin/pdfs/summer06.pdf. Accessed February 28, 2008

49. Blackett WB, Pelton RM. Two disciplinary actions announced: American Academy of Neurology Board approves four PCC recommendations. *AANS Bull*. 2006;15(2):36–37. Available at: www.aans.org/bulletin/Issue.aspx?IssueId=31198. Accessed March 7, 2008

50. American Association of Orthopedic Surgeons. AAOS expert witness program. Available at: www3.aaos.org/member/expwit/expertwitness.cfm. Accessed February 28, 2008

51. Weintraub MI. Expert witness testimony: an update. *Neurol Clin*. 1999;17(2):363–369

52. McAbee GN. Peer review of medical expert witnesses. *J Child Neurol*. 1994;9(2):216–217

53. *Fullerton v Florida Medical Association*, 938 So2d 587 (Fla Dist Ct App 2006)

54. *Austin v American Association of Neurological Surgeons*, 253 F3d 967 (7th Cir 2001), *cert denied*, 534 US 1078 (2002)

55. Cohen FL. The expert medical witness in legal perspective. *J Leg Med*. 2004;25(2):185–209

56. McAbee GN. Improper expert medical testimony: existing and proposed mechanisms of oversight. *J Leg Med*. 1998;19(2):257–272

57. DeVille KA. The jury is out: pre-dispute binding arbitration agreements for medical malpractice claims. *J Leg Med*. 2007;28(3):333–395

58. Fraser JJ; American Academy of Pediatrics, Committee on Medical Liability. Technical report: alternative dispute resolution in medical malpractice. *Pediatrics*. 2001;107(3):602–607

59. Mello MM, Studdert DM, Kachalia AB, Brennan TA. Health courts and accountability for patient safety. *Milbank Q*. 2006;84(3):459–492

60. Boothman RC. Apologies and a strong defense at the University of Michigan Health System. *Physician Exec*. 2006;32(2):7–10

61. Guha SJ. "Fixing" medical malpractice: one doctor's perspective of a non-system in need of national standardization. *N C Med J.* 2000;61(4):227–230

62. Meadow W, Lantos JD. Expert testimony, legal reasoning, and justice: the case for adopting a data-based standard of care in allegations of medical negligence in the NICU. *Clin Perinatol.* 1996;23(3):583–595

63. Rosenbaum JT. Lessons from litigation over silicone breast implants: a call for activism by scientists. *Science.* 1997;276(5318):1524–1525

64. Dodds PR. The plaintiff's expert. *Conn Med.* 1999;63(2):99–101

65. Weinstein J. Improving expert testimony. *Univ Richmond Law Rev.* 1986;20(3):473–497

66. *Meyer v McDonnell*, 392 A2d 1129 (Md Ct Spec App 1978)

67. Freeman JM, Nelson KB. Expert medical testimony: responsibilities of medical societies. *Neurology.* 2004;63(9):1557–1558

68. MacLennan A, Nelson KB, Hankins G, Speer M. Who will deliver our grandchildren? Implications of cerebral palsy litigation. *JAMA.* 2005;294(13):1688–1690

Resolving Malpractice Disputes Without Litigation: Alternative Dispute Resolution

David Marcus, MD, FAAP

· ·

KEY CONCEPTS

- Negotiation
- Mediation
- Arbitration
- Pretrial Screening Panel
- Full-Disclosure/Early Offer Program
- Certificate/Affidavit of Merit
- Health Courts
- University of Michigan Approach to Patient Injuries
- Other Methods
- Barriers to Alternative Dispute Resolution

Given the steep cost of litigation (financial, personal, and professional), pediatricians should be aware of other means of resolving malpractice actions and be able to evaluate the potential risks and benefits associated with specific alternative dispute resolution (ADR) processes.

Negotiation

Negotiation, the most frequently used method of ADR, is defined as the process whereby 2 or more disputing parties confer together in good faith so as to settle a matter of mutual concern.[1] The approach to negotiation may be positional or principled.

In *positional negotiation,* divergent parties incrementally concede their position until a compromise is reached. In *principled negotiation,* the parties generate options focused on their interests to arrive at an agreement based on objective criteria. Negotiation serves as the basis for mediation, an important ADR method used in medical malpractice cases.[2]

Negotiation has its advantages. Disputants remain in control of the process. Negotiated resolutions tend to have greater durability than agreements reached by other methods. The process of negotiation can be educational for both parties and therefore may prevent subsequent discord in the relationship. However, sometimes negotiation alone is not enough to resolve medical malpractice actions. Most negotiated resolutions are reached when disputing parties are large, vertically structured corporations. In these instances, negotiations are conducted by senior members of the opposing corporations or high-level corporate agents with the authority to resolve the dispute. Because the negotiators were not involved in the original conflict, they have sufficient personal and emotional distance to compromise.[3] Medical malpractice litigation often involves individuals (patient versus physician); typically, disputants are not huge, corporate entities. Traditionally, physicians have been in relatively small corporations; therefore, it can be difficult to get the kind of dispassionate perspective that is conducive to successful resolution via negotiation alone.

Mediation

Mediation is an extension of direct negotiation between parties, using a neutral third party to facilitate the process. As a facilitator, the mediator has no authority to impose a solution on the parties, nor are the results of the process binding on the disputing parties. The mediator acts by identifying issues, proposing solutions, and encouraging accommodation on both sides. Mediation can be effective in medical malpractice cases in which the patient and physician want to preserve their relationship or in which poor communication led to the dispute. The advantages of mediation over litigation are its decreased costs, more confidential proceedings, and the degree of control enjoyed by the disputing parties over the process and outcome. In resolving allegations of medical negligence, patients tend to favor mediation because it provides a forum in which they can express their concerns and may lead to an acknowledgment of the problem—sometimes in the form of an apology.[4]

Mediation has its limitations. In many jurisdictions, mediation is voluntary and only can be pursued if both parties agree to it. Mediators do not have the same authority as judges and therefore cannot compel the release of information; nor can their decisions be imposed. The mediator has only as much power as the disputing parties permit and as such, can go no further than the disputants themselves are willing to go.

Arbitration

In arbitration, the parties agree to submit their dispute to a neutral third party, usually an arbiter or arbitration panel. The arbiter conducts a hearing in which each side presents evidence. The arbiter then makes a determination on liability or renders a decision of award. Often the parties agree in advance whether the arbiter's decision will be binding.[5] However, the decision of the arbiter is subject to limited appellate review for procedural error, arbiter bias, or fraud. Arbitration can be private, arising from the terms of a contract between the parties, or judicially mandated by statute or rule.

Potential advantages of arbitration over trials for resolving malpractice claims are speed (arbitration can be initiated as soon as the dispute arises), simpler and less expensive proceedings (in arbitration, the rules of evidence are less stringent and the processes are often more streamlined than court proceedings), and privacy (arbitration hearings are more private than trials). An advantage not to be overlooked is the opportunity to use a uniquely skilled arbiter. Unlike a judge, the arbiter may possess technical skills or scientific knowledge directly related to the subject of the dispute; this could be a distinct advantage when the dispute is enmeshed in an extremely complex or esoteric content area such as medicine. However, by choosing an arbitration panel over a court trial, the defendant physician sets aside certain rights. For example, in arbitration, there is no right to a trial by jury and no judicial instruction on the law. Similarly, documents from arbitration proceedings are not as complete as court proceedings. This can become problematic, as arbitration panels need not explain the basis of their decisions.

Arbitration has been applied in medical malpractice for more than 20 years. In some states, it is required by statute; in California, by contract between managed care organizations (MCOs) and enrollees. Challenges to medical malpractice arbitration awards in some of these states have been upheld by their highest courts. Despite this, arbitration remains an underused ADR method in medical malpractice cases across the country.[6–8]

Pretrial Screening Panel

The pretrial screening panel is an ADR method that was uniquely developed for medical malpractice cases. About half of the states have statutes establishing pretrial screening panels that review malpractice claims and render a nonbinding advisory opinion on the merits of the claim prior to a suit being filed. Panel composition varies considerably from state to state. In some states, only physicians sit on pretrial screening panels; other states restrict panels to attorneys; still other states require that the members of a pretrial screening panel include physicians, attorneys, judges, or laypersons. The panel reviews the merits of the malpractice case and offers an opinion on the physician's liability. In some states, the panel reviews the claim before legal action is taken. In other states, the suit must be filed in court before it is sent to the panel.

States vary on whether the panel renders an opinion on damages. Furthermore, state law determines whether the findings of the pretrial screening panel can be admitted as evidence should the claim go to trial and if so, how much weight the panel's findings should be given. The purpose of the pretrial screening process is 2-fold: to eliminate non-meritorious claims and to encourage settlement of meritorious claims prior to litigation.[9] The earliest malpractice pretrial screening panels date back to the 1960s. In New Mexico, a 1962 statute introduced a voluntary pretrial review panel; in the mid-1970s, during the malpractice litigation crisis, the statute was revised to make pretrial screening mandatory. Consequently, from 1976 to 1996, New Mexico panels have heard more than 2,100 medical malpractice cases; nearly three fourths of those cases were resolved without a trial.

A major disadvantage of pretrial screening panels is the nonbinding nature of most ADR methods. In many states, the plaintiff can still litigate after the pretrial screening panel decision is made. Thus, the pretrial screening panel may, in effect, further delay final resolution of the claim. While there is some evidence that screening panels are effective in eliminating low-merit cases, others contend that panels are victims of their own existence, as they can become clogged with frivolous claims that otherwise would not be pursued.[5]

Full-Disclosure/Early Offer Program

Several health systems and medical liability insurers have developed programs that involve full disclosure of medical errors combined with early offers of compensation. The primary goal is to disclose information to the patient about the adverse occurrence, with careful explanation of what occurred and why it occurred, along with a plan of how to avoid such errors in the future. If the medical institution has determined that the error occurred because of negligence, an apology may be offered when appropriate, and compensation will be offered for injuries suffered because of the event. Legal representation is recommended to ensure that the offer is fair.[10]

Certificate/Affidavit of Merit

As of 2009, certificate/affidavit of merit programs[11] are required in 25 states and are useful in stopping malpractice claims in their early stages. Most of the states require the plaintiff to provide an affidavit that the case has been initially reviewed by a medical expert who believes there is a basis for the claim. In Florida, if a defendant rejects the claim, the defendant must also submit an affidavit that a medical expert feels there is a lack of reasonable grounds for the medical malpractice suit.

Health Courts

A health court[12] is the use of trained judges who have health care expertise, selected through a process ensuring independence, such as appointment by a nonpartisan screening commission. These judges are required to remain current through continuing training and education in health care issues. They make rulings about the standard of care as a matter of law. To be consistent, consideration is given to clinical guidelines based on evidence-based practice standards.

Health courts are also given guidance by neutral experts delivering unbiased testimony on the standard of care. These experts are chosen and compensated by the court and not by opposing parties. Health courts also can involve administrative tribunals overseen by states. Local review boards consisting of medical experts review the details of the cases and in clear, non-contestable cases award damages according to a compensation schedule. If the board feels that no award is merited, the case is dismissed. These rulings may establish precedent on future cases.

University of Michigan Approach to Patient Injuries

The University of Michigan has developed a program that incorporates several different ADR methods to approach potential and actual claims. It begins by addressing situations that could lead to potential claims by setting realistic expectations on the part of the patient, starting with the informed consent process and improving patient education while creating understanding of reasonable outcomes and realistic expectations.

Michigan has mandated a compulsory 6-month pre-suit notice period, which has been a great benefit to the University of Michigan program. The document of notice must contain a significant amount of information, which is reviewed extensively. It allows for time to meet with the family or patient and possibly for the patient to reconsider intent to sue. The university Risk Management Department analyzes the information; this analysis is sent to a separate medical committee made up of several medical specialties, nursing, and hospital administration. The committee is used to answer 2 questions: was the given care reasonable under the circumstances, and did the care adversely affect the outcome?

Once the committee has completed its review, negotiations are held with the patient or family and it is determined whether to drop the claim, mediate and settle the claim, or litigate. The hospital has been allocated funds to pay a claim in an expedited manner, incorporating the full-disclosure/early offer program.

Since the program began in 1999, the rate of claims has decreased, from 136 claims in 1999 to 61 claims in 2006. Claims are also being moved through the system at a rapid rate with a marked decline in open claims (262 in 2001 to 83 in 2007). Processing time has dropped from 20.3 to 8 months, and litigation costs have decreased by more than half. In 2006, a survey of physicians and trial lawyers showed a very high satisfaction rate in both groups.[9,11]

Other Methods

Several other ADR methods are suited to resolving medical malpractice disputes but are seldom used in this setting. These include early neutral evaluation, mediation-arbitration, mini-trial, neutral fact finder, ombudsman, private judging, and summary jury trial. Many of these ADR techniques were developed for and are primarily used in the commercial or corporate environment. With the ongoing consolidation of health care entities into massive corporations, these methods may become more commonly used in medical malpractice claims.

Barriers to Alternative Dispute Resolution

A major impediment to physician use of ADR in medical malpractice is the mandatory reporting of all malpractice payments to the National Practitioner Data Bank (NPDB). It is important that physicians understand that any malpractice payment (eg, settlement, award) made on their behalf, even those derived from an ADR process, must be reported to the NPDB. Entries in the NPDB are specific to the physician on whose behalf the payment was made and are permanent. Every time a physician seeks new employment or renews clinical privileges at a hospital, that physician's NPDB file may be queried by authorized entities. Although physicians can furnish a note of explanation to their NPDB files, many prefer to take the odds of litigation, which tends to favor the physician defendant.[6] Repeated efforts to open the NPDB to the public have not succeeded thus far. This could change as patient rights initiatives continue to gain momentum and other data banks of disciplinary actions taken against health care practitioners already open to the public (eg, Medicare/Medicaid programs exclusions, Occupational Safety and Health Administration/Clinical Laboratory Improvement Amendments sanctions, adverse actions taken by state medical licensing boards) continue to proliferate.

Summary

Various ADR methods are available to resolve medical malpractice claims.[13] Many promise to work more effectively and fairly than the current tort system. Litigation is adversarial, traumatic, and often detrimental to the physician-patient relationship. Litigation stress can take an enormous toll on the plaintiff and defendant. The expense of litigation prevents equal access to the system; sometimes patients who have suffered damages from medical negligence are not able to secure representation because their claim is too small. Not only is the US tort system the most expensive in the world, its awards return less than $0.50 on the dollar to the people the system is designed to help. Furthermore, a relationship between patient injuries and malpractice may or may not exist. The literature has noted that malpractice claims are more likely to be triggered by

mal-occurrence (bad outcome) than malpractice (bad medicine) and that many patients injured by negligent care never file malpractice suits. Alternative dispute resolution techniques often are described as bilateral tort reforms because they can make it cheaper for physicians to defend unfounded claims and easier for plaintiffs to prevail on meritorious claims. Given the persistent problems in medical malpractice litigation for both sides, it is surprising that ADR methods remain underused, especially when reforms based on ADR potentially make the tort system more equitable and affordable to plaintiffs and defendants.

It is important for pediatricians to understand ADR processes, their relative advantages and disadvantages, and suitability to certain kinds of disputes. Moreover, physicians must clearly understand the degree of privacy, level of autonomy afforded the disputants, and binding nature of each ADR method. Beyond knowing the strengths and weaknesses of specific ADR strategies, physicians also must weigh the long-term consequences associated with ADR. For instance, physicians that predominately rely on ADR when faced with malpractice claims may end up with several entries in their NPDB file because ADR payments made on behalf of physicians are not exempt from mandatory NPDB reporting. Unless a more reasonable reporting trigger or payment threshold can be introduced to the NPDB, defendant physicians may prefer to take their chances in court rather than employ ADR to resolve malpractice cases. Helping pediatricians understand the implications of ADR methods may empower them to work more effectively with defense counsel in selecting the best strategy for resolving malpractice allegations.

References

1. Brearton JJ, Hinck KE, Lott E, Nazario S. Alternative dispute resolution. *American Jurisprudence*. Vol 4. 2nd ed. Rochester, NY: Lawyers Cooperative Publishing; 1995: 7–23

2. Fraser JJ Jr. Medical malpractice arbitration: a primer for Texas physicians. *Tex Med*. 1997;93(1):76–80

3. Trachte-Huber EW, Huber SK. *Alternative Dispute Resolution: Strategies for Law and Business*. Cincinnati, OH: Anderson Publishing Co.; 1996

4. Grenig JE. *Alternative Dispute Resolution*. 3rd ed. St. Paul, MN: Thomson/West; 2005

5. Metzloff TB. Alternative dispute resolution strategies in medical malpractice. *Alaska L Rev*. 1992;9(2):429–457

6. Gibofsky A. Alternative dispute resolution. In: Sanbar SS, Firestone MH, Buckner F, Gibofsky A, eds. *Legal Medicine*. 6th ed. St. Louis, MO: Mosby; 2004:66–73

7. Metzloff TB. The unrealized potential of malpractice arbitration. *Wake Forest L Rev*. 1996;31:203–230

8. Deville KA. The jury is out: pre-dispute binding arbitration agreements for medical malpractice claims: law, ethics, and prudence. *J Leg Med*. 2007;28(3):333–395

9. Boothman RC, Blackwell AC, Campbell DA Jr, Commiskey E, Anderson S. A better approach to medical malpractice claims? The University of Michigan experience. *J Health Life Sci Law*. 2009;2(2):125–159

10. Boothman RC. Apologies and a strong defense at the University of Michigan Health System. *Physician Exec*. 2006;32(2):7–10

11. Rogoff AR, Ahonkhai IT. Impact of venue and certificate of merit reforms. *Physician News Digest*. June 13, 2003. http://www.physiciansnews.com/2003/06/13/impact-of-venue-and-certificate-of-merit-reforms. Accessed June 15, 2011

12. Peters PG. Health courts? *Boston U L Rev*. 2008;88(1):227–289

13. Fraser JJ Jr, American Academy of Pediatrics Committee on Medical Liability. Technical report: alternative dispute resolution in medical malpractice. *Pediatrics*. 2001;107(3):602–607

CHAPTER 16

Pediatric Patient Safety

Daniel R. Neuspiel, MD, MPH, FAAP

KEY CONCEPTS

- Reporting Errors
- Disclosing Errors to Patients and Families
- Apologies for Errors
- Researching Pediatric Errors
- Specific Problems
- Specific Settings
- Specific Pediatric Populations at Risk
- Solutions
- American Academy of Pediatrics Activities

We have learned a great deal about the effect of medical errors on children since 1999, when the Institute of Medicine (IOM) published *To Err Is Human: Building a Safer Health System.* The IOM revealed that errors in health care are a leading cause of death and injury.[1] While there are still many gaps in our understanding, a number of successful models have been effective in identifying and preventing pediatric medical errors.

The IOM report concluded that fundamental change was needed to shift health care from a culture that seeks to name and blame those committing errors to one that promotes safety. Beyond disclosing flaws in health care delivery, the report suggested ways to address the problem. It challenged health care to redesign its processes and systems to identify and address errors, establish performance standards, and set safety expectations.

To that end, patient safety advocates contend that all health care systems should be designed to prevent harm. The first step is to identify errors and study their pattern of occurrence within delivery systems to reduce the likelihood of harm to patients. Other steps toward creating a culture of patient safety depend on nonpunitive error reporting, research, and realigning health care workers and patients with shared responsibility to enhance patient safety.

Patient safety experts within the American Academy of Pediatrics (AAP) have recently issued revised recommendations to ensure a comprehensive, accelerated approach toward pediatric patient safety,[2] including

1. Raising awareness and improving working knowledge of pediatric patient safety issues and best practices throughout the pediatric community
2. Acting and advocating for elimination of preventable pediatric medical harm using information on pediatric-specific patient safety risk
3. Improving health care outcomes for children by adhering to proven best practices for improving pediatric patient safety

Reporting Errors

Patient safety pioneer and pediatric surgeon Lucien Leape wrote that "fear and lack of belief that it results in improvement"[3] are the 2 primary reasons that errors are not reported. Most health care professionals are concerned about anonymity and confidentiality of medical error reporting. Some believe that providing any information about a serious adverse event may place health care professionals and facilities at increased risk of litigation. Fear of punishment, sanction, and litigation contribute to hesitation in reporting errors.

Anonymous reporting has been advocated to promote more complete reporting of errors. Though easier in theory, anonymous reporting has some limitations. First of all, true anonymity may be compromised when data in the report provide enough information for others to identify the specific situation and individuals involved. Also, anonymous reporting may result in omission of important data that may be difficult to obtain. When further information is required about a particular adverse incident, the reporter cannot be contacted for more details.

Confidential reporting facilitates the ability to conduct follow-up interviews and obtain more information from those involved in a specific event by potentially eliminating the fear of reporting. The promise of confidentiality is based on the premise that data will be accessible only to those who need it. This requires staff and leadership commitment to a safety culture in which unintentional errors are not punished. However, clinicians may not entirely trust such a system, fearing the disclosure of confidential information that could lead to punishment and litigation. Furthermore, when confidential data are collected and shared with a third party, there are concerns related to discovery during a lawsuit.

The focus of peer-review evaluation should be the reporting of errors, near misses, and general patient safety concerns in hospitals and offices. Before implementing such programs, it is important to determine whether state and federal protections from liability related to peer review already in place for hospitals would be extended to office-based practices.

Several organizations have established methods for reporting and studying medical errors. The American Academy of Family Physicians has used a Web-based anonymous error reporting system and has delineated the legal and practical barriers that impede its effectiveness as a more robust quality improvement tool.[4]

Disclosing Errors to Patients and Families

After a significant medical error, patients and their families have repeatedly verbalized their desire to know what happened, why, and what will be done so it does not happen again. This may be the only reason they file a malpractice claim. Establishing trust with early disclosure could reduce tensions and save time, resources, and strain on families and physicians.[5]

Gallagher et al[6] argue that a transformation in how the medical profession communicates with patients about harmful medical errors has begun, with strong backing from external organizations such as the National Quality Forum and the Joint Commission. They predict that full disclosure of these events will likely be a standard practice in the next several years, and that this change may help to restore public trust in the health care system. Matlow et al[7] also present a compelling argument for complete disclosure of medical errors.

A survey of 439 pediatric attending physicians and 118 residents by Garbutt et al[8] examined attitudes and experiences in error disclosure. More residents than attendings felt that disclosure would be difficult and wanted additional training in this skill. Despite nearly all respondents endorsing disclosure of serious and minor errors to families, many noted factors that might make them less likely to do so.

Attending pediatricians were less likely than residents to be deterred from disclosing an error after considering the following factors: if the family was unaware of it, if they thought the family would not want to know about it or would not understand the information, or if they thought they might get sued. Loren et al[9] also noted significant variation among pediatricians in disclosing serious medical errors, and reported more willingness to disclose errors that were already apparent to the family.

Many investigators have suggested that disclosure of errors will reduce physician litigation risk and settlement amounts.[5,7] However, Studdert et al[10] disagree and explain that there is great uncertainty that disclosure will provide protection from malpractice suits. They present an algorithmic model of the legal consequences of disclosure and determine that predictions of reduced litigation volume or cost do not withstand close scrutiny. They argue that while "disclosure is the right thing to do; so is compensating patients who sustain injury as a result of substandard care." They suggest that growth in transparency about medical injuries will increase tensions between these 2 aims, and that transition toward full disclosure should proceed with prudent planning.

Apologies for Errors

A physician may be hesitant to apologize about an error if doing so can be used as an admission of wrongdoing in a legal action.[5] In response to this, several states have enacted statutes protecting apologies from admission as evidence in malpractice litigation, as shown in Table 16-1. Most states now protect a physician statement such as "I'm sorry," but may not protect admissions of fault.

Table 16-1. States With Apology Laws[11]

State	Statute	State	Statute
Arizona	ARS 12-2605 (2005)	Montana	Code Ann 26-1-814 (Mont. 2005)
California	Evidence Code 1160 (2000)	Nebraska	Neb Laws LB 373 (2007)
Colorado	Revised Statute 13-25-135 (2003)	New Hampshire	RSA 507-E:4 (2005)
Connecticut	Public Act No. 05-275 Sec 9(2005) amended (2006) CT Gen Stat Ann 52-184d	North Carolina	General Stat 8C-1, Rule 413
Delaware	DE Code Ann Tit 10, 4318 (2006)	North Dakota	ND HB 1333 (2007)
Florida	Stat 90.4026 (2001)	Ohio	ORC Ann 2317.43 (2004)
Georgia	Title 24 Code GA Annotated 24-3-37.1 (2005)	Oklahoma	63 OK St 1-1708.1H (2004)
Hawaii	HRS Sec 626-1 (2006)	Oregon	Rev Stat 677.082 (2003)
Idaho	Title 9 Evidence Code Chapter 2.9-207	South Carolina	Ch 1, Title 19 Code of Laws 1976, 19-1-190 (2006)
Illinois	Public Act 094-0677 Sec. 8-1901, 735 IL Comp Stat 5/8-1901 (2005)	South Dakota	Codified Laws 19-12-14 (2005)
Indiana	IN Code Ann 34-43.5-1-1 to 34-43.5-1-5	Tennessee	Evid Rule 409.1 (2003)
Iowa	HF 2716 (2006)	Texas	Civil Prac and Rem Code 18.061 (1999)
Louisiana	RS 13:3715.5 (2005)	Utah	Code Ann 78-14-18 (2006)
Maine	MRSA tit 2908 (2005)	Vermont	S 198 Sec 1 12 VSA 1912 (2006)
Maryland	MD Court & Judicial Proceedings Code Ann 10-920 (2004)	Virginia	Code of VA 8.01-52.1 (2005)
Massachusetts	ALM GL ch 233, 23D (1986)	Washington	Rev Code WA 5.66.010 (2002)
Missouri	MO Ann Stat 538.229 (2005)	West Virginia	55-7-11a (2005)
		Wyoming	WY Stat Ann 1-1-130

Pediatricians should discuss with their malpractice carriers or risk managers specific institutional policies and state disclosure statutes in effect.

Researching Pediatric Errors

Research on the descriptive epidemiology of medical errors in pediatrics has expanded considerably. Medical errors result more frequently from the organization of health care delivery and the way that resources are provided to the delivery system than from individual human error.[12] These findings underscore that changes to system design are essential to efforts to reduce medical errors.

Specific Problems

One way of studying medical errors is to categorize them by the point at which they occur in the health care process, such as communication, diagnostic, treatment, and sedation errors.

Communication Errors

Many clinicians see patients with limited English skills. Often, translation is done by family members of the patient or ad hoc volunteers.[13] Unfortunately, errors in translation and medical interpretation are common in these situations. Flores et al found 31 medical interpretation errors per pediatric clinical encounter, with most having potential consequences. Those committed by ad hoc interpreters were significantly more likely to have potential clinical consequences than those committed by hospital interpreters.[14] Even English-speaking patients may have limited understanding of the language of health care, so assessment of health literacy has been advocated to improve safety.[15]

Lack of use of appropriate interpreters may violate federal and state laws. Title VI of the Civil Rights Act of 1964 requires that health care facilities receiving federal funds provide "meaningful access" by persons with limited English proficiency (LEP) without additional cost.[16] Title III of the Americans

with Disabilities Act of 1990 also mandates accommodations for persons with disabilities and applies to patients with LEP.

Signs of limited health literacy should be noted, including forms not filled out completely, frequently missed appointments, noncompliance with medications or tests, and inability to name medications, explain their purposes and timing of administration.[17] Written information for patients should be at or below a sixth-grade reading level. Handouts should not be all uppercase, should contain only one large font style, and should include only need-to-know content. The American Medical Association has proposed 6 steps to improve interpersonal communication with patients.

1. Slow down in communicating with patients.
2. Use plain, nonmedical language.
3. Show or draw pictures.
4. Limit the amount of information and repeat it.
5. Use the teach-back technique by asking patients to repeat instructions.
6. Encourage questions.

Diagnostic Errors

A review of 7,186 closed malpractice claims involving pediatricians from 1985 to 2009 indicated that the most prevalent medical misadventure was diagnostic error, according to the Physician Insurers Association of America.[18] Failure to diagnose was given as the primary issue in 32.4% of claims reported between 1985 and 2009. For claims closed in 2009 alone, diagnostic errors comprised 43.5% of primary misadventure reports. Among pediatric claims paid in 2009, 61.5% reported diagnostic error as the primary allegation.

For claims involving errors in diagnosis, meningitis was the most prevalent condition that was incorrectly diagnosed by pediatricians, followed by appendicitis, specified non-teratogenic anomalies, pneumonia, and newborns with brain damage. Among this group of claims, errors in diagnosing meningitis resulted in the highest percentage of paid claims (51.65%) as well as the highest average payment ($438,428).

Another prevalent medical misadventure reported was *no medical misadventure,* categorized as a situation in which there is an absence of an allegation of any inappropriate medical conduct on the part of the insured, primarily because the physician had little or no contact with the patient or family. This was followed by improperly performed procedures, failure to supervise or monitor case, medication errors, failure or delay in referral or consultation, and failure to recognize a complication of treatment.

In a survey of 726 academic and community pediatricians and pediatric residents from November 2008 to May 2009, 54% of physicians reported making a diagnostic error at least once or twice per month.[19] The rate among trainees was 77%. Errors harmful to patients were reported to occur at least once or twice annually by 45% of respondents. The most frequently reported process lapse was failure to gather clinical information through the history, physical examination, or review of the medical record. The most commonly reported system error was inadequate coordination of care and teamwork. Among specific errors, the most frequent were viral infections diagnosed as bacterial, followed by misdiagnosis of adverse reactions to medications, psychiatric disorders, and appendicitis. Strategies deemed to be effective in preventing diagnostic errors were access to electronic health records (EHRs) and closer patient follow-up.

Treatment Errors

Treatment errors in pediatrics may involve immunizations, sedatives, and other medications. A medication error is any preventable event that may cause or lead to inappropriate medication use or cause a patient harm. An adverse drug event (ADE) is an injury resulting from the use of a drug. Adverse drug events may result from medication

errors, but most do not. Medication errors may also occur from allergic reactions, particularly when patients are not regularly asked about known medication allergies whenever prescriptions are given, and when allergies are not documented.

Medication errors may occur at any of the following stages:

- Suboptimal ordering or prescribing—overdosing and under-dosing
- Transcription
- Dispensing
- Administration (eg, wrong dose, drug, timing, technique)
- Patient/caregiver noncompliance
- Overlooked adverse effects

Children are at higher risk for medication errors than most other demographic groups.[20-23] Some reasons for this are

- Off-label drugs without standard dosing are often used.
- Doses by weight or body surface area are subject to miscalculation in children because of varied size.
- Pharmacokinetics of some drugs are age dependent.
- Drugs are more commonly prepared for adult use and need the extra step of compounding for pediatric use.
- Children have limited ability to understand and communicate adverse symptoms.
- Children are often treated in adult settings by staff who are not trained in safe pediatric medication practices or whose pediatric skills have waned.
- Adolescents may have particular challenges because of confidentiality issues, with lack of adult assistance in supervision of medication administration.

Medication error was reported as the primary malpractice allegation in about 5% of the closed malpractice claims involving pediatricians from

1985 to 2009.[18] The most prevalent conditions associated with medication error cases were asthma, well-child visits, bronchitis, convulsions, and epilepsy. Indemnity by severity of injury in medication error claims is presented in Table 16-2.

Sedation Errors

Over recent decades there has been an increase in the use of sedation during pediatric procedures, raising concern for patient safety. Airway obstruction or hypoventilation leading to hypercapnia and hypoxemia are important patient safety issues that can lead to significant long-term effects. Coté et al[24] analyzed critical incidents and identified several features associated with adverse sedation events and poor outcome. Adverse outcomes such as permanent neurologic injury or death occurred more frequently in an ambulatory-based facility. Deficient resuscitation and inadequate and inconsistent physiologic monitoring were more often associated with nonhospital settings. Failure to use or respond appropriately to pulse oximetry was a factor contributing to poor outcome in all settings studied. The reviewers noted the following other factors: inadequate pre-sedation medical evaluation, lack of an independent observer, medication errors, and inadequate recovery procedures. Uniform, specialty-independent guidelines for monitoring children during and after sedation; age- and size-appropriate equipment and medications for resuscitation; and health care professionals trained in advanced airway assessment and management training and skilled in pediatric resuscitation were cited as necessary corrective actions.

Specific Settings

Another way to study medical errors is to assess the frequency and severity of adverse events in select patient care settings.

Errors in Hospital Inpatient Settings

Inpatient pediatric medical errors have been reviewed by several recent investigators.[21,25,26] In the Harvard Medical Practice study, there were 12.91 adverse events per 1,000 hospital discharges for all patients from birth through 15 years of age.[27] Among all adverse events, 27.6% were assessed to be due to negligence. Kaushal et al[28] studied medication errors in 2 academic pediatric centers. Among 10,778 orders reviewed, 616 medication errors (5.7%) were identified. One in 5 of these were near misses, and 1% of errors caused patient harm. Adverse drug events were identified in 2.3% of admissions, and 19% were determined to be preventable. Serious errors were more frequent in critical care settings. These investigators estimated that adverse pediatric events occurred 3 times more frequently than those in hospitalized adults.

Table 16-2 . Closed Pediatric Malpractice Claims, 1985 to 2009—Medication Error by Severity of Injury[18]

Severity of Injury	Closed Claims	Paid Claims	Average Indemnity	Total Indemnity
Emotional only	11	1	$17,000	$17,000
Insignificant	18	6	$10,833	$65,000
Minor temporary	42	11	$24,735	$272,083
Major temporary	71	21	$23,427	$491,962
Minor permanent	25	7	$46,739	$327,173
Significant permanent	29	8	$182,030	$1,456,242
Major permanent	22	7	$483,712	$3,385,985
Grave	40	16	$495,659	$7,930,543
Death	80	26	$170,885	$4,443,000

Subsequent comprehensive studies of medication errors and ADEs in pediatric settings have shown similar findings.[29] Marino et al[30] studied 3,312 orders and discovered 784 errors (23.7%), 83% of which occurred at the prescribing stage. Holdsworth et al[31] examined 1,197 admissions by chart review and found 7.5 actual ADEs and 9.3 potential ADEs per 1,000 patient days. There were more ADEs in children with extended lengths of stay, more complex medications, and more severe illness. Woods et al[23] studied more than 3,700 pediatric admissions, including newborns, and detected ADEs in 1%, of which 60% were determined to be preventable. A study by Takata et al[32] included 12 children's hospitals and reported ADEs in 11.1% of patients, 15.7 per 1,000 patient days, and 1.23 per 1,000 medication doses.

Although the majority of patient safety issues within the hospital setting involve medication errors, the picture is not complete without widening the scope to include other events such as slips and falls, sharps injuries, and other occurrences. Most hospitals are not childproof. Uncovered electric outlets and dangling window blind cords pose a threat to young children. Even furniture such as examining tables, rolling stools, and sharp cupboard corners can be safety hazards for infants and toddlers. Hospitalized pediatric patients need to be in beds or cribs that are appropriate for their age and developmental stage. Unfortunately, falls from beds and cribs in pediatric settings happen all too commonly.

Emergency Department

Barata et al[33] and O'Neill et al[34] reviewed sources of error in pediatric emergency department (ED) settings, including improper patient identification, lack of experience of adult emergency staff with pediatrics, and challenges with performing technical procedures and calculating medication doses in children. Errors may occur because of communication, including between prehospital and ED staff;

among ED staff, particularly during change-of-shift sign-off; between ED and inpatient staff; and between ED staff and family members. Other important sources of error in the ED include diagnostic mistakes, medication errors, and environmental deficits, such as equipment malfunction. In a pediatric ED in Canada, 100 prescribing errors and 39 medication administration errors occurred per 1,000 patients.[35]

Several investigators have studied antipyretic dosing errors in children seen in pediatric EDs. Li et al[36] reported that most surveyed caregivers gave inaccurate doses of acetaminophen or ibuprofen, especially to infants. McErlean et al[37] found that 53% of children received an improper antipyretic dose at home. Goldman[38] determined that most parents under-dosed their children with acetaminophen, leading to unnecessary emergency visits. Losek[39] reported that 22% of acetaminophen dose orders were outside accepted recommendations.

Office Setting

Most pediatric care is practiced in the office setting, yet information on errors in pediatric ambulatory care has been slow to emerge.[40] Adverse events and near misses appear to occur frequently, but there is little information on types of errors, risk factors, or effective preventive strategies.

The Learning from Errors in Ambulatory Pediatrics study, sponsored by the Pediatric Research in Office Settings collaborative of the AAP, studied the range of medical errors in pediatric ambulatory care.[41] There were 147 medical errors reported from 14 practices. The largest group of errors was related to medical treatment (37%), with other errors in patient identification (22%), preventive care including immunizations (15%), diagnostic testing (13%), patient communication (8%), and less frequent causes. Among medical treatment errors, 85% were medication errors. Of these, 55% were related to ordering, 30% failure to order, 11% administration, 2% transcribing, and 2% dispensing errors.

In a prospective cohort study at 6 Boston, MA, area pediatric practices over a 2-month period, 57 preventable ADEs occurred in the care of 1,788 patients, a rate of 3%.[42] While none of these events was determined to be life threatening, 8 (14%) were serious. Parenteral drug administration was associated with 40 (70%) of these ADEs. Improved communication between providers and parents and between pharmacists and parents were found to be the strategies with the most potential to prevent these errors. Children with multiple prescriptions were at higher risk of preventable ADEs.[43]

Medication samples have been dispensed with inadequate documentation.[44] Among new prescriptions for 22 common medications in outpatient pediatric clinics, 15% were issued with potential dosing errors.[45] Data from the US 1997 National Immunization Survey showed that 31% of children were under-immunized for at least 1 vaccine; also, 21% of children were over-immunized for at least 1 vaccine, at costs conservatively estimated at $26.5 million.[46]

Specific Pediatric Populations at Risk

In newborns and young infants, lack of mature hepatic, renal, and immune systems may increase the risk of medication errors.[47] During lengthy stays in neonatal intensive care units, weight and maturational changes raise the need for close attention to medication dosing.

Flores and Ngui[48] discussed specific racial and ethnic risk factors for pediatric errors. They note the higher prevalence of risk factors for medical errors among racial and ethnic minorities, including younger age, more prematurity and low birth weight, greater disease complexity and severity, and more fragmented care with greater use of EDs. More frequent errors of omission and suboptimal practice have been reported in these populations, including disparities in asthma treatment,

psychiatric referrals, and neonatal care. Language barriers have led to greater likelihood of medical errors with the use of nonprofessional interpreters, increased risk of hospitalization, and resource utilization.

Leyva et al[49] studied Latino children and parents in the Bronx, NY, and determined that most parents with LEP were not able to understand routinely dispensed written medication instructions. They concluded that pediatric health care professionals should not assume that Spanish-speaking Latino parents who are comfortable speaking English will understand prescription labels written in English, or that Latino parents who speak Spanish will understand drug information written in Spanish.

Solutions

Reducing Medication Errors

Leonard has suggested some practices to help prevent medication errors and ADEs.[21]

- Obtain a thorough list of the patient's current medications and ask parents to bring medications at every visit.
- Obtain an accurate list of the patient's allergies and adverse reactions at every visit.
- Print legibly.
- Avoid the use of unsafe abbreviations.
- Obtain an accurate patient weight.
- Mind your decimals.
- Include indication for therapy on orders and prescriptions.
- Educate patients and families.

Joint Commission Initiatives

The Joint Commission has published a do-not-use list to prevent medication errors (Table 16-3). This applies to all orders and all medication-related documentation that are handwritten, including free-text computer entries, or on preprinted forms.

Table 16-3. Official Do-Not-Use List[50]

Do Not Use	Potential Problem	Use Instead
U	Mistaken for 0 (zero), 4 (four), or cc	Write "unit."
IU	Mistaken for IV or 10	Write "International Unit."
Q.D., QD, q.d., qd Q.O.D., QOD, q.o.d., qod	Mistaken for each other. Period after Q mistaken for I and Q mistaken for I.	Write "daily" or "every other day."
Trailing zero (x.0 mg) Lack of leading zero (.x mg)	Decimal point is missed.	Write x mg or 0.x mg.
MS MSO4 and MgSO4	Can mean morphine sulfate or magnesium sulfate. Confused for each other.	Write "morphine sulfate" or "magnesium sulfate."

The 2010 Joint Commission National Patient Safety Goals are all relevant to pediatrics.

1. Identify patients correctly, using at least 2 identifiers.
2. Use medicines safely, including labeling medicines in syringes and cups.
3. Prevent infection, using accepted hand-cleaning guidelines.
4. Check patient medicines, with an updated medication list provided to the patient and for her or his medical record.

The Joint Commission has also initiated the Speak Up campaign to prevent pediatric errors by helping patients become more informed and involved in their care.

World Health Organization Patient Safety Solutions

The World Health Organization Collaborating Centre for Patient Safety Solutions issued 9 *Patient Safety Solutions* in 2007.[51] Most of these are relevant to a variety of pediatric settings. These include

1. *Look-alike, soundalike medication names.* Confusing drug names are one of the most common causes of medication errors and is a worldwide concern. With tens of thousands of drugs currently on the market, the potential for error created by confusing brand or generic drug names and packaging is significant.

2. *Patient identification.* The widespread and continuing failures to correctly identify patients often lead to medication, transfusion, and testing errors; wrong person procedures; and the discharge of newborns to the wrong families.

3. *Communication during patient handoffs.* Gaps in handoff communication between patient care units, and between and among care teams, can cause serious breakdowns in the continuity of care, inappropriate treatment, and potential harm for the patient.

4. *Performance of correct procedure at correct body site.* Considered totally preventable, cases of wrong procedure or wrong site surgery are largely the result of miscommunication and unavailable or incorrect information. A major contributing factor to these types of errors is the lack of a standardized preoperative process.

5. *Control of concentrated electrolyte solutions.* While all drugs, biologics, vaccines, and contrast media have a defined risk profile, concentrated electrolyte solutions used for injection are especially dangerous.

6. *Ensuring medication accuracy at transitions in care.* Medication errors occur most commonly at transitions. Medication reconciliation is a process designed to prevent medication errors at patient transition points.

7. *Avoiding catheter and tubing misconnections.* The design of tubing, catheters, and syringes currently in use is such that it is possible to inadvertently cause patient harm through connecting wrong syringes and tubing and then delivering medication or fluids through an unintended wrong route.

8. *Single use of injection devices.* One of the biggest global concerns is the spread of HIV, hepatitis B, and hepatitis C via reuse of injection needles.

9. *Improved hand hygiene to prevent health care–associated infection.* It is estimated that at any point, more than 1.4 million people worldwide are suffering from infections acquired in hospitals. Effective hand hygiene is the primary preventive measure for avoiding this problem.

Electronic Health Records

Electronic health records offer potential protections from medical errors, including reminders about periodic screening, links with clinical practice guidelines, computerized practitioner order entry (CPOE) and clinical decision support. Using CPOE, practitioners enter medication and procedure orders directly into a computer for electronic processing. Clinical decision support is a knowledge-based tool integrated with patient data into the work flow of practitioners with the aim of improving quality of care. Whether EHRs live up to their great potential to reduce and prevent medical errors is contingent on how this new technology is implemented.[52,53]

Ambulatory Safety Teams

In the pediatric ambulatory setting, medical errors may be more readily discovered and prevented by initiating a nonpunitive reporting system and enlisting other staff members using a team-based approach. Neuspiel et al[54] reported a successful effort in improved reporting of pediatric errors using a voluntary, anonymous, nonpunitive, team-based system. This was paired with root-cause analysis, rapid redesign, and monitoring of changes made in response to each error. In the first year, 80 errors were reported, compared with only 5 during the prior year with a traditional incident reporting system. Reports originated from physicians (45%), nurses (41%), other staff (9%), and parents and patients (5%). Errors were classified as involving office administration (34%), medications and other treatment (24%), laboratory and diagnostic testing (19%), and communications (18%). Many changes were made in the practice to improve patient safety.

Agency for Healthcare Research and Quality

The US Agency for Healthcare Research and Quality has been active in research and advocacy in promoting patient safety, issuing "20 Tips to Help Prevent Medical Errors."[55]

American Academy of Pediatrics Activities

Safety Initiatives

The AAP has launched the Safer Health Care for Kids Web site (www.aap.org/saferhealthcare) for physicians, allied health professionals, administrators, parents, and caregivers who are seeking pediatric patient safety information and strategies. This site includes resources for pediatric-specific patient safety guidance, Web-based seminars on various pediatric patient safety topics, links to recent news on pediatric patient safety, links to patient safety experts, useful tips for providers to improve safety for their patients, and advice for parents.

Patient safety is also addressed in the AAP by the Education in Quality Improvement for Pediatric Practice, Chapter Alliance for Quality Improvement, and Quality Improvement Innovation Network programs, as well as by educational presentations at national and regional meetings.

Guidelines

American Academy of Pediatrics clinical practice guidelines are developed using an evidence-based approach, combining the best research available with expert consensus on best practice. Experts in the content area and in guideline development join together to create recommendations that are timely and easily implemented in practice. These guidelines are published in *Pediatrics,* posted on www.aappolicy.org, and updated in a published compendium *(Pediatric Clinical Practice Guidelines & Policies).*

Summary

Promoting safety requires changing the culture of medicine to recognize that mistakes occur often, the potential for harmful errors exists, a nonpunitive approach to error reporting is key to knowing about them, and teamwork and communication are central to preventing harm. The promotion of patient safety has become a major goal of the AAP. Leadership on this issue has come from many areas, including the Steering Committee on Quality Improvement and Management and the Committee on Medical Liability and Risk Management. Patient safety should be viewed as an essential component of a broader commitment to promoting health and providing optimal health care for all children.

References

1. Kohn LT, Corrigan JM, Donaldson MS, eds. *To Err Is Human: Building a Safer Health System.* Washington, DC: National Academy Press; 2000
2. American Academy of Pediatrics Steering Committee on Quality Improvement Management, Committee on Hospital Care. Principles of pediatric patient safety: reducing harm due to medical care. *Pediatrics.* 2011;127(6):1199–1210
3. Leape LL. Why should we report adverse incidents? *J Eval Clin Pract.* 1999;5(1):1–4
4. Phillips RL, Dovey SM, Hickner JS, Graham D, Johnson M. The AAFP Patient Safety Reporting System: development and legal issues pertinent to medical error tracking and analysis. In: Henriksen K, Battles JB, Marks ES, Lewin DI, eds. *Advances in Patient Safety: From Research to Implementation: Volume 3. Implementation Issues.* Rockville, MD: Agency for Healthcare Research and Quality; 2005;121–134. AHRQ Publication No. 05-0021-3. http://www.ncbi.nlm.nih.gov/books/NBK20535/pdf/A4255. pdf. Accessed May 19, 2011
5. Pelt JL, Faldmo LP. Physician error and disclosure. *Clin Obstet Gynecol.* 2008;51(4):700–708
6. Gallagher TH, Studdert D, Levinson W. Disclosing harmful medical errors to patients. *N Engl J Med.* 2007;356(26):2713–2719
7. Matlow A, Stevens P, Harrison C, Laxer RM. Disclosure of medical errors. *Pediatr Clin North Am.* 2006;53(6): 1091–1104
8. Garbutt J, Brownstein DR, Klein EJ, et al. Reporting and disclosing medical errors: pediatricians' attitudes and behaviors. *Arch Pediatr Adolesc Med.* 2007;161(2):179–185. http://archpedi.ama-assn.org/cgi/reprint/161/2/179. Accessed May 19, 2011
9. Loren DJ, Klein EJ, Garbutt J, et al. Medical error disclosure among pediatricians: choosing carefully what we might say to parents. *Arch Pediatr Adolesc Med.* 2008;162(10):922–927. http://archpedi.ama-assn.org/cgi/reprint/162/10/922. Accessed May 19, 2011
10. Studdert DM, Mello MM, Gawande AA, Brennan TA, Wang YC. Disclosure of medical injury to patients: an improbable risk management strategy. *Health Aff (Millwood).* 2007;26(1):215–226
11. Sorry Works! Coalition. States with apology laws. http://www.sorryworks.net/lawdoc.phtml. Accessed March 29, 2011
12. Leape LL, Bates DW, Cullen DJ, et al. Systems analysis of adverse drug events. ADE Prevention Study Group. *JAMA.* 1995;274(1):35–43
13. Kuo DZ, O'Connor KG, Flores G, Minkovitz CS. Pediatricians' use of language services for families with limited English proficiency. *Pediatrics.* 2007;119(4):e920–e927. http://pediatrics.aappublications.org/cgi/reprint/119/4/e920. Accessed May 19, 2011
14. Flores G, Laws MB, Mayo SJ, et al. Errors in medical interpretation and their potential clinical consequences in pediatric encounters. *Pediatrics.* 2003;111(1):6–14. http://pediatrics.aappublications.org/cgi/reprint/111/1/6. Accessed May 19, 2011
15. Nielsen-Bohlman L, Panzer AM, Kindig DA, eds. *Health Literacy: A Prescription to End Confusion.* Washington, DC: National Academies Press; 2004

16. US Department of Health and Human Services. Guidance to federal financial assistance recipients regarding Title VI prohibition against national origin discrimination affecting Limited English Proficiency persons. *Fed Regist.* 2003;68(153):47311–47323

17. Weiss BD. *Health Literacy and Patient Safety: Help Patients Understand.* 2nd ed. Chicago, IL: American Medical Association Foundation; 2007

18. Physician Insurers Association of America. *A Risk Management Review of Malpractice Claims—Pediatrics.* Rockville, MD: Physician Insurers Association of America; 2010

19. Singh H, Thomas EJ, Wilson L, et al. Errors of diagnosis in pediatric practice: a multisite survey. *Pediatrics.* 2010;126(1):70–79

20. Kozer E, Scolnik D, Macpherson A, et al. Variables associated with medication errors in pediatric emergency medicine. *Pediatrics.* 2002;110(4):737–742. http://pediatrics. aappublications.org/cgi/reprint/110/4/737. Accessed May 19, 2011

21. Leonard MS. Patient safety and quality improvement: medical errors and adverse events. *Pediatr Rev.* 2010;31(4):151–158

22. Woods DM, Johnson J, Holl JL, et al. Anatomy of a patient safety event: a pediatric patient safety taxonomy. *Qual Saf Health Care.* 2005;14(6);422–427. http://www.ncbi.nlm. nih.gov/pmc/articles/PMC1744098/pdf/v014p00422.pdf. Accessed May 19, 2011

23. Woods D, Thomas E, Holl J, Altman S, Brennan T. Adverse events and preventable adverse events in children. *Pediatrics.* 2005;115(1):155–160

24. Coté CJ, Notterman DA, Karl HW, Weinberg JA, McCloskey C. Adverse sedation events in pediatrics: a critical incident analysis of contributing factors. *Pediatrics.* 2000;105(4):805–814

25. Landrigan CP. The safety of inpatient pediatrics: preventing medical errors and injuries among hospitalized children. *Pediatr Clin North Am.* 2005;52(4):979–993

26. Sharek PJ, Classen D. The incidence of adverse events and medical error in pediatrics. *Pediatr Clin North Am.* 2006;53(6):1067–1077

27. Leape LL, Brennan TA, Laird N, et al. The nature of adverse events in hospitalized patients. Results of the Harvard Medical Practice Study II. *N Engl J Med.* 1991;324(6):377–384. http://www.nejm.org/doi/ pdf/10.1056/NEJM199102073240605. Accessed May 19, 2011

28. Kaushal R, Bates DW, Landrigan C, et al. Medication errors and adverse drug events in pediatric inpatients. *JAMA.* 2001;285(16):2114–2120. http://jama.ama-assn.org/ content/285/16/2114.full.pdf+html. Accessed May 19, 2011

29. Kaushal R, Jaggi T, Walsh K, Fortescue EB, Bates DW. Pediatric medication errors: what do we know? What gaps remain? *Ambul Pediatr.* 2004;4(1):73–81

30. Marino BL, Reinhardt K, Eichelberger WJ, Steingard R. Prevalence of errors in a pediatric hospital medication system: implications for error proofing. *Outcomes Manag Nurs Pract.* 2000;4(3):129–135

31. Holdsworth MT, Fichtl RE, Behta M, et al. Incidence and impact of adverse drug events in pediatric inpatients. *Arch Pediatr Adolesc Med.* 2003;157(1):60–65. http://archpedi. ama-assn.org/cgi/reprint/157/1/60. Accessed May 19, 2011

32. Takata GS, Mason W, Taketomo C, Logsdon T, Sharek PJ. Development, testing, and findings of a pediatric-focused trigger tool to identify medication-related harm in US children's hospitals. *Pediatrics.* 2008;121(4):e927–e935. http:// pediatrics.aappublications.org/cgi/reprint/121/4/e927. Accessed May 19, 2011

33. Barata IA, Benjamin LS, Mace SE, Herman MI, Goldman RD. Pediatric patient safety in the prehospital/emergency department setting. *Pediatr Emerg Care.* 2007;23(6):412–418

34. O'Neill KA, Shinn D, Starr KT, Kelley J. Patient misidentification in a pediatric emergency department: patient safety and legal perspectives. *Pediatr Emerg Care.* 2004;20(7):487–492

35. Kozer E, Berkovitch M, Koren G. Medication errors in children. *Pediatr Clin North Am.* 2006;53(6):1155–1168

36. Li SF, Lacher B, Crain EF. Acetaminophen and ibuprofen dosing by parents. *Pediatr Emerg Care.* 2000;16(6):394–397

37. McErlean MA, Bartfield JM, Kennedy DA, Gilman EA, Stram RL, Raccio-Robak N. Home antipyretic use in children brought to the emergency department. *Pediatr Emerg Care.* 2001;17(4):249–251

38. Goldman RD, Scolnik D. Underdosing of acetaminophen by parents and emergency department utilization. *Pediatr Emerg Care.* 2004;20(2):89–93

39. Losek JD. Acetaminophen dose accuracy and pediatric emergency care. *Pediatr Emerg Care.* 2004;20(5):285–288

40. Neuspiel DR, Hyman D, Lane M. Quality improvement and patient safety in the pediatric ambulatory setting: current knowledge and implications for residency training. *Pediatr Clin North Am.* 2009;56(4):935–951

41. Mohr JJ, Lannon CM, Thoma KA, et al. Learning from errors in ambulatory pediatrics. In: Henriksen K, Battles JB, Marks ES, Lewin DI, eds. *Advances in Patient Safety: From Research to Implementation; Vol. 1. Research Findings.* Rockville, MD: Agency for Healthcare Research and Quality; 2005:355–368. AHRQ Publication No. 05-0021-1. http://www.ncbi.nlm.nih.gov/books/NBK20472/pdf/A1209. pdf. Accessed May 19, 2011

42. Kaushal R, Goldmann DA, Keohane CA, et al. Adverse drug events in pediatric outpatients. *Ambul Pediatr.* 2007;7(5):383–389

43. Zandieh SO, Goldmann DA, Keohane CA, Yoon C, Bates DW, Kaushal R. Risk factors in preventable adverse drug events in pediatric outpatients. *J Pediatr.* 2008;152(2):225–231

44. Dill JL, Generali JA. Medication sample labeling practices. *Am J Health Syst Pharm.* 2000;57(22):2087–2090

45. McPhillips HA, Stille CJ, Smith D, et al. Potential medication dosing errors in outpatient pediatrics. *J Pediatr.* 2005;147(6):761–767

46. Feikema SM, Klevens RM, Washington ML, Barker L. Extraimmunization among US children. *JAMA.* 2000;283(10):1311–1317. http://jama.ama-assn.org/content/283/10/1311.full.pdf+html. Accessed May 19, 2011

47. Chedoe I, Molendijk HA, Dittrich ST, et al. Incidence and nature of medication errors in neonatal intensive care with strategies to improve safety: a review of the current literature. *Drug Saf.* 2007;30(6):503–513

48. Flores G, Ngui E. Racial/ethnic disparities and patient safety. *Pediatr Clin North Am.* 2006;53(6):1197–1215.

49. Leyva M, Sharif I, Ozuah P. Health literacy among Spanish-speaking Latino parents with limited English proficiency. *Ambul Pediatr.* 2005;5(1):56–59

50. Joint Commission. *Facts About the Official "Do Not Use" List.* http://www.jointcommission.org/assets/1/18/Official_Do%20Not%20Use_List_%206_10.pdf. Accessed May 19, 2011

51. World Health Organization. Patient safety solutions. http://www.who.int/patientsafety/implementation/solutions/patientsafety/en/index.html. Accessed May 19, 2011

52. Lehmann CU, Kim GR. Computerized provider order entry and patient safety. *Pediatr Clin North Am.* 2006;53(6):1169–1184

53. Longhurst CA, Parast L, Sandborg CI, et al. Decrease in hospital-wide mortality rate after implementation of a commercially sold computerized physician order entry system. *Pediatrics.* 2010;126(1):14–21

54. Neuspiel DR, Guzman M, Harewood C. Improving error reporting in ambulatory pediatrics with a team approach. *Advances in Patient Safety: New Directions and Alternative Approaches: Vol. 1. Assessment.* Rockville, MD: Agency for Healthcare Research and Quality; 2008:1–7. AHRQ Publication No. 08-0034-1. http://www.ncbi.nlm.nih.gov/books/NBK43643/pdf/advances-neuspiel_43.pdf. Accessed May 19, 2011

55. Agency for Healthcare Research and Quality. *20 Tips to Help Prevent Medical Errors.* http://www.ahrq.gov/consumer/20tips.pdf. Accessed May 19, 2011

CHAPTER 17

Medical Licensure, Specialty Boards, and Practitioner Data Banks

Jose Luis Gonzalez, MD, JD, MSEd, FAAP

KEY CONCEPTS

- Regulation and Licensure of Health Care Professionals
- American Board of Pediatrics Certification
- Data Banks
- Effectiveness of Data Banks
- Know What Is Out There

Physicians today are increasingly scrutinized in their professional and clinical skills as well as in their technical competence through access-restricted national data banks and a variety of physician profile registries accessible to the public. Expansion of the Internet has increased the availability of online information about physicians. Not only are patients tracked in disease registries and other electronic records, but physicians and other health care practitioners are now themselves tracked as to their clinical performance through federal, state, and payer-specific databases. Pediatricians need to understand the purposes behind these information storage systems, how the systems operate, and what their individual rights and responsibilities are. This chapter explains practitioner data banks and how they fit into the restricted-access and freely open physician profile categories, and suggests what pediatricians should do to keep their professional reputations intact.

Regulation and Licensure of Health Care Professionals

All 50 states and the District of Columbia mandate the medical licensure of allopathic and osteopathic physicians before they can practice in the state.[1] Although they vary greatly, most states also have established licensure practice requirements for other health care professionals such as dentists, registered nurses, podiatrists, dental hygienists, pharmacists, optometrists, physician extenders, audiologists, and speech pathologists. State licensure laws specify the applicable minimum qualifications each of these professionals must possess to practice the profession in the state. They also prescribe penalties for those who practice without appropriate licensure and define the circumstances under which a license to practice may be revoked, suspended, or limited.

Failure to adhere to state licensing requirements can result not only in fines or prohibitions on future practice by state licensing boards but also in criminal penalties.[1] Additionally, health care facilities are often required by state law to ensure that professionals providing health care services therein are properly licensed.

The primary public policy rationale advanced in support of state licensure laws is the state's need to protect the health and welfare of its citizen patients. This rationale asserts that laypersons are at a disadvantage in accurately evaluating the skills and expertise of medical personnel and in determining the risks of substandard care. Of relevance, patient care often occurs on short notice, when any effective inquiry into a professional's qualifications is impossible. Further rational argument concludes that any additional economic costs incurred by licensing procedures are, therefore, more than offset by the costs of poor health care at the hands of unqualified and perhaps dangerous practitioners.

State-specific requirements for initial medical licensure differ, but most permit licensure during residency training for American medical graduates. Longer training requirements are required for international medical graduates.[1] However, other policies of state boards vary greatly. Endorsement, formerly known as reciprocity, refers to the issuance of a medical license to physicians who hold licenses to practice in other states or jurisdictions. Each state has strict endorsement requirements, and fees can vary significantly from state to state. Most boards require physicians licensed in their state to renew every year or every 2 years, although a few have longer intervals. Completion of a specified number of hours of CME is required for maintaining licensure in most states.

American Board of Pediatrics Certification

Besides state statutes that mandate professional licensure, a number of professional associations have created their own voluntary, complementary systems for credentialing members. These systems are often based on a set of minimum standards for educational attainment, success on examinations, and a duration of practical, relevant work experience. For example, the American Board of Medical Specialties[2] assists specialty boards in the development and use of standards for certifying physicians in, currently, 24 areas of medical practice. Although these private associations cannot bar an individual from professional practice, as can state licensure agencies, most (but not all) hospitals now require initial and ongoing maintenance of certification

(MOC) within specified times for credentialing medical staff.[3] No less important, certification by a professional organization can also significantly improve career prospects. In fact, when assessment of a physician's expertise is necessary, hospitals and other health service providers will generally interpret professional board certification as a reliable indicator of competence.[4,5] Many hospitals will not permit continued hospital staff privileges if board certification has not been attained within a certain number of years after training.

Young physicians will frequently confuse 2 important pediatric organizations—the American Board of Pediatrics (ABP) and the American Academy of Pediatrics (AAP).[6] The ABP is an independent, nonprofit organization whose certificate is recognized throughout the world as signifying a high level of physician competence. The ABP was founded in 1933. The Board of Directors of the ABP consists of pediatricians distinguished in the fields of education, research, and clinical practice, as well as one or more nonphysicians, who have a professional interest and recognized expertise in the health and welfare of children and adolescents. The ABP strives to improve learner training, establishes the requirements for certification, and sets the standards for its examinations.[7]

Certification by the ABP has one objective—to promote excellence in medical care for infants, children, and adolescents. Certification represents dedication to the highest level of clinical skills and professionalism in patient care. American Board of Pediatrics certification provides a standard of excellence by which the public can select pediatricians and pediatric subspecialists. Although ABP certification is voluntary, nearly all qualified pediatricians seek this recognition. Since its inception, the ABP has awarded more than 93,000 certificates in General Pediatrics and almost 19,000 certificates in pediatric subspecialties.[7] American Board of Pediatrics certificates are awarded in General Pediatrics and in the following subspecialty areas: Adolescent Medicine, Pediatric Cardiology, Child Abuse Pediatrics, Pediatric Critical Care Medicine, Developmental-Behavioral Pediatrics, Pediatric Emergency Medicine, Pediatric Endocrinology, Pediatric Gastroenterology, Pediatric Hematology-Oncology, Pediatric Infectious Diseases, Neonatal-Perinatal Medicine, Pediatric Nephrology, Pediatric Pulmonology, Pediatric Rheumatology, Hospice and Palliative Medicine, Medical Toxicology, Neurodevelopmental Disabilities, Sleep Medicine, Sports Medicine, and Pediatric Transplant Hepatology. Other pediatric subspecialty certification is offered by organizations other than the ABP (eg, child neurology certification from the American Board of Psychiatry and Neurology). Information on pediatric certification may be obtained by visiting the ABP Web site at https://www.abp.org/MOCVerification/VerificationServlet or by calling the ABP at 919/929-0461.

After 1988, certificates issued by the ABP have been time limited and require evidence of licensure as well as the successful completion of the ABP board-certifying examination at initial application and every 7 years for reissue. Starting in 2003, MOC was added as an additional requirement for periodic recertification and was designed for pediatricians who wish to demonstrate to patients, colleagues, and health care organizations their ongoing pursuit of professional development, which results in quality patient care. In turn, compliance with MOC requirements enables the ABP to assure the general public, licensing boards, payers, and regulatory agencies that its board-certified pediatricians and pediatric subspecialists or diplomates have the knowledge and skills necessary to deliver quality care.

As has been the case with initial certification for the last decade, the MOC is based on the 6 core competencies established by the Accreditation Council for Graduate Medical Education (ACGME) (patient care, medical knowledge, practice-based learning and improvements, interpersonal and communication skills, professionalism, and system-based practice) and evaluated during residency and fellowship training.[8] Further, the MOC also consists of 4 primary parts.

- Professional Standing (holds a valid, unrestricted medical license)
- Lifelong Learning and Self-Assessment (assesses and enhances knowledge in areas important to their practice through relevant activities)
- Cognitive Expertise (successfully completes a secure examination)
- Performance in Practice (participates in approved quality improvement projects designed to assess and improve the quality of patient care)[7]

These apply equally to general pediatrics and pediatric subspecialty recertification.

Beginning in 2010, however, periodic recertification changed to continuous certification, and the ABP recognizes 2 distinct classifications of certified pediatricians and pediatric subspecialists: those who have permanent certificates, and those who are certified *and* meet current MOC requirements. Permanent certificate holders will be designated as current or not current with MOC requirements. The ABP recertification process recognizes the ABP position that its defined process of maintenance of certification and periodic secure testing are required for the maintenance of current, high-quality medical care.

Starting with the examinations administered in 2014 for pediatrics and pediatric subspecialties, candidates will no longer have unlimited time to become certified. To assure the public that the candidate possesses the competencies verified at the time of completion of training, the training required for certification must be completed within the 7-year period prior to the examination. If this period is not met, the candidate must complete additional training prior to applying for certification.

American Board of Pediatrics Diplomate Versus American Academy of Pediatrics Fellow

A board-certified pediatrician possesses a certificate from the ABP and is referred to as a diplomate of the ABP. Most board-certified pediatricians, however, are also members of the AAP, a nonprofit, charitable organization dedicated to improving the health care of children through CME, advocacy, research, practice and risk management, and policy development.[6] Many pediatricians-in-training join the AAP as resident fellows. After residency training, they may continue their affiliation with the AAP as candidate fellows, a time-limited category of membership, while they pursue board certification. On achieving board certification, pediatricians can apply for full membership status to become a Fellow of the AAP and be entitled to use this designation in all formal communications (eg, certificates, publications, business cards, stationery, signage). Thus, John Doe, MD, FAAP, is a Fellow of the AAP.

Data Banks

Federal data banks are electronic data systems that serve as central repositories for collecting and dispensing information on various adverse actions taken against physicians and other health care practitioners. Two government-sponsored and government-maintained mandatory reporting systems are currently in effect: the National Practitioner Data Bank (NPDB), implemented by the Health Care Quality Improvement Act of 1986 (HCQIA), and the Healthcare Integrity & Protection Data Bank (HIPDB), which was established as a health care fraud and abuse data collection program under section 1128E of the Social Security Act, as added by the Health Insurance Portability and Accountability Act of 1996 (HIPAA).[9] Although the NPDB and HIPDB share similar reporting requirements and functional objectives,

as well as dispute and appeals processes, they are nonetheless separate and sufficiently different to dictate separate discussion (Table 17-1).

National Practitioner Data Bank

The NPDB contains reports of adverse licensure, clinical privileges, private accreditation organizations, and Drug Enforcement Administration actions—as well as Health and Human Services (HHS) Office of Inspector General Medicare and Medicaid exclusions—taken against physicians and dentists. The HCQIA also mandates submission of negative quality-of-care reports to the NPDB from the aforementioned entities as well as hospitals and other health care systems, such as health maintenance organizations, state medical and dental boards, and professional societies with formal peer review.[10] Actions that affect clinical privileges must have a duration of at least 31 days to be reportable. Denial or voluntary resignations of clinical privileges by a new or existing medical staff member are similarly reportable when such actions involve or replace a peer-review process or judgment.[10]

The NPDB also collects and stores reports of medical professional liability payments made by or for the benefit of any state-licensed health care practitioners (eg, physicians, dentists, nurses, chiropractors, emergency medical technicians, physician extenders) regardless of whether payment was made as a settlement agreement or as a judicial verdict.[10] Although the US Congress clearly stated in the law that "[a] payment in settlement of a medical malpractice action or claim shall not be construed as creating a presumption that medical malpractice has occurred,"[11] federal lawmakers obviously felt that hospitals and licensing boards should be aware of all medical professional liability payment information so they could apply as they saw fit in their competency review processes.

Table 17-1. Data Banks: Who Must Report and Who Can Access?[10]

Expanded NPDB (HCQIA and Section 1921)	HIPDB (Section 1128E)

Who Reports?
• Medical malpractice payers
• State health care practitioner licensing and certification authorities (including medical and dental boards)
• Hospitals
• Other health care entities with formal peer review (HMOs, group practices, MCOs)
• Professional societies with formal peer review
• State entity licensing and certification authorities
• Peer-review organizations
• Private accreditation organizations
• DEA
• HHS OIG
 	
What Information Is Available?
• Medical malpractice payments (all health care practitioners)
• Any adverse licensure action (all practitioners or entities)
  – Revocation, reprimand, censure, suspension, probation
  – Any dismissal or closure of proceedings by reason of the practitioner or entity surrendering the license or leaving the state or jurisdiction
  – Any other loss of license
• Adverse clinical privileging actions
• Adverse professional society membership actions
• Any negative action or finding by a state licensing or certification authority
• Peer-review organization negative actions or findings against a health care practitioner
• Private accreditation organization negative actions or findings against a health care or entity
• Adverse actions against DEA certification
• Medicare exclusions
 	
Who Can Query?
• Hospitals
• Other health care entities, with formal peer review
• Professional societies, with formal peer review
• State health care practitioner licensing and certification authorities (including medical and dental boards)
• State entity licensing and certification authorities[a]
• Agencies or contractors administering federal health card programs[a]
• State agencies administering state health care programs[a]
• State Medicaid fraud control units[a]
• US Comptroller General[a]
• US Attorney General and other law enforcement[a]
• Health care practitioners and entities (self-query)
• Plaintiff's attorney/pro se plaintiffs (under limited circumstances)[b]
• Quality improvement organizations[a]
• Researchers (statistical data only)
• DEA
• HHS OIG
	Who Reports?
	• Federal and state government agencies
	• Health plans
	
	What Information Is Available?
	• Licensing and certification actions (practitioners, providers, and suppliers)—revocation, reprimand, suspension (including length), censure, probation, voluntary surrender, any other negative action or finding by a federal or state licensing or certification agency that is publicly available information
	• Health care–related civil judgments (practitioners, providers, and suppliers)
	• Health care–related criminal convictions (practitioners, providers, and suppliers)
	• Exclusions from federal or state health care programs (practitioners, providers, and suppliers)
	• Other adjudicated actions or decisions (practitioners, providers, and suppliers)
	
	Who Can Query?
	• Federal and state government agencies
	• Health plans
	• Health care practitioners, providers, and suppliers (self-query)
	• Researchers (statistical data only)

Abbreviations: DEA, Drug Enforcement Administration; HCQIA, Health Care Quality Improvement Act of 1986; HHS, Health and Human Services; HIPDB, Healthcare Integrity & Protection Data Bank; HMO, health maintenance organization; MCO, managed care organization; NPDB, National Practitioner Data Bank; OIG, Office of Inspector General.
[a]Eligible to receive only those reports authorized by section 1921.
[b]Eligible to receive only those reports authorized by HCQIA.

Of similar importance, the HCQIA additionally requires all medical malpractice payers to report to the NPDB within 30 days all payments made on behalf of a physician, *including residents and interns,* or a licensed health care practitioner to settle or satisfy a judgment in a medical professional liability case.[11] This payment information must also be reported to the state medical board in the state where the incident occurred.

In its 2006 annual report (the most recent report available),[12] the NPDB noted that 69.3% of all practitioners reported were physicians, including MDs, DOs, and residents and interns. Dentists and dental residents comprised 13.3% of the practitioners' group, while 9.2% were nurses and 2.8% were chiropractors. Physicians also had 78.8% of malpractice payment reports in the NPDB.[12] About two thirds of physicians with reports (66.5%) had only a single report, 85% had 2 or fewer reports, 97.1% had 5 or fewer, and 99.5% had 10 or fewer.[12] Only 6.2% of physicians had a medical malpractice report and an adverse action report. Allopathic and osteopathic interns and residents made up only 0.8% of all cumulative physician malpractice payment reports in the NPDB.[12] Almost 90% (89.3%) of these physicians-in-training had only 1 report, while 3.8% had 2 reports and 8 (0.04%) had 3 or more.[12]

Unlike these mandated reporting requirements, medical professional liability payments made by individuals on their own behalf from their personal finances, not from practice or corporate funds, are not reportable. Likewise, if there is no payment made on behalf of the physician (or health care practitioner) by a payer or the individual practice or corporation, no report to the NPDB is required.[10]

Even if a malpractice payment from a formal legal action is avoided, an adverse professional action may still need to be reported to the NPDB and state licensing board. In this regard, the NPDB definition of a *medical professional liability action* is very broad and encompasses written complaints or demands from a potential plaintiff for compensation, even if no formal legal action is ever filed. For example, although a simple refund of professional service fees by an individual practitioner is not by itself considered to be a malpractice payment, if the refund results from a written demand for monetary payment for damages incurred, it is reportable to the NPDB if paid by the practice, corporation, or malpractice insurer. Similarly, even though submission of an adverse report to the NPDB is not generally required when a physician is formally dismissed from the lawsuit before a settlement or judgment, this exemption does not apply if the physician is dismissed from the lawsuit in consideration of a payment by a third party as a condition to the settlement.[10]

Reports to the NPDB on adverse liability actions may be submitted electronically on the standard Medical Malpractice Payment Report (MMPR) available through the NPDB Web site.[10] Only statutorily qualified, registered entities can access the MMPR to file a report (Table 17-1). Besides certain demographic information on the physician or dentist, the submitted form must also contain the date of the alleged act or acts, the jurisdiction where the claim was filed, the date of judgment or settlement, and the amount and date of payment. In addition, the report must also include a narrative of 2,000 characters or less, written by the entity that makes the payment on the physician's behalf (eg, hospital, insurance carrier), describing the acts or omissions that gave rise to the negligence action[10] and including a classification of the claim according to codes established by the US HHS, Health Resources and Services Administration (HRSA), Bureau of Health Professions, Division of Practitioner Data Banks (DPDB).[10]

Because of the subjective nature of the narrative, a prudent physician will initiate a discussion about the narrative's proposed content with the hospital or insurance carrier *before* the NPDB report is filed. These discussions between a physician and the entity filing the report are fully appropriate. Although the MMPR must clearly describe the allegations made in the claim,[12] the narrative may also state that the claim was paid only for nuisance value or that there was no admission at the time of judgment or settlement of the claim that the standard of care was violated. Even if a plaintiff's attorney offers to drop the physician as a defendant as part of the settlement process (if the physician is a hospital employee), physicians should still provide the hospital or insurance company with recommended language to use in the description of the alleged negligent event as soon as it appears likely that the case may be settled outside of court. In fact, a physician's negotiating power is greatest before a final settlement is reached. Once a payment is made, the deadline for reporting to the NPDB leaves little time for any negotiations as to the narrative's descriptive language.[10]

Physicians need to know what the MMPR will say before agreeing to settle. This is of particular importance for malpractice insurance policies that do not require agreement by the covered physician before the insurance carrier or hospital is legally able to settle with the aggrieved party. If the practitioner is consulted about the NPDB report before it is filed, it may decrease the likelihood of a dispute being filed by the physician about the report. Although there is an expectation by physicians that hospitals and insurance carriers would indicate, when appropriate, that the case was without medical merit and settled simply for financial reasons, NPDB annual reports have actually commented on more than one occasion that submitted narrative descriptions of cases settled for economic reasons may inaccurately reflect the presence of substandard health care.[10,12]

On receipt of an MMPR made on behalf of a physician or dentist, the NPDB will send the report's named practitioner a notification of a report in the NPDB. Although the NPDB routinely waives the 60-day time limit for filing a dispute in the interest

of ensuring a complete and accurate report,[10] physicians should promptly check the accuracy of all the information in the submitted report. When disputing NPDB reports, a 4,000-character statement may be filed with the NPDB describing the basis of the dispute and expressing the physician's view of the professional liability claim, payment, or both. Whereas the dispute process allows the practitioner who is the subject of the report to question its factual accuracy, the process cannot be used to protest the insurer's settlement decision or to appeal the reported adverse action.

Special care should be used in crafting the statement for the NPDB, as this statement will be released unedited along with the NPDB report in response to subsequent queries from registered entities. To dispute an NPDB report or file an appeal, physicians should access the NPDB Web site (www.npdb-hipdb.hrsa.gov) or contact the help line for detailed information on the appeals process and physicians' rights and responsibilities. The toll-free number is 800/767-6732, or 800/SOS-NPDB.[10]

State medical and dental licensing and disciplinary boards, agencies administering federal or state health care programs, state Medicaid Fraud Control Units, and certain law enforcement entities all have access to NPDB information. Hospitals and other health care system facilities that conduct peer review and provide health care services, as well as utilization and quality improvement peer-review organizations, are also capable of querying the NPDB electronic data depository. Of specific importance, individual medical and dental practitioners and entities can submit self-queries on the NPDB Web site for their own provided profiles (Table 17-1).

Hospitals are mandated to query the NPDB on a practitioner's initial application for clinical staff privileges and every 2 years thereafter for all active medical staff members. However, even though medical and dental interns, residents, or fellows may hold licenses to practice the profession, hospitals are not required to check the NPDB about these individuals unless they are being considered for appointment to the clinical staff or are granted clinical privileges beyond the aegis of the residency program, such as moonlighting in the nursery or emergency department.[10] Otherwise, these trainees are considered as students in supervised programs of graduate medical education.[8]

Attorneys are not permitted to directly access the NPDB. They may, however, request data bank reports if independent evidence confirms that they are parties to a legal claim alleging that a hospital or another health care facility failed to query the data bank about a particular physician as mandated for credentialing for clinical privileges. Information acquired from the NPDB under these circumstances, however, can only be used in that particular lawsuit and only against the named facility. If inappropriately obtained or used, HCQIA statutory language provides for strong penalties for breaches of confidentiality.[11] In contrast, although permissive legislation has been introduced in Congress from time to time, the public does not at present have access to the NPDB.

Notwithstanding anxious implications of relatively widespread access to practitioners' adverse liability data, the average pediatrician has little to fear from the NPDB.[12] Most credentialing bodies already require applicants to disclose a greater level of information than that contained in NPDB reports. For example, before hospital privileges are granted or malpractice insurance coverage is issued, applicants are frequently obligated to disclose all open and closed medical professional liability claims, even if the claim was dropped or settled without payment.[5] Conversely, the NPDB only contains reports on closed claims with payments attributable to a specified practitioner.[10]

Healthcare Integrity & Protection Data Bank

The HIPDB was created by HIPAA[13] as a data-collection program to help deter fraud and abuse in health care delivery. Health care fraud burdens the nation with enormous financial costs and threatens health care quality and patient safety. The United States spends more than $2 trillion annually on health care. Of that, the National Health Care Anti-Fraud Association has estimated that at least 3%, or more than $60 billion, is lost every year to health care fraud.[14]

The HIPDB serves as a national fraud and abuse data repository for the reporting and disclosure of certain final adverse actions taken against practitioners and other health care providers and suppliers, including licensing and certification actions, health care–related civil judgments and criminal convictions, health plan contract terminations, and exclusions from federal or state health care programs. As of December 31, 2002 (the most recent report available), physicians (21.1% of 132,022 cumulative reports) and registered nurses (13.5%) made up the greatest proportion of practitioners reported as individuals.[15] Fifty-three percent of physicians and 54.1% of registered nurses had only a single report, while 25% of physicians and 27.7% of nurses had 2 reports. A significant majority (76%) of all physician reports were for state licensure actions, such as the suspension, probation, or revocation of the medical license. Most other reports (18.7%) were for actions excluding participation in a state or federal health care program including, but not limited to Medicaid or Medicare (9.9%).[15]

The HIPDB is primarily a flagging system that alerts certified users that a comprehensive review of a practitioner's, provider's, or supplier's past actions may be in order. This data repository is intended to augment, not replace, traditional forms of fraud and abuse review and investigation,[16–18] serving primarily as an important supplement to the comprehensive and careful review by health care plans and federal and state agencies of prior fraudulent activities. Unlike the NPDB, medical liability claims and civil suit settlements in which no findings or admissions of liability have been made are not reported to the HIPDB.[9,10] The HIPDB, like the NPDB, is not accessible to the public (Table 17-1).

As a nationwide flagging system, the HIPDB provides another resource for federal and state agencies, as well as law enforcement agencies, state licensing boards, and health care plans, to conduct extensive, independent investigations of the qualifications of health care practitioners, providers, or suppliers they seek to investigate, license, hire, or credential, or with whom they seek to contract or affiliate. Although information in the data bank serves to alert federal or state agencies and health care plans that there may be a problem with the credentials of a particular practitioner, provider, or supplier, this information should only be considered in association with relevant data from other official and reliable sources. To be eligible to report or query the HIPDB, an entity must be a health care plan or a federal or state governmental agency. Health care practitioners, providers, and suppliers are also permitted to self-query the HIPDB (Table 17-1).

When the HIPDB processes a report, a Report Verification Document is sent to the reporting entity and a notification of a report in the data bank is sent to the reported individual or entity. As with the NPDB, the health care professional who is the subject of the data bank record has the option to append a 4,000-character subject statement or dispute the report.[10] All data repository reports should be reviewed closely for accuracy.

State Physician Data Banks

Many states currently collect and store a wide range of professional data on physicians, including practice information (eg, primary work setting, address), information on medical education and residency training, CME hours, state medical board disciplinary actions, revocation or restriction of hospital privileges, medical professional liability judgments, settled claims, and criminal convictions.[19] Precipitated by public pressure, an increasing number of states presently offer or are considering offering consumer access to these physician profiles for the stated purpose of providing the information needed to enable informed decisions on consumers' own health care. Access is commonly available via the Internet, but a few states offer the information by way of a toll-free telephone number. Although publicly accessible state data banks differ in the types of physicians' professional information they contain and are able to provide, they are still only minimally used.[19]

On a national basis, at least one organization collects professional physician information and is willing to sell it. Although the Federation of State Medical Boards (FSMB) has collected this information for approximately 40 years, it is only recently that FSMB has allowed public access to its files. For a fee, the FSMB will send consumers a report on all disciplinary actions taken against an individual physician.[1]

Effectiveness of Data Banks

The HIPDB has been operational since 1999, and the NPDB has been collecting and storing records for more than 20 years.[10] Every few years, Congress holds hearings on the need to open the NPDB to the public, yet the debate remains the same—consumers do not think data repository programs can be effective unless the general public can query the system for information on their own physicians, particularly in reference to malpractice data. Conversely, health researchers, policy analysts, and providers caution Congress that the raw data can be misleading and that malpractice payments are more likely to indicate the level of patient disability after an adverse outcome than actual physician malpractice.[10,12]

To this last point, a report by the US Government Accountability Office (GAO) in November 2000 concluded that "[t]he data in medical malpractice payment reports—representing about 80% of the information in NPDB—generally did not meet HRSA's criteria for completeness. For example, over 95% of the medical malpractice reports that were reviewed did not note whether the standard of patient care had been considered when the claim was settled or adjudicated."[20] Although there are no recent, supportive external reports, and in spite of the presumption that data accuracy contained in NPDB malpractice payment reports and HIPDB data collection can only have improved over the years, the GAO findings underscore the importance of physician vigilance in monitoring their stored professional information by regular self-querying.[10]

Know What Is Out There

1. Become familiar with the 2 federal practitioner data banks. Obtain and store copies of data sheets and guidebooks, and make sure you know your rights and responsibilities under these programs.

2. Conduct periodic self-queries to request your data bank files. Both data banks can be accessed via an integrated Web-based inquiry program at www.npdb-hipdb.hrsa.gov.

3. Review all reported information contained in your NPDB and HIBDP files for accuracy. If inaccuracies are found, strongly consider filing a dispute.

4. Search for your name in other physician data banks (eg, state medical licensure, managed care organization provider sites, other physician grading sites) to know and be aware of what kind of professional information patients may be able to access about you and your practice.

Summary

Health care practitioner data banks are not likely to go away. In fact, consumers now desire more information than ever about their health care providers, and regulatory agencies increasingly demand more comprehensive screening and credentialing of medical and dental practitioners from health care employers and service facilities. Physicians thus face the huge challenge of complying with increasing professional monitoring and reporting requirements, while at the same time remaining vigilant in ensuring that their individual data bank records are accurate and complete.

Because the information collected and maintained by the NPDB and HIPDB can markedly affect a practitioner's reputation and livelihood, the integrity of the information must be of great concern to all physicians. It is, therefore, important that federal agencies overseeing these data repositories develop thorough and standardized procedures to verify the accuracy and completeness of the information reported and obtain corrections promptly from reporting agencies when necessary. However, it remains prudent for all physicians to periodically request copies of their personal information from the NPDB and HIPDB.

References

1. State-specific requirements for initial medical licensure. Federation of State Medical Boards Web site. http://www.fsmb.org/usmle_eliinitial.html. Updated July 2010. Accessed June 15, 2011

2. American Board of Medical Specialties Web site. http://www.abms.org. Accessed June 15, 2011

3. Freed GL, Dunham KM, Singer D. Use of board certification and recertification in hospital privileging: policies for general surgeons, surgical specialists, and nonsurgical subspecialists. *Arch Surg.* 2009;144(8):746–752. http://archsurg.ama-assn.org/cgi/reprint/144/8/746. Accessed June 15, 2011

4. American Hospital Association Web site. http://www.aha.org. Accessed June 15, 2011

5. Texas Society for Medical Services Specialists Web site. http://www.tsmss.org. Accessed June 15, 2011

6. American Academy of Pediatrics Web site. http://www.aap.org. Accessed June 15, 2011

7. American Board of Pediatrics Web site. https://www.abp.org. Accessed June 15, 2011

8. Accreditation Council on Graduate Medical Education Web site. https://www.acgme.org. Accessed June 15, 2011

9. Health Resources and Services Administration. National Practitioner Data Bank for adverse information on physicians and other health care practitioners: reporting on adverse and negative actions. Final rule. *Fed Regist.* 2010;75(18):4655–4682

10. The Data Bank: National Practitioner Data Bank and the Healthcare Integrity & Protection Data Bank Web site. http://www.npdb-hipdb.hrsa.gov. Accessed June 15, 2011

11. Health Care Quality Improvement Act (HCQIA) of 1986, as amended. 42 USC §11101 et Seq

12. US Department of Health and Human Services, Health Resources and Service Administration, Bureau of Health Professions, Division of Practitioner Data Banks. *National Practitioner Data Bank 2006 Annual Report.* 2006. http://www.npdb-hipdb.hrsa.gov/resources/reports/2006NPDBAnnualReport.pdf. Accessed June 15, 2011

13. Social Security Act, §1128E, as added by the Health Insurance Portability and Accountability Act (HIPAA) of 1996, §221(a). Pub Law No. 104–191

14. Testimony of Daniel R. Levinson, Inspector General, before the House Energy and Commerce Committee, Subcommittee on Health, US House of Representatives. Health Care Reform: Opportunities to Address Waste, Fraud, and Abuse. June 25, 2009. http://oig.hhs.gov/testimony/docs/2009/06252009_testimony_health_reform.pdf. Accessed June 15, 2011

15. US Department of Health and Human Services, Health Resources and Service Administration, Bureau of Health Professions, Division of Practitioner Data Banks. *Healthcare Integrity and Protection Data Bank 2002 Annual Report.* 2002. http://www.npdb-hipdb.hrsa.gov/resources/reports/2002HIPDBAnnualReport.pdf. Accessed June 15, 2011

16. US Department of Health and Human Services, Department of Justice. *Health Care Fraud and Abuse Control Program Annual Report for FY2008.* 2009. http://oig.hhs.gov/publications/docs/hcfac/hcfacreport2008.pdf. Accessed June 15, 2011

17. US Department of Health and Human Services, Office of Inspector General. *State Medicaid Fraud Control Units Annual Report, Fiscal Year 2008.* http://oig.hhs.gov/fraud/medicaid-fraud-control-units-mfcu/annual_reports/mfcu_2008.pdf. Accessed June 15, 2011

18. *Medicare Fraud and Abuse Resource Reference.* Centers for Medicare and Medicaid Services Web site. http://www.cms.hhs.gov/MLNProducts/downloads/Fraud_and_Abuse.pdf. Accessed June 15, 2011

19. Barrett S. Physician credentials: how can I check them? *Quackwatch.* November 19, 2009. http://www.quackwatch.org/04ConsumerEducation/QA/mdcheck.html. Accessed June 15, 2011

20. United States General Accounting Office. *National Practitioner Data Bank: Major Improvements are Needed to Enhance Data Bank's Reliability. Report to the Chairman, Subcommittee on National Economic Growth, Natural Resources and Regulatory Affairs, Committee on Government Reform, House of Representatives.* Washington, DC: United States General Accounting Office; 2000. GAO-01-130. http://www.gao.gov/new.items/d01130.pdf. Accessed June 15, 2011

Resources

Federation of State Medical Boards

Founded in February 1912, the FSMB is a national nonprofit association with membership consisting of more than 70 medical licensing authorities in 50 states, the District of Columbia, and other sites. Its primary purpose is to facilitate the work of its member organizations.

For further information on medical licensure, contact

Federation of State Medical Boards
400 Fuller Wiser Rd, Suite 300
Euless, TX 76039
817/868-4000
Fax: 817/868-4099
www.fsmb.org

Federal Health Care Data Banks

General descriptions of the data banks are included in this chapter; additional information is available from

www.npdb-hipdb.hrsa.gov
800/767-6732

NPDB Guidebook
www.npdb-hipdb.hrsa.gov/resources/
NPDBGuidebook.pdf

HIPDB Guidebook
www.npdb-hipdb.hrsa.gov/resources/
HIPDBGuidebook.pdf

American Board of Pediatrics

For further information on board certification, contact

American Board of Pediatrics
111 Silver Cedar Ct
Chapel Hill, NC 27514
919/929-0461
Fax: 919/929-9255
abpeds@abpeds.org
https://www.abp.org

American Academy of Pediatrics

Further information on the benefits and privileges of membership in the AAP may be obtained by contacting

American Academy of Pediatrics
Division of Member Services and Relations
141 Northwest Point Blvd
Elk Grove Village, IL 60007-1019
847/434-4721
Fax: 847/228-7035
www.aap.org

CHAPTER 18

Career Transitions: Residency Through Retirement

Jose Luis Gonzalez, MD, JD, MSEd, FAAP

KEY CONCEPTS

- Residency Training
- Employment Changes
- Retirement

It requires a lifelong commitment to become a pediatrician. It takes continued vigilance to prevent pediatric careers from being jeopardized by inadequate or interrupted professional liability insurance coverage. Continuous tort liability insurance (medical malpractice with tail coverage) is one of the most important and expensive features of medical practice today. Maintaining adequate coverage requires time, attention to detail, and ongoing self-learning to be certain that pediatricians are appropriately and continuously insured. Medical liability risk begins with a resident's first patient encounter and continues throughout a physician's professional lifetime. Depending on each state's statute of limitation laws for exempting minors, the period during which a malpractice action can be filed by an aggrieved patient can, in fact, extend well beyond the time of the clinical encounter and even beyond the alleged negligent provider's retirement. This chapter will review many of the key concepts and potential career hurdles surrounding the successful and smooth transition from residency, through practice, into retirement.

Residency Training

Physicians begin to hone their medical knowledge and clinical skills early in their postgraduate medical education under the tutelage of experienced clinicians. During their training, however, residents must also begin to grapple with the real presence of medical malpractice and to develop an understanding of the medical tort liability landscape and hopefully, the essentials of appropriate health care delivery risk management.

Are Residents at Risk?

Because pediatric residents and fellows are closely supervised during training by experienced faculty, their medical malpractice liability risks are theoretically less than that of practicing pediatricians. Under the legal doctrine of respondeat superior, "let the master answer," the educational institution conducting the residency program is responsible for the medical care provided by its residents during training-related activities. Therefore, the institution is liable for defense costs, settlements, and awards for malpractice attributed to physicians-in-training. Residents' and Fellows' trainee status, coupled with their lack of financial assets, often precludes residents from being targeted in a malpractice suit. In those instances in which residents are named in a malpractice complaint, they often are dropped from the case early in the legal proceedings or later in the process following their depositions. Physicians-in-training, however, are not entirely immune from malpractice risks and may actually find themselves as ancillary parties caught in the legal battle to allocate responsibility for an adverse outcome among supervising physicians and the graduate medical education (GME) hospital.

Tort case law addressing the standard of care expected from a resident has evolved over the years but still differs amongst the states. At one time it was thought that because residents were students, they should not be held to the same standards as practicing physicians. Rather, the level of performance expected was that of the "average" resident at a comparable stage of training. Although some state jurisdictions still use this "applicable to his class" resident standard,[1] in an increasing number of jurisdictions, this notion has evolved to current expectations that because of the high level of supervision provided by attending faculty, a resident should provide care at the same level as a physician fully trained and competent by professional standards to practice in his or her specialty.[2,3] In addition, in assessing the medical liability of physicians-in-training, other courts have likewise struggled as to whether residents should be held to the level of expertise expected of general practitioners or specialists.[4] With this as background, it is clear that residents need to understand various key principles of medical liability and risk management likely to affect their practices.

Although more than a decade old, an article documenting the malpractice experiences of pediatric residents at a GME-accredited children's hospital over a 25-year period is characteristic of the liability risk exposures of medical trainees.[5] In their review, the authors found that residents were named in 26% of the hospital's malpractice cases.[5] Residents, however, were rarely named alone; rather, they were usually named as codefendants along with the hospital, attending physicians, or both. In addition, and as confirmed by the National Practitioner Data Bank (NPDB) reported incidence data described on page 222, most residents were dropped as malpractice defendants before the cases were settled or adjudicated at trial.

Some medical malpractice experts have expressed concern that the number of tort liability claims against residents appears to be increasing. In a 1991 *Academic Medicine* article,[6] medical malpractice suits naming residents as defendants were reported to have quadrupled from 1975 through 1989, with the highest incidences in northeastern states. Common issues giving rise to litigation included the question of who owed the duty of care to the injured patient (29% of 136 cases reviewed), correctness of the standard of health care provided, and failure to supervise the resident appropriately.[6] Comparably, from 2001 to 2007, approximately 3 in 10 pediatricians, on average, have had suits or claims brought against them for medical negligence at least once during their careers in medicine.[7] The American Academy of Pediatrics (AAP) Periodic Survey of Fellows has consistently revealed that 1 in 10 pediatricians was party to a malpractice suit resulting from care delivered during residency training. Of greater interest, the survey's mean number of months elapsing between the alleged error or negligent event and malpractice complaint being filed was 32.4 months, or nearly 3 years.[7] It is therefore quite likely that pediatric residents named as codefendants in medical liability cases will have already completed their residency by the time the plaintiff files a claim.

It is similarly possible that former residents may be unaware that they have been included as defendants in a malpractice claim for care provided during their training. Depending on the specifications of the medical malpractice insurance policy, the insurer may be able to settle with the injured patient without the consent or knowledge of physician defendants. In fact, pediatricians might actually find out about the settlement only after payment is reported to the NPDB.[8] The NPDB was established by federal legislation effective September 1, 1990, and requires reporting of all malpractice actions when there is a settlement or judgment payment made for the benefit of a defendant physician or resident (see Chapter 17). The Health Resources and Services Administration Bureau of Health Professionals noted in its 2006 annual report[9] that the NPDB contained information on 1,246 malpractice payments made for the benefit of residents and interns, the equivalent of 1% of all malpractice payments made on behalf of physicians. The long-term effects on subsequent employability and insurability of having a malpractice payment reported to the NPDB so early in a physician's career have yet to be studied.

Communication and Supervision

Residents deliver health care under the direct or indirect supervision of attending physicians. In this context, timely and frequent communication between the resident and attending physician is essential for quality care and effective risk management. Further, as noted earlier, an increasingly commonly adopted legal standard of care expected of a resident is the same as that of an attending physician. Given this standard, attending physicians need to clearly outline for and discuss with residents their evaluation and management expectations for patient care. In turn, residents must adhere to these expectations and closely and repeatedly monitor patient clinical courses. Any significant deviations in a patient's clinical course, unexpected or deficient responses to therapy, or new physical or diagnostic findings must be promptly communicated to the supervising physician. In situations in which the need to communicate may be uncertain, it is best to err on the side of contacting the attending physician rather than placing patients at unnecessary risk. Effective risk management principles dictate that the patient or family should be informed as appropriate and documentation entered in the medical record that the attending physician has been consulted. Failure to communicate in situations in which it is clearly indicated puts the resident and attending physician at risk of increased liability in the event of a poor outcome.

Telephone Medicine

(For a more complete discussion of telephone medicine medical liability risk management, refer to Chapter 5.)

Responsibility for the management of telephone calls from parents or other caregivers in Accreditation Council for Graduate Medical Education (ACGME)-certified training institutions frequently falls to residents. In spite of the increased number of nurse telephone advice programs now in functional existence using clinical guidelines and treatment protocols, physicians and usually pediatricians are repeatedly held ultimately responsible for the care provided to patients and subsequent outcomes. In addition, many pediatricians in smaller communities continue to personally respond to the majority of medical advice calls, especially after hours. As an integral part of pediatric practice, training in telephone management should be an essential component of pediatric residency education. Unfortunately, regardless of this evident educational need, residents too regularly graduate without the pertinent knowledge or appropriate skills to accurately assess and effectively manage telephonic health care complaints.[10] Even though residents may participate in telephone advice centers during training, this experience in telephone management is frequently lacking and, when present, is far from standardized or consistent in duration or teaching method across GME pediatric residency programs.[10]

As with any new skill, residents need to approach telephone management with an informed lifelong learning attitude. Whereas some telephone health care concerns will be straightforward and easily resolved, others will be far more difficult and complex. For the latter situations, it is imperative that residents have available adequate supervising physician backup to provide appropriate guidance and feedback. A system for accurate and timely recording and post-call review of all telephone medical advice given is likewise essential not only for documenting care quality and reducing legal risk but also for providing educational feedback to residents.

Procedures

During training, residents will characteristically receive instruction on the performance of various pediatric-directed invasive procedures, including but not limited to, lumbar puncture, catheter placement, circumcision, suturing, and endotracheal intubation.[11] Although some of these procedures may be performed without informed consent under emergency circumstances, in nonemergency situations it is legally mandatory that physicians and residents obtain informed consent from a patient's parent or legal guardian. Considering its importance to quality patient care, residents must be taught early in their training the basic elements of appropriate informed consent, including an explanation of the need to perform the procedure, who will be performing the procedure, benefits to the patient, potential complications, alternatives, and risks of not doing the procedure. All these elements must be fully explained to the consenting party in language that is nontechnical and understandable by a layperson. Informed consent discussions should always be documented on a standard consent form or distinctly described in the medical record. Consent and confidentiality issues are extremely complex, especially for adolescent patients. (For more information, see Chapter 9.)

Moonlighting

Residents' participation in non-training program activities is typically known as *moonlighting*. Such resident activities may include an agreement to provide coverage in a training program facility during nonprogram time or for providing health care services in a non-training facility, such as an emergency department (ED), hospital, or outpatient setting. Residency programs, however, frequently have established policies that prohibit or limit the types of acceptable non-training program moonlighting activities and, as such, this information

should be clearly addressed during residency program orientation.[11–13]

Residents must understand and adhere to the moonlighting policies of their particular training program. Residents that elect to engage in nonprogram activities must be certain that they have adequate liability coverage in place prior to providing any patient care.[13] Even though the provision of such coverage is typically the responsibility of the nonprogram employer, residents must never presume that it will be provided. Written verification of coverage type and exceptions, including tail coverage, should be obtained prior to the initial patient moonlight encounter. The essentials of effective risk management outlined throughout this chapter apply equally to the nonprogram setting, especially because for many, if not most of these moonlighting activities, residents are on their own without direct supervision. Such independent practice heightens the importance of special risk management challenges, including malpractice liability exposure, faced by residents during training.

Risk Management Training

Improved risk management training during residency could reduce tort liability risks for trainees, as well as practicing physicians, during and after residency. Common allegations for malpractice cases involving residents are similar to those of attending physicians and include adverse outcomes or complications from diagnostic or therapeutic procedures, errors in medication dosing or administration, and failure to diagnose or treat in accordance with the prevalent standards of care. In-hospital malpractice allegations commonly derive from care delivered in the general inpatient setting or ED. The rate and consequences of adverse medication errors, however, are reported as being much greater within critical care areas.[14] Interestingly, this same study also showed that when adjusted for the number of medications provided, this difference became nonsignificant.[14]

Alternatively, although less frequently severe and at much lower overall rates, incidences of sub-standard outpatient care delivery are still quite numerous as a result of the much-increased number of physician-patient encounters in provider office settings.

Given the severity of pediatric malpractice indemnity payments, the permanent nature of adverse reports stored in data bank repositories, and the longer statute of limitations for incidents involving minors in many states, in 2011 the AAP strengthened and reaffirmed its recommendations on the provision of professional liability coverage for all pediatric residents and Fellows throughout training.[13] Furthermore, the AAP also firmly believes that pediatric residents and Fellows should be fully informed by their training institutions of the rights and responsibilities afforded to them by the professional liability coverage provided, as well as appropriately educated on the importance of maintaining adequate professional liability coverage throughout their careers in medicine.

Without a clear understanding of the specifics of professional liability insurance, such as coverage limits and exclusions and the need for prior acts and supplemental tail or nose policies, practicing pediatricians of long standing may find themselves without effective liability coverage for claims filed post-residency for incidents occurring during residency. Fortunately, effective July 2007, the ACGME has implemented rules that require training programs' sponsoring institutions to provide residents with professional liability insurance that includes coverage for "…claims reported or filed after the completion of the program(s)…."[12]

The ACGME requires sponsoring training institutions to provide medical liability coverage for residents during training and include a clear, written summary description of the type of liability policy, and other pertinent coverage information, furnished by the training program for its residents.[12]

(For a more complete discussion of the various types of medical liability policies available, see Chapter 3.) The ACGME also mandates that liability coverage for residents must further include coverage for malpractice claims made after a resident leaves the training program, frequently called tail coverage, so long as "…the alleged acts or omissions of the residents are within the scope of the program."[12] The AAP has in fact long recommended that this post-residency tail coverage and its exclusions should be distinctly detailed in the residents' employment contracts.[13] Physicians-in-training should be aware that this malpractice coverage may not apply to moonlighting activity.

The ACGME program requirements for GME in pediatrics recommend, under the competency of Systems-based Practice, that pediatric residency curricula must incorporate structured educational experiences in risk management.[11] Throughout the required 6 competencies addressed in these program requirements, the ACGME Residency Review Committee for pediatrics has additionally listed a number of medicolegal topics as "must-contain" residency training components, including confidentiality, informed consent, communication, professional behavior, quality improvement, medical record documentation, and billing and coding.[11] Similarly, the AAP Committee on Medical Liability and Risk Management has long recommended that a general overview of risk management concepts, including benefits and limitations of liability insurance coverage, should be discussed during residency training.[15] In support of these recommendations, the 2007 AAP Annual Survey of Graduating Residents confirmed a persistent deficiency in the education of pediatric residents on many of these important medicolegal concepts.[7,16] No less significant was the survey's documentation of only limited curriculum instruction on a variety of other just-as-worthwhile risk management issues, such as vaccine injury liability, expert witness testimony, and medical malpractice litigation.[7] Finally, although coverage of risk communication skills, informed consent, and medical record documentation appear to be a widespread component in a notable majority of pediatric training programs,[16] there is no current evidence to support a standardized and consistent approach to the methods of educational delivery. Several of these issues related to risk exposure during residency warrant special consideration.

Notification of a Claim

On receipt of notification as a named defendant in a malpractice suit, residents must immediately notify their program director to initiate the process of contacting the training institution's insurance carrier. As with all legal actions, timely communication is critical to laying the groundwork for a successful defense. Because in most instances, the insurance carrier or hospital will furnish legal counsel for all parties involved, it is important that hospital risk management, a representative from the insurance carrier, and the representing attorney confer early on with the involved physician or resident defendant(s) to review the health care case in question and develop a general sense of relevant liability issues. Based on their initial assessment of the claim's liability risk, the malpractice insurance carrier will set aside a dollar amount or *reserve* to cover most potential settlements or judgments. In malpractice proceedings, physicians, including residents, are heavily dependent on the assistance of legal counsel. Fortunately, insurance carriers and hospitals also have a significant financial interest in the aggressive defense of all malpractice actions and thus typically employ highly skilled legal counsel to represent involved parties. However, although hospital- or insurance carrier–provided counsel usually work diligently to protect physicians' interests and keep them well informed of a case's progress, if settlement prior to trial is being con-

sidered, it is essential that residents and practicing physicians have at least a basic knowledge of the immediate and long-term career and practice implications of such a decision, particularly as it relates to the NPDB.

Employment Changes

Pediatricians are particularly vulnerable to malpractice litigation because of the long statute of limitations associated with medical care rendered to patients younger than the age of majority.[17] The *tail* is the length of time from when an incident involving a minor occurs to when a malpractice claim can be filed. All states have established a statute of limitations applicable to minors that allows an extended time for a medical malpractice tort claim involving a minor to be filed. This lag time is measured in years for all physicians that care for minor patients, but for pediatricians the statute of limitations can be measured in decades, given the very young age of many of the minor patients they treat. In some states, the limitation period begins when the alleged damaging incident actually occurred, while in others the statute of limitations does not begin until after the injury is discovered or should have been discovered.[17]

Given their prolonged risk exposure, it is a compliment that pediatricians are not accused of medical malpractice as frequently as many other specialists.[18,19] However, as could be anticipated from the much longer, often lifelong effects of an adverse outcome on younger patients, when pediatricians are sued, the stakes are often significantly higher. The Physician Insurers Association of America, whose member companies insure 60% of all physicians in private practice in the United States, reported in 2010 that from 1985 to 2009, pediatricians had the fifth highest average indemnity payment paid per filed claim at $271,784, a value 27.8% higher than the $212,722 average for all physicians.[18]

Pediatricians seeking new employment or a change in career paths, particularly early in their careers, should always ensure that there are no gaps in their malpractice insurance coverage. If the policy that was in force during training or from their prior employer was a claims-made or claims-paid policy, the resident or physician should negotiate tail coverage from the residency training program or prior employer, or nose coverage from the prospective employer.[20] Furthermore, pediatricians considering a claims-made or claims-paid policy through a new carrier should always anticipate the need for liability coverage for the subsequent tail. If a new employer has offered to pay premiums for professional liability insurance, it is reasonable to request that the employer also be financially responsible for providing tail coverage. Similarly, it is reasonable for employers to specify a minimum length of employment as conditional to the provision of the requested or offered tail coverage.[20]

Part-time Employment

Part-time employment options for physicians have gained favor in recent years, spurred on by the rewards of spending additional time with family, friends, and community and spiritual activities.[21] The number of pediatricians employed part-time has increased from 15% in 2000 to 23% in 2006.[22] Fortunately, an increasing number of medical liability insurers now offer programs with discounts to physicians who limit the number of hours they practice or who need coverage for only certain portions of their practice. Others, however, still contend that it is not the number of hours the physician works that determines liability risk but rather the kinds of procedures the physician performs. As resident pediatricians join the post-residency workforce, they must consider and evaluate available coverage policies and initiate discussions on the various options with insurers to determine the best coverage at the best price long before a final selection has to be made.

Leave of Absence

Physicians can request the temporary suspension of liability coverage for extended absences from practice because of illness, disability, family leave, or military service. Insurance policies typically stipulate in writing how long a policy can remain in suspension before it is terminated, and many carriers provide reductions in premiums while the coverage is suspended. It is usually better for the physician to suspend coverage than cancel it, especially if the policy is claims-made. Under the latter circumstances, it is strongly recommended that canceling the policy while on leave should be associated with the concurrent purchase of tail coverage so as to avoid an increased liability exposure from the resultant coverage lapse. Similarly, depending on the reason for the leave of absence, pediatricians may experience difficulty purchasing coverage when returning to practice or may be forced to do so at a much greater premium expense.

Disability or Death

Most insurers will forgive the costs of tail coverage for a physician who becomes disabled or dies while a claims-made policy is in effect.[13]

Retirement

At the point of retirement, a physician terminates a claims-made policy, at which time tail coverage goes into effect. Similar to temporary suspension of coverage, many medical liability insurers have programs that reduce the outlay for tail coverage when a physician terminates a claims-made policy. Some carriers will also offer to incorporate the total costs of tail insurance into yearly premiums over a predefined number of years while the claims-made policy is in effect. A few will actually provide free tail coverage to physicians who remain with the company for a certain number of years, usually a minimum of 5.

A significant number of pediatricians are choosing to remain in practice after age 65.[23] Working at 65 to 69 years of age was, in fact, found to be quite common in a recent article reporting the results of a 2006 survey of AAP members, with 46% of respondents practicing full-time and 27% part-time. Results for the 70- to 74-year-old cohort were, respectively, 25% and 35%.[23] Physicians who have been insured by the same company for a specified number of years will often qualify for free tail coverage once they retire at or after the age prescribed by the policy. In addition, the Federal Tort Claims Act medical malpractice program for free clinics, as authorized by Section 194 of the Health Insurance Portability and Accountability Act of 1996, states that if a volunteer health care professional meets certain criteria, he or she may receive medical malpractice liability coverage through the federal government, in much the same way federal employees do.[24] To be eligible, the volunteer health care professional must be sponsored by the free clinic, provide a qualifying health service as described by statute to the individual at the health clinic while acting within the scope of his or her volunteer responsibilities, be properly licensed to provide such service, and not receive any compensation for the service provided.[24]

Nonetheless, the inclusion of free or reduced tail coverage provisions along with free retirement, death, or disability benefits are important considerations that should not be overlooked when purchasing medical liability insurance. For physicians hoping to retire in a few years, the advantages of staying with a company for sufficient years to qualify for free or reduced tail benefits will likely outweigh switching to another carrier, even if their premiums are lower.

References

1. *Phelps v Physicians Insurance Company of Wisconsin, Inc.,* 2005 WI 85, 282 Wis2d 69, 698 NW2d 643 (2005)
2. Kachalia A, Studdert DM. Professional liability issues in graduate medical education. *JAMA.* 2004;292(9):1051–1056. http://jama.ama-assn.org/content/292/9/1051.full.pdf+html. Accessed June 16, 2011
3. Kern SI. Residents' mistakes can hurt you. *Med Econ.* 2007;84(20):24
4. King JH. The standard of care for residents and other medical school graduates in training. *Am U L Rev.* 2006;55(5):683–751
5. Grupp-Phelan J, Reynolds S, Ling LL. Professional liability of residents in a children's hospital. *Arch Pediatr Adolesc Med.* 1996;150(1):87–90
6. Helms LB, Helms CM. Forty years of litigation involving residents and their training: II. Malpractice issues. *Acad Med.* 1991;66(12):718–725
7. American Academy of Pediatrics. *Periodic Survey of Fellows #69: Experiences with Medical Liability: Executive Summary.* Elk Grove Village, IL: American Academy of Pediatrics; 2007. http://www.aap.org/research/periodicsurvey/PS69exsummedicalliability.pdf. Accessed June 16, 2011
8. The Data Bank: National Practitioner Data Bank and Healthcare Integrity & Protection Data Bank Web site. http://www.npdb-hipdb.hrsa.gov. Accessed June 16, 2011
9. US Department of Health and Human Services, Health Resources and Service Administration, Bureau of Health Professions, Division of Practitioner Data Banks. *National Practitioner Data Bank 2006 Annual Report.* http://www.npdb-hipdb.hrsa.gov/resources/reports/2006NPDBAnnualReport.pdf. Accessed June 16, 2011
10. Ottolini MC, Greenberg L. Development and evaluation of a CD-ROM computer program to teach residents telephone management. *Pediatrics.* 1998;101(3):e2
11. Accreditation Council for Graduate Medical Education. *ACGME Program Requirements for Graduate Medical Education in Pediatrics. Section IV.A.5.f).(7).(a).* Effective July 1, 2007. Chicago, IL: Accreditation Council for Graduate Medical Education; 2007. http://www.acgme.org/acWebsite/downloads/RRC_progReq/320_pediatrics_07012007.pdf Accessed June 16, 2011.
12. Accreditation Council for Graduate Medical Education. *ACGME Institutional Requirements. Section II.D.4.f).(1)-(2).* Effective July 1, 2007. Chicago, IL: Accreditation Council for Graduate Medical Education; 2007. http://www.acgme.org/acWebsite/irc/irc_IRCpr07012007.pdf. Accessed June 16, 2011
13. American Academy of Pediatrics Committee on Medical Liability. Professional liability coverage for residents and fellows. *Pediatrics.* 2000;106(3):605–609

14. Cullen DJ, Sweitzer BJ, Bates DW, Burdick E, Edmondson A, Leape LL. Preventable adverse drug events in hospitalized patients: a comparative study of intensive care and general care units. *Crit Care Med*. 1997;25(8):1289–1297

15. McAbee GN, Deitschel C, Berger J, American Academy of Pediatrics Committee on Medical Liability and Risk Management. Pediatric medicolegal education in the 21st century. *Pediatrics*. 2006;117(5):1790–1792

16. Donn SM. Medico-legal education of pediatric residents remains inadequate. *AAP News*. 2008;29(7):16

17. Shea KG, Scanlan KJ, Nilsson KJ, Wilson B, Mehlman CT. Interstate variability of the statute of limitations for medical liability: a cause for concern? *J Pediatr Orthop*. 2008;28(3): 370–374

18. Physician Insurers Association of America. *Claim Trend Analysis. 1985-2009*. Rockville, MD: Physician Insurers Association of America; 2010

19. Kane CK. Medical liability claim frequency: a 2007-2008 snapshot of physicians. *Policy Research Perspectives*. Chicago, IL: American Medical Association; 2010. http://www.ama-assn.org/ama1/pub/upload/mm/363/ prp-201001-claim-freq.pdf. Accessed June 16, 2011

20. American Medical Association. *Medical Professional Liability Insurance: The Informed Physician's Guide to Coverage Decisions*. Chicago IL: American Medical Association; 1998

21. Landers SJ. Part-time work appeals to pediatricians. *Am Med News*. January 11, 2010. http://www.ama-assn.org/ amednews/2010/01/11/prsa0111.htm. Accessed June 16, 2011

22. Cull WL, O'Connor KG, Olson LM. Part-time work among pediatricians expands. *Pediatrics*. 2010;125(1):152–157. http://pediatrics.aappublications.org/content/125/1/152. full.pdf+html. Accessed June 16, 2011

23. Merline AC, Cull WL, Mulvey HJ, Katcher AL. Patterns of work and retirement among pediatricians aged ≥ 50 years. *Pediatrics*. 2010;125(1):158–164. http://pediatrics. aappublications.org/content/125/1/158.full.pdf+html. Accessed June 16, 2011

24. Public Health Service (PHS), 42 USC §2339(o), as added by the Health Insurance Portability and Accountability Act (HIPAA) of 1996, SEC 194, §221(a). Pub Law No. 104-191, 42 USC §201

CHAPTER 19

Volunteer Activities

Robert A. Mendelson, MD, FAAP

KEY CONCEPTS

- Medical Liability Insurance Coverage
- Federal Protection
- State Options for Limiting Volunteer Medical Liability
- Retired Pediatricians
- Liability While Volunteering Abroad

Many pediatricians provide volunteer services. Findings from American Academy of Pediatrics (AAP) Periodic Survey of Fellows #60, from 1989, 1993, and 2004, revealed that the percentage of pediatricians participating in volunteer community child health activities increased from 48.6% to 57.8% to 79.6% over that period (Table 19-1).[1] *Community child health activities* were defined as providing clinical services at health fairs, camps, public health clinics, schools, and child care centers. Child health activities also included working in child protective agencies and other government health programs, as well as nonprofit organizations as consultants and child health advocates.

The central liability issues facing physicians who provide volunteer health services are

1. Concerns that patients served by volunteer programs may be a higher malpractice liability risk than customary patients.
2. The physician's malpractice insurance may not cover volunteer settings or services provided there.

Literature on liability risk in caring for the uninsured indicates that the elderly and poor are likely to be among those who experience negligence and do not sue, presumably because their low socioeconomic status impedes their ability to secure legal representation.[3] Burstin et al stated that "poor and uninsured patients are significantly less likely to sue for malpractice, even after controlling for the presence of medical injury."[4] Nevertheless, it is a commonly held belief among physicians that socioeconomic and health care insurance status are likely determinants of medical malpractice litigation after an adverse outcome.

Data from AAP Periodic Survey of Fellows conducted in 1987, 1990, 1992, 1995, 2001, and 2007 were analyzed to determine whether there is a relationship between health care insurance status and medical malpractice litigation directed at pediatricians from 1987 to 2007.[5] The AAP Committee on Medical Liability and Risk Management initiated portions of these surveys to track pediatricians' experiences with malpractice claims and lawsuits filed against them during this period. Table 19-2 shows the distribution of health care insurance status of patients filing malpractice claims or suits from 1987 to 2007 by survey year.

In all survey years, the majority of responding pediatricians reported that patients filing medical malpractice claims or suits carried private health insurance, although the percentage decreased significantly in 2007 compared with 1987 and 2001. Additionally, patients filing claims or suits who had no health insurance fell dramatically from 1987 to 2001 and from 2001 to 2007.

Table 19-1. Pediatric Participation in Community Child Health Activities[2]

Participation	1989	1993	2004	P value 1989/1993[a]
Any community activity, no. (%)[b]	353 (56.6)	498 (59.4)	387 (45.1)	<.001/<.001
Volunteer only, no. (%)	171 (48.6)	284 (57.8)	297 (79.6)	<.001/<.001
Paid only, no. (%)	58 (16.5)	79 (16.1)	31 (8.3)	.001/.001
Volunteer and paid, no. (%)	123 (34.9)	128 (26.1)	45 (12.1)	<.001/<.001

[a]P values are calculated for 1989 or 1993 survey results versus 2004 survey results.
[b]In 2004 and 1993, pediatricians were asked about their participation in community activities during the past 12 months; in 1989 they were asked about current participation.

Table 19-2. Health Insurance Status of Patients Filing Claims or Suits[5]

Plaintiff's insurance type	(% of pediatricians reporting)					
	1987	1990	1992[a]	1995[a]	2001[a]	2007[a]
Private health insurance[b]	66.9	62.9	65.9	59	63.5	57.3
Public health insurance (eg, Medicaid)[c,d]	17.9	17.5	20.1	24.6	28	39.7
No health insurance[b,e]	15.2	19.6	14	16.4	8.5	3
TOTAL	100	100	100	100	100	100

[a]1992, 1995, 2001, and 2007 data exclude residents and all claims that occurred during residency.
[b]$P<.05$, 2007 versus 2001.
[c]$P<.01$, 2007 versus 2001.
[d]$P<.05$, 2007 versus 1987.
[e]$P<.01$, 2007 versus 1987.

These data seem to refute the adage that a significant number of pediatric malpractice lawsuits are filed by plaintiffs with no health care insurance. Moreover, they suggest that there has been an increase in the success of enrolling patients into the public health care insurance sector, such as Medicaid and the State Children's Health Insurance Program. In fact, access to legal services may be comparable to access to health care services. Further study of this seems warranted.

What are the implications of these results? First, the majority of patients filing pediatric malpractice lawsuits are still privately insured. Second, the proportion of patients filing pediatric malpractice claims who have public insurance has been steadily increasing. Third, the proportion of patients filing pediatric malpractice claims who have no insurance is quite small and has been steadily decreasing.

Pediatricians need to be aware of these findings and should consider them in formulating risk management strategies. The relationship between health care insurance status and likelihood of filing a medical malpractice lawsuit appears to be shifting and should be explored further.

Medical Liability Insurance Coverage

Volunteer activities can be covered via the physician's professional liability insurance policy. Most insurers ask that physicians advise the company about the types and locations of volunteer activities involving medical practice in which they participate. Any changes in volunteer activities should be reported to the insurer to ascertain that coverage is available.

Federal Protection

The Volunteer Protection Act of 1997 (VPA)[6] is a federal law that exempts a volunteer of a nonprofit organization or governmental entity from liability for harm caused by an act or omission of the volunteer on behalf of such organization or entity if

1. The volunteer was acting within the scope of his or her responsibilities at the time.
2. The volunteer was properly licensed or otherwise authorized for the activities or practice in the state in which the harm occurred.
3. The harm was not caused by willful or criminal misconduct, gross negligence, reckless misconduct, or a conscious, flagrant indifference to the rights or safety of the individual harmed.
4. The harm was not caused by the volunteer operating a motor vehicle, vessel, aircraft, or other vehicle for which the state requires the operator or owner to possess an operator's license or maintain insurance.

The act prohibits the award of punitive damages against a volunteer unless the claimant establishes by clear and convincing evidence that the harm was proximately caused by an action of a volunteer that was willful or criminal misconduct, or a conscious, flagrant indifference to the rights or safety of the individual harmed. The act also makes each volunteer liable for noneconomic loss only in the amount proportional to the percentage of responsibility for the harm for which that defendant is liable. The act is silent on liability for economic losses. The act requires the judge or jury to determine such percentage of responsibility. The act also *preempts* (supersedes) state law to the extent that such laws are inconsistent with this law unless existing state law affords additional protection.

The VPA established a national minimum standard for other volunteer immunity laws. By granting immunity to a volunteer clinician acting within her duties in a nonprofit organization, the VPA protects volunteers from civil liability via immunity except in cases of willful misconduct or gross negligence. Thus, the licensed physician would be immunized from liability for most alleged acts of medical malpractice. The VPA does not prevent claimants from bringing any claims against volunteer physicians; it simply provides protection against certain types of damage awards.

Volunteering at Free Clinics

The Volunteer Medical Act was passed as Section 194 of the Health Insurance Portability and Accountability Act of 1996.[7] It created a Federal Tort Claims Act (FTCA) medical malpractice program for free clinics. This federal law authorized the FTCA to provide medical malpractice protection for volunteer professionals at free clinics. Under the Public Health Service Act, the Department of Health and Human Services (HHS) can deem volunteers to be employees of the US Public Health Service Commissioned Corps, thus extending medical malpractice coverage to them.

The Health Insurance Portability and Accountability Act of 1996 states that if a volunteer meets certain criteria, he may receive medical malpractice liability coverage through the federal government, in much the same way federal employees do.

In March 2004, Congress appropriated funds that allowed the HHS to create this much-needed program. There is no cost to free clinics or clinicians, but free clinics must meet certain criteria to participate in the program.

1. A free clinic is a health care facility operated by a nonprofit private entity that in providing health care, does not accept payment from any third-party payer (including from any insurance policy, health plan, or federal or state health benefits program).
2. In providing health care, a free clinic does not impose charges on patients to whom service is provided or on patients according to their ability to pay.

3. A free clinic may accept patients' voluntary donations for health care service provision, and is licensed or certified to provide health services in accordance with applicable law.

A volunteer free clinic health professional

1. Provides services to patients at a free clinic or through off-site programs or events carried out by a free clinic.
2. Is sponsored by a free clinic.
3. Provides a qualifying health service.
4. Does not receive compensation for provided services from patients directly or from any third-party payer.
5. May receive repayment from a free clinic for reasonable expenses incurred in service provision to patients.
6. Is licensed or certified to provide health care services in accordance with applicable law.
7. Provides patients with written notification before service provision of the extent to which her legal liability is limited.

The following services are covered:

1. Acts or omissions arising from health care services required or authorized under Title XIX of the Social Security Act (ie, Medicaid), regardless of whether the service is included in the state Medicaid plan in effect for the volunteer free clinic
2. Acts or omissions stemming from medical, surgical, dental, or related care provided at a free clinic site or through off-site programs or events
3. Acts or omissions related to health care service occurring on or after the effective date that the HHS secretary approves the FTCA-deeming application submitted by the free clinic on behalf of its volunteers

Free clinics and their FTCA-deemed volunteer health care professionals must satisfy several program requirements. These include credentialing and privileging systems, patient notification of limited liability, risk management systems, and periodic review of medical malpractice claims history.

Only volunteer health care professionals who are licensed or certified are eligible for FTCA-deemed status. Such personnel can be divided into 2 categories.

1. A *licensed independent practitioner* is a physician, dentist, nurse practitioner, nurse midwife, or any other individual permitted by law and the organization to provide care and services without direction or supervision, within the scope of the individual practitioner's license and consistent with individually granted clinical privileges.
2. *Another licensed or certified health care practitioner* is an individual who is licensed, registered, or certified but is not permitted by law to provide patient care services without direction or supervision (eg, laboratory technicians, social workers, medical assistants, licensed practical nurses, dental hygienists).

Claims Processing

Those alleging acts of medical malpractice must file an administrative claim with the HHS prior to instituting any court action. On receipt of the claim, the HHS will determine whether FTCA medical malpractice coverage applies to the particular claim if the alleged act or omission giving rise to the claim

1. Involved a volunteer free clinic health care professional with deemed FTCA status pursuant to the Public Health Service Act
2. Involved a health care service qualifying for FTCA coverage
3. Occurred at a free clinic or a covered off-site program or event carried out by the free clinic

For more information on the FTCA, as well as application instructions and eligibility requirements, visit http://bphc.hrsa.gov/ftca/freeclinics.

State Options for Limiting Volunteer Medical Liability

The growing number of uninsured coupled with the high costs of medical liability insurance compelled a number of states to adopt legislation to limit the liability of volunteer health care workers.

Civil Immunity

The most common way for states to protect volunteer physicians is to provide them with civil immunity for voluntary care. Nearly two thirds of all states have civil immunity statutes for volunteer physicians. Most volunteer physician statutes have 4 elements that must be met for the physician to qualify for civil immunity.

1. The physician must be licensed in the state in which the physician volunteers.
2. The physician must not accept any compensation for the voluntary care given.
3. The voluntary care must be provided through a nonprofit or state agency.
4. The care must not include gross negligence or wanton and willful disregard.

State Purchase

States can purchase medical liability policies for volunteer physicians as another way to increase participation in volunteer programs. This is an attractive alternative because it encourages physicians to volunteer, and it also allows patients to recover legitimate damages if malpractice occurs. In Minnesota, malpractice insurance is purchased by licensing boards to cover volunteer physicians. In Connecticut, the Department of Health is authorized to do so, whereas in Kentucky, money has been made available through legislation to cover malpractice insurance. In Tennessee, insurance carriers have been mandated not to exclude coverage for voluntary services. Unfortunately, state budgetary struggles make this approach difficult to implement and maintain.

Clinic/Agency Purchase

Another alternative for states is to require the free clinic, school, or other nonprofit agency to pay for volunteer physician liability coverage. During the current budget problems in many states, this could be an attractive option. The drawback is that it passes the burden of paying for medical liability insurance onto governmental or nonprofit organizations that may not be able to afford the insurance costs.

State Indemnification

State indemnification laws extend a state government's sovereign immunity to volunteer physicians. Sovereign immunity is "a judicial doctrine that precludes bringing suit against the government without its consent."[8] States can include individuals working on the state's behalf under this umbrella of protection. A state's tort claims act could be expanded to include volunteer physicians.

Under this type of program, a state would permit a harmed party to sue for restitution, but the physician would be covered under sovereign immunity. The harmed individual would then recover from a special state liability fund. States could cap damage awards from the fund and require volunteer physicians to carry a less-expensive liability plan that would cover any damage awards that exceed the state liability fund cap.

Good Samaritan Laws

Expanding a state's Good Samaritan law is another option for states looking to protect volunteer physicians from liability concerns. Expansion is necessary because these laws only offer liability protection for emergency care. Good Samaritan laws provide physicians with an affirmative defense when an action is brought against them for care that might be covered under the statute. Good Samaritan laws are civil liability shields, so expansions of these laws could leave harmed parties without legal recourse.

Retired Pediatricians

Many senior physicians are interested in providing voluntary care in underserved communities. However, a physician must have a valid medical license, usually in the state in which the physician chooses to volunteer. The expense of maintaining active licensure can be of concern to retired physicians, particularly when they only want to provide free care to medically underserved populations. When physicians retire outside of the state in which they have practiced medicine, the issue becomes even more complex.

While some feel that licensure requirements should be eased for physicians who only provide volunteer medical services, it is important that each state maintain equivalent quality standards for all physicians, whether the medical care is free or compensated.

States have addressed 2 factors that can discourage physicians from seeking or maintaining a medical license to provide volunteer care—licensing fees and documentation requirements. Several states have implemented special volunteer licensing provisions. For instance, Florida, Georgia, and Maryland offer volunteer licensures without an annual fee to those serving the poor without compensation at nonprofit clinics or in underserved areas. Other states have reduced annual fees for volunteer licenses. In situations in which physicians relocate when they retire to a state in which they do not hold a medical license, state-to-state licensing reciprocity may be an option. For example, Arizona and Wyoming allow physicians who hold a license in another state to obtain a license to practice on a volunteer basis in their jurisdiction. Some states have limited the amount of documentation of ongoing continuing medical education credits necessary to maintain a license for volunteer medical services.

Unfortunately, a little more than half of all US states offer no special licensing provisions for retired or volunteer physicians. Acknowledging that the high cost of medical liability insurance is likely to be prohibitive for retired physicians practicing on a volunteer basis, currently 43 states and the District of Columbia have some sort of charitable immunity legislation, 7 of which specifically mention retired physicians (Table 19-3).[9]

Table 19-3. State Licensure and Liability Policies for Volunteer Physicians

State	Volunteer/Limited License Offered	Liability Law for Volunteer Physicians
Alabama	No provisions for volunteer or retired	Medical professional who offers services in established free medical clinic is not liable for acts or omissions except for wanton misconduct. Requires notification of patients.
Alaska	No provisions for volunteer or retired	No statute
Arizona	Pro bono license is available for no fee. Must hold an active license from any state or territory or an active or inactive Arizona license. License is restricted to 60 days of practice per year.	Arizona law establishes immunity for volunteers acting in good faith and within the scope of volunteer duties for government entities or nonprofit corporations, organizations, or hospitals. Vicarious liability of the organization can be established if the volunteer was working in the scope of official duties and functions.
Arkansas	No provisions for volunteer or retired	Immunity for volunteer from civil liability unless gross negligence or willful misconduct. For immunity to apply, the patient must acknowledge the physician's immunity from civil suit. If the volunteer has liability insurance, liability is limited to the limit of the insurance policy. Statute references retired volunteer physicians.

Table 19-3. State Licensure and Liability Policies for Volunteer Physicians (continued)

State	Volunteer/Limited License Offered	Liability Law for Volunteer Physicians
California	Volunteer Service License, no fee Retired license, no fee	No statute
Colorado	No provisions for volunteer or retired	No civil liability except for wanton misconduct or willful negligence. Patient must have notice of limited liability.
Connecticut	No provisions for volunteer or retired	Charitable immunity for nonprofit volunteer. Specifically references volunteer health care professional, retired physicians, and certain health care settings, and is limited to certain services.
Delaware	No provisions for volunteer or retired	Charitable for nonprofit volunteer. Specifically references volunteer health care professional, retired physicians, and certain health care settings, and is limited to certain services.
District of Columbia	No provisions for volunteer or retired	Licensed physicians who in good faith provide health care or treatment at or on behalf of a free health clinic without the expectation of receiving or intending to receive compensation shall not be liable in civil damages for any act or omission in the course of rendering the health care or treatment, unless the act or omission is an intentional wrong or manifests a willful or wanton disregard for the health or safety or others. To qualify for this immunity, physicians must require prospective patients to sign a written statement witnessed by 2 persons in which the parties agree to the rendering of the health care or treatment. Free clinic that cannot afford liability insurance and its volunteers can be part of a federal indemnity program and are considered district employees for indemnification purposes.
Florida	Limited license is available for retired physicians wishing to volunteer services, no fee. Must practice in a government or 501c(3) organization in an area to be determined to be an area of critical need by the board.	Volunteer for a nonprofit is not liable except for gross or negligent misconduct. Patients must receive prior notice of limited liability.
Georgia	Volunteer in medicine license, no fee	Volunteer for a nonprofit or government organization, such as a physician who renders care without the expectation of compensation, is granted civil immunity except for gross or negligent misconduct. Patients must receive prior notice of limited liability.
Hawaii	No provisions for volunteer or retired	Not liable unless wanton misconduct or willful negligence if the organization carries liability insurance of less than $200,000 for single occurrence OR if the organization has less than $50,000 in assets.
Idaho	No provisions for volunteer or retired	Health care practitioner at charitable clinic is immune from liability—if liability insurance exists, person is liable to the extent of the policy. Patient must receive prior notice of limited liability.
Illinois	No provisions for volunteer or retired	A physician who volunteers services at a free medical clinic to the indigent is exempt from civil liability except for wanton misconduct or gross negligence. Patients must receive prior notice of limited liability.

Table 19-3. State Licensure and Liability Policies for Volunteer Physicians (continued)

State	Volunteer/Limited License Offered	Liability Law for Volunteer Physicians
Indiana	Retired inactive status—can practice with no restrictions as long as there is no compensation. Fee of $100 every 2 years. Must be fully licensed in Indiana prior to application. Physicians from other states wishing to volunteer in Indiana are limited to 30 days of practice per year with a limited-scope license.	A health care practitioner, including a retired physician, who voluntarily provides health care at a medical clinic or health care facility is immune from civil liability arising from the care provided, unless in delivering care the practitioner's acts or omissions constitute a criminal act, gross negligence, or willful or wanton misconduct.
Iowa	No provisions for volunteer or retired	Iowa legislators established a volunteer physician program within the Iowa Department of Public Health that provides for immunity from liability in certain circumstances. These circumstances include instances in which a physician, registered with the department as being part of the program, provides free medical care at specific hospitals and clinics. While delivering free care under the program, physician is considered an employee of the state and receives certain immunity from liability.
Kansas	Exempt status for retired physicians to provide direct patient care gratuitously. Reduced fee.	Volunteer of a nonprofit is not liable if the organization has liability insurance, health care not specifically named.
Kentucky	No provisions for volunteer or retired	Volunteer for a nonprofit is not liable except for wanton misconduct or gross negligence.
Louisiana	No provisions for volunteer or retired	Health care worker providing free care in a community health clinic is not liable for acts or omission in rendering care or an act or failure to act in providing or arranging for further services. This immunity from liability is valid only if the patient was notified of the limited liability.
Maine	Retired physician license for those doing volunteer work. Fee is $75.	Maine grants civil liability immunity for physicians (including retired) who voluntarily render uncompensated medical care for a nonprofit organization or agency of the state, except in the case of wanton misconduct or willful negligence.
Maryland	Special volunteer license with no fee. Must submit form to the volunteer agency and attest to the fact that this license will be used only in volunteer capacity.	Maryland provides civil immunity from personal liability to volunteers who render certain services under special circumstances. Circumstances include health care practitioners or physicians who render health care services voluntarily and without compensation to any person seeking health care through a charitable organization charted to provide health care services to homeless and indigent patients. Such volunteers are not liable for any amount in excess of any applicable limit of insurance coverage in any suit for civil damages for any act or omission resulting from the rendering of such services, unless the act of omission constitutes willful or wanton misconduct, gross negligence, or intentionally tortuous conduct.
Massachusetts	No provisions for volunteer or retired	Limit on liability to $20,000 for a charitable organization. Health care worker not liable for volunteer care.

Table 19-3. State Licensure and Liability Policies for Volunteer Physicians (continued)

State	Volunteer/Limited License Offered	Liability Law for Volunteer Physicians
Michigan	No provisions for volunteer or retired	Law protects physicians from liability for care provided as a result of a referral from a free clinic. Patients must receive prior notice of limited liability.
Minnesota	No provisions for volunteer or retired	Physicians in certain charitable health care settings performing limited services are immune.
Mississippi	License for retired physicians who wish to volunteer services. Valid for 1 year. No fee.	Mississippi grants immunity from liability for any civil action to a licensed physician who, in good faith on a charitable basis, voluntarily provides medical or health services to any person without the expectation of payment. Immunity will be extended if the physician and patient execute a written waiver in advance of the rendering of medical services, specifying that such services are provided without the expectation of payment and that the physician shall be immune from liability, unless the act or omission is the result of the physician's gross negligence or willful misconduct.
Missouri	Limited license for retired physicians who have practiced for at least 10 years. Some restriction on services physician can offer—eg, no controlled substances. Fee not to exceed $25.	Volunteer at a nonprofit is immune to liability with the exception of willful or wanton misconduct or gross negligence. Physicians specifically mentioned.
Montana	No provisions for volunteer or retired	A health care practitioner who provides free services is not liable for civil damages with the exception of wanton misconduct, so long as patients receive prior notice of limited liability.
Nebraska	No provisions for volunteer or retired	Directors, officers, and trustees of nonprofit organizations are immune from liability; no specific mention of physicians or volunteers in the organization. No charitable immunity for volunteer health care practitioner.
Nevada	Special volunteer license requires acknowledgment of no compensation and care only for indigent. No fee. Renewable annually. New legislation.	Civil immunity for physicians including retired physicians who offer free care or provide emergency obstetric services except for willful or wanton misconduct.
New Hampshire	No provisions for volunteer or retired	A volunteer in a nonprofit organization is immune from civil liability as long as the volunteer is documented by the organization. Exception for wanton misconduct. Additionally, New Hampshire grants certain retired physicians immunity from civil liability for volunteer health education services.
New Jersey	Special volunteer license, but must practice under the supervision of a fully licensed physician. No fee.	Volunteer health care practitioners are not personally liable for damages caused except if there is gross negligence or wanton misconduct.
New Mexico	No provisions for volunteer or retired	No statues for charitable immunity. Grants immunity only to public employees including physicians, psychologists, or dentists providing services to the corrections department and children, youth, and families department. Only mention of immunity for directors of charitable organizations.
New York	No registration renewal fee for non-compensated physicians. Must file affidavit of non-compensation. Some restrictions on practice.	No statutes for volunteers of a nonprofit or volunteer organization

Table 19-3. State Licensure and Liability Policies for Volunteer Physicians (continued)

State	Volunteer/Limited License Offered	Liability Law for Volunteer Physicians
North Carolina	Limited volunteer license to serve indigent. Reduced fee.	Volunteers for charitable organizations are not liable for loss or damages or death except in cases of willful misconduct and wanton negligence.
North Dakota	No provision for volunteer. Offer retired Emeritus status for $150 per year but cannot practice or prescribe (more honorary).	A health care practitioner who renders services at a free clinic is not liable in a personal injury civil action, except for willful or wanton misconduct.
Ohio	Volunteer certificate for those who are retired and have practiced for at least 10 years. No fee. Some restriction on services, eg, cannot deliver babies, perform surgery. Valid for 3 years.	Ohio provides retired physicians and other health care professionals and shelters or health care facilities with qualified immunities from civil liability for providing free diagnoses, care, and treatment to indigent or uninsured patients at certain facilities. Patients must receive prior notice of limited liability.
Oklahoma	Volunteer license	A volunteer of a charitable or nonprofit organization is not liable but in cases of willful misconduct. However the organization is liable. Oklahoma enacted a provision that relieves volunteers of liability for punitive damages when providing services to nonprofit organizations unless those volunteers are currently offering the same service for profit.
Oregon	Emeritus status license for retired volunteers. Must first have active full license. $50 per year.	A physician who volunteers services to a charitable organization is not liable for damages with the exception of gross negligence.
Pennsylvania	Volunteer license for retired physicians. No liability insurance requirement. Can be renewed every 2 years. Requires verification from the director of the approved clinic that the physician has been authorized to provide volunteer services.	A physician who holds a volunteer license under the volunteer health services act (retired physician) is not liable for damages with the exception of substandard care. This immunity is valid only if such a statement of immunity is posted in a conspicuous place in the clinic. This immunity does not apply to institutional health care organizations that hold vicarious liability for the volunteer license holder.
Rhode Island	Active Emeritus status for physicians who are 70 years or older and who have practiced for 15 or more years in Rhode Island. Reduced fee of $25 for license.	A person who volunteers without compensation in a nonprofit or charitable organization is not liable, with the exception of gross negligence.
South Carolina	Volunteer limited license for practice in underserved areas. Renewable annually. No fee. Must practice under a supervisory physician.	South Carolina law provides that no licensed health care practitioner, who provides voluntary medical services without compensation, is liable for any civil damages arising out of acts or omissions resulting from the services rendered, unless due to gross negligence or willful misconduct. Immunity extends only if the agreement to provide voluntary, uncompensated services is made before the rendering of services by the provider.
South Dakota	No provisions for volunteer or retired	South Dakota provides immunity from civil liability for health care professionals volunteering health care services at free clinics. The immunity extends to damages or injuries arising from care provided in good faith and within the scope of the provider's official function. Immunity does not apply to gross negligence and willful misconduct.
Tennessee	Volunteer license is available for those who practice in a nonprofit clinic. No fee.	Liability insurance companies for health care providers may not exclude those who volunteer their services. No specific language for nonprofit or charitable volunteer immunity, only directors.

Table 19-3. State Licensure and Liability Policies for Volunteer Physicians (continued)

State	Volunteer/Limited License Offered	Liability Law for Volunteer Physicians
Texas	Voluntary charity care license—must sign affidavit that care will be given for free. Renewable annually, no fee. No restrictions of practice.	The act provides physician volunteers immunity for performing nonemergency care for certain charitable organizations. Volunteer is a person rendering services for a charitable organization who does not receive compensation in excess of reimbursement for expenses incurred. This includes a person serving as a director, officer, trustee, or direct service volunteer including a volunteer health care practitioner. A volunteer health care practitioner is an individual who voluntarily provides health care services without compensation or expectation of compensation and who meets 1 of 10 types of health care practitioners included in the law. The first option is that the volunteer health care practitioner is an individual licensed to practice medicine under the Medical Practice Act. A second alternative is that the volunteer health care practitioner is a retired physician who is eligible to provide health care services, including a retired physician who is licensed but exempt from paying the required annual registration fee. Patients must receive prior notice of limited liability.
Utah	No provisions for volunteer or retired	A health care practitioner who volunteers services at a health care facility and a facility that sponsors uncompensated health treatment are not liable in a malpractice suit.
Vermont	No provisions for volunteer or retired	No specific mention of charitable immunity or volunteer health care practitioner in particular.
Virginia	No provisions for volunteer or retired	Virginia law grants immunity from liability to health care practitioners who provide health care services to patients of a clinic that is organized for the delivery of health care services without charge and allows such providers, hospitals, and clinics to charge a reasonable minimum fee and still be afforded immunity, except for gross negligence.
Washington	Retired active status license. Can be used for uncompensated practice of up to 90 days per year. Reduced fee. Two-year license.	Limited liability for physicians in certain settings. Charitable immunity exists for retired physicians.
West Virginia	A volunteer license to work in a volunteer clinic can be applied for if the physician holds an active license. No fee. Renewable annually.	A physician with a volunteer license (retired physician) who renders service to needy people is immune from civil liability. Exception for gross negligence.
Wisconsin	No provisions for retired or volunteer. If practice is fewer than 240 hours per year, does not have to pay into Injured Patients and Families Compensation Fund.	Volunteers of nonprofit corporations are not liable; no specific mention of physicians other than in emergency and athletic circumstances.
Wyoming	Retired volunteer license statute. Must show proof of license in good standing immediately prior to retirement in any jurisdiction for minimum of 10 years. No fee but must sign affidavit that they are not being compensated each year.	Nonprofit is liable for negligence of its volunteers. The volunteer is not individually liable unless gross misconduct or negligence. No specific mention of volunteer health care practitioners.

Liability While Volunteering Abroad

While many medical liability concerns for volunteers have been addressed to some degree in the United States, international medical liability proves to be a different issue. Typically, overseas medical liability is not covered by standard professional liability insurance carriers in the United States.

Liability insurance coverage for overseas volunteering is almost impossible to obtain at this time with the exception of a few overseas trusts. Most nonprofit organizations that send physicians abroad have volunteers sign a waiver stating that no medical liability insurance is available within the program.

Hopefully, this is because good medicine is being practiced and patient and personal safety are being observed.

Summary

Voluntary pediatric service in underserved areas can be challenging. Medical liability coverage for volunteer activities is spotty at best and often difficult to obtain. Yet pediatricians should take some comfort in knowing that contrary to conventional wisdom, those without health insurance are not more litigious than patients with health insurance. The literature bears this out. Because volunteerism is so important, federal and state governments as well as nonprofit organizations have taken steps to limit volunteer physician liability and encourage participation. Well-chosen volunteer assignments often provide remarkable personal and professional rewards.

References

1. American Academy of Pediatrics. *Periodic Survey of Fellows #60: Pediatricians' Involvement in Community Child Health Services/Activities: Executive Summary.* Elk Grove Village, IL: American Academy of Pediatrics; 2005

2. Minkovitz CS, O'Connor KG, Grason H, et al. Pediatricians' involvement in community child health from 1989-2004. *Arch Pediatr Adolesc Med.* 2008;162(7):658–664. http://archpedi.ama-assn.org/cgi/reprint/162/7/658. Accessed May 20, 2011

3. Studdert DM, Thomas EJ, Burstin HR, Zbar BI, Orav EJ, Brennan TA. Negligent care and malpractice claiming behavior in Utah and Colorado. *Medical Care.* 2000;38(3):250–260

4. Burstin HR, Johnson WG, Lipsitz SR, Brennan TA. Do the poor sue more? A case-control study of malpractice claims and socioeconomic status. *JAMA.* 1993;270(14):1697–1701

5. American Academy of Pediatrics. *Periodic Survey of Fellows #69: Experiences With Medical Liability.* Elk Grove Village, IL: American Academy of Pediatrics; 2007. http://www.aap.org/research/periodicsurvey/PS69exsummedicalliability.pdf. Accessed May 20, 2011

6. Volunteer Protection Act of 1997, Pub L No. 105-19, codified at 42 USC 14501

7. Health Insurance Portability and Accountability Act of 1996 (Title II, §194), Volunteer services provided by health professionals at free clinics, Pub L No. 104-191

8. Garner BA, ed. *Black's Law Dictionary.* 9th ed. St Paul, MN: West Publishing Co; 2009

9. Plested WG III, American Medical Association. *Report of the Board of Trustees: Licensure and Liability for Senior Physician Volunteers.* http://www.ama-assn.org/ama/pub/about-ama/our-people/member-groups-sections/senior-physicians-group/physician-volunteers.page. Accessed May 20, 2011

Resources

American Academy of Pediatrics Section on International Child Health (www.aap.org/Sections/ich)

American College of Surgeons Operation Giving Back provides resources and guidance to would-be medical volunteers. Information on volunteer liability, including an interactive map outlining state volunteer liability laws, is available at www.operationgivingback.facs.org/resources/liability.php.

Office of the Civilian Volunteer Medical Reserve Corps (www.medicalreservecorps.gov)

CHAPTER 20

Medical Liability and Child Abuse

James L. Lukefahr, MD, FAAP; Sandeep K. Narang, MD, JD; and Nancy D. Kellogg, MD, FAAP

KEY CONCEPTS

- Reporting Suspected Child Abuse or Neglect
- Authorization to Diagnose and Treat Suspected Child Abuse Victims in the Absence of Parental Consent
- Release of Medical Records to Child Abuse Investigators
- Providing Court Testimony About Suspected Abuse or Neglect

A 2010 national incidence survey estimated that more than 1.25 million, or 1 in 58, US children experienced child abuse or neglect in 2006—an incidence of 1.7%.[1] US child protective services agencies received reports of approximately 3.6 million children who may have been maltreated that year, and substantiated 905,000 of those children to be victims, representing 1.2% of the total child population.[2] These figures indicate that child abuse is widespread and similar in incidence to many childhood conditions regularly treated by pediatricians, such as streptococcal pharyngitis[3] or urinary tract infection.[4] Thus, pediatricians, regardless of specialty or practice environment, will inevitably encounter abused children during their professional practice.

All physicians and child health professionals have ethical and legal responsibilities to advocate on behalf of vulnerable patients. This chapter will review the most common liability issues that may be encountered by general pediatricians in carrying out their duty to respond to suspected child abuse. Because most legal guidelines for child abuse reporting and treatment are governed by state law and vary widely among jurisdictions, this discussion will necessarily be of a general nature. Physicians should review the legal codes pertinent to their state and community or consult knowledgeable attorneys if they have particular concerns.

Reporting Suspected Child Abuse or Neglect

Requirement to Report

In all US states, territories, and commonwealths, physicians and other health care workers are mandated by law to report suspected child maltreatment to designated child-protection authorities or local law enforcement agencies.[5] Most states require a report to be made when the physician, in her official capacity, *suspects* or has *reason to believe* that a child has been abused or neglected. Note that in these jurisdictions, incontrovertible proof or diagnostic certainty is not required prior to making the report. In some states, however, the standard for reporting is that the professional has knowledge of or observes a child being subjected to conditions that would reasonably result in harm to the child. Most states do not recognize physician-patient privileged communication as an exception to the requirement to report.

Sexual Activity and Age of Consent

Physicians should become familiar with state statutes that govern when sexual activity involving minor children is reportable, and which agencies are responsible for receiving such referrals. Generally, sexual activity between a child and a family member or caregiver should be reported to child protective services. Nonconsensual sexual activity between adolescents and sexual contact involving a child and an adult nonfamily member are usually reported to law enforcement, but in some states child protection agencies also investigate such referrals.[6]

State laws vary considerably regarding the reporting of sexual activity between 2 minor children. Some states mandate reporting of sexual activity between 2 minors with more than a specified age difference. Other states incorporate an age-based criterion, or *age of consent,* by which physicians or other professionals are required to report any sexual contact involving a child younger than a specified age. Reporting laws in other states rely on the clinician's judgment as to whether the sexual activity was abusive, psychologically or physically. In general, sexual activity involving minor children is reported to law enforcement rather than child protection agencies. However, if a family member participated in or failed to protect the child from the activity, such a circumstance would remain a matter to be reported to a child protection agency.

The pediatrician should recognize that when states use age-based criteria that define sexual activity as child abuse, those may differ from age-based criteria used to define when sexual activity is a criminal offense.

Protection of Confidentiality

Although all jurisdictions have statutory provisions to protect the confidentiality of reporters, in practice that protection is often difficult to maintain for physicians, who may be asked or required to prepare summaries or affidavits, or to testify in court as to the findings that led them to report suspected abuse.

Protection of Reporters From Liability

All US jurisdictions provide some form of immunity from liability for persons making reports of suspected abuse or neglect in good faith.[7] The term *in good faith* implies that the reporter, to the best of his knowledge, genuinely suspected a child was being abused or neglected. Some state statutes specify a *presumption* of good faith, meaning that the good faith of the reporter is assumed unless it is disproved, and 5 states provide absolute immunity from liability (in one case, the absolute immunity is limited to health care practitioners) for reports of suspected abuse or neglect.

Many state statutes specifically deny immunity for any reporter who knowingly makes a false or malicious report, and more than half specify civil or criminal penalties for false reporting.

Immunity may also apply to other stages of abuse reporting and management, such as testifying or consulting with child protective services in case evaluation and management; specific state statutes should be consulted.

Liability for Failing to Report

Almost all states and territories list penalties for mandatory reporters who fail to report suspected abuse or neglect as required by law. These penalties may be in the form of fines or imprisonment. In most jurisdictions they are classified as misdemeanors, but some states regard repeat failures to report, or failure to report serious abusive injuries, as potential felony offenses.[8] Although uncommon, failure to report can also subject a health care practitioner to licensure review. Whenever a report is made, the reporter is advised to document in the medical record the reference number provided by the agency receiving the report.

Delegation of Reporting Responsibility to Others or Interference With Other Reporters

In some states, a mandated reporter's responsibility to report may not be delegated to others (eg, a treating physician may not order a nurse or hospital social worker to report abuse), nor can a supervisor interfere with a subordinate's decision to report (eg, an attending physician may not order a resident, student, or nurse to refrain from reporting possible abuse).

Authorization to Diagnose and Treat Suspected Child Abuse Victims in the Absence of Parental Consent

Examination and Diagnostic Testing

The 1986 federal Emergency Medical Treatment and Active Labor Act (EMTALA) mandates that hospitals and other emergency facilities perform a medical screening examination of anyone who presents for emergency care, irrespective of whether consent of the patient, parent, or guardian has been obtained.[9] Should a physician determine that an emergency condition exists, the law mandates that laboratory and radiologic procedures and subspecialty consultation be obtained as necessary for diagnostic purposes—again, prior to or without obtaining consent if necessary.

In addition, many states authorize physicians to examine children who are suspected victims of abuse or neglect without the consent of parents, guardians, or even the children themselves. This authorization may include performing a complete physical examination, including for sexual abuse; photodocumentation; and obtaining necessary laboratory or radiologic studies. However, the exact wording of such authorization varies considerably among jurisdictions; pediatricians are encouraged to become familiar with statutes pertinent to their practice locations.

Treatment of Child Abuse Victims

In addition to diagnostic measures, EMTALA mandates that hospitals and other emergency facilities provide emergency medical treatment up to and including surgical intervention or transfer to a tertiary facility, irrespective of patient or parent consent (although attempts to contact the parent or otherwise obtain such consent should be documented).[9]

In a situation in which a child requires treatment under less than urgent circumstances (eg, an ill child whose parents have refused a medication or a blood product that must be administered within several hours), the physician is advised to contact the local child protection agency and recommend that the child be taken into emergency state custody. Legal processes in such cases vary widely among jurisdictions, particularly with regard to situations that arise outside normal business hours, and the physician is encouraged to become familiar with the steps to follow in her practice locale.

Release of Medical Records to Child Abuse Investigators

Release of medical records and other protected health information to third parties is regulated by the Health Insurance Portability and Accountability Act of 1996 (HIPAA). This law specifies that states may establish rules allowing release of health information to child abuse investigators, and that these rules take precedence over limits imposed by HIPAA if the HIPAA limits are more stringent.

Most states require that a mandated reporter who files a report of suspected abuse or neglect also release relevant records or prepare a statement that substantiates the report. Release of records by a physician, clinic, or hospital who is not the reporter but who has information pertinent to the investigation is generally regarded as allowed under HIPAA, even if it is not specifically authorized by state statutes.[10] Release of information after an investigation is concluded (eg, for a criminal trial or follow-up hearing weeks or months after the investigation is completed) requires consent from the legal guardian of the child or an acceptable legal mandate from the court, such as a valid subpoena or a court order signed by a judge.

A physician is not required to release information to the parent of the child if the physician has a reasonable belief that the child may be endangered once the information is released.[10] For example, if abuse by a parent is suspected and release of information may subject the child to further abuse or otherwise jeopardize the investigation, the physician may elect not to release information to the parent. Similarly, if the physician believes that a parent is protecting or collaborating with an abuser, the physician may decline to release information to that parent. However, the physician is reminded to document the decision not to release the records (and the justification), just as he should remember to document any time protected health information is released.

Providing Court Testimony About Suspected Abuse or Neglect

Once an investigation of suspected child abuse commences, the physician may be ordered, via a subpoena or court order, to testify in one or more legal settings.

Legal proceedings involving child protection agency investigations generally take place in civil or family courts and address whether a finding of abuse is valid, the safety of the child, appropriate arrangements for visitation and supervision of child-parent interactions, and service plan for the family. Follow-up hearings on these issues may take place several times within the first year of the referral. At those hearings, physicians may be asked to describe the child's condition or injury, the severity of or prognosis for the injury, and their interactions with the family.

In child protection legal proceedings, the physician may encounter attorneys representing the parents, child, or child protection agency. The court will usually appoint a guardian or attorney ad litem or a court-appointed special advocate to represent the child's interest. In criminal proceedings, the physician will usually encounter a prosecutor and a defense attorney. Prior to releasing or discussing patient information with any of these individuals (or their office representatives), the physician should request that they provide legal documentation (eg, a release of information from the legal guardian, an appropriate subpoena or court order).

Criminal proceedings occur less frequently and are generally held several months or even years following the initial referral to reporting agencies. The purpose of the criminal trial is to determine a defendant's guilt in causing or allowing the abuse or neglect. The physician may be asked to describe the child's injury or condition and likely mechanisms, and to opine whether the explanation offered is compatible with the characteristics of the child's injury.

Finally, physicians may be required to testify in lawsuits involving monetary compensation for negligence by individuals or institutions that may have resulted in abuse or neglect of a child. These cases are rare.

Testifying in court can be a daunting experience. Before the scheduled trial or hearing date, the physician should communicate with the attorney requesting her testimony to discuss the medical findings, explain her conclusions or professional opinions about them, review her expertise and training, and understand the questions that the attorney plans to ask. Usually, a physician who has received a subpoena will have to appear in person to testify. In some jurisdictions, telephone or videoconference testimony is allowed for certain legal proceedings.

At all times when testifying or otherwise interacting with legal and judicial officials, the physician should have prepared by carefully reviewing relevant patient records and should confine statements to areas within her expertise and knowledge. The physician should convey the most current evidence-based medical information honestly, impartially, and without personal bias or agenda in strict adherence to established ethical boundaries.[11] Failure to properly prepare for testimony opens the physician to embarrassment on cross-examination; while quite rare, the filing of a grievance with professional boards; or even more rarely, a lawsuit.[12]

Compensation for court testimony depends on whether the physician is a *fact* or an *expert* witness, and is subject to statutory limitations in some jurisdictions. The physician should be familiar with local rules and practices and should consult with an attorney for advice in specific situations.

Conclusion

Every US state and territory requires physicians and other health professionals to report suspected child maltreatment to designated authorities. State and federal law generally protects physicians from liability pursuant to reporting suspected abuse or neglect, allows physicians to diagnose and treat abuse victims without parental consent when necessary, and authorizes the release of pertinent medical records to child abuse investigators. The details of these protections and authorizations vary from state to state, so a physician should consult an attorney familiar with state and local regulations for advice in specific situations.

Acknowledgment

The authors wish to acknowledge the assistance of James Pawelski, director, American Academy of Pediatrics Division of State Government Affairs.

References

1. Sedlak AJ, Mettenburg J, Basena M, et al. *Fourth National Incidence Study of Child Abuse and Neglect (NIS–4): Report to Congress.* Washington, DC: US Dept of Health and Human Services, Administration for Children and Families; 2010. http://www.acf.hhs.gov/programs/opre/abuse_neglect/natl_incid/nis4_report_congress_full_pdf_jan2010.pdf. Accessed June 16, 2011

2. US Department of Health and Human Services, Administration on Children, Youth and Families. *Child Maltreatment 2006.* Washington, DC: US Government Printing Office; 2008. http://www.acf.hhs.gov/programs/cb/pubs/cm06/cm06.pdf. Accessed June 16, 2011

3. Pfoh E, Wessels MR, Goldmann D, Lee GM. Burden and economic cost of group A streptococcal pharyngitis. *Pediatrics.* 2008;121(2):229–234. http://pediatrics.aappublications.org/content/121/2/229.full.pdf+html. Accessed July 14, 2011

4. Jakobsson B, Esbjorner E, Hansson S. Minimum incidence and diagnostic rate of first urinary tract infection. *Pediatrics.* 1999;104(2):222–226

5. US Department of Health and Human Services, Administration for Children and Families Child Welfare Information Gateway. *Mandatory Reporters of Child Abuse and Neglect: Summary of State Laws.* Washington, DC: Children's Bureau; 2010. http://www.childwelfare.gov/systemwide/laws_policies/statutes/manda.cfm. Accessed June 16, 2011

6. Madison AB, Feldman-Winter L, Finkel M, McAbee GN. Commentary: consensual adolescent sexual activity with adult partners—conflict between confidentiality and physician reporting requirements under child abuse laws. *Pediatrics.* 2001;107(2):e16

7. US Department of Health and Human Services, Administration for Children and Families Child Welfare Information Gateway. *Immunity for Reporters of Child Abuse and Neglect: Summary of State Laws.* Washington, DC: Children's Bureau; 2008. http://www.childwelfare.gov/systemwide/laws_policies/statutes/immunityall.pdf. Accessed June 16, 2011

8. US Department of Health and Human Services, Administration for Children and Families Child Welfare Information Gateway. *Penalties for Failure to Report and False Reporting of Child Abuse and Neglect: Summary of State Laws.* Washington, DC: Children's Bureau; 2009. http://www.childwelfare.gov/systemwide/laws_policies/statutes/reportall.pdf. Accessed June 15, 2011

9. American Academy of Pediatrics Committee on Pediatric Emergency Medicine. Consent for emergency medcal services for children and adolescents. *Pediatrics.* 2003;111(3):703–706. http://pediatrics.aappublications.org/content/111/3/703.full.pdf+html. Accessed June 16, 2011

10. American Academy of Pediatrics Committee on Child Abuse and Neglect. Policy statement—child abuse, confidentiality, and the Health Insurance Portability and Accountability Act. *Pediatrics.* 2010;125(1):197–201. http://pediatrics.aappublications.org/content/125/1/197.full.pdf+html. Accessed June 16, 2011

11. Council on Ethical and Judicial Affairs. Medical testimony, 9.07. In: *Code of Medical Ethics of the American Medical Association: Current Opinions with Annotations: 2010-2011 ed.* Chicago, IL: American Medical Association; 2010:337–341

12. Richards EP, Walter C. When are expert witnesses liable for their malpractice? *IEEE Eng Med Biol Mag.* 2000;19(2):107–109

CHAPTER 21

Health Care Fraud, Waste, and Abuse

Jose Luis Gonzalez, MD, JD, MSEd, FAAP, and William M. McDonnell, MD, JD, FAAP

KEY CONCEPTS

- Definitions
- Enforcement Programs
- Key Laws and Regulations
- Risk Management Strategies
- What to Do if Audited
- Assessing Unmet Compliance Needs

The National Health Care Anti-Fraud Association estimates that at least 3%, or $60 billion, of the $2 trillion spent annually on health care in the United States is lost to fraud.[1] The enormity of this problem in our current system of health care cannot be overstated or ignored. Along with increased recognition of this important problem has come an emphasis on enforcement. Enforcement actions by the federal government returned more than $2.5 billion to the Medicare trust funds in 2009.[2] A broad range of medical business practices, including billing and payment, practice structures, and business relationships such as referral practices, are increasingly subject to enhanced scrutiny. Pediatricians who intentionally or inadvertently violate fraud, waste, and abuse rules may face a broad range of serious penalties.

Definitions

Fraud

The US Department of Health and Human Services (HHS) Office of Inspector General (OIG) defines *fraud* as an intentional deception or representation made by individuals who know or believe the deception or representation to be false, knowing that it could result in some unauthorized benefit (usually a financial payment) to themselves or others. Examples of fraud in the physician's office may include but are not limited to

- Requiring that patients return at a future date for a procedure that could have been performed on the same day
- Billing for services not provided, including no-shows
- Billing for services provided to one member that were in fact provided to another
- Billing more than one payer for the same service
- Taking a kickback in money, in-kind, or other valuable compensation for referrals
- Completing a certificate of medical necessity for a patient who does not need the service or who does not have a professional physician-patient relationship with the practitioner

Waste and Abuse

Simply defined in the health care delivery context, *waste* is the inappropriate or inefficient use of health care resources. Alternatively, Medicare defines *abuse* as a practice that directly or indirectly results in unnecessary costs to Medicare or other public health programs. Unlike fraud, no willful intent need be proven for abuse. The Centers for Medicare & Medicaid Services (CMS) uses 3 criteria to establish the abusive nature of an act.

- Lack of medical necessity
- Failure to conform to professionally recognized standards
- Charging unfair prices for services

Enforcement Programs

Though often difficult to measure prospectively, the extent of fraud, abuse, and waste becomes too easily evident through retrospective audits and medical chart reviews. Increasingly sophisticated technologies have increased auditors' ability to recognize improper payments, aberrant trends, and inappropriate utilization patterns. Prevention and education are key in stopping fraud, waste, and abuse. Even if health care fraud, waste, and abuse are decreased by only a few percentage points, billions of taxpayers' dollars could be saved and used for funding necessary and appropriate services. Ultimately, the antifraud goals of the CMS and other enforcement agencies are to minimize payment errors, close inappropriate payment loopholes, and provide greater value for beneficiaries and taxpayers.

Information on health care fraud, waste, and abuse trends and patterns is shared among federal, state, and private payers. Depending on the source of health care dollars and site of care, civil monetary penalties or sanctions may be levied on the adjudicated provider. Alternatively, practitioners may be referred to the US Office of the Attorney General for criminal prosecution.

At the federal level, the False Claims Act (FCA) has served as an effective means of combating fraud in government health care service programs since its enactment in 1986.[3] The FCA allows a private citizen with knowledge of fraud to file a qui tam, or whistle-blower suit, on behalf of the government. If the claim is successful, the whistle-blower can collect up to 30% of the money recovered. Recent bills[4-6] have enhanced and simplified enforcement of the FCA, giving government prosecutors greater power to investigate fraud allegations, limiting available defenses by prospective defendants, and loosening the strictures on whistle-blower suits. Total FCA recoveries since January 2009 have topped $3 billion.[7]

Office of Inspector General enforcement initiatives are updated annually. The 2009 OIG list demonstrates a shift in focus to physician billings, the need for accurate and complete medical documentation, and proper, accurate coding. Examples of the 2009 initiatives include but are not limited to[2]

- *Physicians at Teaching Hospitals* monitors the involvement of attending physicians in teaching hospitals during resident-delivered patient care and ensures that billings are reflective of the correct level of service provided to the patient.
- *Physician relationships with Medicare health maintenance organizations* reviews provider payment methods to determine if managed care capitation plans hinder patient access or decrease quality of care.
- *Physician certification of durable medical equipment* examines how well equipment needs of patients are documented.
- *Hospital ownership of physician practices* monitors the referral relationships between a hospital and its owned physician practices to check for overutilization of inpatient or outpatient hospital services.
- *Accuracy and carrier monitoring of coding* measures the accuracy of evaluation and management (E/M) coding by physicians in the

nonhospital setting as well as whether carriers are monitoring this process.

- *Use of modifiers* examines whether a separate service was performed and documented when claim modifiers are submitted.
- *Use of diagnosis codes* compares claims against medical records to see if diagnosis codes match the reason for ordering tests and providing various services.
- *Physician credit balances* monitors physicians' handling of Medicare and Medicaid credit balances (eg, overpayments, duplicate payments) and refunds to patients or carriers.
- *Multiple discharges* reviews hospital records for duplicate billings submitted for inpatient or observation discharge management.
- *Anesthesia services* monitors anesthesiologists' compliance with Medicare and Medicaid rules that govern residents' and nurse anesthetists' supervision and billing.
- *Critical care services* monitors adherence to guidelines for reporting critical care services.
- *Billing service companies* reviews agreements between physicians and billing companies to ensure that Medicare and Medicaid standards are met.
- *Improper billing of psychiatric services* monitors reporting of mental health services to ensure accuracy with guidelines (eg, billing for psychotherapy services instead of using inpatient hospital codes; billing for psychological tests by the test performed, not by the hour; billing for individual psychotherapy when the service was performed in a group setting; providing psychotherapy services to patients who are not able to receive services because of their mental status).

Additional information on OIG antifraud initiatives is available at http://oig.hhs.gov/fraud.asp.

The federal Payment Error Rate Measurement program monitors improper payments to providers on the basis of sampled Medicaid claims in 17 states per year, with each state, including the District of Columbia, chosen once every 3 years. Although an improper payment does not necessarily indicate fraud, the federal definition of *improper payment* is broad and includes payments made or denied in error, under appeal or active fraud investigation, or otherwise unresolved. Of 1,356 medical reviews randomly analyzed for 2006 and 2007, 4 types of errors accounted for 78% of the total errors and 95% of improper Medicaid overpayments.[8] Prominent among the causes for these overpayments were insufficient or absent documentation and the provision of medically unnecessary services.

Another payment recapture audit is the Recovery Audit Contractor (RAC) program. In 2006, the Tax Relief and Health Care Act[9] made permanent the RAC program for identifying improper Medicare payments in all 50 states. Recovery Audit Contractors may review the 3 preceding years of a provider's claims and also conduct medical record reviews. Payment for RACs is based on a percentage of recovered overpayment amounts from providers. The 2010 health care reform bills[5,6] provide for the expansion of RACs to Medicaid claims.

Lastly, the Deficit Reduction Act of 2005[10] established the federal Medicaid Integrity Program. This program directs the CMS through the use of contractors to conduct nationwide recovery audits of Medicaid claims. Unlike RAC audits, these auditors are not limited to a 3-year look-back period or compensated by a percentage-fee arrangement.

The OIG also publishes an annual work plan that lists OIG areas of interest in Medicare and Medicaid, under the rubric of "physicians and other health professionals," that have been identified for fraud monitoring and review. Previous OIG work plans have included, among others, the following areas of interest for focused monitoring:

- Coding of E/M services
- Use of modifiers with National Correct Coding Initiative edits
- End-stage renal disease monthly capitation payment relative value units

- Place-of-service errors
- Long-distance physician claims
- Care plan oversight
- Billing for diagnostic tests
- Radiation therapy services
- Billing for services and supplies incident to physicians' services
- Ordering physicians excluded from Medicare and Medicaid programs
- Evaluation and management services provided during the global surgery period

For additional past and current OIG areas of interest and general information, visit http://oig.hhs.gov/publications/workplan.asp.[11]

Key Laws and Regulations

An array of civil and criminal penalties under a number of statutory and regulatory structures (eg, Health Insurance Portability and Accountability Act of 1996 [HIPAA],[12] Emergency Medical Treatment and Active Labor Act,[13] medical malpractice judgments and settlements) may be applied to fraudulent or abusive physician practices. The legal standard generally applied for assessing these penalties is *knowing or reckless disregard;* some, such as the FCA, however, provide for recovery against the physician who "knew or should have known" that claims were inappropriate.[3] Examples of activities that may result in enforcement actions under various available laws and regulations include

- Submission of claim charges in excess of services or supplies provided
- Billing Medicare or Medicaid based on a higher fee schedule than used for other payers
- Providing medically unnecessary services
- Submitting bills to Medicare or Medicaid that are the coverage responsibility of another insurance plan
- Routine waiver of a patient's co-payment or deductible

- Coding all visits at the same level regardless of the level of service actually provided
- Unbundling of claims—billing separately for services that are correctly billed as a group under one code
- Billing claims under the wrong provider number

Federal Laws

Fraud, waste, and abuse enforcement programs are based on several key federal laws. It is crucial to understand these laws because violating them can result in a wide range of penalties. For example, the Social Security Act (SSA)[14] establishes basic fraud and abuse enforcement guidelines for Medicare and Medicaid. Violations of these guidelines can result in civil penalties, criminal charges, or both, as well as in administrative sanctions that disallow fraudulent provider's participation in Medicare or Medicaid for a period of up to 5 years. Imposed financial penalties for improperly filed claims can reach as high as $50,000 per individual claim violation.

False Claims Act

The FCA[3] applies when a false claim is made against the US government. A *claim* is defined as any request or demand for money or property made by a contractor, such as a Medicaid or Medicare provider. No specific intent to defraud is required. Civil enforcement actions under the FCA can result in civil sanctions or penalties levied on practitioners for each fraudulent claim. Penalties can range from $5,000 to $11,000 per false claim plus triple the amount of overpayment. The FCA also includes provisions for whistle-blower suits that any citizen can initiate against a practitioner on behalf of the US government (eg, disgruntled employees forced to participate in incorrect billing practices, patients who do not agree with a physician's charges, auditors or inspectors who think billing practices suggest fraud or abuse). The whistle-blower has full protection from the employer, and if a conviction is obtained and monetary penalties are involved, the whistle-blower receives a portion of the money recovered from the fraudulent practitioner.

Health Insurance Portability and Accountability Act of 1996

The Health Insurance Portability and Accountability Act of 1996[12] carries civil and criminal enforcement options. This act makes it a felony to knowingly defraud any health care system. Although criminal prosecution under HIPAA requires proof beyond a reasonable doubt of specific intent to defraud, civil enforcement requires only a *preponderance of the evidence.* As with the FCA,[3] providers may be fined up to $10,000 per false claim plus triple the amount of overpayment as part of HIPAA civil enforcement actions. (Services that have been under-coded may not be used to offset overpayments.) However, should the civil investigation reveal specific intent to defraud, federal investigators and prosecutors can proceed with criminal indictments against the alleged fraudulent practitioners even if the fraud concerns improper payments obtained from private (ie, nongovernment) health insurance plans.

Anti-Kickback Enforcement Act of 1986

The Anti-Kickback Enforcement Act of 1986[15] makes it unlawful for Medicare and Medicaid providers to knowingly and willfully solicit, receive, offer, or pay anything of value to induce referrals of items or services payable by a federal health care program. The kickback prohibition applies to all sources of referrals, even patients. For example, advertising that co-payments will be routinely waived would implicate the anti-kickback prohibition. However, physicians can waive a co-payment if an individual determination that the patient cannot afford to pay is made.[16] Other suspect arrangements may arise within the context of physician-industry collaborative agreements because these carry a potential risk for overutilization of health care products marketed by the collaborating industry. In evaluating these proposals, physicians need to match services requested to compensation offered. If the physician's contribution is tied to referrals for a particular device or supply or to an above–fair-market-value compensation for services provided, the "consulting" arrangement is suspect and likely to violate antikickback statutes.[16] To assist in distinguishing between legitimate and questionable industry relationships, the OIG has developed *Compliance Program Guidance for Pharmaceutical Manufacturers.*[17]

Kickbacks in health care can lead to over-utilization of services, increased costs, patient steering to a specific source of services, and corruption of medical decision-making. A violation of the antikickback law constitutes a felony punishable by a maximum fine of $25,000, imprisonment up to 5 years, or both. Under this statute, the OIG may also exclude violators from doing business with Medicare and other federal health care programs and impose civil monetary penalties of up to $50,000 plus triple the amount of the provider's remuneration. Proof of patient harm or financial loss to Medicare or Medicaid is not required. Practices may obtain copies of all relevant OIG special fraud alerts and advisory opinions that address the application of the antikickback statute.[18] Application of this information can ensure that compliance policies and procedures reflect current OIG positions and opinions.

Stark Law and Regulations

The so-called physician self-referral Stark regulations[19] protect against financial arrangements that improperly constitute self-dealing by physicians. Stark regulations are very technical. Business relationships can sometimes unduly influence physicians' decisions and lead to steering patients to a source of services in which physicians have a financial interest. It is thus generally recommended that all business arrangements, including corporate structure, wherein physician practices refer business to an outside entity (eg, hospitals, hospices, nursing facilities, home health agencies, durable medical equipment suppliers, vendors) be reviewed to avoid potential Stark law violations. The regulations require that physicians, with the assistance of legal counsel familiar with the physician self-referral statutes, scrutinize the terms of each business agreement, the business relationships between parties, and the formulas for determining revenue from the agreement. The OIG describes certain characteristics that, taken separately or together, could indicate a problematic or suspect contractual arrangement under Stark law. Examples of suspect contractual arrangements that may provide the basis for law enforcement action include[19]

1. *New line of business.* The physician-owner expands into a related line of business that is dependent on referrals from or other business generated by that physician-owner's existing business.
2. *Captive referral base.* The new business mostly serves the provider-owner's existing patient base.
3. *Little or no bona fide business risk.* The provider-owner's primary contribution to the venture is referrals, and the provider-owner does not operate the new business itself or commit substantial resources to the new business.
4. *Status of manager/supplier.* Without the contractual arrangement, the provider-manager or supplier of the new business would be a competitor of the new line of business.
5. *Scope of services provided by manager/supplier.* The provider-manager or supplier provides certain key services to the new business such as day-to-day management, billing, and personnel and related services.
6. *Remuneration.* The business arrangement's practical effect is to provide the provider-owner with the opportunity to bill insurers and patients for business otherwise provided by the manager/supplier of the new business, and payments to the owner take into account the value and volume of business (ie, number of referrals to the new business) the provider-owner generates.

7. *Exclusivity.* The parties agree to a non-compete clause.

Proof of specific intent to violate the law is not required. Penalties for Stark law violations can include fines as well as exclusion from participation in federal health care programs. Practices may obtain copies of all relevant OIG special fraud alerts and advisory opinions that address the application of the physician self-referral regulations.[18] Similarly, the CMS also issues opinions to parties who seek advice on the Stark law.[20]

State Laws

Many states have enacted their own, often more stringent, antifraud and anti-abuse legislation to further control fraud, waste, and abuse within that state's public health care delivery programs. In addition, state Medicaid programs have established state-specific Medicaid fraud control units to enforce these measures. The Medicaid Alliance for Program Safeguards has created the Medicaid Fraud Statutes Web site,[21] which contains a comprehensive listing of individual state's statutory citations used to prosecute civil or criminal fraudulent health care activities.

Risk Management Strategies

Medical Record Documentation

Providers can play a vital role in decreasing fraud, waste, and abuse by following a few basic practice guidelines. First among these is *document*. Physicians exert significant influence over what services their patients receive; documentation serves as support for the service claims submitted to public and private insurers for payment. Claim payments, in turn, are based for the most part on the physician's representation on the claim documents.[16] Appropriately, physicians are held accountable for the completeness and accuracy of the documentation for all services they order or provide.

Inadequate or inappropriate documentation can precipitate more time-consuming and costly problems down the road and could raise a suspicion of fraud or abuse when reviewed by an outside party.

One of the most important prerequisites for practice risk management and compliance with fraud, waste, and abuse laws is the appropriate and accurate documentation of provided diagnosis and treatment services. A written compliance plan should specify that medical record documentation should conform to the following principles and guidelines:

- The medical record should be complete and legible.
- The documentation of each patient encounter should include the reason for the encounter; any relevant history and physical examination findings; past and present diagnoses; prior diagnostic test results; assessment, clinical impression, or diagnosis; plan of care; and date and legible identity of the observer. Appropriate health risk factors should also be identified and documented.
- If not documented, the rationale for ordering diagnostic and other ancillary services should be easily inferred by an independent reviewer or third party.
- The patient's progress, any changes in treatment and the response to them, as well as any revisions in diagnosis should be documented.
- All pages in the medical record should include patient name as well as an identifying patient number or birth date.
- Prescription drug management should include the name of the medication, dosage, and instructions.
- Clinically important telephone calls with, among others, family members and other providers should be documented, including date, time, and instructions.
- Anticipatory guidance, patient education, and counseling must be documented when performed.

- Any addenda should be dated, initialed, and signed.
- Consent forms should be dated, the procedure specified, and the form signed by the patient. Documentation should also include a detailed summary of the discussion addressing the procedure, risks, and any other relevant information.
- Avoid abbreviations, but when used, they should be clear and explicit.
- Patient noncompliance should be described and documented.
- Allergies and adverse reactions should be prominently displayed.
- Immunization and growth charts must be included and maintained.
- Problem and medication lists should be complete and current.

Specific examples of potentially suspicious documentation include

- Lack of documentation to support services rendered
- Lack of laboratory result documentation for tests billed
- Incomplete history or physical examination
- Lack of follow-up on services billed or rendered

Coding and Billing

Suspicion of fraud may be raised by irregular billing patterns. When a claim for services performed is submitted for payment, its submission serves to certify that the provider has earned the payment requested and complied with billing requirements.[16] An attempt by a health care provider to collect unearned money may constitute a violation of applicable fraud and abuse laws. Understanding the risk exposure, physicians should have reasonable knowledge of national standards for coding procedure and terminology.[22] The following risk areas associated with coding and billing have been among the most frequent subjects of OIG investigations and audits and should be addressed in establishing a practice's fraud and abuse compliance program:

- Billing for items or services not provided or not provided as claimed
- Submitting claims for equipment, medical supplies, and services that are not reasonable and medically necessary
- Double billing
- Billing for non-covered services as if covered
- Known misuse of provider identification numbers, which results in improper billing
- Billing for unbundled services
- Failure to properly use coding modifiers
- Consistently under-coding or over-coding services

Other areas that may trigger an audit include

- The profile of services reported as provided differing from payer profiles of physicians of a similar specialty
- Consistently utilizing only 1 E/M service code within a category of service
- Repeated use of unspecified *International Classification of Diseases, Ninth Revision, Clinical Modification (ICD-9-CM)* codes or use of codes that are not consistent with the service the billing provider's specialty usually provides
- Submitting physician claims for surgical services that are not consistent with correlate claims submitted by the facility where surgical services are provided
- The number of procedures or services reported exceeding hours in a day
- Prior history of a high number of denials for services billed

Provider Education

Most physicians strive to render high-quality medical care to their patients. Physicians decide what health services and supplies their patients receive,

what drugs they use, and what specialists they are referred to. In turn, health care payers, public and private, rely on physicians for the medical necessity and accuracy of provided or prescribed services. Failing this trust, insurers have broad capabilities to investigate and audit providers when they have a reasonable suspicion of fraud, waste, or abuse.[16] Given the setting, physicians need to understand how to comply with federal and state fraud, waste, and abuse laws and regulations by identifying red flags that could trigger potential liability. Paramount in this risk management progression is ongoing provider education.

The OIG has recently developed and made available a road map to assist physicians in maneuvering and complying with the recognized complex system of fraud, waste, and abuse statutes and regulations.[16] Although intended to primarily address Medicaid and Medicare, the information and direction provided within these educational modules can be easily applied to all health care payers.

Compliance Programs

A compliance program is a fraud management plan created for a specific health care service delivery entity (eg, practice, clinic, hospital) that establishes strategies to prevent, detect, and resolve fraudulent conduct that does not conform to

- Federal and state antifraud statutes and regulations
- Federal, state, and private payer health care program requirements
- The provider organization's own ethical and business policies

Any effective compliance program should develop and maintain written compliance policy standards and procedures that will be followed by the practice and that clearly and distinctly describe the lines of responsibility of each and every practice employee for implementing the compliance program. Strictly followed, these standards and procedures should be reasonably capable of reducing the prospect of fraudulent activity within the practice, including the early identification of any incorrect billing processes. The OIG has developed an educational Compliance Program for Individual and Small Group Physician Offices.[23]

In its compliance guidelines for individual and small group medical offices, the OIG describes 7 fundamental elements of physician practice compliance programs, as well as the principles that each physician practice should consider when developing and implementing an effective compliance program.[23] These guidelines are not mandatory, nor do they represent an exclusive document of required elements of a compliance program. They are, however, a resource to be considered along with other OIG educational outreach activities and other federal agency efforts to promote compliance. The OIG considers the 7 elements of a compliance program to be[23]

- Conduct internal monitoring and auditing.
- Implement compliance and practice standards.
- Designate a compliance officer or contact.
- Conduct appropriate training and education.
- Respond appropriately to detected offenses and develop corrective actions.
- Develop open lines of communication.
- Enforce disciplinary standards through well-publicized guidelines.

Practices should take reasonable steps to respond to each of these elements, depending on practice size and resources.

Kickbacks and Self-referrals

Kickback and self-referral risk areas that should be addressed in practice compliance program policies and procedures include but need not be limited to[23]

- Offers of inappropriate inducements to patients (eg, waiving coinsurance or deductible amounts without a good-faith determination that the patient is in financial need; failing to make

reasonable efforts to collect cost-sharing amounts)
- Financial arrangements with outside entities or facilities to which the practice may refer public health care program business
- Joint ventures, consulting contracts, or medical directorships with entities supplying goods or services to the physician practice or its patients
- Office and equipment leases with entities or facilities to which the physician refers
- Soliciting, accepting, or offering any gift or gratuity of more than nominal value from or to those who may benefit from the physician practice's referral of public health care program business

Retention of Records

Compliance program written policies and procedures should include a standardized process for the creation, distribution, retention, and destruction of patient health care documents. In designing a record-retention system, privacy concerns and federal and state regulatory requirements must be taken into consideration. In addition, the following record-retention guidelines should be followed[23]:

- The length of time that practice medical records are to be retained should be clearly specified. Federal and state statutes should be consulted for applicable time frames.
- Minor patient records may need to be retained indefinitely.
- Medical records should be secured against loss, destruction, unauthorized access, unauthorized reproduction, corruption, and damage.
- The disposition of medical records in the event the practice is sold or closed should be distinctly stipulated.

In addition to maintaining appropriate and thorough medical records on each patient, the OIG further recommends that the practice also maintain the following types of documents[23]:

- All records and documentation (eg, billings, claims) required for participation in federal, state, and private payer health care programs
- All records necessary to demonstrate the integrity and effectiveness of the physician practice compliance process
- All efforts to comply with applicable federal and state health care laws and regulations, including
  - All records associated with requests for advice from a government agency charged with administering a federal health care program, and any written or oral response
  - A log of all other oral or written inquiries between the practice and government-contracted third parties

Practices with written compliance programs report having better control of internal procedures, improved medical record documentation, and streamlined practice operations. Pediatric practices benefit from having compliance initiatives that serve to tighten billing and coding operations and medical record documentation. Compliance programs not only help prevent erroneous or fraudulent claims but also lend support to the fact that a physician practice is making a good-faith effort to submit clean and accurate claims. In fact, an effective compliance program serves to send an important message to physician practice employees. By establishing standardized internal communication systems for reporting questionable activities and resolving problems, fraud and abuse compliance programs discourage individuals from bringing whistle-blower suits under the FCA. Similarly, if a practice becomes aware of an overpayment or other potentially fraudulent situation, the compliance program may lead to an internal administrative practice resolution rather than a formal false claim legal action, thereby saving the practice money by preventing costly civil suits and criminal investigations.[23]

Additional practice benefits of an effective compliance program outside the fraud and abuse context are also likely. Compliance programs frequently result in improved medical record documentation and accuracy of billing and coding, with reduced claim denials and a more effective and efficient service payment process. They can also provide ongoing, timely education for practice physicians and employees on a wide range of practice management topics.

Designation of a Compliance Officer or Contact

Effective administration of a fraud, waste, and abuse compliance program requires the designation of an individual or individuals to be responsible for overseeing its ongoing implementation. Qualifications that the compliance officer should possess include[23]

- Independence of position so as to safeguard against potential conflicts of interest between the performance of assigned employment duties and those expected of a compliance officer
- Effective oral and written communication skills with employees, physicians, and individuals external to the practice
- Experience in billing and coding

One or more practice employee may be designated for the responsibility of monitoring compliance; alternatively, a practice may outsource all or part of the functions of a compliance officer to an external third party. The primary responsibilities of a compliance officer, whether or not a practice employee, consist of but may not be limited to[23]

- Overseeing and monitoring implementation of the compliance program
- Assessing the particular practice situation and determining what best suits the practice in terms of compliance oversight
- Establishing methods, such as periodic internal audits, to improve practice quality of services and to reduce practice vulnerability to fraud and abuse

- Regularly revising the compliance program, including in response to changes in the needs of the practice, federal and state laws and regulations, and policies and procedures of government and private payer health plans
- Developing, coordinating, and participating in training programs that focus on the elements, individually or altogether, of a compliance program; ensuring that training materials are accurate, current, and literally appropriate
- Regularly checking the HHS OIG List of Excluded Individuals/Entities[24] and the General Services Administration Excluded Parties List System[25] with respect to all practice employees, medical staff, and external, independent contractors
- Monitoring practice staff employees and physicians to verify they remain knowledgeable and compliant with pertinent federal and state fraud and abuse statutes, regulations, and practice standards
- Immediately investigating any reports or allegations concerning possible unethical or improper business practices and, as appropriate, monitoring subsequent corrective actions, compliance, or both
- Maintaining an updated record of compliance-related activities, including, at a minimum, documentation of compliance meetings, offered educational activities with attendance records, and internal audit results, paying particular attention to documenting violations found by the compliance program and resulting remedial actions

Although the OIG has not made compliance programs mandatory in private medical offices, it has made it clear that an organization under investigation may be given more sympathetic treatment if a practice-appropriate compliance program is in place.[26] In this context, if an investigation occurs, an established compliance program that is effective and meets government requirements will demonstrate to OIG investigators that the practice is using a thorough, well-documented approach to limit fraud; may cause investigators to be more inclined to resolve the problem civilly rather than criminally; and may influence the OIG decision whether to exclude a provider practice from participation in federal health care programs.

The OIG recognizes that there is no one-size-fits-all compliance program, especially in view of the large variations among physician practices. Acknowledging these differences, the OIG encourages physician practices to participate in other compliance programs, such as those of local hospitals or other settings in which physicians provide health care services. A physician's participation in another provider's compliance program could be a way, at least in part, to satisfy recommended elements of the physician practice's own compliance program. Whether independently or in collaboration with other providers, physician practices should always consider OIG guidelines when developing and implementing a compliance program.

Compliance programs are only effective if fully integrated into daily practice operations; programs should be customized to the particular practice and require compliance efforts that are realistic, achievable, and sustainable. Physician practices should view compliance programs as analogous to practicing preventive medicine.

What to Do if Audited

Should your practice be audited, the following tips will help you and your practice traverse the process:

- Contact legal counsel as soon as possible. Though counsel may not be needed, attorneys with experience in external audits can provide sound advice for getting a practice through the audit process.
- Designate one physician or staff member to serve as the primary contact with auditors. Keep in mind, however, that all physicians and staff members will likely need to work with auditors to some extent.
- If time requirements for producing copies or gathering requested medical records are unreasonable, contact the auditors for an extension. Make certain that there is justification for the extension request.
- Keep copies of all written communication (eg, letters, directives, memos, e-mails) with auditors, including postmarked envelopes and the original notice.
- Fully document and store all verbal communication with auditors.
- Provide only the information requested, and maintain copies of what you provide to auditors in a separate file. Information unrelated to the program being audited, such as services provided when the patient was under a different commercial plan or was uninsured, should not be included.
- Maintain a log of all records provided to auditors and when. Request and record the name of the individual acknowledging receipt, as applicable.
- Do not alter, cross out, or otherwise obscure any documents or medical records. If additional, new, or changed information needs to be included in any document or medical record, this must be done as a separate, dated, and signed entry.

- Request that auditors provide the practice with an opening and closing conference. At the initial meeting, ask for the individuals' credentials and job titles and ask them to summarize the purpose of the visit.
  - Obtain specific contact information in case questions arise or follow-up is needed.
  - Obtain, in writing, the expected date of a written summary of audit findings.
- Respond only to direct questions from auditors. If the review is conducted in your office, hold it in a separate location away from patients, staff, and business operations.

Assessing Unmet Compliance Needs

The following questions should help assess your unmet practice compliance needs:

1. Are the necessary, up-to-date tools to do the job available?
   - *Current Procedural Terminology, ICD-9-CM,* and Healthcare Common Procedure Coding System manuals
   - US HHS OIG road map[16]
   - Documentation guidelines for E/M
2. Are employees and medical physician staff trained, and do they understand their compliance responsibilities?
   - Are they required to attend educational programs? Are attendance records maintained?
3. Are compliance policy and procedure manuals updated regularly, and do employees know their location and have easy, unlimited access?
4. Are lines of communication between employees and the designated compliance individual(s) open for sharing suggestions, questions, or possible fraudulent situations?
5. Are encounter forms used to report provided services and charges? Are they updated at least yearly?

6. If the services of a billing agency are used
   - Has the agency been checked against government health program exclusion lists?
   - Are claims submitted by the billing agency checked for accuracy?
7. Are denied claims (explanations of benefits) from payers reviewed regularly by practice staff and physicians?
   - Are certain claims being reduced or denied regularly? If so, why?
   - Are codes being changed? If so, where in the process does the change occur?
8. Is there a system for regular internal practice audits and reviews of compliance policies and procedures?
9. Do the practice's physicians understand that they are responsible for their own fraudulent acts as well as those acts committed by practice employees?
10. Is there anyone who might want to report the practice for fraudulent activity?
    - An unhappy patient
    - A disgruntled employee
    - A terminated ex-employee

Final Words

Most physicians strive not only to render high-quality care to their patients but also to deliver these services only as medically indicated and to submit accurate and appropriate claims for payment. However, in a system of increasing regulations, the journey between practice of medicine and payment for services is innately perilous. At times, a practice may find itself following billing methods that it subsequently realizes were wrong, or engaged in business relationships with other health care providers that may be perceived as fraudulent or otherwise problematic by payers or government enforcement agencies. In these circumstances, it is important to[16]

- Seek knowledgeable legal counsel.
- Determine, as comprehensively as possible, the amount of money collected in error from patients or payers, and return overpayments.
- Consider reporting the unintentional wrongdoing using OIG self-disclosure protocols.[27]

The OIG Provider Self-Disclosure Protocol provides a vehicle for physicians to voluntarily disclose self-discovered evidence of potential fraud. The terms of the protocol allow providers to collaborate with government fraud investigators to minimize or possibly wholly avoid the significant costs and practice disruptions inherent to a full-blown fraud and abuse investigation.[27]

The SSA clearly states that payment for services provided to patients depends on whether those services are "reasonable and necessary for the diagnosis or treatment."[14] The SSA further states that only the providing physician can furnish the information that is "necessary in order to determine the amounts due" for services rendered to the patient.[14] While mistakes do occur, deliberate ignorance, persistent overutilization, and bad faith mistakes may each rise to the level of fraud and serve as indicators of potential legal liability.[28] Alternatively, physician compliance and practice self-auditing provide the groundwork and guidance for proper billing and payment, ethical practice structures and business relationships, and avoidance of inappropriate or inefficient use of health care resources.[28]

References

1. Testimony of Daniel R. Levinson, Inspector General, before the Senate Special Committee on Aging, US Senate. Combating Fraud, Waste, and Abuse in Medicare and Medicaid. May 6, 2009. http://www.hhs.gov/asl/testify/2009/05/t20090506d.html. Accessed July 14, 2011

2. US Department of Health and Human Services, US Department of Justice. *Health Care Fraud and Abuse Control Program Annual Report for Fiscal Year 2009.* 2010. http://www.justice.gov/archive/dag/pubdoc/hcfacreport2009.pdf. Accessed June 17, 2011

3. Federal False Claims Act. 31 USC §§3729–3733

4. Fraud Enforcement and Recovery Act of 2009, Pub L No. 111–21

5. Patient Protection and Affordable Care Act (PPACA), Pub L No. 111-148

6. Health Care and Education Reconciliation Act of 2010, Pub L No. 111-152

7. Department of Justice Office of Public Affairs. *Justice News.* March 23, 2010

8. HHS OIG Audit Report. Office of Audit Services. April 14, 2010. http://oig.hhs.gov/reports-and-publications/oas/hrsa.asp. Accessed July 14, 2011

9. Tax Relief and Health Care Act of 2006, Pub L No. 109-432

10. Deficit Reduction Act of 2005, Pub L No. 109-171

11. Office of the Inspector General (OIG) Work Plan Fiscal Year 2010. OIG Web site. http://oig.hhs.gov/publications/docs/workplan/2010/Work_Plan_FY_2010.pdf. Accessed June 17, 2011

12. Health Insurance Portability and Accountability Act (HIPAA) of 1996, Pub L No.104-191

13. Emergency Medical Treatment and Active Labor Act (EMTALA), 42 USC §1395dd

14. Social Security Act, 42 USC §1395y (a)(1)(A); §1395l(e) (2009)

15. Anti-Kickback Enforcement Act of 1986, 42 USC §1320a–7b(b)

16. US Department of Health and Human Services, Office of Inspector General. *A Roadmap for New Physicians: Avoiding Medicare and Medicaid Fraud and Abuse.* http://oig.hhs.gov/compliance/physician-education/index.asp. Accessed June 17, 2011

17. US Department of Health and Human Services, Office of Inspector General. *Compliance Program Guidance for Pharmaceutical Manufacturers.* 2003. http://oig.hhs.gov/fraud/docs/complianceguidance/042803pharmacymfgnonfr.pdf. Accessed June 17, 2011

18. US Department of Health and Human Services, Office of the Inspector General. Advisory Opinions. http://oig.hhs.gov/compliance/advisory-opinions/index.asp. Accessed June 17, 2011

19. Physician Self-Referral Laws and Regulations. 42 USC §1395nn and at 42 CFR §411.350–§411.389

20. Physician Self Referral Advisory Opinions (AOs). Centers for Medicare & Medicaid Services Web site. Updated May 26, 2011. http://www.cms.gov/PhysicianSelfReferral/95_advisory_opinions.asp. Accessed June 17, 2011

21. How to Report Fraud Overview. Centers for Medicare & Medicaid Services Web site. http://www.cms.gov/FraudAbuseforConsumers. Accessed June 17, 2011

22. American Medical Association. *Current Procedural Terminology (CPT), Professional Edition.* Chicago, IL: American Medical Association; 2011

23. US Department of Health and Human Services, Office of Inspector General. OIG compliance program for individual and small group physician practices. *Fed Regist.* 2000;65(194):59434–59452. http://oig.hhs.gov/authorities/docs/physician.pdf. Accessed July 14, 2011

24. US Department of Health and Human Services, Office of Inspector General. List of Excluded Individuals/Entities LEIE Downloadable Databases. http://oig.hhs.gov/exclusions/exclusions_list.asp. Accessed June 17, 2011

25. Excluded Parties List System (EPLS). EPLS Web site. https://www.epls.gov. Accessed June 17, 2011

26. US Department of Health and Human Services, Office of the Inspector General (OIG) Web site. http://oig.hhs.gov. Accessed June 17, 2011

27. US Department of Health and Human Services, Office of Inspector General. Self-Disclosure Information. http://oig.hhs.gov/compliance/self-disclosure-info/index.asp. Accessed June 17, 2011

28. Mantese T, Nowakowski G. The audit alter ego: coding for reimbursement. *American Health Lawyers Association Connections.* 2011;15(1):33–36. http://www.healthlawyers.org/News/Connections/CurrentIssue/Documents/2011%20Analysis/Pages%20from%20AC_Jan2011_Analysis.pdf. Accessed June 17, 2011

Index

278

Index

· ·

Key *Online* **Resources**

FROM THE AMERICAN ACADEMY OF PEDIATRICS

Digital Solutions for Your Practice or Institution

Pediatric Care Online™ integrates access to a wealth of must-have pediatric resources—wherever you are!

Pediatric Care Online™ quickly provides evidence-based information and action-oriented recommendations on your desktop, laptop, tablet, or smartphone. It integrates multiple pediatric resources, including the Point-of-Care Quick Reference, *AAP Textbook of Pediatric Care*, AAP Policy, *Red Book*® content, Bright Futures, Interactive Periodicity Schedule, and many more! This point-of-care solution is optimized for mobile browsing, and selected modules are available for download to your mobile device. *Pediatric Care Online*™ is continually updated to keep you current and regularly enhanced to serve you even better. And it is an approved source that may be searched through the AAP PediaLink Internet Point of Care Search CME activity.

www.pediatriccareonline.org • Item #PCO • Individual Subscription Price: $289 • Member Price: $249

3-month trial access cards for individuals are available through your Mead Johnson representative or by calling 888/363-2362.

Find *Pediatric Care Online*™ on Facebook at www.facebook.com/pco.

Link up with *Red Book*® *Online*—the authority on pediatric infectious diseases!

Red Book® *Online* extends beyond the print edition to provide instant access to pediatric infectious disease solutions not available in print or any other platform. Features include the complete text of the current print edition; embedded links that update and enhance content between print editions; a visual library of more than 2,400 full-color images; powerful text and image searching; and a variety of other dynamic resources specific to infectious diseases and vaccination. *Red Book*® *Online* is an approved source that may be searched through the AAP PediaLink Internet Point of Care Search CME activity.

www.aapredbook.org • Item #ON2006 • Individual Subscription Price: $114.95 • Member Price: $99.95

Find *AAP Red Book*® on Facebook at www.facebook.com/aapredbook.

Patient Education Online is a trusted print-on-demand library.

Patient Education Online puts more than 300 pediatric health care handouts right at your fingertips so you always have the most current information as needed. This extensive, easy-to-read collection spans birth through adolescence and includes brochures, Bright Futures well-child visit handouts, CDC Vaccine Information Statements, injury and violence prevention resources, and more! Almost all ready-to-print materials are available in English and Spanish. *Patient Education Online* may help meet the professional meaningful use requirement for patient-specific education resources.

www.patiented.aap.org • Item #ONPE-IND • Individual Subscription Price: $249.95 • Member Price: $199.95

Accelerate payment and coding compliance with *AAP Pediatric Coding Newsletter*™.

AAP Pediatric Coding Newsletter™ is a monthly print and online advisory service to help you maximize payment, save time, and implement best business practices to support quality patient care. It provides broad coverage of coding and documentation practices for pediatric primary care and subspecialty services.

www.coding.aap.org • Item #SUB1005 • Individual Subscription Price: $219.95 • Member Price: $199.95

For individual subscriptions, please visit our Online Bookstore at **www.aap.org/bookstore.**

For institution or practice-wide site licenses, please contact **aapsales@aap.org.**